DRUGS & Life

fourth edition

DRUGS & Life

Harry Avis
Sierra College

WCB McGraw-Hill

Boston   Burr Ridge, IL   Dubuque, IA   Madison, WI   New York   San Francisco   St. Louis
Bangkok   Bogotá   Caracas   Lisbon   London   Madrid
Mexico City   Milan New Delhi   Seoul   Singapore   Sydney   Taipei   Toronto

WCB/McGraw-Hill

A Division of The **McGraw·Hill** *Companies*

DRUGS AND LIFE, FOURTH EDITION

 This book is printed on recycled, acid-free paper containing 10% postconsumer waste.

3 4 5 6 7 8 9 0 QPD/QPD 9 3 2 1 0

ISBN 0–697–29424–2

Vice president and editorial director: *Kevin T. Kane*
Publisher: *Edward E. Barteil*
Developmental editor: *Shirley R. Oberbroeckling*
Senior marketing manager: *Pamela S. Cooper*
Project manager: *Mary Lee Harms*
Production supervisor: *Sandy Ludovissy*
Freelance design coordinator: *Mary L. Christianson*
Senior photo research coordinator: *Carrie K. Burger*
Supplement coordinator: *Tammy Juran*
Compositor: *ElectraGraphics, Inc.*
Typeface: *10/12 Times Roman*
Printer: *Quebecor Printing Book Group/Dubuque, IA*

Freelance designer: *Elise Lansdon*

The credits section for this book begins on page 247 and is considered an extension of the copyright page.

www.mhhe.com

Contents

Five   Stimulants: Cocaine, Amphetamine, and the Xanthines   77

Six   Marijuana   97

Seven   Nicotine   109

Eight   Hallucinogens and Inhalants   127

Preface

When I began to write the fourth edition of this textbook, I had convinced myself that I would not have to make too many changes. After three previous tries I should have solved most of the difficult problems, such as which issues to emphasize and which topics to cover. I found out as I started on the first chapter, however, that I was going to be writing a virtually new text. The primary reason was the information explosion brought about by the Internet and the almost overwhelming amount of new research that became available as a result. In addition, much of my own thinking has changed as a result of studying this literature. With great regret, I have had to shorten or eliminate many of the sections that dealt with the sociopolitical and historical aspects of drug use. Much of the new research has focused on the neurochemical and biological basis of drug use and abuse, so I have expanded the sections that cover these topics.

1. In the first chapter, I begin with the concept of addiction and have included discussions of expectancy theory and the role of religion. The impact of managed health care on treatment of drug abuse has been enormous, and this topic is covered as well.

2. In my own teaching, I found that it took me longer than I would have liked to cover the basic material in chapters 2 and 3 in the previous edition, so I combined the two with the hope that I have not eliminated any essential topics. In some areas dealing with neurochemical changes at the synapse I have gone into greater detail, because I think the detail is essential as a background for understanding the other chapters.

3. The two chapters on alcohol have been substantially rewritten and updated with new findings and recent research studies. I have gone into greater detail on the effects of alcohol on bodily functions and have used more specific examples.

4. When writing about the neurobiological aspects of drug use, I have used the recent work on the "reward pathway" from the substantia nigra to the nucleus accumbens as a unifying principle. I think it is very important for students to understand how drugs work in the brain.

5. In the chapter on stimulants I have tried to anticipate what many researchers feel will be the next trend of drug abuse, the use of methamphetamine. Crank abuse has become endemic in California and other parts of the western United States. All of the available intelligence reports indicate that it is making inroads elsewhere as well. Cocaine abuse is still an important topic, but use seems to be declining except among hard-core users.

6. The social issues surrounding marijuana use are in a state of rapid flux. I wish I were prescient and could predict what will happen in the next few years. I suspect there will be a major shift in the way the general public views this drug.

7. As I write this, the tobacco industry is reeling from recent congressional actions. Again I wish I knew what was going to happen in this country regarding tobacco use and the tobacco industry.

8. In another major change, I have combined the narcotics chapter and the chapter on legal drugs. As a result I have deleted some information on over-the-counter drugs. I believe this change is in keeping with my emphasis on drugs that have psychoactive properties.

9. The last chapter has been improved by using social policy as the underlying theme. I include drinking and driving in this chapter, because I think it is a major social issue.

10. In the third edition I introduced a study guide for the first time. Because it has met with considerable approval, I am including the guide in this edition. Moreover, I have listed Internet addresses of the important sites that relate to drug use and abuse. The study guide includes an exercise in each chapter that requires the student to use appropriate Internet sources. I am confident that this will help the student become familiar with the vast amount of information available online.

I hope the reader will agree with my changes. Wherever possible I have chosen the most recent review articles instead of older sources. The interested student or instructor can use these references to find the older literature.

I have tried to be realistic and objective. While I have

strong opinions about many of the topics I have discussed, I have tried to present several points of view with equal emphasis. At the same time I have tried to make the text interesting and have included a number of topics that I think the student will enjoy reading. I have received several compliments whose gist was that the text was not preachy or heavy-handed. Drug abuse is never funny, but neither does it have to be unrelentingly grim. I think my occasional use of humor is justified.

It is my sincere hope that this edition will be useful to the student for many years to come. Several readers have written to me indicating that they have kept a copy of the book for reference and have found it valuable. The changes I have made should make the book even more of a "keeper." No book is without errors, and, of course, I take full responsibility for any that are found.

Harry Avis, Ph.D.
Department of Psychology
Sierra College
5000 Rocklin Road
Rocklin, CA. 95677

Pedagogical Aids

Chapter Objectives at the beginning of each chapter provide the student with a list of concepts to be aware of when reading and studying the chapter.

NEW to this edition! After each major section, a *Stop and Review* feature asks questions on the material, allowing students to make sure they understand the main concepts.

In Depth and *What Do You Think?* boxes contain additional information for specific content on current concerns or controversies.

A *Chapter Summary* assists students in the review process with the major concepts.

Key Terms are bolded in the text and defined after the summary in each chapter.

The *References* section at the end of each chapter contains the latest materials, allowing the students access to further readings and research.

The *Student Study Guide* at the end of the text contains study guide information for each chapter. There is an outline of the objectives for each chapter; a list of the key terms; a summary of the key concepts; and a self-test consisting of multiple-choice, true/false, and critical thinking questions.

NEW to the study guide is material on the Internet and research questions using the Internet resources listed.

Supplemental Material

For the Instructor

Instructor's Manual and Test Bank

Prepared by Harry Avis, the *Instructor's Manual* includes tips for teaching and various resources available. The test bank includes multiple choice, true/false, and essay questions for each chapter.

Microtest

This software provides a unique combination of user-friendly aids that enable the instructor to select, edit, delete, or add questions, as well as construct and print tests and answer keys. The computerized test bank package is available to qualified adopters of the text for PC and Macintosh computers.

Photo CD-ROM for Drugs

The CD-ROM includes 39 images on the nervous system, methods of drug administration, alcohol, tobacco, cocaine, opioids, stages of change, and recovery/prevention. Contact your sales representative for details.

Web Sites

Information about WCB/McGraw-Hill drug and health books is available on the Internet. Go to *http://www.mhhe.com/hper/health/* and discover a variety of material.

For the Student

HealthQuest

HealthQuest by Gold/ Atkinson/ Conley/ McDermott is an interactive CD-ROM allowing exploration of your health and wellness status. The modules on tobacco, alcohol, and other drugs give you the opportunity to input your data and receive feedback on your personal drug level. *HealthQuest* can be packaged with the text. Contact your sales representative for details.

Taking Sides: Clashing Views on Controversial Issue in Drugs and Society

Raymond Goldberg from the State University of New York at Cortland has brought together 36 selections dealing with 18 current controversial drug issues for debate. *Taking Sides* is the perfect tool to encourage critical thinking. *Taking Sides* can be packaged with the text. Call your sales representative for details.

Annual Editions: Drugs, Society, and Behavior

This series of articles is a collection of facts, issues, and perspectives designed to provide the reader a framework for examining current drug-related issues. *Annual Editions* can be packaged with the text. Your sales representative can help you with the details.

Web Sites

Information about WCB/McGraw-Hill drug and health books is available on the Internet. Go to *http://www.mhhe.com/hper/health/* and discover a variety of material.

Acknowledgments

No one has ever written a textbook without the help of a variety of people. The comments I received from my reviewers helped me during the writing process of the fourth edition of *Drugs and Life.*

Reviewers

John H. Reed
Manchester Community-Technical College

Judy Hagan
Fort Peck Community College

Faye Evans
Thomas Nelson Community College

Victor Etta
Chicago State University

Denise Denton
Iowa State University

Jerry Lotterhos
East Carolina University

Joseph Donnelly
Montclair State University

Wayne Jones
Southeastern Oklahoma State University

Elin Cormican
Mohawk Valley Community College

Chapter One

An Overview

Chapter Objectives

When you have finished studying this chapter, you should

1. Understand why the term *addiction* is such a difficult concept to define.
2. Know the difference between pharmacological and behavioral definitions of addiction.
3. Understand what craving is and how it differs from withdrawal.
4. Know the definition of substance abuse according to the *DSM-IV*.
5. Be able to distinguish among four kinds of tolerance.
6. Be able to state the criteria used in the Comprehensive Drug Abuse Prevention and Control Act to list drugs on various schedules.
7. Know why heroin, LSD, and marijuana are Schedule I drugs while cocaine is Schedule II.
8. Understand why nicotine and marijuana are often placed in their own separate categories.
9. Know what the two major drug surveys are and how they differ.
10. Be able to describe how drug use changes across the life span.
11. Be able to describe the three kinds of drug use.
12. Know the stages of recovery and the role that relapse plays.
13. Be able to state the three primary reasons for relapse.
14. Distinguish between lapse and relapse.
15. Be able to show the differences between inpatient and outpatient treatment.
16. Be able to differentiate between negative and positive reinforcement.
17. Know what role religion plays in drug use.
18. Be able to describe how availability affects drug choice and use.
19. Know why *expectancy* has become an important concept in explaining drug use.
20. Be able to define the term *dual diagnosis* and show how it complicates treatment.

A man of good constitution can drink two bottles of wine a day throughout a long lifetime; but he would not stand the same quantity of coffee for so long. He would become an idiot or die of consumption. In Leicester Square, London, I have seen a man whom the immoderate use of coffee had reduced to the state of a helpless cripple.

Brillat Savarin, 1826

Let, then, every man who has drunk too deeply from the cup of pleasure, every man who has devoted to work a considerable part of the time due to sleep, every man tormented with some fixed idea which deprives him from the liberty of thinking, let all such people, we say, prescribe to themselves a good pint of chocolate mixed with amber . . . and they will see wonders.

Brillat-Savarin, 1830
(As quoted in Gattey, 1986)

According to the National Household Survey on Drug Use, illegal drug use in the United States reached a peak in 1979, when 17.5 percent of those over the age of 12 admitted to having used an illegal drug within the last year. The low point was 1992, when the figure was 9.7 percent. Since then, however, illegal drug use has begun to increase once again. The latest figures available (for 1997) indicate that 11.2 percent admitted to using an illegal drug (*National Household Survey on Drug Abuse*, 1998). Table 1.1 shows

TABLE 1.1 Trends in Percentage of Young Adults (18–25) Reporting Drug Use in the Past Year

Drug	1979	1982	1985	1988	1991	1992	1993	1994	1995	1996	1997
Any illicit drug	45.5	—	37.4	29.1	26.6	24.1	24.2	24.6	25.5	26.8	28.3
Marijuana	44.2	37.4	34.0	26.1	22.9	21.2	21.4	21.8	21.8	23.8	22.3
Cocaine	17.0	15.9	13.6	10.5	6.7	5.5	4.4	3.6	4.3	4.7	3.9
Alcohol	84.6	80.6	84.2	79.6	80.7	75.6	76.9	78.5	76.5	75.3	75.1
Cigarettes	—	—	49.9	50.9	46.9	46.8	43.7	41.1	42.5	44.7	45.9

— indicates that an estimate is not available
Notice that use has increased since 1994 for all drugs except alcohol. None of the percentages for the past few years comes close to 1979. National Household Survey on Drug Abuse (1998)

the results of that survey looking specifically at young adults 18–25. While drug use in 1997 is much lower than in 1979, use of illegal drugs has begun to increase. You should also see that alcohol use has decreased much less than marijuana use. How can this continuing use of illegal drugs be explained? After all, these young adults were exposed to numerous drug education programs in school. Has the War on Drugs turned into a stalemate? Does the recent increase mean that we are losing the war? Are the young adults who admit to this use drug abusers or merely experimenters?

Before we begin to look at these and other questions, we need to examine the meaning of some terms that will be used throughout this book. Virtually everyone who is quoted on the subject uses terms like *addiction, legalization,* and *drug abuse* very freely. Is everyone talking about the same thing? Does it make sense to talk about heroin addiction and addiction to the Internet in the same sentence? Just how much drug use is drug abuse? What is drug abuse itself?

The term *addiction* is a good place to start. Until recently, the definition of addiction was simple: addiction occurs when the user develops **tolerance** and **dependence** (O'Brien, 1996). *Tolerance* means that the body has become adapted to the presence of a drug with the result that a given amount of a drug has less of an effect than when the user first tried it. *Dependence* means that physiological changes have taken place so that the drug is necessary for normal functioning—without the drug, the user experiences **withdrawal,** a process also known as **detoxification.** If drug use is resumed before detoxification is finished, the symptoms disappear. We will call this **pharmacological addiction** (see fig. 1.1). If these were the only problems associated with addiction, treatment would consist solely of detoxification. But of course, physical withdrawal is just the beginning of recovery. In addiction, pharmacological addiction does not explain why users report strong cravings for drugs that cause little or no physical dependence (O'Brien, 1997).

Newer definitions of addiction presently emphasize out-of-control use. A person is addicted if he or she (1) takes more drug than originally intended, (2) continues drug use

despite serious personal and legal problems, and (3) after long periods of **abstinence** has a **relapse** and begins using again (Heyman, 1997). We will call this **behavioral addiction.** The terms *craving* and *drug-seeking behavior* encompass the three criteria above and are more commonly used. The American Psychiatric Association avoids the term *addiction* entirely, using instead the terms *substance abuse* and *substance dependence* in its official publications (American Psychiatric Association, 1994). The fourth edition of the *Di-*

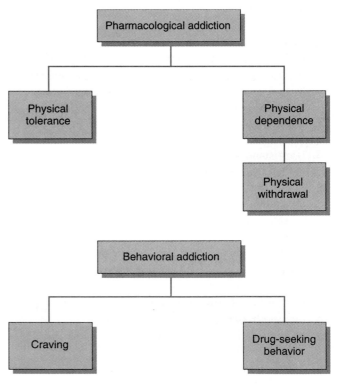

Two different views of addiction

FIGURE 1.1
The older view of addiction emphasizes the physiological basis of drug abuse. The newer view takes into consideration psychological factors.

agnostic and Statistical Manual of Mental Disorders (DSM-IV) is the standard reference used to classify psychological disorders, including substance-abuse disorders. The *DSM-IV* definition of substance dependence (table 1.2) is very close to our definition of behavioral addiction. Substance abuse seems to involve behavior that causes significant problems without causing dependence.

Let us look at two drugs from the viewpoint of the old and newer definitions. **Caffeine** is a widely used drug, and you might be surprised to learn that it is "addicting" by the older, pharmacological definition (Strain, Mumford, Silverman, & Griffiths, 1994). However, very few caffeine users meet the criteria for the newer definition of addiction. Who continues to drink coffee even though it causes serious personal problems? Do you know anyone who has relapsed after not drinking coffee for several months? All the same, the prolonged use of caffeine is considered a significant enough problem that the American Psychiatric Association lists the drug in an appendix of the *DSM-IV* and says that the question of caffeine dependence "deserves further study."

Cocaine is widely considered an addicting drug, yet physical withdrawal from this drug is mild. Tolerance occurs when the user is using heavily, but cocaine is not used every day for long periods (Gold, 1997). According to the pharmacological definition, then, cocaine is not a particularly addicting drug. But obviously the definition is wrong—because cocaine abuse has been a serious problem in the United States. Users relapse, they use in spite of serious personal and occupational problems, and some users report that the craving for the drug is strong weeks after they have stopped using (Schuckit, 1995).

Distinguishing between the two types of addiction helps explain the use of narcotic drugs such as morphine. Virtually everyone taking narcotics for several weeks will experience dependence with physical withdrawal. Nevertheless, fewer than 1 percent of patients taking properly prescribed narcotic drugs go on to develop an addiction (Stimmel, 1997). Taking narcotics for nonmedical reasons, though, rapidly leads to behavioral addiction (Stimmel, 1997). As you will read in chapter 9, this distinction has dramatically changed physicians' attitudes toward prescribing narcotic pain medication. The patient's report of pain is now accepted as the criterion to be used in deciding how much and how often to prescribe. Long-term medication with narcotics is now being used to relieve the pain of a number of chronic conditions including headache and low back pain (Ziegler, 1994;

TABLE 1.2 Some Common Substance-Related Disorders

Substance Dependence	Substance Withdrawal	Substance Abuse
A maladaptive pattern of substance use leading to impairment or distress with three or more of the following during the last year:	A condition, resulting from substance use, with all of the following three characteristics:	A maladaptive pattern of substance use leading to impairment or distress, with one or more of the following within the last year:
1. Tolerance—either needing more of the substance to achieve the same effect, or reverse tolerance.	1. Development of symptoms due to a cessation or reduction in substance use that has been heavy or prolonged.	1. Recurrent substance use leading to a failure to fulfill role obligations at work, school, or home.
2. Withdrawal.	2. The symptoms cause distress or impairment in social, occupational, or other areas of functioning.	2. Recurrent use in physically hazardous situations (drinking and driving, for example).
3. Use of the substance in larger amounts or over a longer period of time than intended.	3. Symptoms are not due to a medical condition or a mental disorder.	3. Recurrent use-related legal problems, such as arrest for disorderly conduct.
4. Persistent desire or unsuccessful attempts to cut down on substance use.		4. Continued use despite social or interpersonal problems recurrently being caused or made worse by the substance.
5. Spending a great deal of time in activities necessary to obtain the drug (such as going to many doctors for prescriptions), or using the substance, or recovering from its use.		
6. Important social, occupational, or recreational activities are given up or reduced because of its use.		
7. Use is continued despite the existence of physical or psychological problems caused or made worse by the substance.		

Source: American Psychiatric Association: *Diagnostic and Statistical Manual of Mental Disorders, Fourth Edition*, Washington, DC, American Psychiatric Association, 1994.

Brown, Fleming, & Patterson, 1996). Once the patient is stable, there seems to be little or no impairment in everyday activities even at high doses of these drugs (Zacny, 1995).

Stop and Review

1. What is the difference between pharmacological addiction and behavioral addiction?
2. Explain why drug use that produces dependence does not always lead to addiction.
3. The *DSM-IV* does not use the term *addiction.* What two terms does it use instead?

Another term is widely used in discussions of addiction. We read of the *disease* of alcoholism, instead of alcohol addiction. Have you ever heard of "the disease of nicotinism"? We think of heroin addicts, cocaine addicts, and people who are nicotine dependent; only alcohol abuse is described as a disease. Neither of the terms *disease* or *addiction* is used anywhere in the *DSM-IV*, even though the disease concept of alcoholism is widely accepted (Royce & Scratchley, 1996). In the chapters that follow we will see how the use of these terms affects our attitudes toward the user and our willingness to provide treatment.

In addition to the confusion over addiction and the disease concept, the term *tolerance* has more meanings than the one just described. In table 1.3 you can read the several definitions of the term. Each of these will be used in the appropriate context. For example, behavioral tolerance is seen in the drinker who learns to compensate for obvious effects of alcohol on speech and movement. Cross-tolerance occurs between several of the hallucinogenic drugs, such as mescaline and LSD. Someone who has taken several doses of LSD, for example, will not be affected by psilocybin, the active chemical in psychedelic mushrooms.

The term *dependence* can also have more than one meaning. *Physical dependence* refers to a biological change that occurs as a result of drug use. Without the drug, physical symptoms of withdrawal appear. Quite often these symptoms are opposite to the effects of the drug. The narcotic drugs produce constipation, and withdrawal from these drugs produces diarrhea. The antianxiety drugs such as Xanax and Valium reduce anxiety, and an increase in anxiety is seen during withdrawal. The term *psychological dependence* has a meaning similar to **craving.** Long-term users of a drug might feel a craving for the drug for months or even years after they have gone through physical withdrawal. In fact, this craving is more often the cause of relapse than the physiological withdrawal (Halikas, 1997). Former cigarette smokers will recognize this distinction easily (Killen & Fortman, 1997).

Craving is not an easy term to define scientifically. Often described as a "compelling urge," an "irresistible impulse," or an "overpowering desire," craving has both subjective and neurobiological aspects (Halikas, 1997). The subjective feeling is the heart of the problem of definition. Is craving a wish, a desire, or a compelling urge? It cannot be "irresistible," because not everyone always gives in. It might be related to neurochemical changes, due to prolonged drug use, that trigger a desire for the drug under certain circumstances. Perhaps the precise definition does not matter very much, since it is a term that everyone understands, especially as a significant aspect of drug use and addiction.

Perhaps the most imprecise term is the word *drug* itself. Penicillin, morphine, and birth control pills are drugs, but we don't usually think of them as being the same. We are mainly concerned with drugs that affect behavior and/or emotions. As used in this text, a **psychoactive drug** will be defined as any chemical substance taken into the body that affects psychological functioning. Keep this in mind, however: Many drugs that we ordinarily do not think of as psychoactive can affect behavior and emotion. For example, antihistamines are sold as sleeping pills as well as to reduce the symptoms of allergies.

TABLE 1.3 Definitions of Tolerance

Physiological tolerance	An adaptive mechanism at the biochemical level that affects the rate of drug metabolism and elimination. It can also involve postsynaptic receptor sensitivity or the second messenger system.
Behavioral tolerance	The process of acquiring, through learning, the ability to disguise the physiological effects of a drug. With alcohol, for example, behavioral tolerance might involve strategies for appearing sober by avoiding difficult speech sounds or by practicing walking a straight line.
Acute tolerance	The physical adaptation to a drug that occurs during a single episode of use. Acute tolerance occurs when the second administration of a drug has less effect than the first. It can also mean that a drug might have different effects when it is absorbed and when it is being metabolized.
Cross-tolerance	The development of physiological tolerance to a class of drugs after exposure to one drug in the class. For example, someone who has taken LSD will show less of a response to psilocybin if it is taken when the LSD has begun to wear off.
Reverse tolerance	The process by which a person becomes more sensitive to a drug rather than less sensitive. It can occur as a result of damage to organs, such as a liver that can no longer metabolize a drug. It can also occur for unknown reasons (as with cocaine).

TABLE 1.4 Controlled Substances

Schedule	Description	Examples
I	Virtually all the drugs in this group are illegal. All of them have a high potential for abuse and currently do not have an accepted medical use. These drugs are not prescribable.	Benzylmorphine, dihydromorphine, heroin, LSD, marijuana, mescaline, nicocodeine, peyote.
II	Like Schedule I drugs, these have a high potential for abuse and can lead to serious physical and psychological dependence. Unlike Schedule I drugs, however, they have an accepted medical use. Most of them are stimulants, narcotics, or depressants. Prescriptions for them cannot be renewed.	Amphetamine, cocaine, codeine, meperidine, morphine, secobarbital.
III	Drugs in this group have a lower potential for abuse than those in Schedules I and II, but they can nevertheless lead to dependence. Prescriptions for Schedule III drugs can be refilled up to five times in six months if the prescriber authorizes it.	Acetaminophen with codeine, aspirin with codeine, methyprylon (sleeping drug), benzphetamine (appetite suppressant), phendimetrazine (appetite suppressant),
IV	The drugs in this group have a potential for abuse lower than for Schedule I–III drugs. The regulations for refilling prescriptions are the same in most states as for Schedule III drugs.	Chloral hydrate (sleeping drug), diazepam (antianxiety drug, muscle relaxant), ethchlorvynol (sleeping drug), phenobarbital (anticonvulsant), prazepam (antianxiety drug).
V	These drugs have a low potential for abuse. For the most part, they are preparations that contain small amounts of narcotics.	(Note: These are all brand-name combination preparations.) Lomotil (antidiarrheal), Parepectolin (antidiarrheal), Cheracol (cough suppressant), Robitussin AC (cough suppressant), Tussi-Organidin liquid (cough suppressant).

Professionals in the field commonly use the phrase *alcohol, tobacco, and other drugs (ATOD)*. Does the use of this phrase mean that ATOD should be viewed as one kind of drug use? Aren't there distinctions? After all, alcohol and tobacco are legal. A distinction is made between legal and illegal drugs, but this distinction says more about the attitude of society toward a drug than about the drug itself. Drugs are not classified as legal or illegal because of their relative danger; overdoses of alcohol all too frequently are fatal, but no one has ever died of an overdose of LSD. Drugs are not classified on the basis of the addiction potential; smoking cigarettes clearly leads to severe physical dependence, smoking marijuana does not. Table 1.4 shows the legal classification of drugs as described by the Comprehensive Drug Abuse Prevention and Controlled Substances Act of 1972.

The basic criteria for classifying drugs under the Controlled Substances Act are simple: does the drug have a medical use, and does the drug have a potential for dependence. Schedule I drugs have no recognized medical use and have a high abuse potential. Heroin is a Schedule I drug in the United States even though it is used medically in other countries. Marijuana is a Schedule I drug even though its abuse potential is less than for some of the drugs lower on the list. LSD is a Schedule I drug even though true physical dependence does not occur with its use. As a result of what you will come to know as "designer drugs," any drug with a certain molecular structure is automatically a Schedule I drug even if it hasn't been created yet. It is placed on Schedule I as soon as it is first synthesized. The Controlled Substance Act of 1972 is a legal, not a scientific system that specifies legal penalties for possession, sale, or manufacture.

The most common way to classify drugs is based on their effects. Some drugs increase the activity of the nervous system and are called stimulants, some decrease the activity of the nervous system and are called depressants. Table 1.5 shows a common classification based on the effects of drugs. Keep in mind, however, that these distinctions are somewhat arbitrary. At low doses, alcohol (a depressant) suppresses the part of the brain that enables us to consider our actions, thus many people feel stimulated. High doses of cocaine (a stimulant) cause respiratory arrest and death. Yet another problem is how to classify nicotine and marijuana, which do not readily fall into any of the other categories and so are generally given their own separate classes. There are also large individual differences in responses to taking a drug. Drugs that are stimulants for most of us, calm a person with attention deficit disorder.

Stop and Review

1. Make sure that you know the various types of dependence and tolerance.
2. What are the two criteria used in the Controlled Substances Act of 1972 to classify a drug?
3. Why are nicotine and marijuana given separate listings in table 1.5?

TABLE 1.5 The Principal Psychoactive Drugs

Mode of Action	Drug	Street/Trade Names
Stimulant	Cocaine	Coke, crack, Aunt Nora, Racehorse Charlie
	Amphetamine	Benzedrine, Dexedrine, bennies, thrusters
	Methamphetamine	Crystal, crank, gofast, ice
	Xanthines	Coffee, tea, chocolate
Depressant	Alcohol	Gin, beer, wine
	Barbiturates	Yellow jackets, Nembutol, Seconal, sodium pentothal
	Benzodiazepines	Disco biscuits, blue martinis, Ativan, Xanax, Librium, Valium
Cannabis	Marijuana	Skunk, righteous bush, grass, Lord Randolph's wedding weed, indica, sativa, sins, shake, ditch weed, bo-bo, blunt, catnip, and many, many others
	Tetrahydrocannabinol (THC)	Marinol
	Hashish	Hash
Hallucinogens	LSD	Acid, fry, snowman, shields, yellow dimple, vodka acid
	Psilocybin	'Shrooms, silly putty
	Mescaline	Peyote, half-moon
	Phencyclidine	PCP, angel dust, mad dog, gorilla biscuits
	Amphetamine-like drugs	MDA, MDMA, DOM, 45-minute psychosis, XTC, Adam
Narcotics	Opium	Paregoric
	Codeine	Codeine sulfate, Tylenol with codeine
	Morphine	Morphine
	Heroin	Bozo, Aunt Hazel, red chicken, Tango and Cash, snow, etc.
Stimulant-Sedatives	Nicotine	Tobacco

Source: Drugs and Crime Data Center and Clearinghouse.

Who Uses Drugs

If you were to ask people on the street if they had ever used drugs, most would probably answer no, because most people assume the term means illegal drugs. However, according to the definition of psychoactive drugs you just read, the right answer would almost definitely be yes. As you can see in table 1.6, 83.5 percent of young adults 18–25 questioned reported that they had used alcohol at least once in their lives. Even if you were asking about illegal drugs, table 1.6 shows that 45 percent answered yes to the question "Have you ever used an illegal drug?" The most commonly used illegal drug is marijuana, followed by cocaine. Nearly half of young adults admit to marijuana use and nearly 10 percent to cocaine use. Were all of these people addicted? Obviously not, but does this mean that there is a safe level of drug use? How much marijuana can you smoke without becoming dependent? How much alcohol can a person drink without becoming an alcoholic? What level of cocaine use constitutes addiction? We will deal with these questions in the chapters to follow. Keep in mind, for now, that the answer to the question "Who uses drugs?" is: virtually everyone.

You should be wondering where these figures come from and how accurate they are. No medical tests exist that can detect whether a person used a drug several years ago or even several weeks ago. You will see that it is difficult even to detect heavy current use of some drugs. The data that you read in the media and in this text largely come from questionnaires, which means that these percentages represent those who *admit* to using drugs. Even though common sense

would tell us that people who use illegal drugs or misuse legal ones are likely to lie about it, most researchers feel that these numbers are reasonably accurate (Harrison, Haaga, & Richards, 1993).

The questionnaires are answered anonymously, the wording does not reflect any disapproval of use, and people are surprisingly willing to admit to a wide range of socially disapproved behaviors. One exception to this general rule of honesty is reporting on lifetime use; about 20 percent of people who admit to recent drug use deny that use a few years later (Harrison, Haaga, & Richards, 1993). Does it surprise you that most of the "forgetting" was done by infrequent users? These questionnaires are always voluntary, and certain groups of potential users are likely not to be sampled, so the figures are probably a little low. The data are most useful in detecting trends. Given that there is, at present, no other way of determining drug use that is nearly as accurate, these figures are as good as we can get.

The two most widely cited drug surveys are the Monitoring the Future survey and the National Household Survey on Drug Abuse. Because of their long history, they are seen as definitive. The Monitoring the Future survey samples high school students, while the National Household Survey questions a random sample of people over the age of 12. The Monitoring the Future survey is school-based; the National Household Survey is administered in people's homes. A direct comparison of the two for young people shows that rates of drug use obtained in the school survey are larger than those obtained in the household survey (Gfroerer, Wright, & Kopstein, 1997). The household survey is administered to

Why Does Western Society Use Alcohol and Not Hallucinogens?

You will read in chapter 3 that fermented alcoholic beverages such as beer and wine are mentioned in the first written historical records, dating back five thousand years. Evidence exists that the use of mind-altering plants is even more ancient. These plants that we refer to as hallucinogenic may have played a role in the development of moral, ethical, and religious systems (Dobkin de Rios, 1984; Wasson, Kramrisch, Ott, & Ruck, 1986). Why does our culture view the use of alcohol as acceptable while making the use of hallucinogens illegal?

The question becomes even more complicated when we consider cultures such as the Maya and Aztec of what is now Latin American. These highly sophisticated societies had both alcoholic beverages and hallucinogenic substances. The hallucinogens were revered and considered holy, while alcohol played a small role (Devereaux,1997). Although the dangers of excessive drinking have been recognized in all cultures that have learned to ferment alcohol, there is no evidence of abuse of hallucinogenic substances in any of the cultures that have been studied (Dobkin de Rios, 1984).

Many theories have been proposed to explain how our culture came to use alcohol to the virtual exclusion of hallucinogenic substances (McKenna, 1992; Devereaux, 1997). Both alcohol and mind-altering plants were known to Western society, and there is evidence that mind-altering plants were used before alcohol (Devereaux, 1997). What factors do you think might be responsible for alcohol becoming the predominant drug of our culture? Here are some ideas to consider:

1. Alcohol in the form of wine has symbolic significance in our predominant religious system, Christianity.
2. Greek society, which was familiar with both alcohol and mind-altering plants, was supplanted by the Romans, whose overwhelmingly favorite drink was wine.
3. Alcohol kills bacteria, and wine and beer are much safer drinks when the only alternative is contaminated water.
4. Beer and (to a lesser extent) wine contain nutrients and vitamins that may have supplemented a meager diet.

young people while parents are in the house, though not in the same room; the school survey is administered anonymously in the classroom. Would you be as likely to answer truthfully if you knew your parents were nearby?

Drug Use across the Life Span

Just as the risk of having an automobile accident varies with age, drug use of any kind also changes with age. For most people, drug use reaches its peak during late adolescence and early adulthood (Chen & Kandel, 1995). Specifically, marijuana and alcohol use reach their peak before age 21, while the peak of cocaine use is a few years later. The only drug use that does not show a decline with age is cigarette smoking. The age of onset of drug use is also an important consideration. Children are beginning drug use at an earlier age than ever before. For most young people, the first drug is cigarettes, followed by alcohol and marijuana. The earlier drug use begins, the greater the risk for abuse (Zhang, Wieczorek, & Welte, 1997).

TABLE 1.6 Trends in Percentage of Young Adults (18–25) Reporting Drug Use in Their Lifetime

Drug	1979	1982	1985	1988	1991	1992	1993	1994	1995	1996	1997
Any illicit drug	69.0	—	62.9	58.1	53.9	50.9	50.2	46.3	45.8	48.0	45.4
Marijuana	66.1	61.3	57.6	54.6	48.8	46.6	45.7	41.9	41.4	44.0	41.5
Cocaine	27.2	27.4	24.3	19.6	17.8	15.7	12.5	12.1	9.8	10.2	8.9
Alcohol	—	—	—	—	—	85.8	86.6	86.3	84.4	83.8	83.5
Cigarettes	—	—	75.3	75.2	71.4	9.0	67.1	69.1	67.7	68.5	67.7

— data not available

Note that those who report ever using any illegal drug has declined but the percentage reporting use of alcohol and cigarettes has remained fairly constant. You should also note that the percentage using alcohol and cigarettes is far higher than the percentage reporting illegal drug use. Nevertheless, nearly half of young adults have used an illegal drug at least once.

Abuse of drugs can develop at any age. Studies have identified alcohol abusers in the fourth grade (Loveland-Cherry, Leech, Laetz, & Dielman, 1996). Children at risk for later substance abuse can be identified as early as kindergarten (Masse & Tremblay, 1997). Nor is abuse of drugs (especially alcohol) rare among the elderly (Adams, Barry, & Fleming, 1996). Elderly abusers are not necessarily those who drank or used heavily throughout a lifetime; abuse can begin late in age (Gambert, 1997). Substance abuse does not follow a clear pattern during the life span. Some people are abusers early in life, others at middle age, and some during the retirement years. For example, alcohol abusers will go through periods of abstinence or moderate use that might last for months or years, interrupted by a period of heavy use (Schuckit, 1996).

The vast majority of people who try a drug do not go on to abuse it. The major risk period begins about age 12 and is mostly over by 22 (DeWitt, Offord, & Wong, 1997). The average user's illegal drug use is **experimental use,** defined as ten or fewer experiences. Experimental users do not go on to regular use for a number of reasons—the drug is not readily available, the user does not like the effect of the drug, the user matures or has changes in lifestyle that do not support continued use, and so on. Experimental users might have been motivated by curiosity, might be more willing to take risks, or might have lived a lifestyle that encouraged drug use. Experimental use is not usually harmful. In fact, at least one study shows that those who used marijuana in their youth during the 1970s were actually better adjusted than those who had been abstainers or heavy users (Shedler & Block, 1990).

Regular use, also called "social" or "recreational" use, occurs when the user finds that the drug is reinforcing. Regular users incorporate drug use into their living pattern, but it does not usually become a problem for them, either. It might surprise you to know that there are recreational users of just about any drug, legal or illegal. If the drug is illegal, the user might have to be careful to avoid detection, and might deny use if asked. Most people who drink alcoholic beverages are regular users. They drink in social settings, when relaxing, or for the enjoyment of the taste or effects. For some people, though, it appears that drug use becomes associated with relief from negative emotions and situations. These users usually go on to heavy use.

Heavy users have taken regular use to an extreme. They often use in situations that are risky, or might use the drug as a means to escape problems (often brought on by the drug use itself). Their recreational experiences are likely to be limited, and their lifestyle might revolve around the drug use. Heavy drinkers, for example, might avoid social situations and might choose to drink alone or with a few other heavy-drinking companions. Heavy users are at great risk of developing legal, occupational, personal, or health-related problems. Not every heavy user of a drug experiences problems, and some heavy drinkers continue for many decades

(Fingarette, 1988). Most people know at least one person who drank heavily, smoked cigarettes, and lived to a ripe old age. It is important to keep in mind that they accomplished this in spite of their habits, not because of them.

Stop and Review

1. What age group is at greatest risk for using illegal drugs and alcohol?
2. What is the typical pattern of drug use over the life span of an individual?
3. What are the three main patterns of drug use?

Recovery and Treatment

The path to drug abuse is complex, so it should not be surprising that the path to recovery is complex as well. A series of studies has shown that recovery occurs in stages (Prochaska, DiClemente, & Norcross, 1992). As you can read in figure 1.2, the stages of change begin with the **precontemplation stage.** In this stage, abusers have no intention of changing. They do not think about solutions, because they do not think they have a problem. Their family, friends, and employers might see the problem, though. Abusers in this stage might go for treatment because of threats from others, but once the pressure is off they revert to old habits (Willoughby & Edens, 1996).

The second stage is the **contemplation stage.** Abusers now recognize that change is necessary, but they are still struggling with the decision. They justify continuing their drug abuse by thinking about how good alcohol tastes or how much they need the cocaine high. When they consider the effort required to change and what they will have to give up, they choose to continue. Nevertheless, they are concerned about their use.

The third stage is called the **preparation stage.** Abusers now intend to change, and soon. They begin to think about treatment or methods of cutting down. They are still using, but they have crossed the line. They often try to cut down their use or tell others of their decision. Part of the preparation stage is adjusting their beliefs about themselves. They begin to think of themselves as abusers instead of users.

The fourth stage is the **action stage.** Action requires time and energy, often a great deal of time and energy. The action stage does not represent real change, but the abuser is struggling with the issue. People in this stage do not usually think of themselves as in recovery, because their struggle is still very difficult. As a general rule, the action stage usually last six months to a year after the user stops.

Maintenance, the fifth stage, is an active process during which the abuser continues abstinence and tries to prevent relapse. This stage also requires time and energy. The newness of being abstinent has worn off but the temptations remain. The maintenance stage can last for months or a lifetime. Some abusers prefer to call themselves "recovering"

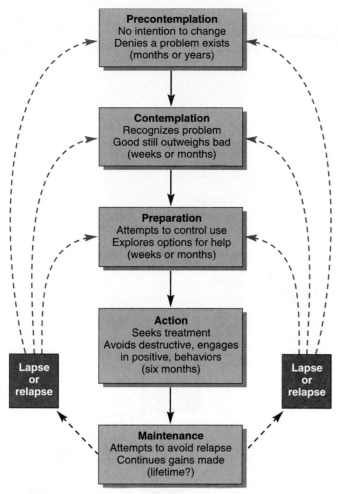

FIGURE 1.2
The stages of change apply to virtually any drug of abuse, including alcohol and nicotine.

Most often relapse occurs when a person is in a high-risk situation and lacks the resources to cope. Three kinds of situations commonly lead to relapse: (1) negative emotional states, such as frustration or boredom; (2) interpersonal conflicts; and (3) social pressures, such as being offered a drink in a situation where it is hard to refuse. Other researchers feel that a lack of social interaction, the family setting, anxiety, and depression should be added to the list (Stout, Longabaugh, & Rubin, 1996). These relapse triggers will not automatically lead to drinking or using. Good coping skills act as a buffer against the temptation to use again (Marlatt, 1996).

Coping skills can be either active or passive. Active skills involve doing something that is incompatible with using or thinking about the recent positive consequences of abstinence. Passive skills involve ignoring the cues or waiting them out. Not surprisingly, active coping skills are more effective than passive ones in preventing relapse (McKay, Maisto, & O'Farrell,1996). You will read about specific relapse prevention methods and relapse triggers for several drugs in subsequent chapters.

It is useful to make a distinction between a lapse and a relapse and even a collapse. A lapse is a single occurrence of use. How the abuser deals with this lapse seems to be important in determining whether he or she will return to heavy use (a relapse). If the user sees it as a sign of weakness, a full relapse is more likely. If the user views it instead as a mistake, figures out why it occurred, and develops coping skills to use when the situation recurs, a return to abusive drinking or use is less likely (Rotgers, 1996). The most positive outcome occurs when the user is faced with a risky situation and copes without using. Such success leads to a greater feeling of self-worth and confidence that one has the ability to weather other crises. Figure 1.3 shows how these two pathways diverge.

Treatment for Substance Abuse

Once the alcohol or drug abuser has decided to change, a number of options are available. No one knows how many people decide to stop smoking, drinking, using heroin or cocaine, and simply do so. The Office of the Surgeon General of the United States (*The Health Benefits of Smoking Cessation,* 1990) claims that 90 percent of cigarette smokers stop on their own without any help. Estimates for other drugs vary, but it is probably safe to say that the majority of abusers of any drug stop without formal or informal treatment (Sobell, Cunningham, & Sobell, 1996; Godlaski, Leukefeld, & Cloud, 1997).

For many people, though, some kind of treatment is necessary. Hospitalization is essential for severely dependent individuals at risk for life-threatening complications of withdrawal. Those who are not physically dependent do not need hospitalization during withdrawal (Booth, Blow,

rather than recovered abusers, in recognition of the fact they are still engaged in the struggle. Relapse is common during this stage, as it is in the previous stage. It is relatively easy to stop using; the problem is staying stopped. In the past few years a great deal of attention has been focused on **relapse prevention.**

Relapse Prevention

Why would a person who has been abstinent for months or even years suddenly start using again? During the short period of time immediately after stopping, when the abuser is going through withdrawal, the reasons are fairly obvious. Taking a drug during the withdrawal period relieves the withdrawal symptoms. Physical withdrawal is complete for all drugs within a relatively short period of time, yet relapse rates in the first year are high for most drugs. Although the exact nature of relapse triggers is still a matter of debate, several situations are generally recognized as being involved (Marlatt, 1996).

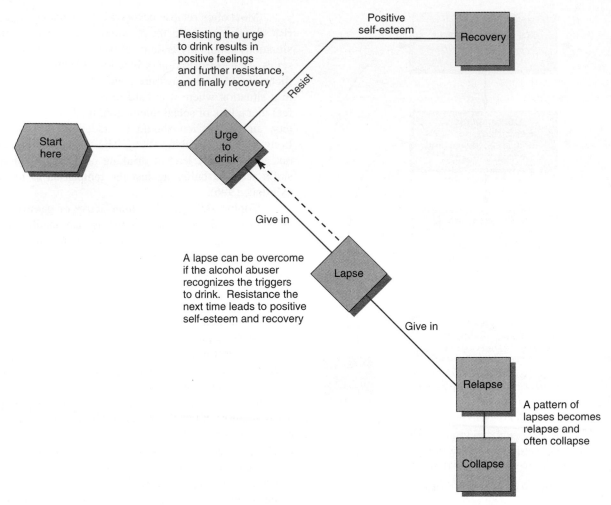

FIGURE 1.3
A summary of several possible pathways to recovery or relapse.

Ludke, & Ross, 1996). After detoxification, the choices are varied. Some inpatient drug programs last for two months, others for two weeks. In an inpatient program, abusers remain in a hospital-like situation, usually confined to the premises, and are closely monitored. They are expected to attend meetings, lectures, and group therapy. Patients are not allowed to wear clothing with any design or decoration that mentions alcohol or drug use. Even the use of caffeine is prohibited or restricted in many programs. Outpatient treatment is more flexible. Patients attend meetings during the day, but return to their own homes at night. Some programs are run in the evening so the patient can continue to work.

A shift has begun to take place in the treatment sector. Inpatient treatment used to be the rule. Such programs can cost thousands of dollars a day, and a one-month program can lead to a staggering bill. In the past, some medical insurance programs would pay for this treatment, but the advent of managed care has changed that. Managed care programs make the not-unreasonable assumption that treatments should work. They also insist that if two treatments

work equally well and one costs thousands of dollars less, they will pay only for the less expensive one. Outpatient treatment does not involve hospitalization, so obviously it is much less expensive (Campbell, Gabrielli, Laster, & Liskow, 1997).

Are the two kinds of programs equivalent? Apparently yes, at least in the short run (McLellan, Hagan, Meyers, Randell, & Durrell, 1997). This might not be saying much, since short-term relapse rates are high for both inpatient and outpatient treatment and numerous questions have yet to be answered. Are substance abusers with more serious problems better off at inpatient centers? Is inpatient treatment more effective with some types of abusers? Are long-term relapse rates the same? These questions have yet to be answered.

Drug abuse does not affect only the abuser. The spouse and children of a married substance abuser have a difficult task coping with the disruption that the abuse typically creates in the family. The abuser is rarely an ideal parent and seldom a good spouse. After recovery begins, the family must learn to deal with someone they might hardly recognize, and the various strategies they developed to compensate for having a substance abuser in the family now have to change (McKay, et al 1996). Family therapy is often useful in helping with these changes. Studies have shown that substance abusers whose treatment includes family therapy fare better than those who have only individual therapy (Stanton & Shadish, 1997).

Relapse is common for substance abusers. As you read earlier, cognitive psychologists have developed various ways of coping with craving. In addition, both psychotherapy and drug treatment are often useful (Borg, 1997; McDuff & Beuger, 1997). Drug treatment might be geared to reducing craving or relieving the depression and anxiety that are common during recovery (Borg, 1997). Some studies suggest that a combination of drug treatment and psychotherapy leads to the best outcome (Carroll, 1997). Drug treatment can be essential during the acute withdrawal stage. A new drug treatment for heroine can eliminate the symptoms of withdrawal. The patient is given several drugs that induce withdrawal and heavy sedation so that the patient sleeps during the entire withdrawal period (Bartter & Gooberman, 1996).

Many substance abusers are depressed in the period after withdrawal, and craving, although difficult to define, is usually strong. Psychotherapy typically focuses on helping the abuser deal with feelings of shame and learn how to function in "straight" society. Antidepressant drugs have been moderately helpful with these patients' emotional problems. Drug treatments that suppress the craving for alcohol (O'Malley, 1996) and drugs that counteract the effects of cocaine are in the development stage; with these treatments, even if the abuser slips, the abused drug will have no effect. Of course, short-term treatment is unlikely to be long-lasting if the substance abuser does not maintain the changes made during early recovery. Groups such as Alcoholics Anonymous and Narcotics Anonymous as well as other social and community resources are necessary to support long-term recovery (Humphreys, Moos, & Cohen, 1997). We will return to these topics in later chapters.

For some people neither inpatient nor outpatient treatment is effective. Such individuals might do well in **therapeutic communities.** These have been in existence for more than thirty years to provide vocational and group counseling as well as social services. Substance abusers in therapeutic communities are expected to stay for long periods of time. They may be employed outside but return to the community each day. The whole living group acts as a "therapist," and peers and staff interact twenty-four hours a day. The goal of the therapeutic community is to promote a change in lifestyle and personal identity. Not every substance abuser needs such a drastic change, but for those who do, success rates are high. Of course, dropout rates are also high. Most therapeutic communities are designed to deal with narcotics abusers (Schuckit, 1995).

Stop and Review

1. What are the five stages of change?
2. What are some factors that lead to relapse?
3. How has managed care changed treatment for drug abuse?

Why Do People Take Drugs?

Most people take drugs. In many cases the reasons are obvious: to relieve headaches, to lower blood pressure, to reduce anxiety, and so on. In other cases the reasons are not so obvious. Why would anyone smoke plant material (marijuana) that causes short-term memory deficit? Why would anyone snort something (cocaine) to get an effect that lasts only for twenty minutes? The question is not why people take drugs, but why people take psychoactive drugs.

Human beings seem to have a need to alter their consciousness. At a theme park we pay money to be spun around like clothes in a dryer. Some people jump from a bridge with only a high-tech rubber band attached to their body to break their fall. Others jump from airplanes or hang-glide or snow ski. The one thing all of these behaviors have in common is that they alter our consciousness—if done well, they give us a feeling of exhilaration. Some drugs do the same thing. Soothing baths and hot tubs relax us. Drugs also can relax us. It appears that we take psychoactive drugs for the same reason we engage in certain other behaviors— to alter our consciousness (Siegal, 1989).

Another way of looking at drug use is that drugs make us feel good. The psychological term for this is **positive reinforcement** (National Institute of Drug Abuse, 1997). People rarely continue to use a drug that makes them feel bad. Alcohol, heroin, cocaine, and amphetamine all increase the release of the neurotransmitter dopamine in a part of the brain that is believed to be involved in reward (Koob & Nestler, 1997)—that is, these drugs make you feel good (at least for a short time). Once drug use is established and the person becomes dependent, the drug might no longer be rewarding, but it serves to relieve unpleasant physical and psychological states. In other words, after prolonged use a drug might no longer make you feel good, but you might need it just to feel normal (see fig. 1.4).

Negative reinforcement is a difficult concept for many people to understand, but it is really quite simple. You take an aspirin to relieve a headache. The effect of the aspirin in relieving your headache is negative reinforcement. If you drink alcohol because it gets rid of your hangover, this, too, is negative reinforcement. The debate among researchers is whether positive or negative reinforcement plays a greater role in drug use and abuse (Carroll, 1997). Both play a role, and positive reinforcement might better explain occasional drug use while negative reinforcement might predominate in drug abuse.

Some people take psychoactive drugs to enable them

The thrill of climbing this grade probably produces an increase in dopamine in this climber's nucleus accumbens. Drugs do the same thing. Which is safer?

to keep going. The caffeine in coffee and the cocaine in a coca leaf serve the same purpose for North Americans and some of the indigenous people of South America. Nicotine can increase alertness, and amphetamines have been used since they were first introduced to ward off sleepiness. The desire to enhance performance is carried to an extreme by those who take steroids or other drugs to gain an edge in athletic competition.

Many parents would like to believe that their children's drug use is due to the company they keep rather than the home they live in. Peer pressure is widely held to be a

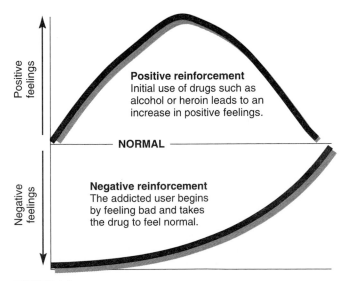

FIGURE 1.4
Many drug users report that they begin by taking a drug to feel good, but end up using to feel less bad. Frequently they report that they get no pleasure from using, only relief.

significant factor in adolescent drug use (Schor, 1996). However, young people typically report that their parents are a greater and longer-lasting influence. In addition, children's personalities influence their selection of friends. Similarity in drug use among peers probably stems from young persons' choice of friends whose drug use is similar to their own. Even during adolescence, the influence of the family is greater than the influence of peers (Schor, 1996).

Religious beliefs also affect drug use. Deeply religious young people are less likely to use drugs, although some do use drugs (Cook, Goddard, & Westall, 1997). Personal devotion seems to be a stronger factor than church attendance or affiliation. In others words, deeply religious young people of any faith are less likely than other young people to use drugs (including alcohol and nicotine). Church attendance itself does not seem to play a role, so getting drug users to go to church is unlikely to have much effect. Personal devotion is also related to conservative beliefs, which also play a role in decreasing the likelihood of using drugs (Kendler, Gardner, & Prescott, 1997).

The media are often criticized for promoting drug use. If you see a movie star or television personality smoking a cigarette or drinking a beer, are you more likely to do the same? Popular music gets its share of blame as well. About a quarter of all music videos portray alcohol or cigarette use (Durant et al., 1997). Does all this smoking and drinking encourage underage adolescents to do the same? The available research does not clearly support a causal relationship between media imagery and drug use. Such research is very difficult to do, because so many factors affect the decision to drink alcohol, smoke cigarettes, or use illegal drugs. If drug-related lyrics in popular music increase along with an increase in drug use, this might mean that the lyrics have influenced users. However, whatever factors actually lead to

Sitting in church doesn't make you religious any more than sitting in a garage makes you a car. Deeply committed religious young people are less likely to abuse drugs. Can you think of reasons why?

an increase in drug use might also influence popular music lyrics.

Cigarette manufacturers and the alcohol industry claim that they are only trying to get you to switch to their brand, not encourage you to start smoking or drinking. As you will read in chapter 7, however, the cigarette industry must recruit a million new smokers per year to replace those that quit or die, and beer is the most popular alcoholic beverage of underage drinkers. Much criticism has been directed at advertisements for smokeless tobacco at sport events that are popular with young adolescents, and beer advertisements rarely show middle-aged drinkers.

If you were a visitor from another planet and got your only impressions of human beings from cigarette and alcohol ads, you would probably think that all humans were in their early twenties, impossibly fit, and quite well off financially. How do these images compare to the public service announcements and pamphlets that are supposed to discourage underage drinking? You will read more about the influence of advertising in chapter 7, but for now you should know that research in this area has led to conflicting conclusions. Under some circumstances, however, it appears that restricting advertisements and counteradvertising can reduce consumption (Saffer, 1996).

The *availability* of a drug has a clear influence on drug use. A person who intends to drink heavily on Sunday will not be deterred by laws that prohibit alcohol sales after midnight on Saturday, but studies have shown that strategies such as increasing prices and limiting the time and places where

alcohol can be purchased do decrease overall consumption (Kenkel & Manning, 1996). Students typically report that marijuana is at least as easy to obtain as alcohol, so it should come as no surprise that marijuana is the most commonly used illegal drug. In 1997, sales of cigarettes from vending machines were severely curtailed and penalties for sale of cigarettes to underage smokers were increased. The principle behind these and other measures, such as an increase in the federal sales tax on cigarettes, is to decrease the availability of cigarettes to young people. The restrictions on smoking in public places not only reduce the danger of being exposed to secondhand smoke but discourage smokers by making the act of smoking more difficult.

The Influence of the Family

Of all the variables studied, the family influences drug and alcohol use the most (Thomas & Schandler, 1996). Family values are currently a hot political topic, but studies have shown for many years that drug abuse is far less frequent when the parents are good role models and a good relationship exists between parents and children. Such negative factors as physical or sexual abuse, family discord, or lack of parental guidance are clearly strong risk factors associated with early drug use and subsequent drug abuse (Thomas & Schandler, 1996).

Personality Factors

Numerous studies have tried to find a "drug-abusing personality," with little success (Schuckit, 1995). Research has shown that some people with personality disorders that produce long-standing difficulties with virtually every part of life are more likely to abuse drugs. Studies have also found personality differences between those in treatment and those who do not have drug problems, but these differences are not seen before the user begins to take drugs (Anthenelli & Schuckit, 1997). Apparently the personality changes occur as a result of the drug use and are not its cause.

Researchers have been more successful in identifying some individual personality characteristics that are associated with drug use and abuse. Three characteristics seem to distinguish at least some abusers: harm avoidance, novelty seeking, and reward dependence (Cloninger, Svrakic, & Przybeck, 1993). The term harm avoidance refers to cautiousness and a low level of willingness to take risks. The term novelty seeking refers to a liking for change and low levels of social and moral inhibition. Finally, the term reward dependence refers to eagerness to help others and a high sensitivity to social cue. Details of how these traits might apply to each drug will be discussed in later chapters.

Cognitive Factors

Shakespeare says in *Hamlet,* "There is nothing that is bad or good, but that thinking makes it so." Thinking or cognition plays an important role in drug use. Psychologists use the term *expectancy* to describe how thinking affects many factors related to drug use. Those who associate drinking with expectations of feeling power, sexual arousal, and relaxation drink more than those who don't, and drinking further reinforces the expectancy (Smith, Goldman, Greenbaum, & Christiansen, 1995). Expectation of the effects of drinking and other drug use begin before use actually begins and is an important factor in determining whether and how much the individual will consume when use begins (Dunn & Goldman, 1996).

The concept of expectancy can explain why some people who smoke marijuana that contains no active chemical or drink what they only think is alcohol report feeling high or intoxicated (Kirsch, 1997). Expectancy theory can also account for craving that occurs long after withdrawal is over. It might seem obvious that what people expect of a drug will influence their use of it. What is not so obvious is that changing these expectancies will decrease use (Goldman, Greenbaum, & Darkes, 1997). Expectancy theory can be extremely complex, but an example should help you gain a basic understanding: A young person has learned that alcohol or some other drug will make them interesting, happy, and sexy. When the person tries the drug, they find that they do feel interesting, sexy, and happy. The memory of this experience is triggered whenever the opportunity to use comes along again (Roerich & Goldman, 1995). There is, by the way, little relationship between what the person thinks the drug will do and what it actually does physiologically. Alcohol is more likely to make one depressed and boring, to say nothing of its effects on sexual behavior.

Sociocultural Factors

Drug use is not confined to any ethnic or cultural group, nor is it seen exclusively in inner-city neighborhoods. You will read about the relationship of individual drugs to sociocultural factors in later chapters. In general terms, however, belonging to some cultural groups is somewhat protective against drug abuse, while other groups seem to encourage it (Ellickson, McGuigan, Adams, Bell, & Hays, 1996). Asian Americans and African Americans are less likely to use either illegal drugs or alcohol (Thomas & Schandler, 1996; James, Kim, & Moore, 1997). Living in a rural area does not necessarily provide a buffer against drug use. There is less use of some illegal drugs in rural areas, primarily because they are unavailable there, but other drug use is virtually the same as in more cosmopolitan parts of the country (Cronk & Sarvela, 1997). Compared to men, women almost invariably drink less alcohol and use illegal drugs less, but when they do drink or use, the negative consequences can be even more severe for them than for men (McGann & Spangler, 1997). In addition, the stigma of being an addict or alcoholic is greater for women. Most treatment services are male-oriented and might not meet women's needs (Ramlow, White, Watson, & Leukefeld, 1997).

Stop and Review

1. What is the difference between positive and negative reinforcement?
2. Which is more important in determining drug use, peer pressure or family influence?
3. How do the following affect the likelihood of drug use: (a) religious background, (b) availability of a drug, (c) media influence, (d) gender?
4. What are the results of the search for the "addictive personality"?
5. What is expectancy and how does it relate to drug use?

Dual Diagnosis

People who have mental disorders are not different from you and me. In fact, they might *be* you and me! Many people with psychological problems use drugs, and many people who use drugs have psychological problems (fig. 1.5). Many people with psychiatric disorders drink alcohol, for example, for many of the same reasons the rest of us do (Carey & Carey, 1995). As many as half of all people with mental disorders are also dependent on at least one drug, and the cost of treating these **dual-diagnosis** patients is much higher than for those without dependence (Dickey & Azeni, 1996). Furthermore, people with both a substance-abuse disorder and a psychological disorder have a poorer outcome than those with only one such problem (Carey, 1996).

The recognition of this problem raises a number of questions that are currently topics of debate. For example, does the abuse precede or cause the disorder? Does the disorder precede or cause the abuse? Is the psychiatric patient using drugs in an attempt at self-medication? Perhaps both the abuse and the psychological problems stem from the

Psychiatric disorder precedes drug use	Drug use precedes psychiatric disorder
1. Individual with a psychiatric disorder begins using drugs for the same reasons as everyone else	1. Drug use brings out psychiatric disorder in susceptible individual
2. Individual with a psychiatric disorder uses drugs as self-medication	2. Long-term or intense short-term drug use *causes* psychiatric disorder
3. Individual uses drugs because of disordered thinking, resulting from psychiatric disorder	3. Withdrawal produces a psychiatric disorder limited to the period of recovery

FIGURE 1.5
Theoretically there are several ways in which drug use and psychological disorders can affect each other. In real life it is often difficult to distinguish which came first, however. Alcohol abusers are often depressed, and depressed people turn to alcohol to self-medicate—which came first?

same cause but are not directly related. There is evidence for all of these positions, and each might be true in specific circumstances. In general, however, disorders such as depression and severe anxiety are most likely to be the result of alcohol abuse (Allan, 1995; Roy, 1996; Marshall, 1997). The relationship between schizophrenia, the most serious psychiatric disorder, and substance abuse is widely recognized, but there is too little research available to draw conclusions (Brunette & Drake, 1997). In the chapters that follow, you will read more about this very important topic.

Summary

After reading this chapter, you should appreciate that the answer to the drug problem in the United States or elsewhere is not simple. Many factors combine to determine whether someone will use or abuse a particular drug, and it is impossible to predict who will do either. Simple slogans make for good advertising copy and good politics, but they have little relevance to the real issues. Keep in mind as well that many people who come from the worst possible backgrounds and have the greatest risk factors successfully avoid becoming drug abusers.

The term *addiction* has many different meanings. Older definitions do not accurately reflect the behavior of drug abusers. Newer definitions of addiction emphasize craving and the role of thinking.

Dependence can be physical or psychological or both. Physical dependence might not lead to behavioral addiction. The classification of drugs by their abuse potential is the basis for our drug laws, but it is flawed. Drugs that have little dependence potential are placed on a higher schedule than some drugs that are widely prescribed.

Most everyone uses some drug or another, and drug use changes across the life span. Many people use a drug but do not become dependent. For those who do become dependent, treatment and recovery are difficult, but not impossible. Relapses are common, but recovery is possible. Recovery involves physical changes and psychological adjustment. Most people benefit from self-help groups. Therapeutic communities try to change a person's entire lifestyle. Medical treatment can eliminate most withdrawal symptoms.

Human beings seem to take drugs (at least initially) for positive reasons. After repeated drug use, the user is motivated by negative reinforcement. Cognitive factors such as expectancy are becoming more widely recognized. Expectations about what a drug will do have a strong effect, but individual personality differences do not seem to predict who will become an abuser.

One of the most important changes in the field is the realization that many drug abusers have psychological problems that are separate from their substance abuse, and many people with psychological problems use drugs. The concept of dual diagnosis promises to be even more important in the future as we learn more.

Key Terms

abstinence   Refraining completely from the use of alcohol or a drug.

action stage   The stage in which a person takes the first steps toward recovery from substance use.

behavioral addiction   Substance abuse characterized by strong craving for and active seeking of the drug being used.

caffeine   A stimulant drug found in coffee, tea, and chocolate as well as other beverages.

contemplation stage   The stage in which a person recognizes that she or he has a substance-abuse problem and seeks information about ways to stop using the drug.

craving   A strong feeling of need for a drug.

dependence   A physiological or psychological need for a drug, expressed by craving and/or withdrawal.

detoxification   The process that occurs during withdrawal when the patient is recovering from substance abuse.

experimental use   Using a drug ten or fewer times.

heavy user   A person who uses a drug to escape problems. The user's lifestyle revolves around the drug.

maintenance stage   A stage in which one actively avoids using a substance while examining the reasons for having previously abused it.

negative reinforcement   A reinforcement that increases the likelihood of a behavior by removing a subjectively unpleasant stimulus. Aspirin that relieves a headache is an example of a negative reinforcer.

pharmacological addiction   The development of physical tolerance and physical dependence on a drug.

positive reinforcement   A reinforcement that is subjectively pleasant and increases the likelihood of a behavior.

precontemplation stage   The period of time when a person uses or abuses a substance and does not acknowledge having a desire to change.

preparation stage   The stage in which a person is aware that she or he has a substance-related problem and evaluates various alternatives to continuing the substance use or abuse.

psychoactive drug   A drug that alters consciousness or mood.

regular use   The user incorporates drug use into their living pattern, but use is not usually a problem. Also called social or recreational use.

relapse   A period of use of a substance after an initial period of abstinence.

relapse prevention   Strategies aimed at preventing a return to drinking or drug use.

therapeutic community   A community of substance abusers with the goal of promoting a change in lifestyle. The abusers usually live in the community for a period of time.

tolerance   The need to increase drug use to achieve the same effect.

withdrawal A physiological condition brought on by the abrupt cessation of use of a drug to which the body has become adapted.

References

Adams, W. L., Barry, K. L., & Fleming, M. F. (1996). Screening for problem drinking in older primary care adults. *Journal of the American Medical Association, 276,* 1964–1967.

Allan, C. A. (1995). Alcohol problems and anxiety disorders: A critical review. *Alcohol and Alcoholism, 30,* 145–151.

American Psychiatric Association. (1994). *Diagnostic and statistical manual of mental disorders* (4th ed.). Washington, DC: Author.

Anthenelli, R., & Schuckit, M. (1997). Genetics. In J. Lowinson, P. Ruiz, R. Millman, & J. Langrod (Eds.), *Substance abuse: A comprehensive textbook* (pp. 41–50). Baltimore: Williams & Wilkins.

Bartter, T., & Gooberman, L. (1996). Rapid opiate detoxification. *American Journal of Drug and Alcohol Abuse, 22,* 489–495.

Blume, S. B. (1997). Women: clinical aspects. In J. Lowinson, P. Ruiz, R. Millman, & J. Langrod (Eds), *Substance abuse: A comprehensive textbook* (pp. 645–653). Baltimore: Williams & Wilkins.

Booth, B. M., Blow, F. C., Ludke, R. L., & Ross, R. L. (1996). Utilization of acute inpatient services for alcohol detoxification. *Journal of Mental Health Administration, 23,* 366–374.

Borg, L. (1997). Pharmacological therapies for substance dependence. *Current Opinion in Psychiatry, 10,* 225–229.

Brown, R. L., Fleming, M. F., & Patterson, J. J. (1996). Chronic opioid analgesic therapy for chronic low back pain. *Journal of the American Board of Family Practice, 9,* 191–204.

Brunette, M. F., & Drake, R. E. (1997). Gender differences in patients with schizophrenia and substance abuse. *Comprehensive Psychiatry, 38,* 109–116.

Campbell, J., Gabrielli, W., Laster, L., & Liskow, B. (1997). Efficacy of outpatient intensive treatment for drug abuse. *Journal of Addictive Diseases, 16,* 15–25.

Carey, K. B. (1996). Substance use reduction in the context of outpatient psychiatric treatment: A collaborative, motivational, harm reduction approach. *Community Mental Health, 32,* 291–306.

Carey, K. B., & Carey, M. P. (1995). Reasons for drinking among psychiatric outpatients: Relationship to drinking patterns. *Psychology of Addictive Disorders, 9,* 251–257.

Carroll, K. M. (1997). Integrating psychotherapy and pharmacotherapy to improve drug abuse outcomes. *Addictive Behaviors, 22,* 233–245.

Chen, K., & Kandel, D. B. (1995). The natural history of drug use from adolescence to the mid-thirties in a general population sample. *American Journal of Public Health, 85,* 41–47.

Cloninger, C., Svrakic, D., & Przybeck, T. (1993). A psychobiological model of temperament and character. *Archives of General Psychiatry, 50,* 975–990.

Cook, C. C., Goddard, D., & Westall, R. (1997). Knowledge and experience of drug use amongst church affiliated young people. *Drug and Alcohol Dependence, 46,* 9–17.

Cronk, C. E., & Sarvela, P. D. (1997). Alcohol, tobacco and other drug use among rural/small town and urban youth: A secondary analysis of the Monitoring the Future data set. *American Journal of Public Health, 87,* 760–764.

Devereux, P. (1997). *The long trip: a prehistory of psychedelia.* New York: Penguin/Arkana.

DeWitt, D., Offord, D., & Wong, M. (1997). Patterns of onset and cessation of drug use over the early part of the life course. *Health Education and Behavior, 24,* 746–758.

Dickey, B., & Azeni, H. (1996). Persons with dual diagnoses of substance abuse and major mental illness: Their excess costs of psychiatric care. *American Journal of Public Health, 86,* 973–977.

Dobkin de Rios, M. (1984). *Hallucinogens: cross-cultural perspectives.* Albuquerque: University of New Mexico Press.

Dunn, M. E., & Goldman, M. S. (1996). Empirical modeling of an alcohol expectancy memory network in elementary school children as a function of grade. *Experimental and Clinical Psychopharmacology, 4,* 209–217.

Durant, R. H., Rome, E. S., Rich, M., Allred, E., Emans, S. J., & Woods, E. R. (1997). Tobacco and alcohol use behaviors portrayed in music videos: a content analysis. *American Journal of Public Health, 87,* 1131–1135.

Ellickson, P. L., McGuigan, K. A., Adams, V., Bell, R. M., & Hays, R. D. (1996). Teenagers and alcohol misuse in the United States: *By any definition, it's a big problem. Addiction, 91,* 1489–1503.

Fingarette, H. (1988). *Heavy drinking: The myth of alcoholism as a disease.* Berkeley: University of California Press.

Galen, L., Henderson, M., & Whitman, R. (1997). The utility of novelty seeking, harm avoidance, and expectancy in the prediction of drinking. *Addictive Behaviors, 22,* 93–106.

Gambert, S. (1997). The elderly. In J. Lowinson, P. Ruiz, R. Millman, & J. Langrod (Eds.), *Substance abuse: A comprehensive textbook* (pp. 692–697). Baltimore: Williams & Wilkins.

Gattey, C. N. (1986). *Excess in food, drink and sex.* London: Harrap Ltd.

Gfroerer, J., Wright, D., & Kopstein, A. (1997). Prevalence of youth substance abuse: The impact of methodological differences between two national surveys. *Drug and Alcohol Dependence, 47,* 19–30.

Godlaski, T. M., Leukefeld, C., & Cloud, R. (1997). Recovery: With and without self help. *Substance Abuse and Misuse, 32,* 621–627.

Gold, M. S. (1997). Cocaine (and crack): Clinical aspects. In J. H. Lowinson, P. Ruiz, R. B. Millman, & J. G. Langrod (Eds.), *Substance abuse: A comprehensive textbook* (3rd ed., pp. 181–198). Baltimore: Williams & Wilkens.

Goldman, M. S., Greenbaum, P. E., & Darkes, J. (1997). A confirmatory test of hierarchical expectancy structure and predictive power: Discriminant validation of the alcohol expectancy questionnaire. *Psychological Assessment, 9,* 145–157.

Halikas, J. A. (1997). Craving. In J. H. Lowinson, P. Ruiz, R. B. Millman, & J. G. Langrod (Eds.), *Substance abuse: A comprehensive textbook* (3rd ed., pp. 85–89). Baltimore: Williams & Wilkins.

Harrison, E. R., Haaga, J., & Richards, T. (1993). Self-reported drug use data: What do they reveal? *American Journal of Drug and Alcohol Abuse, 19,* 423–441.

The health benefits of smoking cessation: A report of the surgeon general. (1990). Washington, DC: U.S. Department of Health and Human Services.

Heyman, G. M. (1997). Resolving the contradictions of addiction. *Behavioral and Brain Sciences, 19,* 561–610.

Humphreys, K., Moos, R. H., & Cohen, C. (1997). Social and community resources and long-term recovery from treated and untreated alcoholism. *Journal of Studies on Alcohol, 58,* 231–238.

James, W. H., Kim, G. K., & Moore, D. D. (1997). Examining racial and ethnic differences in Asian adolescent drug use: the contributions of culture, background and lifestyle. *Drugs: Education Prevention and Policy, 4,* 39–51.

Kendler, K. S., Gardner, C. O., & Prescott, C. (1997). Religion, psychopathology, and substance use and abuse: A multimeasure, genetic-epidemiologic study. *American Journal of Psychiatry, 154,* 322–329.

Kenkel, D., & Manning, W. (1996). Perspectives on alcohol taxation. *Alcohol Health and Research World, 20,* 230–238.

Killen, J. D., & Fortman, S. P. (1997). Craving is associated with smoking relapse: Findings from three prospective studies. *Experimental and Clinical Psychopharmacology, 5,* 137–142.

Kirsch, I. (1997). Response expectancy theory and application: A decennial review. *Applied and Preventive Psychology, 6,* 69–79.

Koob, G., & Le Moal, M. (1997). Drug abuse: Hedonic homeostatic dysregulation. *Science, 278,* 52–58.

Koob, G. F., & Nestler, E. J. (1997). The neurobiology of addiction. *Journal of Neuropsychiatry and Clinical Neurosciences, 9,* 482–497.

Loveland-Cherry, C. J., Leech, S., Laetz, V. B., & Dielman, T. E. (1996). Correlates of alcohol use and misuse in fourth grade children: Psychosocial, peer, parental and family factors. *Health Education Quarterly, 23,* 497–511.

Markou, A., Kosten, T. R., & Koob, G. F. (1998). Neurobiological similarities in depression and drug dependence: a self-medication hypothesis.

Marlatt, G. A. (1996). Taxonomy of high-risk situations for alcohol relapse: Evolution and development of a cognitive behavioral model. *Addiction* (Suppl.), *91,* S37–S49.

Marshall, J. R. (1997). Alcohol and substance abuse in panic disorder. *Journal of Clinical Psychiatry, 58* (Suppl.), 46–49.

Masse, L. C., & Tremblay, R. E. (1997). Behavior of boys in kindergarten and the onset of substance abuse during adolescence. *Archives of General Psychiatry, 54,* 62–68.

McDuff, D. R., & Beuger, M. (1997). Psychotherapy of substance abuse. *Current Opinions in Psychiatry, 10,* 243–246.

McGann, K., & Spangler, J. (1997). Alcohol, tobacco and illicit drug use among women. *Primary Care, 24,* 113–122.

McKay, J. R., Maisto, S. A., & O'Farrell, T. J. (1996). Alcoholics' perceptions of factors in the onset and termination of relapses and the maintenance of abstinence: Results from a 30-month follow-up. *Psychology of Addictive Behaviors, 10,* 167–180.

McKenna, T. (1992). *Food of the gods: the search for the original tree of knowledge.* New York: Bantam Books.

McLellan, A. T., Hagan, T. A., Meyers, K., Randall, M., & Durell, J. (1997). "Intensive" outpatient substance abuse treatment:

Comparisons with "traditional" outpatient treatment. *Journal of Addictive Diseases, 16,* 57–84.

National household survey on drug abuse: Population estimates 1997. (1998). Rockville, MD: Substance Abuse and Mental Health Services Administration, Office of Applied Studies.

O'Brien, C. (1996). Recent developments in the pharmacotherapy of substance abuse. *Journal of Consulting and Clinical Psychology, 64,* 677–686.

O'Brien, C. (1997). A range of research based pharmacotherapies for addiction. *Science, 278,* 66–70.

O'Malley, S. S. (1996). Opiod antagonists in the treatment of alcohol dependence: Clinical efficacy and prevention of relapse. *Alcohol and Alcoholism, 31,* 77–81.

Prochaska, J. O., DiClemente, C. C., & Norcross, J. C. (1992). In search of how people change. *American Psychologist, 47,* 1102–1114.

Ramlow, B. E., White, A. L., Watson, D. D., & Leukefeld, C. G. (1997). The needs of women with substance abuse problems: An expanded vision for treatment. *Substance Abuse and Misuse, 32,* 1395–1404.

Roerich, L., & Goldman, M. S. (1995). Implicit priming of alcohol expectancy memory processes and subsequent drinking behavior. *Experimental and Clinical Psychopharmacology, 3,* 402–410.

Rotgers, F. (1996). Behavioral theory of substance abuse treatment: Bringing science to bear on practice. In F. Rotgers, D. S. Keller, & J. Morgenstern (Eds.), *Treating substance abuse: Theory and technique.* New York: Guilford Press.

Royce, J. E., & Scratchley, D. (1996). *Alcoholism and other drug problems.* New York: Free Press.

Saffer, H. (1996). Studying the effects of alcohol advertising on consumption. *Alcohol Health and Research World, 20,* 266–272.

Schor, E. L. (1996). Adolescent alcohol use: Social determinants and the case for early family-centered prevention. *Bulletin of the New York Academy of Medicine, 73,* 335–356.

Schuckit, M. (1995). *Drug and alcohol abuse: A clinical guide to diagnosis and treatment* (4th ed.). New York: Plenum Medical.

Schuckit, M. (1996). Recent developments in the pharmacotherapy of alcohol dependence. *Journal of Counseling and Clinical Psychology, 64,* 669–676.

Shedler, J., & Block, J. (1990). Adolescent drug use and psychological health: A longitudinal inquiry. *American Psychologist, 45,* 613–630.

Siegal, R. K. (1989). *Intoxication.* New York: Dutton.

Smith, G. T., Goldman, M. S., Greenbaum, P. E., & Christiansen, B.A., (1995). Expectancy for social facilitation from drinking: The divergent paths of high expectancy and low expectancy adolescents. *Journal of Abnormal Psychology, 104,* 32–40.

Sobell, L. C., Cunningham, J. A., & Sobell, M. (1996). Recovery from alcohol problems: With and without treatment: Prevalence in two population surveys. *American Journal of Public Health, 86,* 966–972.

Stanton, M. D., & Shadish, W. R. (1997). Outcome, attrition and family-couples treatment for drug abuse: A meta-analysis and review of the controlled, comparative studies. *Psychological Bulletin, 122,* 170–191.

Stimmel, B. (1997). *Pain and its relief without addiction.* New York: Haworth Medical Press.

Stout, R. L., Longabough, R., & Rubin, A. (1996). Predictive validity of Marlatt's relapse taxonomy versus a more general relapse code. *Addiction, 91* (Suppl.), S99–S110.

Strain, E. C., Mumford, G. K., Silverman, K., & Griffiths, R. R. (1994). Caffeine dependence syndrome: Evidence from case histories and experimental evaluations. *Journal of the American Medical Association, 272,* 1043–1048.

Thomas, C. S., & Schandler, S. L. (1996). Risk factors in adolescent substance abuse: Treatment and management implications. *Journal of Child and Adolescent Substance Abuse, 5,* 1–16.

Wasson, R. G., Kramrisch, S., Ott, J., & Ruck, C. A. (1986). *Persephone's quest: entheogens and the origins of religion.* New Haven: Yale University Press.

Willoughby, F. W., & Edens, J. F. (1996). Construct validity and predictive validity of the stages of change scale for alcoholics. *Journal of Substance Abuse, 8,* 273–291.

Zacny, J. P. (1995). A review of the effects of opioids on psychomotor and cognitive functioning in humans. *Experimental and Clinical Psychopharmacology, 3,* 432–466.

Zhang, L., Wieczorek, W. F., & Welte, J. W. (1997). The impact of age of onset of substance abuse on delinquency. *Journal of Research in Crime and Delinquency, 34,* 253–268.

Ziegler, J. (1994). Opiate and opioid use in patients with refractory headache. *Cephalgia, 14,* 5–10.

Chapter TWO

Biological Basis of Drug Action

Chapter Objectives

When you have finished studying this chapter, you should

1. Be able to label the principle parts of the neuron.
2. Understand what happens at the synapse.
3. Be able to state the lock-and-key principle.
4. Know the difference between the first and second messenger systems.
5. Know how inhibitory and excitatory neurotransmitters work.
6. Know how neurotransmitter action is terminated.
7. Be able to distinguish between agonists and antagonists.
8. Know the function of the following neurotransmitters: acetylcholine, dopamine, norepinephrine, serotonin, the amino acid neurotransmitters, adenosine, the opioid peptides, and anandamide.
9. Be able to describe at least one function for the prefrontal cortex.
10. Know why the diencephalon is so important in understanding drug use.
11. Know where the substantia nigra and nucleus accumbens are and how they relate to drug abuse.
12. Be able to describe at least two functions of the brain stem.
13. Understand how the routes of administration are important in determining a drug's abuse potential.
14. Know the role played by lipid solubility in drug action.
15. Know the advantages and disadvantages of each of the routes of administration.
16. Be able to explain what first-pass metabolism is and why it is important.
17. Understand what a half-life is.
18. Be able to explain how the action of a drug is terminated.
19. Know why gender, age, and weight play a role in determining a drug's actions.
20. Be able to distinguish among set, setting, and placebo effects.

Addiction is a brain disease, and it matters.

Leshner, 1997

Addiction is a sociologic term that has come to mean the presence of compulsive drug seeking behavior. . . . Addiction, when applied in a medical setting, leaves much to be desired. This had been recognized . . . as early as 1967 when, in an attempt to prove a uniformity of terms, [the World Health Organization] recommended the term dependence *be substituted for* addiction. *The prescription of a dependency-producing drug to relieve pain and allow adequate function is not only appropriate but extremely beneficial. Such a person should not be considered to be addicted any more than a diabetic would be considered addicted to insulin, a cardiac patient addicted to Digoxin, an individual with schizophrenia addicted to phenothiazines, or a person with epilepsy addicted to phenobarbital or Dilantin.*

Stimmel, 1997

In Chapter 1 you read of the definitions of addiction, dependence and tolerance. In this chapter you will read of the theories about the neurochemical basis for drug taking as well as the pharmacological variables that affect drug use and abuse. Keep in mind the distinction between addiction and dependence as you read further.

The Neurobiology of Drug Action

Psychoactive drugs work by affecting the chemical messengers in the brain, known as **neurotransmitters.** Neurons, the basic building blocks of the nervous system, communicate with each other across gaps known as synapses. The various neurotransmitters bridge those gaps. The billions of individual neurons in the brain and spinal cord form the various structures of the central nervous system. In the past few years, researchers have learned much about how psychoactive drugs affect our behavior. We will see how this knowledge helps us understand drug use and abuse.

Figure 2.1 shows how the central nervous system is organized. Drugs can also affect individual organs such as the liver, but we will be most concerned with their effect upon the brain. Figure 2.2 shows the structure of a neuron. The neuron transmits information by electrical and chemical processes. At the synapse, which is the major site of drug action, information is transmitted by release of neurotransmitters. The dendrite receives information from other neurons, and the cell body transmits that information to the axon. The axon carries the information to the end button, which releases neurotransmitters into the synapse—the space between that neuron and the cell body or dendrite of another (Waxman, 1996). When you read of "brain chemistry" in the media, the term refers to the action of the neurotransmitters in the synapse.

Events at the synapse are incredibly complicated, and any brief description will be inadequate. All the same, it is helpful to understand certain basic elements of neurotransmitter action. As you can see in figure 2.3, the **vesicles** contain the neurotransmitters. When the nerve impulse reaches the end button, these vesicles move toward the wall of the end button and release the neurotransmitter. The neurotransmitter crosses the synapse and attaches to a **receptor** on the wall of the dendrite. The receptor functions like a lock and the neurotransmitter functions like a key, so we call it the **lock-and-key principle.** When a key fits into and unlocks a lock, a door opens. When the neurotransmitter fits into the receptor, which is an ion channel, the channel changes shape to permit the flow of ions. If the neurotransmitters open enough ion channels on the post synaptic neuron, the neuron fires.

The basic divisions of the nervous system

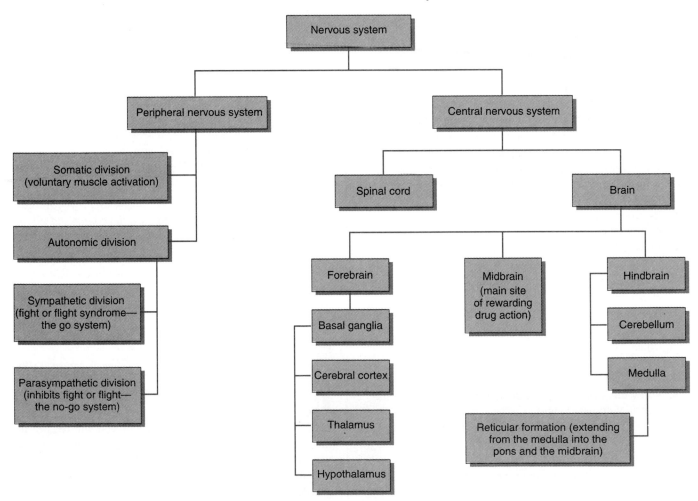

FIGURE 2.1

The two divisions of the nervous system are the peripheral nervous system and the central nervous system.

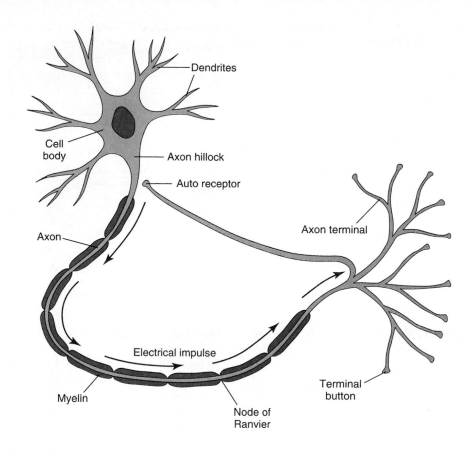

FIGURE 2.2
A "typical" neuron.

Neurotransmitters can affect the receptor (ion channel) in two ways. With the **first messenger system** the neurotransmitter opens the ion channels that are necessary to cause the postsynaptic neuron to fire. Acetylcholine acts by means of the first messenger system at the junction between nerves and muscles. The **second messenger system** is slower and operates indirectly. When the neurotransmitter attaches to the receptor, it causes a release of protein that is attached to the inside wall of postsynaptic neuron. This pro-

tein, in turn, attaches to receptors and changes them so they are more likely to open when neurotransmitters attach to them. Acetylcholine in the brain operates through the second messenger system. The lock and key example just mentioned might help explain first and second messenger systems. Think of a key which turns a lock and opens a door as the first messenger system. Now think of the second messenger system as a two key lock. The first key will not open the door itself, but permits the second key to operate.

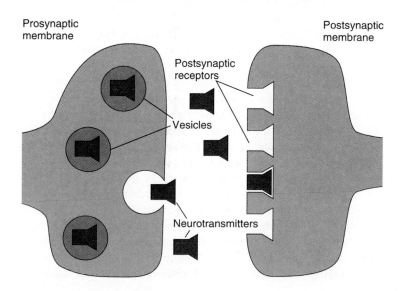

FIGURE 2.3
The lock-and-key principle. The appropriate neurotransmitter, because of its molecular structure, fits like a "key" into the "lock" of the postsynaptic receptor.

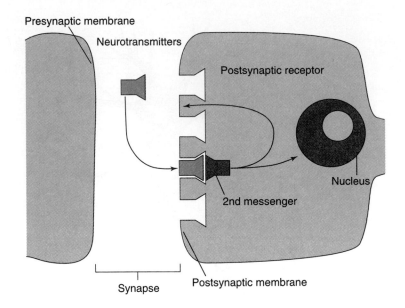

FIGURE 2.4
When the neurotransmitter attaches to the postsynaptic receptor, a *second messenger system* is activated, which alters the permeability of the postsynaptic membrane and affects the cell nucleus.

Several mechanisms in the synapse serve the purpose of maintaining a steady pattern of firing by the neurons. The most important for understanding the effects of drugs are **down regulation** and **up regulation.** If the concentration of neurotransmitters in the synapse is too high, the post synaptic neuron adjusts by decreasing the number of receptors (down regulation). If the concentration is too low the post synaptic neuron increases the number of receptors (up regulation). Since drugs can increase or decrease the levels of neurotransmitters in the synapse, drugs can cause either up regulation or down regulation. These concepts can be difficult to understand, perhaps figure 2.5 will help.

Drugs that increase the action of a neurotransmitter are called **agonists,** and drugs that block the action of a neurotransmitter are called **antagonists.** For example, amphetamine is an agonist because it increases the amount of norepinephrine and dopamine released into the synapse. Cocaine is an agonist because it blocks the reuptake of catecholamines into the presynaptic neuron and increases the amount of neurotransmitter available. Do not confuse inhibition of reuptake with the action of antagonists. Antagonists work by preventing neurotransmitters from reaching the postsynaptic receptor. Naloxone, which is used to counteract the effects of opiates like morphine, displaces the molecules of morphine on the postsynaptic receptor. Therefore, naloxone is an opiate antagonist. Cocaine is an agonist because it blocks the presynaptic receptor.

Stop and Review

1. What is the site of action of most psychoactive drugs?
2. What happens when a neurotransmitter is released in the synapse?
3. What happens during up regulation and down regulation?
4. What do agonists and antagonists do?

Neurotransmitters

At least fifty candidates for neurotransmitters have been proposed, and more are on the way. Researchers have found that even vitamins can function as neurotransmitters (Rebec & Pierce, 1994). Only a few will be discussed here, because too little is known about the actions of most of the others. Keep in mind, as you read this section, that drugs rarely affect only one transmitter system; for instance, a drug might be an antagonist for dopamine but also block norepinephrine and serotonin. In addition, the neurons containing one neurotransmitter might connect with neurons containing other neurotransmitters. For example, dopamine transmission is affected by norepinephrine, serotonin, and GABA (gamma-aminobutyric acid) (Ashby & Tassin, 1995; Kelland & Chiodo, 1997; Walters & Pucak, 1997).

Neurotransmitters can affect the postsynaptic receptor so as to increase the likelihood of the cell firing, making them **excitatory,** or they can decrease the likelihood of the cell firing, making them **inhibitory.** As many as a thousand synapses, some of them excitatory and some inhibitory, might exist on one neuron (Waxman, 1996). Whether the cell fires is a function of all the inhibitory and excitatory neurotransmitters.

The neurotransmitter stays attached to the receptor on the dendrite for a very brief period of time and then is dislodged. Some neurotransmitters are taken up again by the neuron that released it and returned to the vesicle, in a process known as **reuptake.** Other neurotransmitters are metabolized or broken down in the synapse by enzymes. Finally, neurotransmitters can literally leak from the synapse and then be metabolized.

Drugs can affect neurotransmitters at many sites. At the synapse they can bind to the postsynaptic receptor, taking the place of the neurotransmitter but not initiating a nerve impulse. They can bind to the receptor and facilitate firing. They can block the enzyme that breaks down the

(a) Up regulation

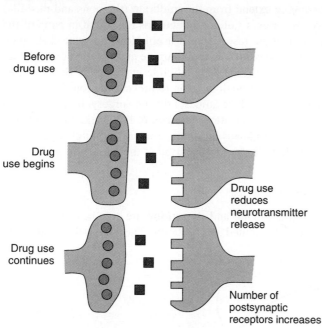

Before drug use

Drug use begins

Drug use reduces neurotransmitter release

Drug use continues

Number of postsynaptic receptors increases

(b) Down regulation

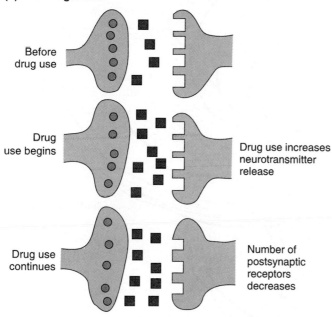

Before drug use

Drug use begins

Drug use increases neurotransmitter release

Drug use continues

Number of postsynaptic receptors decreases

FIGURE 2.5

In up regulation, a drug is taken that decreases the amount of neurotransmitter released. The postsynaptic receptor responds by developing more receptors. In down regulation, the opposite happens. Up and down regulation may account for the actions of drugs like morphine and the antidepressants. If normal release of neurotransmitter is resumed after the person stops taking the drug, a further adjustment must take place because there are now too many receptors (with up regulation) or too few (with down regulation). The period of adjustment may partly explain the prolonged withdrawal symptoms of some drugs of abuse.

neurotransmitter. Finally, drugs can work by preventing re-uptake or by stimulating the release of a neurotransmitter. Figure 2.6 shows how cocaine inhibits the reuptake of dopamine.

Acetylcholine

Found throughout the body and the brain, acetylcholine has widespread effects. There are two different kinds of postsynaptic receptors that are activated by acetylcholine. One resembles the molecule nicotine and is called **nicotinic.** The other resembles molecule called muscarine and is called **muscarinic.** Nicotinic receptors are found primarily on the muscles, whereas muscarinic are found primarily in the brain. Drugs that affect the acetylcholine system can operate at either or both of these receptors (Bissette et al., 1996).

Even though the manner in which acetylcholine exerts its effects was unknown until the twentieth century, drugs that altered the acetylcholine system have been used since the beginning of recorded history. Aided only by trial and error, many of the infamous poisoners of the past centuries used substances that altered acetylcholine to cause instantaneous death, death after hours of agony, or death delayed by weeks or months. They also knew of plants that could make people appear to be insane. The wife of Emperor Augustus, Livia, and the wife of Emperor Claudias were notorious poisoners; Livia managed to kill her husband by incorporating the poison from the deadly nightshade plant into his specially grown figs. Apparently, most of Mark Anthony's army was accidentally poisoned by anticholinergic drugs (which block the action of acetylcholine) found in unfamiliar plants they ate. In his A.D. 36 battle with the Pathans, many in his army died after first going mad (Mann, 1992).

A well-known drug that affects the acetylcholine system is **curare.** Curare blocks the action of acetylcholine at

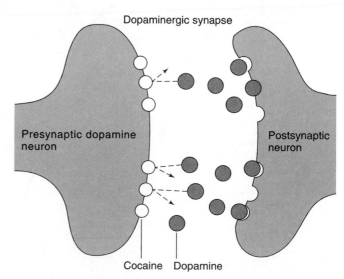

Dopaminergic synapse

Presynaptic dopamine neuron

Postsynaptic neuron

Cocaine   Dopamine

FIGURE 2.6

Cocaine blocks the presynaptic uptake sites. Since dopamine cannot be taken back up, it accumulates in the synapse increasing firing in the postsynaptic neuron.

the neuromuscular junction—preventing acetylcholine from binding to the receptor and preventing the muscle from contracting. Someone shot with a curare-tipped arrow would suffer horribly as their muscles became paralyzed, making them unable to breath, speak, or move. Because curare does cross the blood-brain barrier, the victim is completely aware of everything going on, until he or she loses consciousness and dies of respiratory arrest. Synthetic relatives of curare are widely used in surgery because they reduce the amount of anesthetic needed and cause complete muscle relaxation (Leiken & Paloucek, 1996).

The pathways containing acetylcholine neurons can be seen in figure 2.7. The cholinergic pathway to the hippocampus is believed to degenerate during Alzheimer's disease, and this deterioration can largely account for the memory loss in this disease (Bissette, Seidler, Nemeroff & Slotkin, 1996). Cholinergic systems involved in sleep and dreaming extend from the midbrain (the pons and medulla) to the cortex. Cholinergic neurons are found in parts of the brain that are responsible for emotion and arousal (Comer, 1998). Drugs such as scopolamine and plants such as datura block the action of acetylcholine in the brain. Scopolamine is absorbed through the skin to prevent motion sickness and injected to produce amnesia during surgery. In high doses it produces hallucinations (Leiken & Paloucek, 1997). Datura is used by shamans in South America (Schultes & Hoffman, 1989) but is not widely abused in the United States.

Catecholamines

Norepinephrine and **dopamine** are two neurotransmitters widely distributed in the brain. They are called **catechol-**

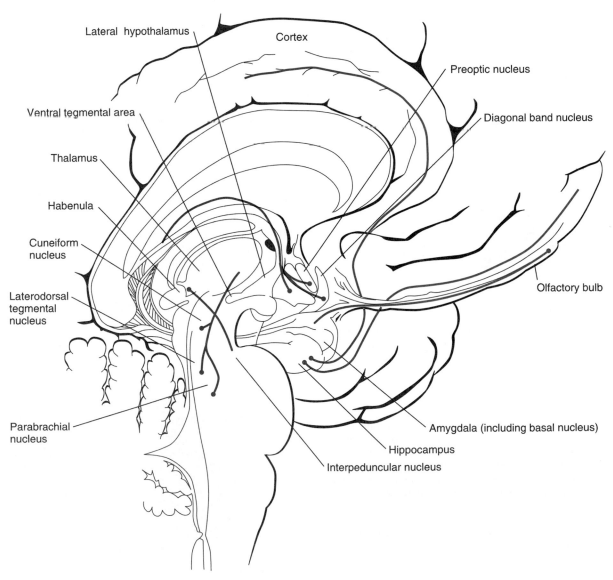

FIGURE 2.7
Acetylcholine is widely distributed in the brain. The pathway to the hippocampus is involved in memory. Other pathways regulate sleep and dreaming.

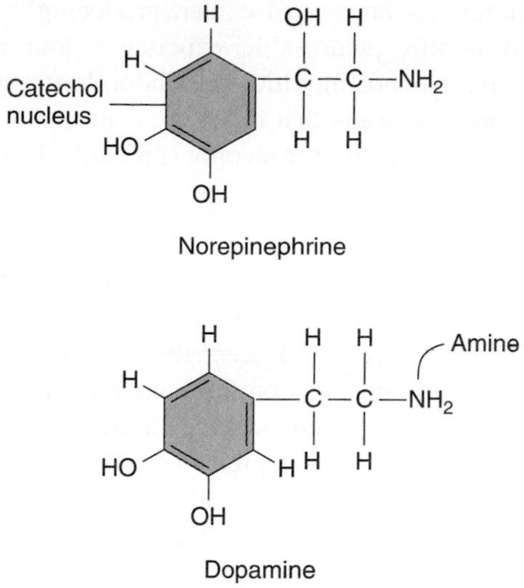

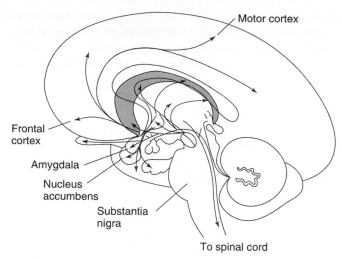

FIGURE 2.8
The catechol nucleus and the amine (NH$_2$) form a catecholamine. As you will read in Chapter 5, amphetamine closely resembles these two neurotransmitters.

FIGURE 2.9
Dopamine has many functions in the brain. It is involved in the reward system and in movement.

amines because they contain a catechol nucleus and an amine group, as you can see in figure 2.8. Epinephrine is another neurotransmitter related to norepinephrine; its action is confined to organs such as the adrenal glands. Adrenalin and epinephrine are the same thing, but the term *adrenalin* used to be a trade name and was replaced by the name *epinephrine.* The primary function of norepinephrine-containing neurons is to regulate sleep and arousal (Waxman, 1996) and reduce anxiety (Comer, 1998).

Dopamine works on the second messenger system and mainly exerts its effect on the glutamate receptors discussed below. It can be either inhibitory or excitatory (Reith, Xu, & Chen, 1997; Carvey, 1998). Virtually all drugs of abuse increase the amount of dopamine released in the nucleus accumbens (Koob & Nestler, 1997). Dopamine is also the primary neurotransmitter in the system that controls movement. The third function of dopamine is to regulate memory and attention (Carvey, 1998). Stimulant drugs like cocaine and amphetamine can produce schizophrenic-like symptoms when taken continuously for several days. The primary dopamine-containing neurons are shown in figure 2.9.

Serotonin

You would have had to have been living in a cave for the last ten years not to have heard of Prozac and its cousins, Zoloft and Paxil. You might know that these drugs are supposed to work by increasing the amount of serotonin in the brain. You might even know that they are referred to as SSRIs (selective serotonin reuptake inhibitors). Without knowing how serotonin modifies behavior, however, you know very little about how these drugs actually work. Figure 2.10 shows the primary pathways for serotonin in the brain. The serotonin pathway from the hindbrain might regulate some aspects of

sleep. There is also a serotonin pathway to the thalamus. The thalamus receives input from sensory systems and sends its output to the cortex. Other serotonin fibers can be seen extending to the limbic system.

Serotonin is an inhibitory neurotransmitter that affects a wide range of behavior. Low levels of serotonin are associated with violence, depression, and suicide (Coccaro, Kavoussi, & Hauger, 1997). Drugs that increase the amount of serotonin in the brain are being used to treat many disorders, ranging from depression in humans to compulsive paw licking in dogs. Serotonin-containing neurons also moderate the dopamine reward system (Crespi, Mannini, & Gobbi, 1997).

Amino Acid Transmitters

Amino acids are used by all cells in the process of protein synthesis. In addition, two of the amino acids, GABA

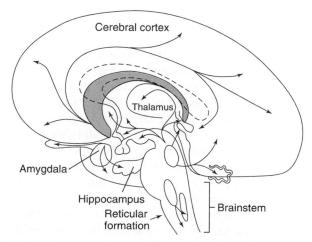

FIGURE 2.10
Serotonin exerts influence on sleep-arousal-emotions + sexuality.

(gamma-aminobutyric acid) and glutamate, are thought to be the major neurotransmitters throughout the brain (Lambert & Grover, 1995). Glutamate is excitatory, GABA is inhibitory. We know more about the drugs that affect GABA than those that affect glutamate. Alcohol and the various antianxiety drugs such as Xanax, Valium, and Librium facilitate the function of GABA in inhibiting cell firing (Snyder, 1996). Blocking the action of glutamate or increasing the action of GABA can result in memory loss. In addition, amino acid neurotransmitters apparently act upon the dopamine reward system (Kiyatkin & Rebec, 1997).

Adenosine

Technically, adenosine is not a neurotransmitter. It is formed as the result of the breakdown of adenosine triphosphate (ATP), the primary energy source for most cells in the body. ATP forms adenosine inside the cell, and the adenosine is transported across the cell membrane. In the extracellular fluid, adenosine interacts with receptors on the cell body and affects the cells' function. Instead of being a neurotransmitter, it is called a **neuromodulator.** Adenosine alters neural transmission at synapses that use other neurotransmitters and is considered inhibitory. It prevents the release of neurotransmitters and diminishes the postsynaptic cell's response to neurotransmitters (Dohrman, Diamond, & Gordon, 1997).

Caffeine, our most popular stimulant, inhibits the release of adenosine. Because it inhibits the action of a substance that itself is inhibitory, neural transmission is increased. Caffeine probably increases dopamine in the reward system in the brain but probably does so in an indirect way (Garrett & Griffiths, 1997). Adenosine also plays a role in determining the behavioral effects of alcohol, and it might be involved in the development of alcohol tolerance (Dohrman et al., 1997).

Opioid Peptides

Like adenosine, the opioid peptides (otherwise known as endorphins) are neuromodulators—they modulate the actions of other neurotransmitters. They are produced by the neurons in the presynaptic area and stored there. The three basic types are called enkephalins (because they are found in the brain) and endorphins and dynorphins (found in the brain and the body). Of the three, enkephalins are the most important for understanding drug action because they regulate pain perception, emotion, respiration, and cardiovascular function (Froelich, 1997). The term **endorphin** is usually used to describe all three of the opioid peptides and will be used here. You should be aware, however, that there are three kinds of opioid peptides and that they have different functions in the brain and the body.

Drugs such as morphine act on endorphin receptors. When given for pain, morphine acts by reducing sensitivity to pain, making the pain more bearable. Acting like endorphins, morphine increases the output of dopamine in the nu-cleus accumbens, the reward center, producing a pleasant feeling. It is this pleasurable experience that narcotics abusers seek. Alcohol modifies the endorphin system in a complex way, and drugs that block the action of the endorphins reduce the craving for alcohol (Froelich, 1997).

Anandamide

Ananda, a Sanskrit word meaning "tranquility," is the name given to one of the endogenous neurotransmitters in the brain, anandamide. Tetrahydrocannabinol (THC), the active chemical in marijuana, acts on the same receptors as anandamide. Just as your brain produces a chemical that does what morphine does, it also produces a chemical that acts like THC. Receptors for anandamide are found primarily in areas of the brain associated with movement, such as the basal ganglia and the cerebellum. These receptors are also found in the hippocampus, a site for memory (Pertwee, 1997). You will read more about the role of THC and anandamide in chapter 6.

Stop and Review

Match the following neurotransmitters with the drugs that affect them:

1. endorphins	_____	a. alcohol
2. acetylcholine	_____	b. antidepressants
3. dopamine	_____	c. cocaine
4. serotonin	_____	d. morphine
5. adenosine	_____	e. THC
6. anandamide	_____	f. caffeine
7. GABA	_____	g. curare

Drugs and the Brain

Drugs exert their primary action on the synapses. The individual neurons form systems and structures throughout the brain that enable us to think, act, and experience emotions. Figure 2.11 shows a cross section of the brain with many of these structures labeled. In the past few years, neuroscientists have made enormous gains in understanding how these structures interact and how drugs influence them.

The brain can be divided in three basic units: the **brain stem,** the **central core,** and the **cerebral cortex.** The cortex is responsible for most of the behaviors we label "human." It enables us to engage in complex cognitive processing, make judgments, initiate action, and withhold unwanted responses. Drugs affect the cortex and so can disrupt our thinking, make us unable to plan ahead, and distort our perceptions. Alcohol abusers often experience difficulties in abstract thinking, stimulant drugs can produce strange sensations, and hallucinogenic drugs alter our perceptions of the world.

Most drugs exert their main effects on the central core and the brain stem. The **limbic system,** the **basal ganglia,** the **reticular formation,** and the **medulla** are interconnected structures where many drugs have their principal ac-

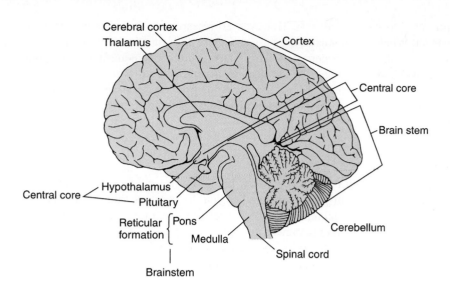

FIGURE 2.11
A cross section of the brain.

tions. These complex groups of brain systems play crucial roles in learning and memory, in biological drives such as hunger and sex, and in the various functions necessary to keep us alive, such as breathing (Pinel, 1997).

Cortex

The **prefrontal cortex,** shown in figure 2.12, is involved in impulse control, attention, and organization of complex information. Just behind it is the motor and sensory cortex, which enables us to feel bodily sensations and to move specific parts of our bodies. The **visual cortex** receives sensory input from the thalamus and enables us to see. The temporal lobe is involved in language production and understanding, facial recognition, and other complex processes.

The Central Core

The central core of the brain can be thought of as having three parts: the **diencephalon,** the **limbic system,** and the **basal ganglia.** The diencephalon is composed of the thala-

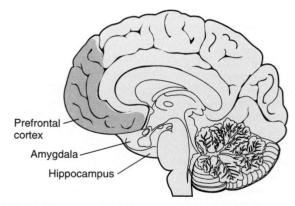

FIGURE 2.12
The prefrontal cortex controls impulses, attention, and complex information organization.

mus and the hypothalamus. The thalamus integrates information coming from the various sensory organs. The hypothalamus is a rich complex of cell bodies that controls eating, drinking, and sexual behavior; by means of connections to the pituitary, it also monitors our hormonal systems.

The limbic system includes the amygdala, which is involved in aggression, the cingulate, which connects the other parts of the limbic system with the prefrontal cortex, and the hippocampus, which is involved in memory. Drugs such as alcohol, marijuana, and the narcotics have strong effects of these structures. They can produce anxiety, depression, memory loss, and aggressiveness by affecting the limbic system along with the hypothalamus. The causes of many of the psychological disorders that are treated by prescription drugs can also be found in these areas.

The basal ganglia coordinate our motor behavior. Recent research has focused on two specific structures in the basal ganglia that have a much different function. The substantia nigra, which actually starts out in the brain stem, sends neurons to the nucleus accumbens, found near the thalamus. Drugs as cocaine, amphetamine, alcohol, nicotine, and the narcotics cause a release of dopamine in the nucleus accumbens (Koob & Nestler, 1997). In rats, dopamine is also released there when the animal experiences a novel situation, eats, or engages in sexual behavior (Rebec, Gradner, Johnson, Pierce, & Bardo, 1997). One theory is that this pathway is the common pathway for the perception of pleasure (Koob & LeMoal, 1997).

Recent studies have suggested that long-term use of alcohol, cocaine, and amphetamine might alter the sensitivity of the dopamine receptors in the nucleus accumbens (Nicola & Malenka, 1997). Heroin and anandamide also alter the functioning of the nucleus accumbens but in a different way (Tanda, Pontieri, & DiChiara, 1997). In fact, any drug that has an abuse potential seems to increase dopamine in the nucleus accumbens (Nestler & Aghajanian, 1997). According to a prominent theory, as drug use continues, dopamine release is altered and the postsynaptic receptors change in number. This alteration can be permanent. When the user stops taking the drug, dopamine release is decreased, and this decrease is the basis for withdrawal and craving. This theory is sometimes called the theory of **dopaminergic supersensitivity** (Nestler & Aghajanian, 1997). The changes that take place in the brain might be long-lasting or even permanent, so the user feels the need for the drug long after going through physical withdrawal.

Another theory suggests that dopamine release in the nucleus accumbens does not result in a feeling of pleasure, but instead signals to the user that an important stimulus is occurring. The stimulus is associated with reward, and the function of the release of dopamine is to draw attention to significant events (Wickelgren, 1997). Dopamine release helps the user to recognize that certain events—such as consuming tasty food, engaging in a sexual act, or the rewarding effects of a drug—are about to occur. Each of the two theories explains some of the behaviors associated with drug taking. The second theory, for example, explains why cues associated with drug taking are perceived as positive. The mere sight of a bottle of liquor or a line of cocaine might cause the brain to go on alert because that sight has been associated in the past with pleasurable experiences (Wickelgren, 1997).

These two theories are currently being debated by researchers. However, all researchers also recognize that for humans, drug use and abuse are a function of more than neurochemistry. Drug abuse cannot be reduced to dopamine output in the nucleus accumbens, no matter what it does there. There are numerous psychological and cultural variables that also need to be considered. You will read of these variables shortly.

The Brain Stem

You can thank your brain stem for the fact that you breathe in your sleep, regulate your heart rate within safe limits, and maintain your blood pressure. The brain stem also acts as a filter to prevent unimportant stimuli from distracting us, puts us to sleep, and enables us to dream. Stimulant drugs like amphetamine and caffeine act on the structures of the brain stem to keep us awake, increase our heart rate and blood pressure, and affect our ability to concentrate. Alcohol is a depressant and a blood alcohol level (BAL) of .40 is usually fatal because the drinker stops breathing. At low doses alcohol irritates the stomach and vomiting is common. At a higher BAL, however, the opposite occurs. When someone drinks rapidly, alcohol is dumped into their intestine. If the BAL reaches about .30, it suppresses the emesis center (as well as the breathing response).

For our purposes, the most important brain stem struc-

What Do You Think? What Do You Think?

Where Do Choice and Free Will Fit Into the Definition of Addiction?

You have read about the physiological basis of addiction. If there is a biochemical alteration in the brain that produces a craving for a drug, can a person who is dependent choose not to use that drug? If not, should they be held legally liable for their actions? Every thought, emotion, and action occurs as the result of some biochemical change in the brain. Does the thought cause the biochemical change, or does the biochemical change cause the thought? At issue is a concept known as *reductionism.* Can a behavior such as drug use be "explained" by biochemical changes in the brain? Take, for example, the fact that cocaine makes the user feel good. Suppose we find that this good feeling is accompanied by an increase in dopamine in the nucleus accumbens. Do users take the drug because it makes them feel good or because it causes a release of dopamine?

No matter how strong the craving for a drug is, the user does not always give in to the craving. Heroin users, for example, will put aside enough heroin for a wake-up shot in the morning. A more familiar example is cigarette smoking. A smoker with a pack of cigarettes does not smoke until all the cigarettes are gone. Usually smokers make sure they have a couple left in the pack when they go to bed so they won't have to buy a new pack first thing in the morning. Another way of saying the same thing is that they choose not to smoke every cigarette in their possession. When smokers quit smoking, they experience withdrawal and craving, yet many succeed in breaking the habit. Once again, they choose not to smoke. Therefore, how important is it that addictive drugs cause craving by altering the biochemical balance of the brain?

The word *willpower* is not used in the addiction field, partly because alcoholics were formerly viewed as "weak" people who simply lacked willpower. The disease concept of alcoholism developed in part as an attempt to avoid such labeling. However, even the staunchest proponents of the disease concept say that people can and must choose not to drink. It is a widely accepted idea that no one can make a drinker stop drinking, they must "want to." Can you think of a way to resolve the apparent contradiction in the view that addiction is a biological disease that is cured by the addict's choosing not to use?

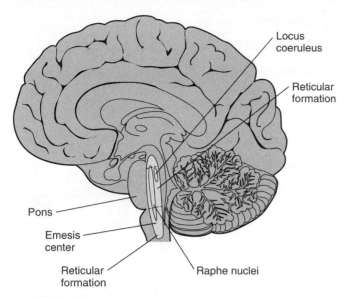

FIGURE 2.13
The brain stem contains structures that are essential to survival. Death due to drug overdose typically occurs when drugs affect this region.

tures are the **medulla** and the **reticular formation,** which actually extends into the midbrain. Figure 2.13 shows these structures. The medulla regulates breathing and heart rate, and the reticular formation alerts us to important sensory stimuli. Most deaths due to a drug overdose are the result of the drug's inhibiting the breathing and heart rate response in the medulla.

Stop and Review

1. You should be able to name two important structures in the cortex, three in the midbrain, and three in the brain stem. If you cannot do this, go back and review this section.
2. Name the dopamine pathway that is thought to mediate the rewarding effects of drugs.
3. What is dopaminergic supersensitivity, and how does it relate to drug abuse?

Pharmacology of Drug Action

Pharmacology, the study of how drugs affect the body, is one of the oldest sciences. Sumerian tablets dating to 3000 B.C. list prescriptions for treatment of many diseases. In the past, many drug treatments consisted of mixtures of many different substances, some of which were effective and some of which were dangerous. Egyptian prescriptions included such "drugs" as jackal fat, boiled thigh bones and crocodile dung along with useful substances such as opium and castor oil (Levine, 1983). Modern science has largely been able to find the useful drugs in the old prescriptions, so we no longer have to take jackal fat and crocodile dung along with our opium.

Drug Action

When a drug is taken, it is absorbed , distributed in the body, broken down (metabolized) and excreted. You need to know how each of these stages occur in order to understand how drugs act. Why is it, for example, that 500 milligrams of some drugs are needed before any effect is seen, while others work at 1/10,000 of that amount? Under some circumstances a drug can reach the brain in seconds, while under other circumstances the same drug may take hours to have an effect. Some drugs can be detected days after use, while others are gone in minutes. Understanding how **absorption, distribution, metabolism** and **excretion** occur will provide an answer.

Absorption and Distribution

Once a drug reaches the bloodstream, it is distributed to all of the tissues and organs of the body. Some drugs, like alcohol, have an affinity for nearly all the cells in the body and so alcohol acts directly. Other drugs primarily work by changing levels of neurotransmitters in the brain which alters the function of various structures in the brain. These drugs can also have widespread effects in the rest of the body because brain structures control various organs and tissues in the body.

The effect of a drug depends on several factors. One of the most important is **lipid solubility.** The layers of fat found in the middle layers of the blood vessels can be a barrier to absorption. Drugs that are highly soluble in lipids (fats) can cross this barrier easily and so are effective at low doses. Lysergic acid diethylamide is a highly lipid soluble and is effective at extremely low doses.

The rate of absorption (and metabolism) of a drug determines the concentration of a drug in the bloodstream. **Titration** is the term used to describe the ability to maintain a given concentration. Experienced users are usually better at titration than inexperienced users. Regular drinkers, for example, may be able to reach and maintain a given blood alcohol level for hours. Less experienced drinkers often drink too much at first and then experience unpleasant effects when their blood alcohol level gets too high.

Routes of Administration

With few exceptions, a psychoactive drug must get into the brain to be effective. The various **routes of administration** enable the drug to get into the bloodstream. From there the drugs are taken up into the brain and other cell tissues. Drug users adopt various routes of administration to produce the most rapid delivery to the brain. Some routes of administration are quite rapid, others rather slow. Each route has advantages and disadvantages (Quinn, Wodak, & Day, 1997).

A user could bypass the bloodstream entirely and inject the drug directly into the brain. This method is used in research laboratories with animals. The drugs are administered through cannula (tubes) or needles, implanted in various parts of the brain. Researchers can target specific areas of the brain and see how drugs affect these structures. This method is not used with humans, obviously, although it is probably safe to say that if such a method were developed, some drug users would try it.

Oral Route

The **oral route** is popular and has the advantage of being convenient. However, the effects of drugs administered orally vary greatly, depending on several factors, among them the concentration of the drug being absorbed. If you remember the process of osmosis from biology class, you will recall that any substance that is in higher concentration on one side of a permeable membrane will diffuse across that membrane until its concentration is the same on both sides. Once the liver begins to metabolize the drug, the concentration outside the cell decreases and the same process occurs in reverse until the drug is completely eliminated from the system.

Stomach content also influences how readily a drug will be absorbed through the oral route. Drugs are more readily absorbed on an empty stomach than on a full one because the food in the stomach will also absorb the drug. Digestive acids in the stomach can interact with the drug, and enzymes that are present can break down or metabolize the drug. Men, for example, have in their stomachs more of the enzyme that metabolizes alcohol than do women. The result is that the alcohol in the stomach of a woman will be absorbed more readily and she will have a higher blood alcohol level than a man who drinks the same amount (Lieber, 1997).

Buccal and Sublingual Routes

Absorption can take place in the mouth (**buccal**) and under the tongue (**sublingual**). The thin layer of cells (**epithelium**) lining the mouth and the intricate network of blood vessels permit rapid absorption. There is no first-pass metabolism with these routes, so the drug reaches the brain quickly. The indigenous people of Bolivia, Colombia, and Ecuador keep wads of coca leaves in their mouths, absorbing cocaine in this way. Chewing tobacco and tobacco pouches deliver nicotine in the same way. Prescription drugs used to treat migraine headaches, panic attacks, and heart conditions are marketed in this form, as are some over-the-counter drugs (Berlin, May-McCarver, Notterman, & Ward, 1997).

Parenteral Route

The term **parenteral** literally refers to any route other than the gastrointestinal route, and it usually indicates injection into the body (fig. 2.14). Injections can be **subcutaneous** (under the skin). There is a rich layer of blood vessels just below the skin. Drugs injected by this route are absorbed rather slowly, but the rate of absorption can be controlled.

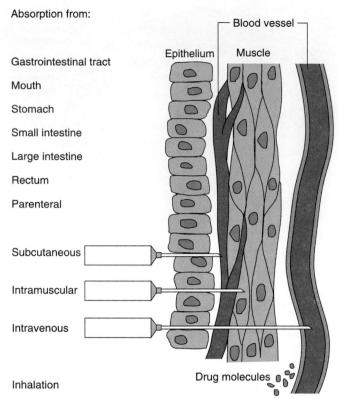

Absorption from:

Gastrointestinal tract
Mouth
Stomach
Small intestine
Large intestine
Rectum
Parenteral

Subcutaneous

Intramuscular

Intravenous

Inhalation

Epithelium Muscle Blood vessel

Drug molecules

FIGURE 2.14
As you can see from this diagram, the parenteral routes of administration are rapid because they put the drug near the bloodstream. Absorption by inhalation is also rapid for the same reason. Absorption along the gastrointestinal tract is relatively slow because the drug must pass through the outer layer of the tract (the epithelium) as well as the muscles that line the tract.

An example would be the use of a local anesthetic in dentistry. Along with the anesthetic, a drug that constricts blood vessels would decrease the rate of absorption and increased the duration of anesthesia. Drug users refer to this route as **skin-popping;** some heroin addicts start their drug-using career with this route. Problems associated with the subcutaneous route include irritation by the substance injected and abscesses as a result of nonsterile needles. The subcutaneous route is used to inject sumatriptan, which constricts blood vessels in the brain and relieves migraine. Several time-release drugs, primarily forms of birth control, are injected under the skin. Injecting subcutaneously is easier than injecting directly into a vein or even a muscle.

The **intramuscular route** is familiar from countless hospital jokes, because injections are often made into a buttock muscle. In fact, any large muscle group will work, including the upper arm and the thigh. The intramuscular route is used when an immediate response is not needed and when a large quantity of the drug must be injected. Drugs dissolved in oil can be injected intramuscularly and remain active for months. Some birth control medication uses this technique.

Most people find it difficult to inject themselves with

a drug. The styrette has been developed for both subcutaneous and intramuscular injection to get around the problem. A styrette is a spring-loaded device ending in a needle and containing a standard dose of a drug. The styrette is placed in contact with the skin, and the button at the top is depressed. This releases the spring and drives the needle into the body, releasing the dose of drug. Styrettes have been developed for subcutaneous as well as intramuscular injection, and one company markets a styrette for injection directly into the penis to treat impotence. In this case, the route of administration is probably a considerable drawback.

The **intravenous route** of administration is most commonly used when speed is important. If you have ever been a patient in a hospital, one of your first experiences was probably to be hooked up to an intravenous catheter in either the hand or the arm. Intravenous drug users inject themselves, usually in the arm. Usually they draw blood back into the syringe to allow it to mix with the drug and then "boot it" by pushing the plunger. Drugs injected intravenously reach nearly every part of the body within one minute. Because the drug is injected into a vein, it travels to the heart, then the lungs, back to the heart, and then through arteries to all parts of the body.

Because precise measurement is possible with intravenous injection, titration is easy and the concentration of the drug is not diluted by stomach contents or digestive acids. **Patient-controlled anesthesia** refers to the administration of anesthetics under the patient's control. The patient can push a button that releases a small amount of painkiller into the bloodstream. Patients can adjust the amount of drug in the bloodstream and achieve a level of pain relief without sedation that is very difficult to obtain by a standard injection. The total amount of the drug that can be injected and the interval between injections can be controlled by medical personnel to prevent overdose (Owen & Plummer, 1997).

Inhalation

The fastest route of administration is **inhalation,** because the inhaled drug goes from the lungs to the heart and then directly into the bloodstream. The blood vessels in the lungs form an extensive network for absorbing oxygen and many other molecules. Small molecules such as anesthetic gases, nicotine, THC, and cocaine are readily absorbed, and the deeper the drug is inhaled, the more contact it makes with the capillaries that make up the network of blood vessels (figure 2.15). Inhalation is highly reinforcing because a large amount of a drug can be absorbed quickly and distributed to the brain and body rapidly (Pickworth & Henningfield, 1997).

An inhaled drug will absorb into the capillaries of the lung as long as the concentration of the drug in the bloodstream is lower than the concentration in the air sacs of the lungs. Conversely, when the concentration is higher in the bloodstream than in the air sacs, the molecules diffuse

the other way. The Breathalyzer test relies on this principle. As long as there is any alcohol in the bloodstream, alcohol will be found in the breath in the same proportion as in the bloodstream. For the same reason, anesthetic gases are absorbed quickly and cause the patient to lose consciousness. As soon as the mask is removed, the pattern reverses, and the gases in the blood diffuse back into the breath, with the result that the patient awakens quickly.

The inhalation route produces effects so rapidly, it is hard to imagine anyone thinking up a way to make it even quicker, but we should never underestimate the ingenuity of drug users. The faster a large quantity of drug gets into the lungs, the more rapidly and completely it will be absorbed. Some cocaine and heroin smokers "shotgun," which means that one user breathes in the smoke from the drug and forcefully blows it into the mouth of another person (Perlman, 1997)! Perhaps the "inspiration" for this method came from reading about the users of hallucinogenic snuff in South America who blow the drug directly into each others nostrils?

Mucosal Route

Any **mucous membrane** provides a route of administration. Rectal suppositories take advantage of this. The Mayans administered hallucinogenic drugs by means of an enema, as their drawings clearly demonstrate. Intravaginal absorption also occurs, and this route might have been behind the folk belief that witches could fly. During the supposed witches' Sabbaths, drugs such as opium, belladonna, and hemlock might have been inserted into the vagina by means of a broomstick. The effect of these drugs combined with the women's expectations might account for the reports of flying. One advantage of these routes (it isn't too hard to think of disadvantages) is that the blood vessels leading from the rectum and the vagina bypass the liver on their way to the heart. Of course, the buccal route is a specialized type of mucosal administration.

One route of mucosal administration is fairly common. **Insufflation** is the technical term for snorting. Most people think of cocaine when they think of snorting a drug, but legal drugs are administered by this route as well. Nicotine nasal sprays have recently come on the market, and many over-the-counter cold medications are absorbed by insufflation. Snorting heroin has recently begun to rival injecting the drug among addicts, and snorting of methamphetamine is common as well. Snorting gets the drug to the heart nearly as quickly as inhalation. Drugs that irritate the mucous lining of the nose can cause serious health problems, and not all drugs can be absorbed in this manner (Quaraishi, Jones, & Mason, 1997).

Transdermal Route

Most drugstores stock various preparations designed to allow the absorption of nicotine through the **transdermal route.** These nicotine patches are worn on the skin, usually

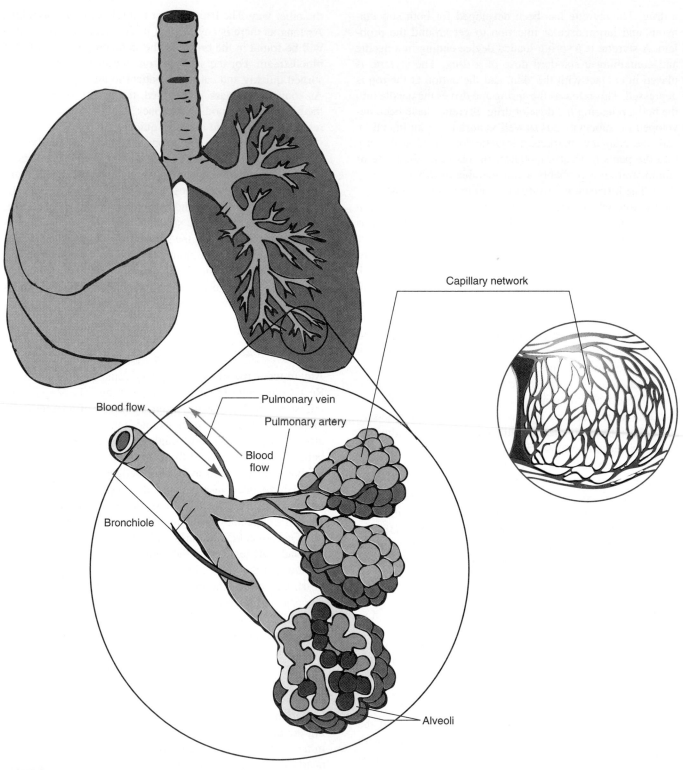

FIGURE 2.15
Drugs inhaled into the lungs are absorbed into the bloodstream through the capillaries in the alveoli. There are thousands of alveoli, allowing rapid absorption.

Labels in figure: Capillary network, Blood flow, Pulmonary vein, Pulmonary artery, Blood flow, Bronchiole, Alveoli

on the chest (fig. 2.16). They allow nicotine to be absorbed slowly and steadily, with the result that nicotine levels can be kept high enough to prevent withdrawal. As you will read in chapter 7, using this method smokers can learn to break the habit of smoking before withdrawal take place. Powerful narcotics such as **fentanyl** are also administered by means of patches. Serious consequences, including death, have been reported when young children place these patches on

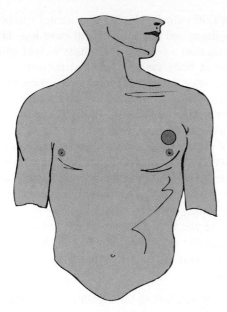

FIGURE 2.16
Transdermal patches are frequently placed on the chest, but other areas of the body are used as well. The transdermal patch that administers the drug scopolamine, used to treat seasickness, is commonly placed behind the ear.

themselves. The skin is an effective barrier, and many drugs cannot be absorbed transdermally, but for those that can, the transdermal route allows rapid absorption and ease of titration (Berlin, May-McCarver, Notterman, & Ward, 1997).

Stop and Review

1. What are the four steps that occur when a drug is taken?
2. What is first-pass metabolism, and how does it explain some of the gender differences in the effects of alcohol?
3. What is titration, and why is it important in understanding drug use?
4. How is the oral route of administration different than buccal and sublingual absorption?
5. Which is the faster route of administration and why?
6. What are the types of parenteral administration?

Metabolism and Excretion

First pass metabolism refers to the passage of a drug through the liver before it reaches the heart and brain. Drugs taken orally and absorbed in the intestine are subject to first pass metabolism which increases the amount of time it takes the drug to get to the brain. Drugs injected into a vein are not subject to first pass metabolism and so take much less time to reach their peak effect. Termination of drug action occurs when the drug is eliminated by the kidneys or metabolized by the liver. Lesser routes of termination include respiration through the lungs and excretion through the skin.

In the kidney, the process of **diffusion** causes the drug to pass into the renal tubules. The drug is then excreted in the urine. The substances produced when the drug is metabolized by the liver are excreted the same way. The elimination of a drug or its metabolites in the urine is the basis for the most common form of drug testing, **urinalysis.** The various methods used for urine tests do not actually measure the presence of the drug, but its metabolites. Because similar but legal drugs are metabolized to the same compounds, a urine test can result in a false positive. False positives occur when some substance other than the drug being tested shows up as positive in the urine.

The **half-life** is the time required for half of the drug to be eliminated. The half-life is the major factor in determining how long the drug will act in the body and the length of time during which its presence can be detected. Some drugs, such as LSD, continue to exert their effect after the drug is gone from the bloodstream; others, such as cocaine, have a shorter duration of action than their half-life would predict. Nevertheless, the half-life of a drug is the usual means of predicting how long the drug can be detected in the body.

Every drinker can remember having a couple of drinks, feeling wonderful an hour later, and then feeling depressed, cranky and irritable as the effects of the alcohol wear off. The **time response curve** accounts for this experience. First is the absorptive phase, when the concentration of alcohol in the blood stream increases. After it reaches peak concentration, the metabolic phase begins and the concentration falls. Some drinkers have more to drink when they begin to feel "down." Heavy drinkers may continue to chase the first "high" for hours, drinking more alcohol each time while feeling less effect. Cocaine and amphetamine abusers are similar. Since the positive psychological effects of cocaine last for only a brief period, abusers can consume quantities of the drug pursuing an ever elusive euphoria. The effects of amphetamine last for hours and amphetamine abusers may continue to use for days going without sleep or food.

Individual Differences

Women absorb drugs differently than men do, young people differently than the elderly and thin people differently than obese. The exact relationship is complex and depends on the drug, but there are some general principles that apply to all drugs.

Age. Infants and young children lack some enzymes, making them more susceptible to the effects of some drugs. In the elderly, the response to a given drug is affected by several factors. First, their heart or cardiac output is decreased, so drugs remain longer in their bloodstream. Both liver and kidney function are decreased, further increasing the length of time the drug is present in their bloodstream. The elderly also typically have a higher ratio of body fat to muscle, which can result in the drugs being stored in the body for a long period of time. Finally, the elderly are often taking several drugs for medical conditions. These drugs can compete in the liver with psychoactive drugs and might interact with them. These issues can complicate an understanding of what constitutes normal drinking in the elderly (Chermack, Blow, Gomberg, Mudd, & Hill, 1997).

Weight. The weight of an individual plays a role in determining the effect of a given dose of a drug as the chart relating weight to blood alcohol level (see Figure 2.17) demonstrates. The percentage of body fat and the amount of muscle are also important. Some drugs are more readily absorbed into fatty tissue (that is, they are lipid soluble) while others are more readily absorbed into muscle. For example, if a person with a high percentage of body fat smokes mari-

juana, the THC (which is highly fat soluble) will be taken up into fatty tissue and the smoker will have less THC in the bloodstream than a person of the same weight with a lower percentage of body fat who smoked the same amount of marijuana. Since the brain absorbs drugs through the blood stream, the more muscular person would be more affected by the THC. Alcohol is not as lipid soluble as THC but is readily absorbed into muscle, so a person with a high percentage of muscle tissue would absorb the alcohol and have a lower blood alcohol level than a drinker who was obese. Since women typically have a higher percentage of body fat than men, the woman's BAL will be higher even if the two weigh the same.

In case you are wondering, obese and muscular people have roughly the same amount of fat in the middle or lipid layer of the blood stream and it makes up a small part of total body fat.

Gender. In addition to the higher percentage of body fat, and generally lower weight, hormonal differences between men and women can affect their responses to a drug. Women and men differ in the concentrations and locations of enzymes that break drugs down. In the last ten years, progress has been made in understanding how drugs affect women, but the amount of research is woefully inadequate (Blume, 1997).

Although it may be difficult to believe, the first nationwide systematic effort to study alcohol, cigarette and illicit drug use in women was not completed and reported until 1997! Some of the results, which were part of the National Household Survey on Drug Abuse, are encouraging: for example, a smaller percentage of adult women than adult males reported use of alcohol, cigarettes, and any illicit drugs. They were also less likely to report heavy use of any of these drugs. On the other hand, adolescent females were just as likely as adolescent males to use alcohol, cigarettes or any illicit drug, and were more likely to report inappropriate, nonmedical use of psychotherapeutics such as analgesics, stimulants, antianxiety drugs, and sedatives (*Substance abuse among women in the United States,* 1997).

Other Factors that Alter Drug Effects

Placebo Effects

Most people think of a **placebo** as an inactive substance that works by the power of suggestion. It seems highly unlikely that placebo effects are solely the result of the patient's expectations, however. Placebos show time-response curves, reverse tolerance, and dose-response effects. Two placebo pills are more effective than one! People taking placebos develop side effects such as nausea, drowsiness, insomnia, and headache. Furthermore, big placebo capsules produce a stronger response than small ones, and yellow capsules are perceived as stimulants and white capsules as pain relievers (Turner et al., 1994). One study compared open administration of placebo (the patient was told they were getting a pain

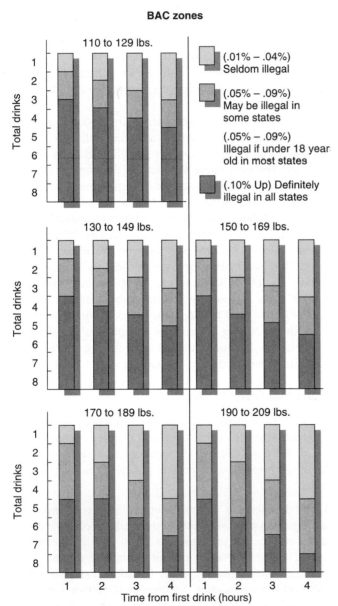

FIGURE 2.17
Weight and blood-alcohol concentration. This chart is conservative and does not take into consideration stomach contents, need, and other factors.

relier) to covert administration of morphine (the patients received an infusion of morphine without their knowledge). The placebo was as effective as 5 mg of morphine (Fields & Price, 1997). To be sure, 5 mg of morphine is a low dose (10 mg is the standard) but it is still remarkable that the patients got as much relief from a placebo they thought was a pain reliever as they did from an infusion of morphine that they didn't even know they were getting!

Set and Setting

The concepts of **set** and **setting** are crucial to understanding the effects of drugs. *Set* refers to expectations about what a drug will do. Set is similar to a placebo effect in that it is the expectation that produces the response. The term *set,* however, usually refers to the manner in which expectations change the effects of a drug. I am experiencing the effects of set if I take two aspirin containing caffeine because I have a headache and go to sleep immediately, and when I take caffeine to stay awake while I am driving and cannot get to sleep when I make it home. Very few people ever take a hallucinogenic drug without some set related to its effects. A person who takes LSD without knowing what substance she or he is ingesting will have a much different reaction than those who know they are taking LSD. In chapter 8 you will read about Albert Hoffman, the discoverer of the effects of LSD, and research sponsored by the United States military that clearly shows such differences.

Setting refers to the circumstances surrounding the use of a drug. Two glasses of wine in a dark, quiet room might make a person sleepy, while the same amount at a party might wake the same person up. Many of the bad experiences people have with various drugs, especially the hallucinogens, can be understood in terms of the effects of the setting. Being under the influence of Ecstasy at a rave is much different from being under the influence of Ecstasy in a police station.

Stop and Review

1. Drug A has a half-life of 10 hours and drug B has a half-life of 36 hours. If you took each drug once a day, which one would build up faster in your body?
2. What is a time-response curve, and why is it important?
3. Name at least five factors that can alter drug effects.
4. Describe the differences among placebo effects, set, and setting.

Summary

The basic building block of the nervous system is the neuron. The synapse is the most important site for drug action. Neurotransmitters released from a neuron cross the synapse and interact with the next neuron. These neurotransmitters operate on the first or second messenger system. When the amount of neurotransmitter changes in the synapse, the neuron responds with up regulation or down regulation. Neurons can be inhibitory or excitatory.

Among the most important neurotransmitters are acetylcholine, the catecholamines, and serotonin. In addition, adenosine, anandamide, the endorphins, and the amino acid neurotransmitters also play a role in drug action.

The most important components of the brain, regarding drug use, are the cortex, the diencephalon, and the brain stem. Each of these has a specific function and affects behavior in many ways. Drugs act through neurotransmitter systems in these areas to exert their effects.

The effect of any drug depends on absorption, distribution, metabolism, and excretion. The route of administration for a drug plays a large role in determining the drug's abuse potential. Inhalation is the fastest route of administration. Most drugs are metabolized mainly in the liver, although some metabolism occurs elsewhere.

Drug effects are modified by a number of factors, including gender, age, weight, and prior experience. Placebos, set, and setting can also exert profound effects.

Key Terms

absorption   The process of taking a drug into the system (usually into the bloodstream).

acetylcholine   A neurotransmitter found in the synapses between neurons and muscles. Also widely distributed in the brain.

agonist   A chemical that increases the action of a neurotransmitter.

antagonist   A chemical that blocks the action of a neurotransmitter.

basal ganglia   A structure in the brain thought to be involved in motor movement.

brain stem   The part of the brain that contains the medulla and reticular formation.

buccal route   A means of absorbing a drug by placing it inside the mouth.

catecholamine   A neurotransmitter, such as norepinephrine or dopamine, that contains a catechol nucleus.

central core   The part of the brain involved in emotion, hunger, and trust.

cerebral cortex   A basic unit of the brain responsible for cognitive processing.

curare   A drug that blocks the action of acetylcholine, preventing muscle contraction.

diencephalon   An area of the brain composed of the thalamus and hypothalamus.

diffusion   The tendency for molecules to move from an area of high concentration to an area of lower concentration.

distribution   The process by which a drug reaches various parts of the body.

dopamine   A catecholamine involved in motor movement and reward, as well as other functions.

dopaminergic supersensitivity   An increase in the firing pattern of dopamine neurons as a function of an increase in dopamine in the synapse.

down regulation   A reduction in the number of postsynaptic receptors.

emesis center   The part of the brain that controls vomiting.

endorphin   The endogenous neurotransmitter in the brain upon which morphine acts.

epithelium   A thin layer of cells, found in various parts of the body such as the mouth.

excitatory neurotransmitter   A neurotransmitter that increases the likelihood that a neuron will fire.

excretion   The process by which a drug is eliminated from the body.

fentanyl   A potent derivative of morphine that is widely used in surgery.

first messenger system   The opening of the postsynaptic ion channel by one of several neurotransmitters.

first-pass metabolism   The metabolism of a drug before it reaches the heart, usually taking place in the liver.

half-life   The amount of time required for half of a dose of a drug to be metabolized.

inhalation   Absorption of a drug in the lungs.

inhibitory neurotransmitter   A neurotransmitter that decreases the likelihood that a postsynaptic receptor will fire.

insufflation   The technical term for "snorting."

intramuscular route   Administration of a drug by injection it into a large muscle group.

intravenous route   A means of administering a drug by injecting it directly into the bloodstream.

ligand-gated channel receptor   An ion channel that opens when a neurotransmitter attaches to it. Part of the first messenger system.

limbic system   A group of structures in the brain that are involved in memory and emotion.

lipid solubility   The degree to which a drug is absorbed into fatty tissue or lipid layers.

lock-and-key principle   The principle that neurotransmitters attach to a postsynaptic receptor and open ion channels, permitting a neuron to fire, in the same manner as a key fits into a lock and allows a door to open.

medulla   A structure in the brain that controls breathing, heart rate, and other vegetative functions.

metabolism   The process by which a drug is converted into another, usually less active, form.

mucous membrane   Cells lining the mouth, vagina, and lower intestinal tract.

mules   People who smuggle drugs inside small packages, suitcases, or their own bodies.

muscarinic postsynaptic receptor   A receptor resembling the molecule muscarine.

neuromodulator   A chemical substance released from a neuron that alters the normal firing pattern of another neuron.

neurotransmitters   Molecules that bind to a synaptic structure and alter the function of the ion channels.

nicotinic postsynaptic receptor   A receptor resembling the molecule nicotine.

norepinephrine   A neurotransmitter in the brain regulating sleep and arousal.

oral route   A method of administering a drug by swallowing it. Absorption takes place in the stomach and small intestine.

parenteral route   The administration of a drug by injecting it directly into the body.

patient-controlled anesthesia   The administration of an anesthetic under the control of the patient according to her or his perceptions of pain.

placebo   A presumably inert substance.

prefrontal cortex   The area of the brain that controls impulses, attention, and organization of complex information.

receptor   An area on a membrane that accepts a neurotransmitter substance or drug.

reticular formation   A structure in the brain stem and central core that is involved in attention.

reuptake   The absorption of a neurotransmitter by the sending neuron. The structure that absorbs the neurotransmitter is called the transporter.

routes of administration   The various means by which a drug is introduced into the bloodstream and distributed throughout the body.

second messenger system   Alteration of sensitivity of the postsynaptic membrane due to release of a protein from the postsynaptic receptor.

set   Expectations about the effect of a drug.

setting   The situation or environment where drug use occurs.

skin-popping   Subcutaneous injection of a drug.

subcutaneous   Under the skin.

sublingual route   A means of absorbing a drug by placing it under the tongue.

transdermal route   The absorption of a drug across the skin barrier without the use of injection.

titration   The regulation of drug intake to maintain a given level of the drug in the body.

up regulation   An increase in the number of postsynaptic receptor vesicles.

urinalysis   A urine test for the presence of a drug or drug metabolite.

vesicles   Presynaptic structures that contain neurotransmitters.

visual cortex   The area of the brain that receives visual sensory input and allows us to see.

References

Ashby, C., & Tassin, J. (1995). The modulation of dopaminergic transmission by norepinephrine. In C. Ashby (Ed.), *The modulation of dopaminergic neurotransmitters by other neurotransmitters.* New York: CRC Press.

Berlin, C. M., May-McCarver, D. G., Nottermen, D. A., & Ward, R. M. (1997). Alternative routes of drug administration: Advantages and disadvantages. *Pediatrics, 100,* 143–152.

Bissette, G., Seidler, F. J., Nemeroff, C. B., & Slotkin, T. A. (1996). High affinity choline transporter status in Alzheimer's disease. In R. J. Wurtman, S. Corkin, J. H. Growdon, & R. M. Nitsch (Eds.), *The neurobiology of Alzheimer's disease* (pp. 32–50). New York: New York Academy of Sciences.

Carvey, P. M. (1998). *Drug action in the nervous system.* New York: Oxford University Press.

Chermack, S. T., Blow, F. C., Gomberg, E. S., Mudd, S. A., & Hill, E. M. (1997). Older adult controlled drinkers and abstainers. *Journal of Substance Abuse, 8,* 453–462.

Coccaro, E. F., Kavoussi, R. J., & Hauger, R. L. (1997). Serotonin function and antiaggressive response to fluoxetine. *Biological Psychiatry, 42,* 546–552.

Comer, R. (1998). *Abnormal psychology.* New York: W.H. Freeman.

Crespi, D., Mennini, T., & Gobbi, M. (1997). Carrier-dependent and Ca2+-dependent 5HT and dopamine release induced by (+)amphetamine, 3,4-methylenedioxymethamphetamine, p-chloroamphetamine, and (+)-fenfluramine. *British Journal of Pharmacology, 121,* 1735–1743.

de Rios, M. (1984). *Hallucinogens: Cross-cultural perspectives.* Albuquerque: University of New Mexico Press.

Devereux, P. (1997). *The long trip: A prehistory of psychedelia.* New York: Penguin/Arkana.

Dohrman, D., Diamond, I., & Gordon, A. (1997). The role of the neuromodulator adenosine in alcohol's actions. *Alcohol Health and Research World, 21,* 136–143.

Fields, H. L., & Price, D. D. (1997). Toward a neurobiology of placebo analgesia. In A. Harrington (Ed.), *The placebo effect* (pp. 93–116). Cambridge, MA: Harvard University Press.

Froelich, J. (1997). Opioid peptides. *Alcohol Health and Research World, 21,* 132–136.

Garrett, B. E., & Griffiths, R. R. (1997). The role of dopamine in the behavioral effects of caffeine in animals and humans. *Pharmacology, Biochemistry and Behavior, 57,* 533–541.

Hiltunen, A. J. (1997). Acute alcohol tolerance in social drinkers: Changes in subjective effects dependent on the alcohol dose and prior alcohol experience. *Alcohol, 14,* 373–378.

Joynt, B., & Mikhael, N. (1985). Sudden death of a heroin bodypacker. *Journal of Analytical Toxicology, 9,* 238–249.

Kelland, M. D., & Chiodo, L. A. (1997). Serotonergic modulation of midbrain dopamine systems. In C. Ashby (Ed.), *The modulation of dopaminergic neurotransmission by other neurotransmitters.* New York: CRC Press.

Kiyatkin, E. A., & Rebec, G. V. (1997). Activity of presumed dopamine neurons in the ventral tegmental area during heroin self-administration. *Neuroreport, 8,* 2581–2585.

Koob, G. H., & LeMoal, M. (1997). Drug abuse: hedonic homeostatic dysregulation. *Science, 278,* 52–56.

Koob, G. F., & Nestler, E. J. (1997). The neurobiology of drug addiction. *Journal of Neuropsychiatry and Clinical Neurosciences, 9,* 482–497.

Lambert, N., & Grover, L. (1995). The mechanism of biphasic GABA responses. *Science, 269,* 928–929, 978–980.

Leiken, J. B., & Paloucek, F. P. (1997). *Poisoning and toxicology handbook.* Cleveland: Lexi-Comp.

Leshner, A. (1997). Addiction is a brain disease, and it matters. *Science, 278,* 45–47.

Levine, R. (1983). *Pharmacology: Drug action and reaction.* Boston: Little, Brown.

Lieber, C. (1997). Pathogenesis and treatment of liver fibrosis in alcoholics: 1996 update. *Digestive Diseases, 15,* 42–66.

Mann, J. (1992). *Murder, magic and medicine.* Oxford: Oxford University Press.

McKenna, T. (1992). *Food of the gods: The search for the original tree of knowledge.* New York: Bantam Books.

Nestler, E., & Aghajanian, G. (1997). Molecular and cellular basis of addiction. *Science, 278,* 58–63.

Nicola, S. M., & Malenka, R. C. (1997). Dopamine decreases excitatory and inhibitory synaptic transmission by distinct mechanisms in the nucleus accumbens. *Journal of Neuroscience, 17,* 5697–5710.

Owen, H., & Plummer, J. (1997). Patient controlled analgesia: Current concepts in acute management. *CNS Drugs, 8,* 203–218.

Perlman, D. C., Perkins, M. P., Paone, D., Kochems, L., Salomon, N., Friedmann, P., & DesJarlais, D. C. (1997). "Shotgunning" as an illicit drug smoking practice. *Journal of Substance Abuse Treatment, 14,* 3–9.

Pertwee, R. G. (1997). Pharmacology of cannabinoid CB1 and CB2 receptors. *Pharmacology and Therapeutics, 74,* 129–180.

Pickworth, W. B., & Henningfield, J. E. (1997). Smokable drugs: Pharmacologic basis for consumer appeal. *Addiction, 92,* 691–701.

Pinel, J. (1997). *Biopsychology.* Boston: Allyn & Bacon.

Quaraishi, M. S., Jones, N. S., & Mason, J. D. T. (1997). The nasal delivery of drugs. *Clinical Otolaryngology, 22,* 289–301.

Quinn, D., Wodak, A., & Day, R. (1997). Pharmacokinetic and pharmacodynamic principles of illicit drug use and treatment of illicit drug users. *Clinical Pharmacokinetics, 33,* 344–400.

Rebec, G. V., & Pierce, C. (1994). A vitamin as neuromodulator: Ascorbate release into the extracellular fluid of the brain regulates dopaminergic and glutaminergic transmission. *Progress in Neurobiology, 43,* 537–565.

Rebec, G. V., Gardner, C. P., Johnson, M., Pierce, R. C., & Bardo, M. T. (1997). Transient increases in catecholaminergic activity in medial prefrontal cortex and nucleus accumbens shell during novelty. *Neuroscience, 76,* 707–714.

Reith, M. E. A., Xu, C., & Chen, N. (1997). Pharmacology and regulation of the neuronal dopamine transporter. *European Journal of Pharmacology, 324,* 1–10.

Schultes, R., & Hoffman, Q. (1989). *Plants of the gods: Origin of hallucinogenic use.* New York: McGraw-Hill.

Snyder, S. (1996). *Drugs and the brain.* New York: Scientific American Library.

Stimmel, B. (1997). *Pain and its relief without addiction.* (2nd ed.). New York: The Haworth Medical Press.

Tanda, G., Pontieri, F., & DiChiara, G. (1997). Cannabinoid and heroin activation of mesolimbic dopamine transmission by a common mu-1 opioid receptor mechanism. *Science, 27,* 2048–2050.

Turner, J. A., Deyo, R. A., Loeser, J. D., Von Korff, M., & Fordyce, W. E. (1994). The importance of placebo effects in pain treatment and research. *Journal of the American Medical Association, 271,* 1609–1614.

Walters, J. R., & Pucak, M. L. (1995). The modulation of midbrain dopamine systems by GABA. In C. Ashby (Ed.), *The modulation of dopaminergic neurotransmission by other neurotransmitters.* New York: CRC Press.

Wasson, R., Kramrisch, S., Ott, J., & Ruck, C. (1986). *Persephone's quest.* New Haven, CT: Yale University Press.

Waxman, S. G. (1996). *Correlative neuroanatomy* (23rd ed.). Stanford, CT: Appleton & Lange.

Wickelgren, I. (1997). Getting the brain's attention. *Science, 278,* 35–37.

Chapter Three

Alcohol: Pharmacological and Physiological Effects of Use and Abuse

Chapter Objectives

When you have finished studying this chapter, you should

1. Know where in the gastrointestinal tract alcohol is absorbed.

2. Be able to discuss three factors that affect absorption in the stomach.

3. Understand how heavy drinking can harm the gastrointestinal tract.

4. Know why the liver is so important for the process of metabolism.

5. Be able to discuss the three common types of liver damage caused by heavy drinking.

6. Be able to name two other organs related to digestion and excretion that are also affected by alcohol.

7. Have your own opinion about the health benefits of drinking alcohol and be able to support your position.

8. Know what effect alcohol has on male and female sexual performance.

9. Be able to describe how alcohol affects the fetus.

10. Know what happens in the brain of someone who drinks heavily.

11. Be able to describe the effects of alcohol on the amino acid neurotransmitter systems.

12. Know how alcohol's effects on serotonin relate to depression and violence.

13. Be able to describe the rationale behind prescribing SSRIs for recovering alcoholics.

14. Understand and be able to discuss the controversy surrounding the disease concept of alcoholism.

15. Know what inherited characteristics make alcohol abuse more common in the sons of alcoholic fathers.

16. Be able to list the genetic markers for alcohol abuse that have been demonstrated in research animals.

17. Understand the concept of recovery without treatment.

18. Be able to describe the main characteristics of alcohol abuse treatment and differentiate between inpatient and outpatient treatment.

19. Know what craving is and understand the important role of motivation in recovery.

It [alcohol] sloweth age, it strengtheneth youth: it cutteth flegme: it abandoneth melancholie: it relisheth the heart: it lighteneth the minde; . . . it helpeth digestion; . . . it pounceth the stone; . . . it puffeth away ventositie; it keepeth and preserveth. . . . the mouth from snaffling, . . . it keepeth the weason from stiffling, the stomach from wambling;. . . . it keepeth the sinews from shrinking . . . and the marrow from soaking.

Adapted from Furnas, 1973, p. 18

For most of recorded history, alcohol has been considered a necessary ingredient of the human diet and an essential and effective medicine. After all, what else do you know of that you can take if your weason begins to stiffle, your stomach to wamble, and you notice your marrow is soaking? Alcohol is still so familiar to most of us that we can forget that it is a powerful drug. The difference between the blood alcohol level (BAL) that produces the most positive effects (.04–.05) and the BAL that is fatal (.40–.50) is very small. Most people drink alcohol occasionally, suffer no consequences, and might even benefit from its use. Others drink excessively and experience serious social, personal, and health problems. It is important to know what alcohol does to the body in both low and high doses. It is also important to know what research has found out about the biology and genetics of alcohol abuse. Media reports and what passes for common knowledge are often wrong or greatly distorted.

Absorption, Distribution, and Metabolism of Alcohol

Alcohol is absorbed primarily in the small intestine, although some absorption takes place in the mouth, esophagus, and stomach. The wall of the small intestine is covered with *villi,* which greatly increase the surface area of the intestinal wall (Bode & Bode, 1997). Figure 3.1 shows the villi and their relationship to the intestine. The speed with which alcohol is absorbed into the bloodstream depends on a number of factors. An empty stomach speeds absorption, the presence of food slows it. Straight alcohol irritates the gastrointestinal tract, so a mixed drink made with carbonated beverage will be absorbed more rapidly than straight shots (Carvey, 1998).

After alcohol is absorbed into the bloodstream, it passes through the liver and travels to the heart, then to the lungs, and then back to the heart. Alcohol is then distributed through the circulatory system and is taken up by most organs. Some alcohol passes from the lungs into the air sacs and the breath, where it can be detected by the Breathalyzer test. (The Breathalyzer analyzes a sample of air from the lungs for the amount of alcohol present. The BAL is then calculated from that percentage.) A small amount of alcohol passes unchanged through the skin barrier, in sweat and urine. These routes eliminate about 10 percent of the alcohol present in the bloodstream (Carvey, 1998).

Metabolism of alcohol begins in the stomach. Alcohol is metabolized by **alcohol dehydrogenase** into **acetaldehyde** and eventually into carbon dioxide and water. Men have more alcohol dehydrogenase in the stomach than women do, which means that women will have a higher blood alcohol level than men after drinking the same amount of alcohol (Bode & Bode, 1997). Even though metabolism of alcohol begins in the stomach, the liver is the primary site for its breakdown. Chapter 2 introduced the concept of first-pass metabolism, referring to the breakdown of a drug on its first circulation through the body. Although the stomach and the liver both participate in first-pass metabolism, the liver subsequently does all the work.

The rate at which alcohol is metabolized is very similar for virtually everyone. Alcohol is eliminated at the rate of .015 percent BAL per hour. This means that someone with a BAL of .15 will not be completely sober until 10 hours after the last drink is absorbed. Heavy drinkers might metabolize alcohol more rapidly because of a second route of metabolism called the microsomal enzyme system (Carvey, 1998). The constant rate of metabolism can create problems for drinkers—they usually feel more sober on the downward slope of the metabolic curve than when alcohol is being absorbed. Figures 3.2 and 3.3 shows what can happen.

Stop and Review

1. Alcohol metabolism begins in the _____ but absorption takes place primarily in the _____.
2. Describe how alcohol is metabolized.
3. Can you explain why the rate of absorption of alcohol is variable but the rate of metabolism is constant?

Physiological Effects

Effects of Alcohol on the Gastrointestinal Tract

The gastrointestinal tract plays an important part in mediating the effects of alcohol. Alcoholic beverages contact the oral cavity, esophagus, and stomach in virtually undiluted form. All of these structures are covered with cells (called mucosa) that secrete mucus. Heavy drinking can damage the mucosal lining and cause lesions in these structures (Bode & Bode, 1997). In the oral cavity, heavy drinking reduces the secretion of saliva and can lead to inflammation of the tongue and mouth, as well as increase the incidence of tooth decay and gum disease. Once in the esophagus, alcohol slows down its rhythmic muscular movement (peristalsis). Heartburn, which is caused by stomach acid leaking past the esophageal sphincter, is common in heavy drinkers because alcohol can damage the sphincter. In fact, the sphincter can be damaged after a single episode of heavy drinking. Heavy drinkers can develop a peculiar abnormality called "nutcracker esophagus" (the name is very descriptive) that can fool physicians into making a diagnosis of chronic heart disease (Bode & Bode, 1997).

One of the most dramatic effects of alcohol on the gastrointestinal tract is esophageal hemorrhage caused when the area between the esophagus and stomach is ruptured

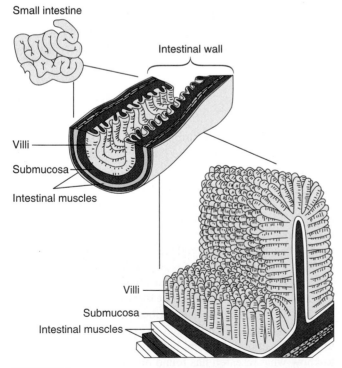

FIGURE 3.1
The villi of the small intestine absorb alcohol and digested food. As you can see, their surface area for absorption is quite large.

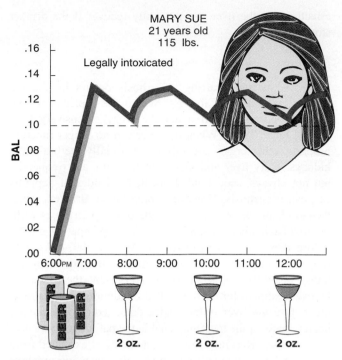

FIGURE 3.2A

Mary Sue drank three beers around 6 P.M. She felt intoxicated so she didn't drink anything else until 8 P.M., when she had just two ounces of wine. She had two ounces of wine at 10 P.M. and at midnight. Although she probably feels fine, she has, in fact, been legally intoxicated since 6:30. The two ounces of wine every two hours was enough to maintain her blood-alcohol level above .10.

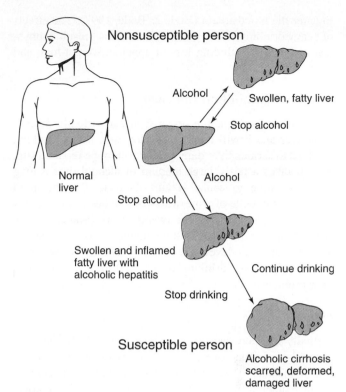

FIGURE 3.3

The liver can metabolize many poisons. For those susceptible to the effects of alcohol, however, excessive alcohol use can lead to cirrhosis.

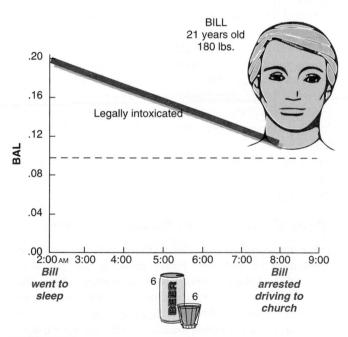

FIGURE 3.2B

On Saturday night Bill celebrated his twenty-first birthday with six shots of tequila and six beer chasers. He went to "sleep" at 2:00 A.M. with a BAL of .20. He woke Sunday morning feeling fine but he has not sobered up yet. On the way to church at 8 A.M., Bill is stopped and arrested; his blood-alcohol level is .11.

(Bode & Bode, 1997). Occasionally this hemorrhaging is the result of repeated vomiting. Esophageal hemorrhage can cause death in a matter of minutes. Cancer of the esophagus, which is almost always fatal, is linked to heavy drinking as well. Apparently the cells lining the esophagus become cancerous as a result of the irritation of alcohol and the resultant increase in secretion of gastric acids (Bode & Bode, 1997). Alcoholic beverages, especially beer and wine, increase secretion of gastric acid. This is not necessarily bad, because gastric acid is necessary for digestion. However, heavy drinking can reverse this effect, and chronic alcohol abuse can lead to a decrease in gastric acid. Gastric acids not only aid in digestion but kill bacteria associated with food (Bode & Bode, 1997). Because of decreased gastric acid, heavy drinkers do not digest food as well and are prone to bacterial infections in the intestine.

Heavy drinking causes its real damage in the intestine. Chronic alcohol abuse affects intestinal motility with the result that diarrhea is common. In high doses alcohol also decreases absorption of glucose, water, and sodium. Carbohydrates, fats, and protein are not absorbed properly and alcohol interferes with intestinal enzymes, especially lactose (Bode & Bode,1997). Many heavy drinkers, therefore, have lactose intolerance. Even a single episode of heavy drinking can lead to intestinal bleeding, and with heavy drinking a complex series of events takes place that results in the intestine being more likely to allow bacteria and toxic substances to enter the bloodstream (Bode & Bode, 1997). The effects of heavy drinking on the gastrointestinal tract result in physical complaints including loss of appetite, weight loss, and malnutrition.

Effects of Alcohol on the Liver

The liver is a remarkable organ. You can virtually destroy your liver and it will regenerate. However, heavy drinking can lead to serious liver damage that cannot be repaired (fig. 3.4). It takes a fairly large amount of alcohol over a long period of time to cause serious damage. The threshold seems to be a bottle of wine, a six-pack of beer, or five or six drinks of liquor per day for twenty years (Maher, 1997). Even then, liver damage is not inevitable—about one-half of all heavy drinkers develop severe liver damage. However, it doesn't take heavy drinking over a lifetime to cause some liver problems.

Fatty Liver

Virtually all heavy drinkers have a fatty liver, and many people will experience one after just a day or two of unusual (for them) intake. The enzymes that metabolize fat also metabolize alcohol, so when alcohol is present, the liver stores the fat until the alcohol is all gone. Fatty liver is not dangerous and leads to few symptoms, other than abdominal discomfort. Fatty liver develops regardless of diet (Lieber, 1997).

Alcoholic hepatitis

Roughly half of all heavy drinkers have one or more bouts of alcoholic hepatitis. It is often mistaken for a bad case of the flu, since the symptoms include fever, nausea, vomiting, and abdominal pain. *Hepatitis* literally means "inflammation of the liver," and it can lead to massive destruction of liver tissue. It can be fatal, but prompt treatment usually is effective and the liver can generally recover if the drinker stops drinking.

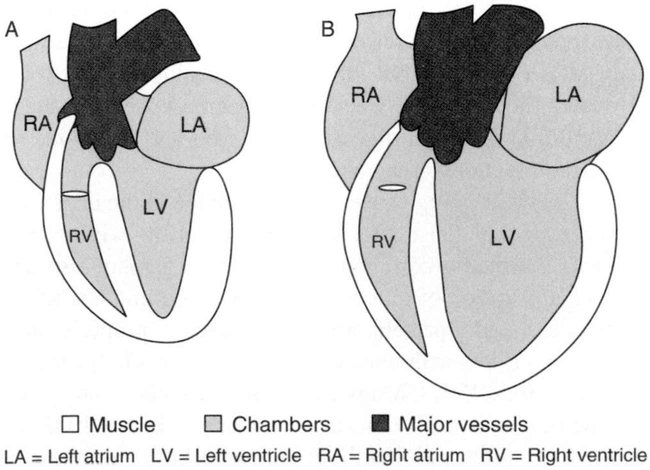

Cirrhosis

Cirrhosis means "scarring." Cirrhosis occurs in about a quarter of all alcohol abusers. Scar tissue replaces normal tissue, blood vessels stiffen, and the liver is extensively damaged (Lieber, 1997). When the liver can no longer function properly, other organs are injured, especially the brain and kidneys. Fatty liver and alcoholic hepatitis are frequently, but not always, sequential. Repeated episodes of hepatitis can cause cirrhosis. However, some heavy drinkers never develop hepatitis or cirrhosis, some develop cirrhosis without first having hepatitis, and some develop hepatitis and die before they progress to cirrhosis (Maher, 1997). As with fatty liver, cirrhosis can develop even if the drinker maintains a healthy diet (Lieber, 1997). At present, there is no effective treatment for cirrhosis. If the individual stops drinking before the liver is too badly damaged, the remaining healthy parts of the liver may enable the patient to live a normal life span. Recently, however, a chemical extracted from soybeans has shown promise in actually reversing previous damage (Lieber, 1997). So far, this research has been conducted only in animals, so it remains to be seen if human clinical trials yield the same results. Successful treatment would benefit many who are abstainers or light drinkers since cirrhosis of the liver can affect nondrinkers as well.

Just how liver damage occurs is far from clear. At least three mechanisms have been identified: lack of oxygen, inflammation, and fibrosis. Lack of oxygen results in the formation of large numbers of free radicals. Normally these are destroyed by antioxidants (such as vitamins A and E). However, with excess alcohol intake the free radicals increase greatly in number and antioxidant production decreases. These two changes lead to massive death of the liver cells (Maher, 1997). Inflammation occurs as a result of hepatitis. Usually the inflammation serves a useful function of producing antibodies and destroying poisons, but when heavy drinking occurs, the inflammatory agents destroy the liver's own tissues. Fibrosis occurs when heavy drinking stimulates the liver's fat-storing cells to produce scar tissue. The fibrosis can lead to cirrhosis (Lieber, 1997).

Effects of Alcohol on the Pancreas and Kidney

The pancreas is the organ that regulates blood sugar and secretes digestive enzymes. Heavy drinking can lead to inflammation of the pancreas, called pancreatitis (Apte, Wilson, & Korsten, 1997). Pancreatitis is extremely painful and the damage it causes affects the digestion and metabolism of food. Pancreatitis shortens the life span but does not usually cause immediate death (Apte, Wilson, & Korsten, 1997). Remember that alcohol reaches all the organs, so tissue damage is also occurring elsewhere in the body and death occurs from damage to other organs such as the liver. The only treatment for pancreatitis is bed rest and fasting. Intra-

□ Muscle　□ Chambers　■ Major vessels

LA = Left atrium　LV = Left ventricle　RA = Right atrium　RV = Right ventricle

FIGURE 3.4
A—Normal heart; B—Enlarged heart.

Should Alcohol Abusers Receive a Liver Transplant?

Organ transplantation now seems routine, but the technical problems were not solved until the 1960s. Even now, the demand for organs greatly exceeds the available supply. Organ transplantation must take place within a few hours after the donor's death. How do doctors decide who gets an available organ? The current rule of thumb is to give it to the person whose life is most in jeopardy, regardless of social class, age, or any criteria other than need. Does this seem fair to you? A seriously ill person of 80 who might expect at most a few more years of life would be chosen over a young child who was less ill.

The case of liver transplants is even more complicated. About 3,000 livers are transplanted every year in the United States, and there are as many as 65,000 potential recipients (Van Thiel, 1996). Excessive consumption of alcohol is responsible for about half of all cases of terminal liver disease. This means that it is almost inevitable that if alcohol abusers compete equally for access to available livers, some alcohol abusers will get a liver before some patients who have non-alcohol-related problems, who will then die. The cost of transplantation can be more than a million dollars; usually this is paid by the patient's insurance. Recovery from alcohol abuse is difficult under the most favorable circumstances, and most drinkers relapse.

Given these facts, why should alcohol abusers be given new livers? If they relapse, they might damage the new liver and could even die, wasting a precious commodity (Kumar et al.,1990). Don't alcohol abusers

have an obligation to prevent their abuse from reaching the point where they develop terminal liver disease (Moss & Siegler, 1991)? Should they not be given a lower priority than patients whose liver damage is not alcohol induced? Would you be as likely to donate your liver at death if you knew it would go to a serious alcohol abuser?

On the other hand, several studies have found that of alcohol abusers who receive a liver transplant, only about 10 percent resumed drinking and none returned to heavy (daily) drinking (Novick, Haverkos, & Teller, 1997). Their survival rates are the same as for those whose liver disease is not alcohol related, and the alcohol abusers were as likely to be employed as nonabusers (Kumar et al., 1990). Alcohol abusers were no more likely than nonabusers to have emotional problems, had the same energy levels, and were just as likely to comply with follow-up medical treatment and medical regimens (Carrington, Tartar, Switala, & Van Thiel, 1996).

Furthermore, if we give alcohol abusers a lower priority than nonabusers, what do we do about other lifestyle-related health conditions? Should smokers get a new lung or a new heart? Should a chronically obese person with heart disease get a lower priority because they "chose" to eat too much? If alcoholism is a disease, then is the alcoholic really responsible for drinking (Van Thiel, 1996)? Isn't it a moral judgment to say that alcohol abusers are"bad"? Should physicians be put in the position of evaluating patients' lifestyles? What do you think?

---

venous fluids help, but no medical treatment has been found to be effective. Heavy drinkers who abstain have fewer and less frequent symptoms and a reduction of pain, but abstention does not cure the disease.

The kidney is another important organ affected by alcohol. The kidneys regulate fluids in the body and produce hormones that regulate blood pressure and red blood cell metabolism. Alcohol consumption can damage the kidney directly or indirectly through the liver. Alcohol increases urine flow by inhibiting the production of antidiuretic hormone (ADH). ADH inhibits urine production, so alcohol increases urine flow by inhibiting the inhibitor of urine production (Epstein, 1997). Increased urine output leads to an imbalance of electrolytes such as sodium, potassium, and chloride ions. Levels of other important elements such as phosphates, magnesium, and calcium are also disrupted. The effect of alcohol on the kidney might play a role in the high blood pressure common to heavy drinkers. When other or-

gans of the body, especially the liver, are damaged by alcohol, the kidneys are affected as well. **Ascites** is a condition brought on by liver and kidney damage that results in the accumulation of fluid (edema). The fluid is stored in the abdomen, where as much as seven gallons can accumulate (Epstein, 1997).

Stop and Review

1. How does heavy drinking damage the gastrointestinal system?
2. What are the three types of liver problems associated with drinking alcohol, and what are their consequences?
3. How does malnutrition result from alcohol damage to the pancreas?
4. What are two conditions that can result when alcohol damages the kidneys?

Effects of Alcohol on the Cardiovascular System

Alcohol reduces the energy capacity of the heart muscle, thus reducing its ability to contract and causing direct damage to the muscle itself. Alcohol can irritate the heart, leading to cardiac arrhythmia. Heavy drinking can lead to premature heartbeats and a disturbance of the heart rhythm called **holiday heart syndrome** (Zakhari, 1997). Because the symptoms are similar to those of a heart attack, emergency rooms see many people with this syndrome after holidays like Thanksgiving, Christmas, and New Year's, hence the name.

Alcohol also contributes to high blood pressure. Even moderate amounts (3 to 4 drinks a day) are associated with an increase in blood pressure. Twice as many heavy drinkers as light drinkers or abstainers have high blood pressure. Alcohol abuse can also increase the risk of cerebrovascular problems (Zakhari, 1997). Alcoholic cardiomyopathy is a serious problem resulting from the damaging effects of alcohol on the heart (fig. 3.5). Because of its weakened condition, the heart must enlarge to pump out sufficient blood. This further weakens the heart and can lead to a heart attack or heart failure.

Alcohol dilates the peripheral blood vessels, a condition familiar to almost every drinker. The dilation produces a feeling of warmth that can be misleading because the increased blood supply to the periphery comes from the inner body. Core temperatures decrease in individuals exposed to cold after consuming alcohol. This decrease leads to feelings of sleepiness and fatigue. A heavy drinker exposed to the cold outdoors in winter will feel warm and sleepy, and might fall asleep outdoors and freeze to death.

After all the discussion of the harmful effects of alcohol on various organs, you might think that at last something good can be said about the effects of alcohol on the heart. After all, the **French paradox** is well known. Even though the French are notorious for eating just the kind of diet that we are told leads to heart disease, the incidence of heart disease in France is quite low. Presumably the wine that so many French drink serves to protect them against heart disease (Constant, 1997). The supposed beneficial effects of drinking (especially red wine, we are told) had led to a marked increase in the sale of wine in the United States. Consumption of wine increased almost 4 percent between 1995 and 1996 alone. Just what is the relationship between alcohol and the heart? Will we really live longer if we have a glass of wine every day? The answer might be yes, no, or maybe, depending on the individual.

Alcohol can be good for the heart or harmful, depending on the amount consumed and the traits of the drinker. Heavy drinking can bring about high blood pressure, disease of the heart muscle, and irregular heart rhythms, while moderate drinking can bring about a decrease in coronary artery disease, which is responsible for nearly 500,000 deaths a year in the United States (Puddey & Croft, 1997). The culprits or heroes are the same: concentration of high- and low-density lipoproteins, blood clot formation, and blood clot dissolution (Bisson, Butzke, & Ebeler, 1995).

Alcohol and cancer

Heavy drinkers have an increased risk of several kinds of cancer, especially of the gastrointestinal tract. Alcohol probably does not cause cancer by itself. Instead it seems to interact with other cancer inducing substances. Heavy drinking by smokers further increases the risk of cancer of the voice box, tongue, and pharynx. Heavy whiskey drinkers have a 25 times greater chance of cancer of the esophagus compared to those who drink about 2 drinks a day. Smokers who drink heavily have a 45 fold increase in this type of cancer. Heavy alcohol consumption is also related to cancers of the colon and rectum. The risk of rectal cancer is greatest for heavy beer drinkers, distilled spirits seem to have no effect (Bode & Bode, 1997).

FIGURE 3.5
Fetal alcohol syndrome can result in numerous facial deformities. They tend to become less noticeable with age, however, and are difficult to identify in mild cases.

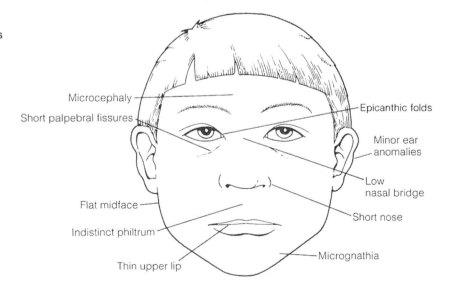

Microcephaly

Short palpebral fissures

Epicanthic folds

Minor ear anomalies

Low nasal bridge

Flat midface

Short nose

Indistinct philtrum

Micrognathia

Thin upper lip

After many years of controversy, researchers have apparently established a link between moderate drinking and breast cancer in women. One study evaluated associations between lifestyle and breast cancer in more than 300,000 women of whom over 4000 contracted breast cancer in the course of the study. The researchers found that women who consumed 2–5 drinks a day were 1.4 times as likely to develop breast cancer as those who did not drink (Smith-Warner, et al, 1998). They reported that there was a 9 percent increase in risk for every daily drink up to about 5 drinks a day. The 1 percent of women who drank even more than that did not show any further increase in risk. Other researchers have reported that the risk was greatest for those who had been drinking in the five years prior to the onset of cancer. In this study, women who drank more than 2 drinks a day were 2.4 times as likely to develop breast cancer as those that drank less (Swanson et al, 1997).

Exactly how alcohol intake is related to breast cancer is not clear, but whatever the relationship, lower rates of drinking are clearly associated with lower rates of breast cancer (Smith-Warner et al, 1998). At this point in this text, you might be asking yourself, does this mean that cutting down on drinking will reduce the risk of breast cancer. Keep in mind that the study showed that those who drank regularly had a higher risk of breast cancer. The researchers did not try to determine the effects of reduced drinking on breast cancer.

Health benefits of drinking

Until very recently, the question of whether moderate drinking increased life span was hotly debated, but the issue now seems clear. Moderate drinkers live longer than heavy drinkers (which is to be expected). They also live longer than abstainers (which is a surprise). Much of the debate centered around the definition of "abstainer." If enough abstainers abstained because they were former heavy drinkers or had other serious health problems, it would reduce the average lifespan of all abstainers. But research that controls for this possibility finds that moderate drinkers live longer (Hanna, Chou, & Grant, 1997). This effect is seen worldwide and has been found with drinkers of both fermented and distilled beverages (Constant, 1997).

What is not clear is how alcohol exerts its beneficial effect. Alcohol appears to increase levels of the so-called good cholesterol, HDL (Figueredo, 1997), and decrease the formation of blood clots that lead to heart attack (Constant, 1997). In addition, red wine might provide an extra benefit because it contains substances known as flavonoids, which are antioxidants. You read earlier that oxidation and the formation of free radicals damage body tissue. The flavonoids appear to reduce the formation of free radicals (Zakhari, 1997).

Light drinking not only reduces the risk of first heart attack, but also decreases the risk of a second heart attack (Miyamae, Diamond, Weiner, Camacho, & Figueredo, 1997) as well as the incidence of angina, a painful condition that occurs when the oxygen supply to the heart is interrupted (Camargo et al., 1997). The beneficial effect is seen in the average population as well as in a group of physicians who are part of a massive ongoing study of health (Camargo et al., 1997). One might expect that physicians would take particular care of themselves and certainly should get adequate health care. The finding that alcohol seems to be beneficial for doctors is therefore even more striking.

Before you stop reading this section and go have a drink for your health. there are many factors that you should consider. The beneficial effect is seen only with light drinking, certainly no more than one or two drinks a day. Any amount of alcohol greater than that can be harmful. Furthermore, many people, such as diabetics, should not drink, and certainly anyone with a family history of alcohol abuse should exercise extreme caution. Drinking even one or two drinks can affect driving ability and other activities. The beneficial effect of alcohol is not large, and could probably be obtained equally as well by cutting down on fats or exercising regularly. The antioxidant effects of red wine can be obtained by drinking purple grape juice (Zakhari, 1997).

Keep in mind that the relationship between alcohol and longevity is correlational. Studies have shown that people who are light drinkers live longer, but no studies to date have shown that nondrinkers who take up light drinking will benefit. There might be something else that light drinkers do that accounts for the increase in lifespan, or there could be a third factor associated with both light drinking and longevity. If you are already a light drinker, there is no reason for you to stop drinking; if you are a heavy drinker, there probably is; but if you don't drink at all, there is no good reason to start.

Effects of Alcohol on the Reproductive System

Shakespeare said it best when describing the effects of alcohol on sexual behavior: "it provokes the desire but takes away the performance." Of course, Shakespeare wasn't the first to notice the effect. None other than Aristotle wrote, "Those who are drunk are incapable of sexual intercourse." The armies of Alexander the Great conquered the known world, but Alexander was notorious for riotous living and reportedly drank so much "that he had no appetite for sexual indulgence" (Abel, 1985).

Alcohol releases inhibitions and increases perceived sexual arousal (Crowe & George,1989). However, physiologically the exact opposite is happening. Increased alcohol levels lead to decreased strength of erections in men and an increase in time to orgasm for women (Malatesta, Pollack, Crotty, & Peacock, 1982). Long-term effects of alcohol are even worse. Alcohol reduces testosterone levels after even a short period of drinking, and heavy drinking in women can lead to a variety of sexual problems (Blume, 1997). Male alcohol abusers can develop testicular atrophy, impotence, and infertility, and increased estrogen (Ellingboe & Varanelli,

1979). The result is decreased body hair, breast development, and the female pattern of body fat. *As many as 60 percent of male alcohol abusers report impotence* (Crowe & George, 1989). Women alcohol abusers experience infertility and menstrual difficulties and are at higher risk for spontaneous abortion. In addition, they often experience earlier menopause (Blume, 1997).

Fetal alcohol syndrome

The harmful effects of alcohol on the developing fetus were first identified in the early 1970s (Finnegan & Kandall, 1997). After more than twenty years of research we now know that alcohol can cause a wide range of physical and behavioral fetal defects. Heavy drinking during pregnancy can lead to fetal growth deficiencies, facial abnormalities (fig. 3.6), and central nervous system damage (Finnegan & Kandall, 1997). The damage caused to the fetal central nervous system seems to persist throughout life. The facial and growth abnormalities might become less noticeable with age. The term **fetal alcohol syndrome (FAS)** is a medical diagnosis used when all three defects are found (Connor & Streissguth, 1995). FAS children also show hearing, speech, and language difficulties (Church, Eldis, Blakeley, & Bawle, 1997).

Alcohol-related neurodevelopmental disorder

Alcohol-related neurodevelopmental disorder (ARND) is much more common and is also more difficult to diagnose. The amount of alcohol consumed does not seem to differentiate between FAS and ARND. More likely the relevant factor is the time during pregnancy when the alcohol is consumed. Drinking during the first trimester is more likely to lead to FAS, whereas ARND can occur when the mother drinks heavily at any time during pregnancy (Connor & Streissguth,1995). Because the damage from ARND refers to changes in the brain, dysfunction due to ARND can be even more severe than FAS. Alcohol causes a reduction an overall reduction in brain volume and a decreased size of the diencephalon. The cerebellum and basal ganglia, both involved in motor function, are disproportionately damaged. The damage seen is different than in children who are equally developmentally disabled for other reasons (Abel, 1996).

Despite many years of research, just how alcohol causes damage is not definitely known. Alcohol does cause impaired blood flow between the mother and the fetus, as well as causing hormonal imbalances. There can also be a direct effect of alcohol on the developing cells of the fetus, because the alcohol readily passes through the placenta and into the blood supply of the fetus (Young, 1997). If the mother is intoxicated, so is the fetus. The fetus is at greater risk because the fetal brain and body are rapidly developing. Just how many babies are born in the U.S. with FAS or ARND is not known, but estimates range from almost 800,000 to 2.6 million annually. The amount of alcohol necessary to produce these deficits also is not known, but consumption of more than five or six standard drinks daily and frequent binge drinking clearly pose the greatest risks (Finnegan & Kandall, 1997).

At this point you might be saying to yourself, Wait a minute, lots of women drank during pregnancy in the past, what about them? Many women did drink during pregnancy and many babies were born with birth defects as a result. FAS and ARND did not *begin* in the early 1970s, it was the relationship between drinking and defects that was demon-

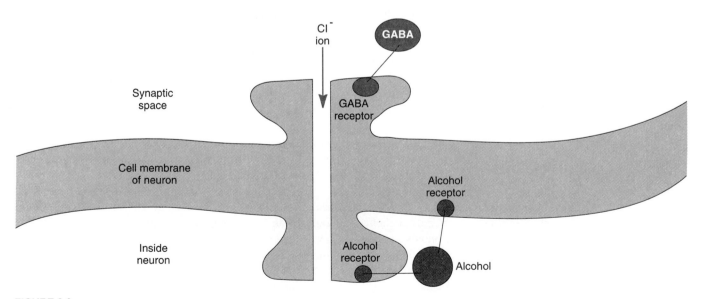

FIGURE 3.6

GABA is an inhibitory neurotransmitter. When it attaches to a receptor, as shown above, it opens the ion channel and allows chlorine ions to enter the neuron. The function of the neuron (the action potential) is inhibited. GABA works on the outside of the neuron. Alcohol works on the same receptors as GABA but on the inside of the neuron and has the same function, to inhibit the firing of the neuron. Alcohol may also work on the membrane of the neuron, as shown.

strated then. Most women who take an *occasional* drink during pregnancy *probably* won't have a baby with alcohol-related birth defects. If you were a health professional, however, would you tell pregnant women it is safe to drink? More to the point, if you were pregnant would you want to take the chance?

Stop and Review

1. Alcohol intake can cause high blood pressure and heart damage, but it can also reduce the risk of heart attack. Can you explain how alcohol can have both effects?
2. How do the effects of alcohol on sexual functioning differ in men and women?
3. What is the difference between ARND and FAS?

Effects of Alcohol on the Brain

Alcohol effects on the structures of the nervous system

Chronic consumption of alcohol can damage the nervous system, particularly the brain. The effects of alcohol can be direct or indirect. Direct effects are the result of alcohol-induced changes in the various neurotransmitter systems as well as alcohol-induced atrophy of neurons and brain shrinkage. Indirect effects are the result of alcohol-induced damage to the liver and other body organs (Oscar-Berman, Shagrin, Evert, & Epstein, 1997).

Even moderate drinking can lead to alcohol effects on the central and peripheral nervous system. The body's ability to regulate temperature is affected with potentially fatal results. While peripheral vasodilation leads to feelings of warmth, the core temperature is reduced and the medulla does not compensate (Oscar-Berman, 1997). When body temperature is reduced, the individual falls asleep and can easily freeze if outdoors in winter. Alcohol affects sleep, particularly REM sleep or dreaming. Even a few drinks of alcohol will reduce REM sleep temporarily, with a rebound after drinking stops.

Of course, virtually everyone is familiar with the effects of alcohol on the cerebellum (the part of the brain that coordinates muscle movements). Even low blood alcohol levels result in some impairment of balance and coordination, and higher doses lead to the all-too-familiar staggering. Another consequence familiar to most people who live with drinkers is that alcohol can increase snoring and breathing difficulties during sleep (Dawson, Bigby, Poceta, & Mitler, 1997). Alcohol acts on the medulla to produce this effect. Although snoring might seem to be more annoying than dangerous, serious consequences can arise in those who are prone to sleep apnea (a disorder in which the person stops breathing during sleep).

Alcohol abuse has been associated with damage to various parts of the brain, especially the frontal lobes (Rosse, Riggs, Dietrich, Schwartz, & Deutsch, 1997). The frontal lobes are responsible for abstract thinking, planning, and carrying out goal-directed behavior. Alcohol abuse can lead to atrophy, impaired circulation, and impaired metabolism in the frontal lobes. Heavy drinkers often show deficits in complex thinking (Oscar-Berman & Pulaski, 1995). The limbic system, particularly the hippocampus and amygdala, are affected by alcohol, and alcohol abusers often are found to have deficits in memory and emotional functioning (Sullivan, Marsh, Mathalon, Lim, & Pfefferbaum, 1995). These measures of brain damage can persist even among abstinent abusers, although some return to normal functioning does occur for some abstinent former abusers (Shear, Jernigan, & Butters,1994). Curiously, there is no clear relationship between the amount of alcohol consumed and evidence for brain damage. Some very abusive drinkers show little or none, whereas some relatively light drinkers show significant damage (Oscar-Berman, Shagrin, Evert, & Epstein, 1997).

Fortunately, the most severe form of alcohol-induced brain damage is becoming rare. The development of **Korsakoff's syndrome** requires extremely heavy drinking along with dietary neglect (Oscar-Berman & Evert, 1997). A genetic factor might also be involved. People with Korsakoff's syndrome cannot form new long-term memories, so they live in an eternal present. A patient who developed Korsakoff's in the 1970s might think now that Nixon is president and that the Vietnam War is still being fought. The long-term memories that had been formed before onset of the illness remain intact, and for the most part intellectual functioning remains normal. However, the disease is devastating because the patients cannot remember what happened to them a few minutes ago.

Patients with Korsakoff's can develop an inflammation of the brain lining known as Wernicke's encephalopathy, which leads to a staggering gait and abnormal eye movements (Oscar-Berman & Evert, 1997). The inflammation damages various parts of the brain, especially the diencephalon and cerebellum. Like Korsakoff's syndrome, Wernicke's encephalopathy is related to dietary factors, particularly to a deficiency in thiamine (Oscar-Berman & Evert, 1997). Both of these conditions are becoming rarer now that we know the dietary components (although they can occur even with good nutrition). Vitamin supplementation is standard practice during medical treatment for any of the many consequences of heavy drinking.

Increasing age aggravates the harmful effects of heavy drinking (Pfefferbaum, et al., 1992). The elderly are at risk for both short-term and long-term alcohol effects on the brain. They have a higher risk of accidents, and the medication taken for problems common to the elderly, such as chronic pain and heart disease, can interact with alcohol (Gambert, 1997). The elderly are particularly prone to hypoglycemia (low blood sugar) because many diseases common to the elderly result in loss of appetite. The failure to eat properly sets the stage for adverse effects when the elderly drink, and they often lack the mechanisms necessary to compensate well (Gambert, 1997).

Alcohol Effects on Neurons and Neurotransmitters

Recent research has focused on the effects of alcohol on neural transmission and especially on neurotransmitter systems. Alcohol can affect the neuron itself as well as nearly all neurotransmitter substances so far studied (Oscar-Berman et al., 1997). No other drug seems to have such a profound effect on the brain. To further complicate matters, each of the neurotransmitter systems interacts with several others. It is not possible to describe all of the changes here, so you will read about only the most important effects on the most important neurotransmitters in the sections that follow.

Alcohol and the GABA System   As you read in chapter 2, GABA is an inhibitory neurotransmitter and it is found throughout the brain. When GABA is taken up by the postsynaptic receptors, it makes the neuron less likely to fire (fig. 3.7). Alcohol acts on the GABA system by helping to open the ion channel on the postsynaptic receptor. The wide distribution of GABA throughout the brain accounts for many of the immediate effects of drinking (Mihic & Harris, 1997). When animals are exposed to alcohol for a period of time, the GABA receptors seem to become resistant to the effects of alcohol. At this point the word *tolerance* should be occurring to you; in fact, it is generally accepted that much of the tolerance to alcohol is mediated through GABA.

Alcohol and glutamate   Glutamate is the other important amino acid neurotransmitter. It is an excitatory neurotransmitter found in nearly all parts of the brain. Alcohol inhibits the functioning of glutamate-containing neurons. This inhibition might be responsible for the effects of alcohol on memory, because glutamate is the neurotransmitter in the hippocampus, the brain structure responsible for converting short-term memory into long-term memory (Gonzales & Jaworski, 1997). As is the case with GABA, chronic exposure to alcohol leads to adaptation and perhaps a change in the number of glutamate receptors (up regulation) (Freund & Anderson, 1996). Therefore, glutamate receptors also seem to play a role in the development of tolerance.

If both GABA and glutamate receptors are important in tolerance, then withdrawal should lead to a rebound. The common symptoms associated with alcohol withdrawal—anxiety, sleeplessness, and even seizures—might represent GABA and glutamate rebound, respectively (Gonzales & Jaworski, 1997). More evidence that the amino acid neurotransmitters are involved in the symptoms of withdrawal comes from the fact that drugs given to reduce the symptoms of withdrawal affect the GABA system. You will read in chapter 9 about the benzodiazepines, such as Librium and Valium. They are prescribed to reduce anxiety and affect a portion of the GABA receptor. They also reduce the symptoms of alcohol withdrawal (Hyatt, Cheever, & Eldot, 1996).

Serotonin and alcohol   You will remember from chapter 2 that serotonin plays an important role in mood and many behaviors. Alcohol abusers have lower levels of the metabolite of serotonin in the cerebrospinal fluid, indicating that they have lower levels of serotonin in the brain (Farren & Dinan, 1996). Chronic exposure to alcohol in mice (and presumably humans) leads to an increase in the number of postsynaptic receptors for serotonin, and this increase could account in part for the tolerance to alcohol as well as to some withdrawal symptoms (Lovinger, 1997).

The drugs known as SSRIs, or selective serotonin reuptake inhibitors, provide another indication that serotonin plays a role in alcohol abuse. Giving the SSRIs to experimental animals leads to a decrease in the amount of alcohol they consume. There is some evidence that the same SSRIs (Prozac, Zoloft, and Paxil) reduce alcohol consumption in alcohol abusers, although the SSRIs do not help many alcoholics (Lovinger, 1997).

Dopamine and alcohol   Dopamine seems to play an important role in the development of alcohol abuse (Noble, 1996). You will remember that dopamine is the neurotransmitter in the nucleus accumbens, which is thought to be the reward center of the brain. Alcohol increases dopamine in the nucleus accumbens and does so in a manner different from natural rewards. When natural rewards such as food are given, the dopamine release increases but rapidly habituates or decreases, even if the reward is continued (DiChiara, 1997). Alcohol-induced dopamine release does not decrease with repeated administration. As a result, according to one theory, the rewarding feeling that results from the release of dopamine is associated with many environmental cues (such as the sight of a bottle or a familiar bar). When the drinker is exposed to these cues, the desire to drink becomes stronger (DiChiara, 1997).

Alcohol induces two changes in dopamine levels in the nucleus accumbens. The first is associated with the taste of alcohol in the mouth, and the second occurs when the alcohol reaches the brain. Ordinary rewards like good-tasting food cause only one release (Lovinger, 1997). The second involves endorphins. Apparently, alcohol increases the release of endorphins, and these in turn act on neurons to produce an increase of dopamine in the nucleus accumbens (DiChiara, 1997).

In chapter 2 you read about the theory of dopaminergic supersensitivity. If the theory is correct, heavy drinking produces an increased output of dopamine in the nucleus accumbens that eventually causes the postsynaptic neuron to down regulate. When the drinker stops, even temporarily, the amount of dopamine released decreases and there are not enough receptors on the postsynaptic neuron. This deficiency leads to craving and a return to drinking.

The endorphin system and alcohol   The endorphin system, discussed in chapter 2, plays a role in the effects that alcohol produces. Drugs that block the action of the endorphins reduce alcohol consumption in animals, including monkeys, rats, and mice (Froelich, 1997). Careful, well-controlled studies have shown that giving endorphin blockers or antagonists to alcohol abusers decreases the frequency of relapse, the desire to drink, and the ability to get "high" from alcohol if they do drink (O'Malley, Jaffe, Rode, & Rounsaville, 1996).

In rats, studies have shown that a single dose of alcohol increases the release of endorphins in the brain; human and animal studies have shown that alcohol increases the output of endorphins from the pituitary (Froelich, 1997). With long-term consumption, the situation is reversed. In rats, prolonged exposure to alcohol reduces the release of endorphins, and similar results have been shown in humans (Froelich, 1997). Animals bred specifically for the tendency to drink alcohol show an increased responsiveness of the endorphin system to alcohol. In humans, alcohol consumption induces an increase in endorphin levels only for those with a family history of alcohol abuse; subjects without such a family history do not increase endorphin output (Froelich, 1997). Do you see the connection between the studies of alcohol-preferring rats and the human studies of people with a family history of alcohol abuse?

Increased levels of endorphins in humans is associated with feelings of euphoria and well-being. Rats and mice will learn a response for which the reward is an injection of endorphins, and they will self-administer endorphins given the opportunity. Although this would not explain all cases of alcohol abuse, the increased responsiveness of the endorphin system might be an inherited trait that increases the probability of drinking (Froelich, 1997). Increases in endorphins might produce euphoria directly or indirectly by increasing dopamine levels in the nucleus accumbens.

Stop and Review

1. How can alcohol damage the brain?
2. Describe the symptoms of Korsakoff's syndrome.
3. Alcohol affects nearly all the neurotransmitter systems in the brain. Three of the most important are the GABA, dopamine, and endorphin systems. Describe how alcohol affects each of these.

Trying to describe the effects of alcohol on one neurotransmitter is a little like trying to remove one stick in a game of pick up sticks. As you probably remember from your childhood, the game consists of trying to remove one stick from a large pile of sticks that are all lying atop one another. Moving one stick often causes other sticks to move because they are intertwined. The same is true for neurotransmitter systems. Each of the neurotransmitters affects the others either directly or indirectly, making it virtually impossible to isolate one effect or another.

Alcohol Abuse

If you have been reading carefully, you may have noticed that the word *alcoholism* has not been used in this textbook until now. The omission was deliberate and follows the thinking of most researchers in this field. The term *alcoholism* has a long

and honorable past, and for many years it was useful because it encouraged people to think of alcohol abuse and dependence as a disease rather than a moral weakness.

The Concept of Alcoholism

The term *alcoholic* is far less pejorative than *drunkard*. However, words are very powerful, and over time these two terms have acquired connotations that are now creating their own problems.

Many researchers use the terms *alcoholism* and *alcoholic* as a sort of shorthand because better terms are not available. In most recent publications, when the term *alcoholism* is used, it is followed by a statement that the term refers to alcohol abuse and dependence as defined by the *DSM-IV*. Even the more ardent defenders of the disease concept of alcoholism have partially changed their viewpoint. Two of these, James Royce and George Vaillant, have suggested using the terms *illness* or *disorder* and calling the condition by names similar to those in the *DSM-IV* rather than use *alcoholism* (Vaillant, 1996; Royce & Scratchley, 1996).

The effort has come about because the terms *alcoholism* and *alcoholic* have never overcome their very negative connotations. Labeling someone an "alcoholic" might make that person unwilling to accept treatment, especially those (alcohol abusers) whose drinking creates a problem but is not so serious that the term *alcohol dependent* is warranted (Royce & Scratchley, 1996). Think about someone you know well who has a drinking problem (yourself?). Wouldn't they feel less burdened if they were told they had a problem with alcohol abuse than if they were called an alcoholic?

Many counselors and others involved in treatment have a strong belief in the usefulness of the concept of alcoholism. Many are recovering themselves and owe their recovery to acceptance of these beliefs. This discussion does not mean that someone who has an alcohol problem can safely drink, or that those who have received such counseling should think that they have been lied to. The terms *alcoholism* and *alcoholic* still have considerable use in the treatment setting, but you should also be aware that they do not have a precise meaning. As Royce and Scratchley (1996) have pointed out, a new way of thinking about alcohol abuse may lead to important research that can help to reduce the terrible toll that alcoholism (or whatever it is called) now takes. Now that you know the reasons the terms were avoided, they will be used, sparingly, because they are less cumbersome than phrases like *those who are alcohol abusers or alcohol dependent.*

Genetic and Biological Factors

The fact that alcohol abuse runs in families has been observed for centuries. Plutarch (A.D. 46–120) observed that "drunks beget drunkards." Why this should be so, however, is a matter of debate. Obviously, growing up with a parent who is an alcohol abuser would provide strong modeling. If the child observes her or his parents using alcohol to cope with virtually every situation, the child is learning that behavior. How can you determine whether alcohol abuse is the result of nature (a genetic characteristic) or nurture (family environment)?

Inheritance and adoption

Genetic factors clearly play a role in alcoholism for many abusers, but certainly not for all. The strongest evidence comes from adoption studies, studies of identical twins, and animal studies in which mice and rats are bred to prefer alcohol. Adoption studies attempt to determine whether an adopted child's drinking pattern is most like that of their biological parents or that of their adoptive parents. Twin studies look for evidence of greater **concordance,** or similarities, between identical twins than between fraternal twins. If identical twins (who are genetically identical) show higher concordance than fraternal twins (who are no more genetically alike than any other two siblings), then it is likely that alcohol abuse is a genetic inheritance involving one or more genes (Anthenelli & Schuckit, 1997).

Type I and Type II

Concordance studies show a higher incidence among identical twins, but the rate is far less than 100 percent. Fifty percent of alcohol abusers have close relatives who abuse alcohol, and another 20 percent have more-distant relatives. Nevertheless, one-third of alcohol abusers have no relative with an abuse or dependence problem (Schuckit, 1994). Twin studies demonstrate that genetics probably plays a role, but that environmental factors are also important.

Adoption studies suggest that there might be two distinct types of alcohol abusers, with different paths to abuse and perhaps different genetic factors. **Type 1 (milieu-limited) alcoholism** can be either male or female. Onset is usually after age 25, and though these abusers can abstain when required to, they show a greatly diminished capacity to control their drinking when they do start. They have at least one parent who was a problem drinker, and they grew up in an environment conducive to heavy drinking. Type 1 alcoholics have fairly mild symptoms and are rarely involved in criminal activity. It appears that they inherit a genetic predisposition that must have an environmental releaser before abuse occurs (Anthenelli & Schuckit, 1997).

Type 2 (male-limited) alcoholism seems to be independent of environmental influence. As the name implies, these abusers are invariably male, and their abuse is more severe and is associated with criminal activity. Type 2 alcoholism shows itself at an early age. These alcohol abusers are impulsive and uninhibited, and they lack social contacts. Males born into families with a Type 2 alcoholic father are nine times as likely to become alcohol abusers as those born into a "normal" family. Being adopted into a family with no history of abuse does not seem to moderate the tendency to become an abuser (Anthenelli & Schuckit, 1997).

Gender differences in inheritance

Readers with a background in psychology might recognize some of these symptoms as being similar to those of antisocial personality disorder. Whether the drinking of Type 2 alcoholics is secondary to their personality disorder is an issue that has not been completely resolved, although the weight of evidence suggests that the two overlap but are not the same (Anthenelli & Shuckit, 1997).

Nearly all of the studies have examined males. When studies are done to measure the inheritance of alcohol abuse among females, the results are less clear. Some studies have found evidence for a genetic link, others have not. Most of those that have found a link indicate that the genetic contribution is roughly 50 percent (Prescott, Neale, Corey, & Kendler, 1997). Studies assessing genetic factors are always difficult to do, and the problems are greater for studies requiring female subjects because fewer women abuse alcohol. It does seem, however, that the same genetic influences apply to both men and women, although they might be stronger in men (Anthenelli & Schuckit, 1997).

Genetic studies with animals

Research on alcohol abuse using laboratory animals has advantages and disadvantages. Animal studies permit a greater deal of control, because social and personality factors can be ruled out. Using animals permits researchers to study changes or differences in the brain, because the animals are killed at the end of the research study. On the other hand, a major drawback is that most laboratory animals do not willingly drink alcohol and those that do, drink very little. The solution was to breed strains of rats that actually prefer alcohol. Several such strains have been developed (Stewart & Li, 1997).

Studies with alcohol-preferring rats demonstrate that, at low doses, alcohol increases their behavioral activity more than it does in nonpreferring rats. They also seem less susceptible to high doses. They become tolerant to alcohol more quickly than nonpreferring rats and could be called greater "risk takers" (Stewart & Li, 1997). The brains of alcohol-preferring rats have lower levels of serotonin and low levels of dopamine. Alcohol releases dopamine in the nucleus accumbens, which is part of the "reward center." Alcohol-preferring rats seem to show increased levels of GABA in this area of the brain. The opioids might also moderate alcohol use. The alcohol-preferring strains of rats show more response to opiates than nonpreferring rats and their drinking is inhibited by naloxone. Naloxone, which blocks the opiate receptors in the brain, has been used with success to treat the craving that many human alcoholics experience (Berg, Pettinati, & Volpicelli, 1997; Stewart & Li, 1997).

The role of inheritance

Assuming there is a genetic component to alcoholism, what exactly is inherited? One possibility is a specific gene that is different in alcoholics and nonalcoholics, such that people with the gene will develop alcoholism and those without it will not. Probably the most studied genetic marker for alcohol abuse is the DRD2 gene, which produces a receptor site for dopamine. In 1990, a study showed that 69 percent of alcohol-dependent subjects, as opposed to 20 percent of the control group, had this gene (Blum, Noble, & Sheridan, 1990). This study has generated a great deal of debate. Some researchers have been able to find an association, others have not. The incidence of the gene clearly is related to the degree of alcohol abuse (Lawford et al., 1997). Not everyone who becomes an alcohol abuser has the gene, and many who have it are not abusers. It seems unlikely that one gene could produce the complex set of behaviors that we refer to as alcohol abuse.

Most researchers would agree that a number of genes in combination (polygenetic influence) produce the characteristics associated with alcohol dependence (Quaid, Dinwiddie, Conneally, & Nurnberger, 1996). Perhaps a threshold number of a certain type of gene is necessary before alcohol abuse is seen (Schuckit, 1994). It also seems likely that what is inherited is not a tendency to become an alcoholic, but a set of characteristics that make it more likely to become an alcohol abuser (Shuckit, 1994). The genetic contribution is, therefore, indirect rather than direct.

Biochemical Markers of Alcohol Abuse

Biochemical markers

One way to study the genetic component of alcohol abuse is to look for biochemical products of genes that are different in alcohol abusers. One such marker has shown promise. **Monoamine oxidase (MAO)** is an enzyme that breaks down many neurotransmitters, including dopamine, norepinephrine, and serotonin, all of which have been implicated in the development of alcohol abuse. Low levels of MAO activity have been associated with Type 2 alcoholism. Low MAO activity has also been found in many men with alcohol abuse that begins early and is severe, whether they can be classified as Type 2 or not (Anthenelli & Schuckit, 1997). It might be that the lower MAO activity is not specific to alcohol abuse but is an indicator of impulsiveness, lack of inhibition, and a predisposition to abuse any drug (Anthenelli & Shuckit, 1997).

Alcohol and flushing

The single genetic factor most strongly related to *reduced* incidence of alcohol abuse is an inherited form of the enzyme that metabolizes **acetaldehyde** (Steinmetz, Xie, Weiner, & Hurley,1997). About half of Asians have a different form of the enzyme **alcohol dehydrogenase.** When they drink, they experience flushing and other unpleasant symptoms. Because this enzyme system is under genetic control, and because Asians are at less risk for alcohol abuse than many other populations, it does have some usefulness as a marker for a group of people who are less likely to become

alcoholic (Anthenelli & Schuckit, 1997). However, remember from the previous discussion that personal and cultural factors are also very important. Some people who flush still manage to become alcohol abusers.

Brain wave activity and alcohol abuse

Another marker that has generated a great deal of research is a measure of the electrical activity of the brain. Sons of alcohol abusers tend to show a distinctive brain-wave response when presented with a particular type of stimulus. This response, called the P3 wave, is smaller in the sons of many alcoholics than in the control population. Once again, not all sons of alcoholics show this wave, and so it is not likely to be a reliable indicator for screening those at risk. The P3-wave difference is considered a genetic marker because it is a response seen more often in the sons of alcohol abusers and it occurs as the result of inheritance alone (Anthenelli & Schuckit, 1997).

Sons of alcohol abusers

Sons of alcohol abusers seem to have a different behavioral response to the effects of alcohol, another presumably inherited trait. The sons of alcoholic fathers (family history positive—FHP) seem to be less affected by alcohol compared to sons of nonalcoholic fathers (family history negative—FHN). When they consume alcohol, FHPs report being less intoxicated and show fewer physical responses such as swaying. They exhibit less change in stress hormones such as cortisol, and show other signs of having a reduced hypothalamic-pituitary-adrenal response (Anthenelli & Schuckit, 1997). Perhaps those at risk for alcohol abuse who are not as affected by alcohol drink more to compensate and the results are abuse and dependence.

Not all FHPs show a reduced response, and some FHNs did so. Follow-up studies of the subjects just described indicate that those who are FHP and show a diminished response had almost a 60 percent risk of alcohol abuse. Many studies have shown that FHPs in general have about a 30 percent chance of developing an alcohol problem. Even the few FHNs who showed a diminished response to alcohol were at greater risk (Athenelli & Schuckit, 1997). It seems unlikely that a single gene could account for this relatively complex response, and it is essential to note that not all of the FHPs who showed the response developed alcohol problems.

Stop and Review

1. Why do some researchers object to the phrase *disease of alcoholism*?
2. Genetic factors undoubtedly play a role in alcohol abuse. Describe two types of alcohol abuse that seem to have a genetic basis.
3. How are genetic factors different for men and women?
4. How do studies with alcohol-preferring rats advance our knowledge of alcohol abuse in humans?

5. How do the sons of alcohol abusers (FHP) differ from other males (FHN)?

Recovery from Alcohol Abuse

How do people who are alcoholics recover? Do they recover, or is alcoholism untreatable? The answer is complicated by the fact that alcohol abusers have a wide range of drinking patterns, come from all socioeconomic groups, and exhibit a wide range of alcohol problems when they decide to stop. An older man who has been drinking a quart of vodka per day for twenty years, neglecting his diet, and living on the street is going to face different problems than a employed woman with a family who has been drinking moderately for ten years and finds that her drinking has increased to the point where she now feels she has become dependent.

Recovery without treatment

It may come as a surprise to learn that some problem drinkers stop without help. Yet recent data suggest that some alcohol abusers do just that. They either abstain completely or return to moderate drinking. A recent study found that roughly 75 percent of the people responding to a survey who reported a previous problem with alcohol moderated their drinking or stopped without help (Sobell, Cunningham, & Sobell, 1996). These findings are so opposed to conventional wisdom that they should be carefully examined.

Formal treatment for alcohol abuse is a recent development. Abusers must have been recovering (and relapsing) for thousands of years without treatment, so they can undoubtedly do so in the twentieth century. The best-known self-help group, Alcoholics Anonymous (AA), was formed less than seventy years ago. Most alcohol abusers do not go to AA, and 90 percent of those who do drop out within a year (Godlaski, Leukefeld, & Cloud, 1997). Relatively few studies have looked at this phenomenon—sometimes called "natural recovery." Having a commitment to change and having the support of family members were related to success (Sobell, Sobell, Toneatto, & Leo, 1996).

Moderation and abstinence

Because there have been so few studies of recovery without treatment, numerous questions remain unanswered. Is there a difference in severity between those entering treatment and those who do not? Are relapse rates the same? Do those who recover without treatment substitute some other organization? Do those who attend a self-help group once or twice and drop out have the same recovery rates as those who attend regularly (Godlaski, Leukefeld, & Cloud, 1997)? Undoubtedly you can think of several other questions to raise.

Another issue is returning to moderate or social drinking after a period of abuse. Again, conventional wisdom says

that this is impossible, yet a sizable number of those who recover without treatment report moderate drinking (Sobell et al., 1996). Are they telling the truth? Did the method of data collection really identify moderate drinking? Did those who moderated have fewer alcohol-related problems as abusers? Have the moderators been drinking for a shorter period of time?

Can alcohol abusers go back to moderate, or social, drinking? Surely it must have happened somewhere at some time, so the answer must be yes. But isn't the real question whether alcohol abusers should attempt or be encouraged to moderate their drinking (rather than stop completely)? Given that relapse rates for alcohol abusers who have completed treatment are 30 to 40 percent in the first year alone, why would anyone want to take the chance? An issue as controversial as this cannot be resolved in the pages of a textbook. There is simply insufficient data to permit anyone to draw definite conclusions. Until the issue is resolved, it seems wise to come down on the side of caution. Drinking alcohol is not necessary for the preservation of life, or even for the enjoyment of life. The risks involved for alcohol abusers who try to drink socially are so great that the few benefits seem inconsequential.

Alcohol abuse treatment

Once a person decides to get help for alcohol abuse, there are several options available. Assuming that the alcoholic has had a competent evaluation, the first decision depends on the severity of his or her drinking. If the evaluation reveals that the person is alcohol dependent, then inpatient treatment might be recommended. Alcohol dependence implies the possibility of physical withdrawal, a medical problem that can be life-threatening. The first stage of treatment for the alcohol dependent is called *detoxification.* Symptoms range from anxiety to **delirium tremens,** during which the person is confused, disoriented, and suffering from delusions and hallucinations (Finn & Crabbe, 1997).

Alcohol withdrawal   Alcohol withdrawal can be thought of as hyperactivity of the autonomic nervous system. To prevent withdrawal symptoms, the alcoholic continues to drink. The initial symptoms are anxiety, tremor, and insomnia. When sleep does occur, it is often disturbed by vivid, unpleasant dreams. The symptoms can begin before BAL reaches zero. The symptoms usually last from one to three days. About 10 percent of alcoholics develop more severe symptoms, including large increases in blood pressure, elevated body temperature, and drenching sweats. The more severe symptoms usually reach a peak on days 3 to 4 and begin to improve by day 5. Patients who develop delirium tremens (about 5 to 10 percent) usually do so by the day 4 (Goodwin & Gabrielli, 1997).

Treatment for withdrawal symptoms usually involves prescribing benzodiazepines such as Xanax or Valium (Hyatt, Cheever, & Eldot, 1996). These drugs are effective because they occupy the same GABA receptor sites as alcohol does and so they permit the alcoholic to taper off slowly and prevent major symptoms of withdrawal. These drugs, along with vitamins and minerals, are given for the first few days and the dose is gradually reduced. Use of the benzodiazepines is sometimes criticized because alcohol abusers are at risk to become dependent on them. Most inpatient treatment centers do prescribe them, however, and make sure that intake is carefully monitored (Goodwin & Gabrielli, 1997).

For alcoholics who do not seem physically dependent, more treatment centers are relying on outpatient treatment (Hubbard, 1997). As you read in chapter 1, outpatient treatment involves intensive counseling and informational lectures during the day, although the patient typically goes home at night. Once through withdrawal, the dependent alcohol abuser might attend the same or similar sessions. With inpatient treatment the patient resides in the facility for two weeks or more; outpatient treatment usually requires a commitment of a month or more (Washton, 1997).

Once the acute period of withdrawal is over, the second phase begins. The body is adapting to the absence of alcohol, therefore, anxiety, insomnia, depression, and hormonal changes are now occurring. There is a period of central nervous system hyperexcitability because a depressant (alcohol) has been withdrawn. This is a difficult time for the alcoholic—craving is high, emotional turmoil is usually present, and the physiological changes are less than pleasant. This phase, sometimes called **post alcohol withdrawal syndrome (PAWS),** can last for several weeks (USDHHS, 1997). The risk of relapse is high during this time, and many abusers get medical treatment to help them remain abstinent.

Medical treatment during recovery

One treatment that works if the patient is highly motivated is **Antabuse (disulfiram)** (Goodwin & Gabrielli, 1997). In use for more than forty years, Antabuse prevents acetaldehyde from being metabolized. If a person taking Antabuse drinks alcohol, the acetaldehyde buildup results in flushing, nausea, vomiting, difficulty in breathing, and an increase in heart rate. You might be surprised how many everyday things we use contain alcohol. People taking Antabuse must avoid many cold medications, mouthwash, hair tonic, and even perfume. Sensitivity to alcohol increases the longer Antabuse is used (Goodwin & Gabrielli, 1997). Furthermore, it could take two weeks to lose this sensitivity after the alcoholic stops taking Antabuse.

Motivation to stop drinking is an important factor in the effectiveness of Antabuse. Those who wish to drink might "forget" to take it for a few days. In the past, it was considered sound practice to require anyone taking Antabuse to drink an amount of alcohol to trigger a response. This "challenge dose" was supposed to demonstrate its effectiveness and increase the motivation to stop. This practice is no longer recommended because serious side effects, including liver problems, can occur and must be monitored.

Newer drugs have recently been developed that deal with the craving for alcohol. **Naloxone,** which blocks the endorphin receptor and is used to precipitate heroin withdrawal in addicts, has proven to be effective in many cases (Berg, Pettinati, & Volpicelli, 1997). Abusers who take naloxone report that their craving is lessened and that if they do slip and take a drink, its effect is greatly reduced (O'Malley, Jaffe, Rode, & Rounsaville, 1996). Like Antabuse, naloxone doesn't work for everyone and seems to be most effective when combined with counseling or psychotherapy. It might be especially useful for high-risk individuals who are in the early stages of problem drinking (Kranzler, Tennen, Penta, & Bohn, 1997; King, Volpicelli, Frazer, & O'Brien,1997). In chapter 4 you will read about the psychological aspects of alcohol abuse and treatment.

Stop and Review

1. What is natural recovery, and how common do you think it is?
2. Why is detoxification a medical problem for those who are alcohol dependent?
3. What happens to the alcohol abuser once the physical withdrawal is over?
4. What kinds of drug treatment are currently used to help alcohol abusers remain abstinent? How do disulfiram and naloxone differ in their actions?

Summary

Alcohol is both absorbed and metabolized along the entire gastrointestinal tract. Most absorption takes place in the intestine. Food can slow absorption, especially if it contains some fat. Gender, age, and body temperature also play a role. Heavy alcohol use can damage the entire gastrointestinal tract. Abuse can lead to hemorrhage, cancer (even though alcohol does not cause cancer), intestinal bleeding, and bacterial infections.

The liver is the primary site of metabolism of alcohol. Alcohol is metabolized into acetaldehyde, which is toxic, and eventually into carbon dioxide and water. Heavy drinking can lead to fatty liver, alcoholic hepatitis, and cirrhosis. The pancreas can also be damaged, and pancreatitis is common with alcohol abuse. Alcohol damage to the kidneys combined with liver damage can lead to ascites.

Alcohol has both good and bad effects on the cardiovascular system. Heavy doses can lead to cardiomyopathy. Low doses reduce clotting time and increase HDL. Along with an increase in antioxidants, these effects can decrease the risk for heart disease. One drink a day seems to reduce the risk of cardiovascular problems.

Alcohol has a negative effect on all aspects of sexuality. Heavy use can lead to impotence in males and gynecological problems in women. It can increase the rate of spontaneous abortion in pregnant women and lead to fetal alcohol effects. Heavy drinking during pregnancy is the leading preventable cause of birth defects.

The effect of light to moderate drinking on thinking and the brain is not clear. Abuse, however, leads to neurological damage and can produce Korsakoff's syndrome. Alcohol affects several neurotransmitter systems, leading to aggression, depression, and impaired thinking. The endorphin system plays a particularly important role.

Alcoholism is difficult to define, so researchers are turning to the terms *alcohol abuse* and *alcohol dependence*. Genetic, environmental, and sociocultural factors all play a role in alcohol abuse and dependence. There are several techniques to identify problem drinkers, and treatment is widely available. Most alcoholics do not go for treatment and relapse is common. Nevertheless, those who really want to can change. It is an open question whether alcohol abusers can return to normal drinking, but most experts would advise against it.

Key Terms

acetaldehyde   A toxic substance formed by the metabolism of alcohol.

alcohol dehydrogenase   An enzyme present in the liver and stomach that metabolizes ethyl alcohol.

alcohol-related neurodevelopmental disorder (ARND)   Changes in the brain of fetus due to the mother's drinking heavily at any time during pregnancy.

antabuse (disulfiram)   A drug that prevents the metabolism of acetaldehyde and helps alcohol abusers stay off alcohol.

ascites   An accumulation of fluid (edema) brought on by liver and kidney damage.

concordance   The degree to which two individuals share the same properties or behaviors. Identical twins show much higher concordance than do fraternal twins, other siblings, and parents.

delirium tremens   Confusion, disorientation, delusions, and hallucinations that occur during severe alcohol withdrawal.

fetal alcohol syndrome (FAS)   A pattern of fetal malformation, including facial deformity, growth deficiency, and limb defects, found in children born to mothers who abused alcohol during pregnancy.

French paradox   The apparent contradictory situation in which the French eat large quantities of high-fat and high-cholesterol foods yet have a low rate of heart problems.

holiday heart syndrome   Cardiac arrhythmia occurring as a result of alcohol abuse.

Korsakoff's syndrome   Brain damage resulting in amnesia and confusion brought on by alcohol abuse and nutritional deficiency.

monoamine oxidase (MAO)   An enzyme that breaks down neurotransmitters in the endbutton. MOA has been implicated in the development of alcohol abuse.

naloxone   A drug that blocks the endorphin receptor; it is used to precipitate narcotic withdrawal.

post alcohol withdrawal syndrome (PAWS)   A group of symptoms occurring in alcohol abusers after detoxification.

Type 1 (milieu-limited) alcohol abuse   Alcohol abuse prompted by a genetic predisposition with an environmental releaser.

Type 2 (male-limited) alcohol abuse   Alcohol abuse with a genetic predisposition. These alcohol abusers (usually male) are impulsive, uninhibited, and lack social contacts.

References

Abel, E. (1985). *Psychoactive drugs and sex.* New York: Plenum Press.

Abel, E. (1996). Brain anomalies in fetal alcohol syndrome. In E. Abel (Ed.), *Fetal alcohol syndrome: From mechanism to prevention* (pp. 51–68). Boca Raton, FL: CRC Press.

Anthenelli, R., & Schuckit, M. (1997). Brain reward mechanism. In J. Lowinson, P. Ruiz, R. Millman, & J. Langrod (Eds.), *Substance abuse: A comprehensive textbook* (pp. 41–50). Baltimore: Williams & Wilkins.

Apte, M. V., Wilson, J. S., & Korsten, M. A. (1997). Alcohol-related pancreatic damage: Mechanisms and treatment. *Alcohol Health and Research World, 21,* 13–20.

Blume, S. (1997). Women: Clinical aspects. In J. Lowinson, P. Ruiz, R. Millman, & J. Langrod (Eds.), *Substance abuse: A comprehensive textbook* (pp. 645–654). Baltimore: Williams & Wilkins.

Bode, C., & Bode, J. C. (1997). Alcohol's role in gastrointestinal tract disorders. *Alcohol Health and Research World, 21,* 76–83.

Camargo, C. A., Stampfer, M. J., Glynn, R. J., Grodstein, F., Gaziano, J. M., Manson, J. E., Buring, J. E., & Hennekens, C. H. (1997). Moderate alcohol consumption and risk for angina pectoris or myocardial infarction in U.S. male physicians. *Annals of Internal Medicine, 126,* 372–375.

Carrington, P., Tarter, R., Switala, J., & Van Thiel, D. (1996). Comparison of the quality of life between alcohol and nonalcoholic patients after liver transplantation. *American Journal on Addictions, 5,* 18–23.

Church, M. W., Eldis, F., Blakley, B. W., & Bawle, E. (1997). Hearing, language, speech, vestibular and dentofacial disorders in fetal alcohol syndrome. *Alcoholism: Clinical and Experimental Research, 21,* 227–237.

Constant, J. (1997). Alcohol, ischemic heart disease and the French paradox. *Clinical Cardiology, 20,* 420–424.

Crowe, L., & George, W. (1989). Alcohol and sexuality. *Psychological Bulletin, 105,* 374–386.

Dawson, A., Bigby, B., Poceta, J., & Mitler, M. (1997). Effect of bedtime alcohol on inspiratory resistance and respiratory drive in snoring and nonsnoring men. *Alcoholism: Clinical and Experimental Research, 21,* 183–190.

DiChiara, G. (1997). Alcohol and dopamine. *Alcohol Health and Research World, 21,* 108–114.

Ellingboe, J., & Varanelli, C. (1979). Ethanol inhibits testosterone biosynthesis by direct action on Leydig cells. *Research Communication in Chemistry, Pathology, and Pharmacology, 24,* 87–102.

Epstein, M. (1997). Alcohol's impact on kidney function. *Alcohol Health and Research World, 21,* 84–92.

Farren, C. K., & Dinan, T. G. (1996). High serum tryptophan associated with evidence for diminished central serotonin function in abstinent alcoholics. *Human Psychopharmacology, 11,* 511–516.

Figueredo, V. M. (1997). The effects of alcohol on the heart. *Postgraduate Medicine, 101,* 165–176.

Finn, D., & Crabbe, J. (1997). Exploring alcohol withdrawal syndrome. *Alcohol Health and Research World, 21,* 149–156.

Finnegan, L., & Kandall, S. (1997). Maternal and neonatal effects of alcohol and drugs. In J. Lowinson, P. Ruiz, R. Millman, & J. Langrod (Eds.), *Substance abuse: A comprehensive textbook* (pp. 513–534). Baltimore: Williams & Wilkins.

Freund, G., & Anderson, K. (1996). Glutamate receptors in the frontal cortex of alcoholics. *Alcoholism: Clinical and Experimental Research, 20,* 1165–1172.

Froelich, J. (1997). Opioid peptides. *Alcohol Health and Research World, 21,* 132–136.

Furnas, J. C. (1965). *The life and times of the great demon rum.* New York: Capricorn.

Gambert, S. (1997). The elderly. In J. Lowinson, P. Ruiz, R. Millman, & J. Langrod (Eds.), *Substance abuse: A comprehensive textbook* (pp. 692–697). Baltimore: Williams & Wilkins.

Godlaski, T., Leukefeld, C., & Cloud, R. (1997). Recovery: With and without help. *Substance Use and Misuse, 32,* 621–627.

Gonzales, R., & Jaworski, J. (1997). Alcohol and glutamate. *Alcohol Health and Research World, 21,* 120–126.

Goodwin, D., & Gabrielli, W. (1997). Alcohol: Clinical aspects. In J. Lowinson, P. Ruiz, R. Millman, & J. Langrod (Eds.), *Substance abuse: A comprehensive textbook* (pp. 142–147). Baltimore: Williams & Wilkins.

Hanna, E. Z., Chou, S. P., & Grant, B. F. (1997). The relationship between drinking and heart disease morbidity in the United States: Results from the National Health Interview Survey. *Alcoholism: Clinical and experimental research, 21,* 111–118.

Hyatt, M., Cheever, T., & Eldot, R. (1996). Diazepam loading for alcohol detoxification. *American Journal on Addictions, 5,* 354–358.

Kranzler, H., Tennen, H., Penta, C., & Bohn, M. (1997). Targeted naltrexone treatment of early problem drinkers. *Addictive Behaviors, 22,* 431–436.

Kumar, S., Stauber, R., Gavaler, J., Basista, M., Dindzans, V., Schade, R., Rabinovitz, M., Tarter, R., Gordon, R., Starzl, T., & Van Thiel, D. (1990). Orthotopic liver transplantation for alcoholic liver disease. *Hepatology, 11,* 159–164.

Lawford, B., Young, R., Rowell, J., Gibson, J., Feeney, G., Ritchie, T., Syndulko, K., & Noble, E. (1997). Association of the D2 dopamine receptor A1 allele with alcoholism: Medical severity of alcoholism and type of controls. *Biological Psychiatry, 41,* 386–393.

Lieber, C. (1997). Pathogenesis and treatment of liver fibrosis in alcoholics: 1996 update. *Digestive Diseases, 15,* 42–66.

Lovinger, D. (1997). Serotonin's role in alcohol's effects on the brain. *Alcohol Health and Research World, 21,* 114–120.

Maher, J. J. (1997). Exploring alcohol's effect on liver function. *Alcohol Health and Research World, 21,* 5–12.

Malatesta, V., Pollack, R., Crotty, T., & Peacock, L. (1982). Acute alcohol intoxication and the female sexual response. *Journal of Sex Research, 18,* 1–17.

Mihic, S., & Harris, R. (1997). GABA and the GABAa receptor. *Alcohol Health and Research World, 21,* 127–131.

Miyamae, M., Diamond, I., Weiner, M. W., Camacho, S. A., & Figueredo, V. M. (1997). Regular alcohol consumption mimics cardiac preconditioning by protecting against ischemia-reperfusion injury. *Proceedings of the National Academy of Sciences of the USA, 94,* 3235–3239.

Moss, A., & Siegler, M. (1991). Should alcoholics compete equally for liver transplantation? *Journal of the American Medical Association, 265,* 1295–1298.

Noble, E. (1996). Alcoholism and the dopaminergic system. *Addiction Biology, 1,* 333–348.

Novick, D., Haverkos, H., & Teller, D. (1997). The medically ill substance abuser. In J. Lowinson, P. Ruiz, R. Millman, & J. Langrod (Eds.), *Substance abuse: A comprehensive textbook.* Baltimore: Williams & Wilkins.

O'Malley, S., Jaffe, A., Rode, S., & Rounsaville, B. (1996). Experience of a "slip" among alcoholics treated with naltrexone or placebo. *American Journal of Psychiatry, 153,* 281–283.

Oscar-Berman, M., & Evert, D. (1997). Alcoholic Korsakoff's syndrome. In P. Nussbaum (Ed.), *Handbook of neuropsychology and aging* (pp. 201–215). New York: Plenum Press.

Oscar-Berman, M., & Pulaski, J. (1997). Association learning and recognition memory in alcoholic Korsakoff patients. *Neuropsychology, 11,* 282–289.

Oscar-Berman, M., Shagrin, B., Evert, D., & Epstein, C. (1997). Impairments of brain and behavior: The neurological effects of alcohol. *Alcohol Health and Research World, 21,* 65–75.

Pfefferbaum, A., Sullivan, E. V., Mathalon, D., & Lim, K. O. (1997). Frontal lobe volume loss observed with magnetic resonance imaging in older chronic alcoholics. *Alcoholism, Clinical and Experimental Research, 21,* 521–529.

Prescott, C. A., & Kendler, K. S. (1996). Longitudinal stability and change in alcohol consumption among female twins: contributions of genetics. *Development and Psychopathology, 8,* 849–866.

Prescott, C. A., Neale, M. C., Corey, L. A., & Kendler, K. S. (1997). Predictors of problem drinking and alcohol dependence in a population-based sample of female twins. *Journal of Studies on Alcohol, 58,* 167–181.

Puddley, I., & Croft, K. (1997). Alcoholic beverages and lipid peroxidation: Relevance to cardiovascular disease. *Addiction Biology, 2,* 269–276.

Quaid, K., Dinwiddie, S., Conneally, P., & Nurnberger, J. (1996). Issues in genetic testing for susceptibility to alcoholism: Lessons from Alzheimer's disease and Huntington's disease. *Alcoholism: Clinical and Experimental Research, 20,* 1430–1437.

Rosse, R., Riggs, R., Dietrich, A., Schwartz, B., & Deutsch, S. (1997). Frontal cortical atrophy and negative symptoms in patients with chronic alcohol dependence. *Journal of Neuropsychiatry and Clinical Neurosciences, 9,* 280–282.

Royce, J. E., & Scratchley, D. (1996). *Alcoholism and other drug problems.* New York: Free Press.

Schuckit, M. (1994). A clinical model of genetic influences in alcohol dependence. *Journal of Studies on Alcohol, 55,* 5–17.

Shear, P. K., Jernigan, T. L., & Butters, N. (1994). Volumetric magnetic resonance imaging quantification of longitudinal brain changes in abstinent alcoholics. *Alcoholism: Clinical and Experimental Research, 18,* 172–176.

Smith-Warner, S. A., Spiegelman, D. Shiaw-Shyuan, Y., van den Brandt, P. A., Folsom, A. R., Goldbohm, A. Graham, S., Holmeberg, L., Howe, G., Marshall, J. R., Miller, A. B., Potter, J. D., Speizer, F. E., Willet, W. C. Wolk, A., Hunter, D. J. (1998). Alcohol and breast cancer in women: a pooled analysis of cohort studies. *Journal of the American Medical Association, 279,* 535–540.

Sobell, L., Sobell, M., Toneatto, T., & Leo, G. (1993). What triggers the resolution of alcohol problems without treatment. *Alcoholism: Clinical and Experimental Research, 17,* 217–224.

Steinmetz, C., Xie, P., Weiner, H., & Hurley, T. (1997). Structure of mitochondrial aldehyde dehydrogenase: The genetic component of ethanol aversion. *Structure, 5,* 701–711.

Stewart, R., & Li, T. (1997). The neurobiology of alcoholism in genetically selected rat models. *Alcohol Health and Research World, 21,* 169–176.

Sullivan, E. V., Marsh, L., Mathalon, D. H., Lim, K. O., & Pfefferbaum, A. (1995). Anterior hippocampal volume deficits in nonamnesic, aging chronic alcoholics. *Alcoholism: Clinical and Experimental Research, 19,* 110–122.

Swanson, C. A., Coates, R. J., Malone, K. E., Gammon, M. D., Schoenberg, J. B., Brogan, D. H., McAdams, J., Potischman, N., Hoover, R. N., Brinton, L. A. (1997). Alcohol consumption and breast cancer risk among women under age 45 years. *Epidemiology, 8,* 231–237.

Vaillant, G. E. (1995). *The natural history of alcoholism revisited.* Cambridge, MA: Harvard University Press.

Valenzuela, C. F. (1997). Alcohol and neurotransmitter interactions. *Alcohol, Health and Research World, 21,* 144–148.

Washton, R. (1997). Structured outpatient groups therapy. In J. Lowinson, P. Ruiz, R. Millman, & J. Langrod (Eds.), *Substance abuse: A comprehensive textbook* (pp. 440–447). Baltimore: Williams & Wilkins.

Young, N. (1997). Effects of alcohol and other drugs on children. *Journal of Psychoactive Drugs, 29,* 23–42.

Zakhari, S. (1997). Alcohol and the cardiovascular system: Molecular mechanisms for beneficial and harmful action. *Alcohol, Health and Research World, 21,* 21–29.

Four

Alcohol: Social and Psychological Aspects of Use and Abuse

Chapter Objectives

When you have finished studying this chapter, you should

1. Know what a standard drink is and decide whether the drinks you have are standard.
2. Know what percentage of people are abstainers, light drinkers, and heavy drinkers.
3. Know why five drinks or more is considered binge drinking.
4. Be able to describe the harmful effects of binge drinking on college students.
5. Be able to discuss the pattern of drinking over the life course.
6. Be able to discuss alcohol use by the following groups: women, gay men and lesbians, the elderly, Native Americans, African Americans, Asians and Latins, the homeless.
7. Know how alcohol affects driving and know what strategies are being used to combat drinking while driving.
8. Be able to discuss the relationship between depression and alcohol abuse.
9. Understand how alcohol affects the family.
10. Be able to describe the role of the family in alcohol-abuse treatment.
11. Know why the search for the "alcoholic personality" has been unsuccessful.
12. Be able to describe how the antisocial personality trait might predispose someone to alcohol abuse.
13. Understand the concept of relapse prevention.
14. Know what triggers for relapse are specific to alcohol.
15. Know why Alcoholics Anonymous has been so successful and what some criticisms of it might be.
16. Be able to name three other groups that offer support for alcohol abusers.

Early on the evening of 25 August 1997, a 19 year old freshman joined a group of fellow pledges to Sigma Alpha Epsilon fraternity at Louisiana State University at a popular off-campus bar. The pledges drank heavily, ordering several pitchers of "Three Wise Men"—a drink made of equal parts 151 proof rum, whiskey, and Jagermeister (a liqueur). When the group returned to the fraternity house, someone called the police, who arrived to find two dozen men passed out. Many were taken to the hospital, by which time one student had died of acute alcohol poisoning. His BAL was .59.

A twenty one year old student living in St. Paul, Minnesota, wanted to party before returning to college for his senior year. He asked a friend to be his designated driver and set out to see how much alcohol he could consume. He fell off the bar stool at the tenth stop of the evening, and the bartender refused to serve him. His friend loaded him in the back seat of the car and drove him home. Because Matt seemed to be resting comfortably, the designated driver let him sleep it off in the back of the car, where he was found dead the next morning of alcohol poisoning.

On 9 February 1997, a fifty year old woman, was returning to England from a trip to Montreal. She was afraid of flying, so she had some drinks before she got on the plane. When the flight attendant refused to serve her any more alcohol, she threw red wine in the steward's face and pulled off his tie. She then took a bottle of whiskey from her luggage and continued to drink. Upon arrival in England she was approached by a constable. She began swearing, kicked him in the groin, and twisted his right thumb back, tearing the tendon and spraining his wrist.

In 1997, on a flight from San Francisco to Chicago, a first-class passenger rammed a steward with a drink cart and broke the copilot's nose with a head butt after he was refused further alcohol. He was subdued by two FBI agents who happened to be on the flight.

Types of Alcoholic Beverages

As you have already seen, alcohol results from two processes: fermentation and distillation. Fermentation is a natural process whereby yeast turns sugar into alcohol. Fermentation continues until the alcohol content of the beverage reaches 12 percent and it then slows dramatically until it reaches 14 percent, at which point the alcohol concentration kills the yeast cells. Any substance containing sugar, or that can be converted to sugar, can be fermented. Grain such as corn, wheat, and rice can be combined with malt, and the fermented result will be beer. In many cultures the making of alcoholic beverages begins with people chewing grain and spitting into a large vat. An enzyme in saliva, ptyalin, changes the starch in the grain to sugar (Siegal & Inciardi, 1995). Naturally present yeast cells ensure that fermentation will take place. The various peoples of Central and South America have made their drinks this way for thousands of years. In many areas, the result is called **chicha.**

Fermented Beverages

Technically, a fermented beverage made by adding malt to grain is called beer. Wine results from the fermentation of fruit with a high sugar content so no "malting" is necessary. State laws differ, but in general beer sold in the United States has an alcohol content of about 5 percent and most wines are 12 percent alcohol. Ale, stout, porter, and malt liquor are malted beverages with a higher alcohol content. Sherry and port are the result of adding distilled liquor to wine, thereby increasing the alcohol content from 12 or 14 percent to 18 to 20 percent. Sometimes called "fortified" wines, they are popular among heavy drinkers with little money because they can be made cheaply and are stronger than wine. Made with care and good ingredients, sherry and port can also be considered prestige drinks with a complex taste and high price to match. You would probably only have to go to your nearby liquor store to find bottles of sherry priced anywhere from $2 to $50.

Distilled Beverages

Distillation involves heating a fermented beverage until the alcohol boils off, condensing the steam and repeating the process until the desired concentration is reached. Distillation works because alcohol boils at a lower temperature than water. The Arab scientists who discovered the process of distillation were looking for the "essence" of wine, which was universally considered to be a valuable medicine. The term *alcohol* is derived from the Arabic *al kohl,* which means (you guessed it) "the essence" (Abel, 1987). The highest possible concentration of alcohol is 95 percent because alcohol absorbs a little water from the air. Most distilled beverages are mixed with water, coloring agents, and other substances that alter their taste. They usually have an alcohol content of 40 to 50 percent.

Until the last century, precise measurement of the alcohol content of a beverage was impossible. Enterprising purchasers, however, developed a method to make sure they weren't getting liquor that was more water than alcohol. The buyer would mix the liquor with an equal amount of gunpowder and touch a match to it. If the mixture contained at least 50 percent alcohol, the gunpowder would light. Today's term **proof** stems from this test. The old phrase was *gunpowder proof,* and the word *proof* in this context meant *test.* Thus, 100 proof (50 percent alcohol) meant that it passed the gunpowder test (Abel, 1987).

The Standard Drink

Just as fashions in clothing change, so do fashions in alcoholic beverages. Rum and whiskey were the favorite liquor in the United States until the end of the nineteenth century (Lender & Martin, 1987). After Prohibition ended, gin and vodka became popular in some areas of the country, whereas bourbon was the favorite in the South (Grimes, 1993). Nearly all liquor sold in the United States is 80 proof, or 40 percent alcohol. Distillation produces the alcohol content; the various characteristics including color and taste depend on the source of the alcohol, the method of distilling, and the type of storage.

Vodka is the simplest type of liquor sold. Look at the label of any bottle of vodka, and you will see that it contains "100% grain neutral spirits." Grain neutral spirits is pure ethanol distilled from some kind of grain. According to federal standards, vodka cannot contain any flavoring and must be produced so that it has no taste or smell. Water is added to bring the alcohol content to the point desired. Because all vodka must contain nothing but grain neutral spirits and water, why does the price of vodka vary from a few dollars a quart to $30 or more?

Gin, responsible for the "gin epidemic" in nineteenth-century England, is grain neutral spirits flavored with juniper berries and other herbs. Bourbon is made from corn and aged in charred oak barrels that give it a characteristic color and taste. Scotch is made from malt and grain, distilled over peat fires, and aged in barrels formerly used to store sherry. Tequila and mezcal are made in Mexico from cactus plants. Brandy is distilled wine, and the "liqueurs" are various types of liquor sweetened with fruit or herbs (Keller, McCormick, & Efron, 1982). Keep in mind, however, that 80 proof liquor contains 40 percent alcohol regardless of what it is called.

The federal government has defined a "standard" drink. It contains 0.60 ounces of pure ethanol. A 12-ounce glass of beer, a 5-ounce glass of wine, and a drink made of 1.5 ounces of 80 proof liquor are considered standard drinks, because they all contain the same amount of pure ethanol (0.6 oz). This standard is often referred to as "equivalency," meaning that the three standard drinks are equivalent. However, some wine glasses contain far more than 5

GIN LANE.

BEER STREET.

Gin originated in Holland and so was not a "British" drink like beer. These engravings also demonstrate a prevailing opinion at the time. The "lower classes" drank gin and got drunk. Middle-class respectable people drank beer and remained sober.

ounces, some beers come in 40-ounce cans, and many people pour liquor by estimating the amount. Alcoholic beverages served in private homes usually contain more than a standard drink (Lemmens, 1994). A person who claims they only have one drink when they come home at night cannot be taken seriously if that "one drink" consists of a 12-ounce tumbler of bourbon.

Stop and Review

1. What is the difference between fermentation and distillation? Why can't fermented beverages have more than 14 percent alcohol content?
2. What is proof, and how does it relate to fermented and distilled beverages?
3. What is equivalency and how is it related to a "standard drink"?

Behavioral Effects of Alcohol

Regardless of how is it imbibed, a standard drink contains 0.6 ounces of ethanol. The effects of alcohol on behavior are dose dependent and nearly linear. This means that, within reasonable limits, a little alcohol produces a small effect and a large dose produces a large effect. The overall effect of alcohol is measured by **blood alcohol level (BAL).** Table 4.1 lists changes in behavior as a function of alcohol use. If you drink and don't recognize the changes in behavior at the var-

ious BALs, remember that alcohol distorts perception. Have you ever seen a videotape of your actions after a few drinks? It can be a sobering experience.

Who Drinks What and How Much

As a society we do not drink nearly as much as we did in the 1830s. Figure 4.1 shows the changes in consumption over the years. We do not drink as much as people in many other cultures, as you can see in table 4.2. The term **per capita** means "per person," so the per capita U.S. consumption of alcohol is the total amount of alcohol consumed divided by the number of people in the United States. Obviously this figure can be misleading, because the amount of alcohol consumed varies widely from person to person. Some of us don't drink at all, some drink very little, some drink a moderate amount, and some drink *a lot.* The 10 percent of drinkers who drink the most heavily account for 50 to 64 percent of all alcohol consumed (DuFour, 1996). Different methods of measuring consumption and differing definitions of alcohol use account for the difference in these figures.

Although a large majority of people in the United States drink, most drink very little. The most recent estimates from the National Household Survey on Drug Use (1997) show that 82.6 percent of Americans have used alcohol at least once, 64.9 percent within the last year and 51.0 percent within the last month. Are you surprised to learn that just about half of all Americans have not had a drink within

TABLE 4.1 Blood-Alcohol Concentrations and Effects on Behavior

BAL	Number of Drinks Consumed	Effects on Behavior
.04	1–2	Impairment of judgment Relaxation of inhibitions Feelings of warmth and relaxation Feelings of being suave, debonair, and chic
.08	3–4	Beginning of loss of coordination Loss of good judgment Feelings of warmth Relaxation of inhibitions Feelings of being tipsy, happy, and clumsy
.12	5–6	Impairment of fine motor skills Delayed reaction time Exaggerated emotions Talkativeness Noticeable clumsiness Behavior becomes sloppy, loud, and boorish
.16	6–8	Slurred speech Blurred vision Serious loss of judgment Serious lack of coordination Double vision Staggering and feelings of being stupid and sick
.20	8–10	Irresistible urge to lie down Inability to walk or dress without help Tears or rage with little provocation Room-spinning, drunk, passed out, or incoherent

Source: Reprinted by permission from pages 43–44 of *Alcohol,* 2nd ed. by Hafen and Brog; Copyright © 1991 by West Publishing Company. All rights reserved.

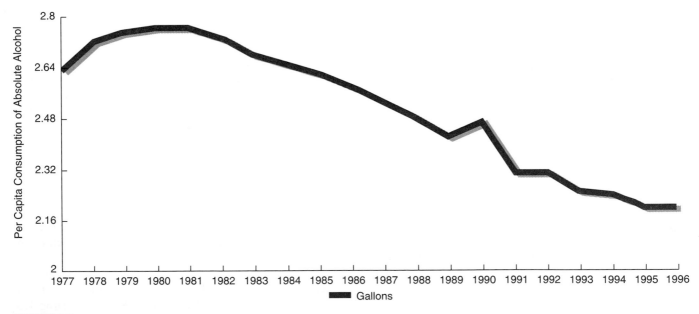

FIGURE 4.1

Table 4.1 Per capita consumption of alcohol (for those over 14) from 1977–1996 measured in gallons of absolute alcohol.
Notice that with the exception of 1990 there has been a consistent downward trend in the consumption of alcohol. As a yardstick, the consumption of absolute alcohol in 1996 translates into approximately 360 12 oz cans of beer (assuming that no other alcohol is consumed) for every man, woman and adolescent over the age of 14

Source: *The Bottom Line on Alcohol in Society,* **18,** 1997

TABLE 4.2 Estimated Per Capita Consumption of Pure Ethanol in Gallons

Country	Amount
Luxembourg	3.32
France	3.05
Austria	2.78
Germany	2.75
Portugal	2.75
Hungary	2.70
Denmark	2.65
Switzerland	2.65
Spain	2.65
Greece	2.43
Belgium	2.42
Italy	2.28
Bulgaria	2.20
Ireland	2.20
United States	2.20

Note: Most of the countries who have higher per capita consumption of absolute alcohol primarily consume beer or wine. Beer is the most popular drink in the United States.
Source: *The Bottom Line on Alcohol in Society,* **16,** pp. 45–46, 1995.

the last month? Most drinkers are. People generally use a **consensus estimate** to predict drinking. If you drink very little, you tend to think that others drink little, and if you drink frequently, you see others as doing the same.

You might be wondering about the accuracy of the various self-reports of alcohol use. Are heavy drinkers likely to admit their use? One way to test the accuracy is to estimate how much alcohol is consumed in a given year based on survey reports and compare this figure to the amount of alcohol sold based on taxes paid. Estimates based on self-report account for only 50 percent of alcohol sold (USDHHS, 1997). Either a lot of people are spilling a lot of drinks, or a lot of people are underestimating their consumption. Which do you think is more likely?

Another way of judging the accuracy of self-report and determining who is fudging on their estimates is to look at what would happen if everyone took up light to moderate drinking. The federal guidelines for "safe drinking" suggest no more than two drinks a day for men and one for women. If all drinkers followed these guidelines, alcohol sales would decline 80 percent (ARIS, 1997)!

Patterns of Drinking

The amount of alcohol a person consumes is not as important as the pattern in which it is consumed. **Binge drinking** (defined as five or more drinks during a drinking session) causes greater social, personal, and physical problems than the same amount spread out over a few days (Single, 1996). Five or more drinks a day seems to be the cut-off point at which problems begin to appear. Most binge drinkers have more than five drinks on a binging day, and some drink a lot more.

Social drinking usually involves having a drink after getting home or stopping at a tavern on the way. Leisure time is another socially acceptable occasion for drinking. In our culture, at least, morning drinking is usually considered a sign of alcohol dependence (Dawson, 1996). The time prescribed for drinking by social norms seems to be early evening, and any major deviation is associated with alcohol-related problems. In one study, only 1.2 percent of regular drinkers reported drinking between 6 A.M. and 11 A.M., while 60 percent reported drinking after 6 P.M. Older drinkers typically began earlier in the day, and younger drinkers were more likely to drink late at night (12 P.M. to 6 A.M.). Early drinking was associated with an increase in interpersonal, social, and legal problems. Late-night drinking showed a strong relationship to alcohol problems as well (Dawson, 1996). It seems that those who have problems associated with drinking not only binge and drink more, but drink when the rest of the population is sober.

In Chapter 3 you read that light to moderate drinking may reduce the risk of heart disease. Several studies have shown that light to moderate drinking has another positive effect. Men (and to a lesser extent women) who drink earn about 7 percent more than those who don't drink! One study found that light to moderate drinkers earn more than heavy drinkers or abstainers, while another (by the same group of researchers, no less) showed that even heavy drinkers earn more (French & Zarkin, 1995; Zarkin, French, Mroz, & Bray, 1998). Keep in mind that these are correlations. If you don't drink, don't start on the assumption you will start to increase your salary. The actual relationship between earnings and consumption of alcohol is not clear and undoubtedly complex.

Alcohol Use in Specific Populations

Alcohol Use and College Students

This textbook is written with college students in mind, so a discussion of the specific issues that students face should begin this section of the chapter. Of course, the traditional definition of a college student as being between 18 and 21 years old is no longer valid. In many colleges, reentry students and those who have delayed their education constitute a significant part of the student body. In community colleges in California, for example, the average age is 27. Older students usually have family responsibilities and occupations. Being more mature, they are less likely to indulge in the more freewheeling lifestyle that is typical of their younger classmates. Therefore, the focus of research into the role that alcohol plays among college students is directed toward the underage drinker.

Drinking alcohol has been a popular pastime among American college students since colleges were first established in the colonial period. Fraternity parties and tailgate parties are nearly always associated with drinking. College drinking songs extol the pleasures of alcohol, and drinking

Alcohol in American History

The Puritans who first settled in New England were no strangers to alcoholic beverages. Drunkenness was condemned and shunned, but the "sinner" was almost always forgiven and allowed to return to society. For the first two hundred years of our country's existence, alcoholic beverages were considered absolutely essential. Most water was unsafe to drink, so alcoholic drinks were common at the breakfast table. The army and navy furnished their soldiers and sailors with two to four ounces of hard liquor first thing in the morning (Lender & Martin, 1987).

After the War for Independence, farmers moved farther "out west" to Kentucky and Western Pennsylvania. It was too expensive to ship the grain they grew back East to market, but they found they could make a substantial profit if they converted it to whiskey. Consumption of alcohol reached a peak in the early 1800s, when the average person consumed more than six ounces per day of hard liquor or the equivalent (Lender & Martin, 1987).

Temperance, Prohibition, and Control of Drinking

The temperance movement tried to reduce the amount of alcohol consumed without eliminating it entirely. Two articles, one by a devout Quaker named Anthony Benezet and another by the famous eighteenth-century physician, Benjamin Rush, brought the issue of excessive drinking to the attention of most Americans for the first time. Benezet's article was entitled *The Mighty Destroyer Displayed, in Some Account of the Dreadful Havoc Made by the Mistaken Use and well as Abuse of Distilled Spiritous Liquors.* It condemned distilled liquor but was silent on cider, beer, and wine. Rush's article, *Inquiry into the Effect of Ardent Spirits,* actually praised cider and wine as healthy and necessary; he, too, saved his wrath for "ardent" or distilled spirits (Blocker, 1989).

The Prohibition movement had its start in 1838 when Massachusetts passed a law forbidding the sale of fewer than fifteen gallons of liquor at one time. The idea was that the poor and the abusers would not be able to afford liquor in such amounts. Enterprising drinkers and sellers soon figured out a way around the law. The purchasers would buy fifteen gallons and one gill (about a half pint) and sell the fifteen gallons back to the buyer. The citizens of Maine passed a law in 1846 banning the manufacture, sale, or *possession for sale* of distilled liquor. Possession for personal use remained legal. The solution soon became obvious. Shopkeepers would sell crackers for a few cents and provide a drink for free (Lender & Martin, 1987).

The Eighteenth Amendment

The Eighteenth Amendment was passed and became law in 1919. Part of the enthusiasm for the law was the result of prejudice against immigrants to the United States, mostly the Irish and German, who brought with them different drinking habits. Prohibition mandated a fine and jail time for manufacture and sale of alcoholic beverages. Anyone could still brew their own beer, make their own wine, or even distill liquor as long as they didn't sell it.

Prohibition actually reduced drinking in the first few years after it was enacted. The most accurate figures indicate that drinking declined by about 50 percent nationwide. However, the lives saved must be weighed against the thousands who died as a result of drinking wood alcohol and contaminated alcohol (Sinclair, 1962). Law enforcement was never able to stop the smuggling and production of illegal alcohol, and organized crime made sure there was a sufficient supply in every major community (Sinclair, 1962).

The repeal of Prohibition in 1933 came about during the Great Depression. The government needed money and realized that taxing alcohol would provide a substantial income. In the end most people realized that they really did want to drink and they were offended by the restrictive moralistic attitudes of those who championed Prohibition (Rorabaugh, 1979). After the repeal of Prohibition, the federal government limited its jurisdiction over alcohol to regulating the production and marketing of alcoholic beverages.

games are notorious (and well known) on many campuses. Recently, a great deal of attention has been focused on alcohol abuse by college students. Have things really changed, or were the alcohol problems of the past simply ignored? No careful studies of the prevalence of drinking and alcohol problems were done until recently, so there is no real way to know. We do know, however, that alcohol use and abuse cause many problems on college campuses, problems that have an impact not only on the drinkers themselves but on everyone associated with higher education (Wechsler, 1995).

The most thorough study, done in 1993, examined drinking and its effects at 140 colleges throughout the United States. One particular finding needs to be emphasized: Drinking varies widely from college to college. For example, binge drinking rates varied from 1 percent of students to 70 percent (Wechler, 1996). Fraternity and sorority residents drink more heavily, as do students with a party-centered lifestyle (Wechsler, Dowdall, Davenport, & Castillo, 1995). Overall, 50 percent of men and 39 percent of women reported binge drinking (Wechsler, Dowdall, Davenport, & Castillo, 1995). Nearly 80 percent of sorority residents and 86 percent of fraternity residents binge (Wechsler, Kuh, & Davenport, 1996). White males were most likely to binge (54 percent), and African American women were least likely (12 percent) (Wechsler, 1996).

Why the emphasis on binge drinking? Those who drink this much (or more) are the most likely to have problems as a result. For example, 64 percent of these reported having a hangover, 30 percent missed class, 36 percent did something they regretted, 27 percent had a memory lapse, and 21 percent had unplanned sex (Wechsler, Dowdall, Davenport, & Rimm, 1995). Heavy drinking affects others as well. Students who do not drink heavily report having been assaulted, having their property damaged, or experiencing unwanted sexual assaults. Nondrinking students at heavy drinking schools were four times as likely to suffer these consequences (Wechsler, Moeykens, Davenport, Castillo, & Hansen, 1995).

Community college students were far less likely to binge than students at four-year colleges. Overall, 29 percent of community college students reported binge drinking (40.1 percent of males and 21.1 percent of females). In fact they drink less overall—more than half of community college students reported that they drank once a month or less and two-thirds reported having no more than one drink a week (Presley, Meilman, & Lyerla, 1995). You can probably think of some reasons for this difference. Community colleges do not have the same degree of on-campus fraternity and social life, which is related to heavy drinking. Many community college students are older (and some are more mature), and the younger students are more likely to live at home. The bad news is that about 10 percent report binging three or more times in the past two weeks.

Just as there are individual differences in the amount people drink, drinking changes across the life span. A dramatic increase occurs in the 18-to-24 group compared to 12- to 18-year-olds. Similarly, a steep decline occurs in those over 35 compared to the 25-to-34 group, and binge drinking is highest at ages 21 to 22. There is a hint in this data that might explain lower rates of binging among noncollege students and lower overall drinking in those over 35. Both groups are more likely to be married.

Alcohol Use by Young Adults

Marriage has an influence on the drinking of both husbands and wives. In fact, the effect begins in the year before marriage (but only if the couple is engaged!). Both men and women reduce their drinking as a result of marriage. Men reduce their drinking most in the presence of their wives and do most of their drinking at home. When their wives are not around, as you might suspect, there is no change in drinking (Leonard & Roberts, 1996). Women reduce their drinking

both at home with their husband and when their husband is not around. For both men and women the reduction continues until the third year of marriage, and then drinking remains stable (Leonard & Roberts, 1996).

Most studies have found that older adults drink less and have fewer drinking problems than younger adults. Nevertheless, 2 to 4 percent of older adults do meet the criteria for alcohol abuse, and as many as 30 percent of older adults in certain groups are alcohol abusers. Roughly one-third to one-half of elderly abusers are late-onset, meaning that their drinking problems began late in life, while the rest are early-onset abusers whose heavy drinking began in adolescence or young adulthood (Brennan & Moos, 1996). Alcohol abusers were more likely to be male and unmarried.

Stop and Review

1. Why is it hard to determine how much alcohol the "average" person consumes?
2. Why is binge drinking considered a particular risk?
3. Why is so much attention payed to alcohol use by college students?
4. What is the effect of marriage on alcohol use by men and women?

Gender Differences in Alcohol Use

As you can see from table 4.3, more men than women drink. This gender difference has narrowed in recent years, and the difference between age at first use has almost disappeared entirely. In 1961 to 1965, only 7 percent of females started drinking between the ages of 10 and 14; by 1995 the percentage had grown to 31 percent. The comparable figures for males are 20.5 percent in 1961 to 65, and 35 percent in 1995. For the age group 15 to 18, the percentage is the same for both males and females—54 percent. Men are also more likely to report being heavy drinkers, by a factor of about four. "Only" 3 percent of women report heavy alcohol use—nevertheless this figure translates to about 3.3 million women who are heavy drinkers (defined as five or more drinks five or more times in the last month). (*Substance Abuse Among Women in the United States, 1997.*)

Even when women and men are matched for weight, equal doses of alcohol will produce a higher blood alcohol level for women. Women have a lower percentage of water in their bodies than men, meaning that a given dose of alcohol will result in a higher concentration. Women have less of the stomach enzyme that metabolizes alcohol, and the hormonal changes during their menstrual cycle might affect absorption (Blume, 1997).

When women do drink heavily, they tend to develop symptoms more rapidly than men, although they begin to drink at a later age (Blume, 1997). Women who consume two to three drinks a day can have health problems that are not seen in men unless they consume three times as much. Women are also at greater risk for developing alcoholic car-

Alcohol and the Writer

Of the seven American writers who have won the Nobel Prize for Literature, five were "alcoholics" Sinclair Lewis, William Faulkner, Ernest Hemingway, John Steinbeck, and Eugene O'Neill (Goodwin, 1988). The quotation marks are used because it is difficult to determine the exact point at which someone should be classified as alcoholic, and the evidence regarding these writers must be circumstantial since none ever were professionally examined. Numerous other writers such as F. Scott Fitzgerald, Jack London, Tennessee Williams, Truman Capote, and Carson McCullers, had equally serious alcohol problems; in fact, very few notable creative writers of the twentieth century escaped the problem (Dardis, 1989).

Would such authors have been better writers, and would they have been more productive, if they didn't drink to excess? Or did the misery and depression that typically accompanies alcohol abuse give them insight into the human condition? Did alcohol fuel their creativity? Relatively few great writers in other cultures have had similar problems. Of course there is no way of knowing what these and other authors could have written had they not been alcohol abusers, but both they and others had long periods in which they did little writing, and several committed suicide. For most, their best work was early in their careers and their later work deteriorated in quality. Was this the result of alcohol abuse and its damage to the body and brain?

Many also had long periods of depression, which can be the result of heavy drinking or can coexist with it. On the other hand, there is evidence to suggest that manic depressive illness in a creative person can enhance creativity (Jamison, 1995). Manic depressives have wide mood swings from elation to depression, with depressive periods tending to become more common (and longer) later in life. Most of us live most of our lives within a fairly narrow range of emotions. Although we are all capable of deep feelings, we don't experience them on an everyday basis. One way to gain these experiences is through literature. Do authors who can produce these feelings in us need to experience them with more regularity than we do? If this is the case, then perhaps alcohol abuse fuels this process, even at the cost of cutting lives and careers short. Even though most observers clearly saw a harmful effect, most of the authors mentioned did not feel that their alcohol abuse hindered their work.

As anyone who has ever tried to write anything knows, writing is a lonely profession, done largely in isolation from others. Perhaps the seclusion triggers the abuse, since we know that solitary drinking is particularly dangerous. Of course, it might be that the genetic and environmental influences that gave these writers the ability to produce great works of literature are somehow tied to a tendency to alcohol abuse.

What do you think?

TABLE 4.3 Percentage of Respondents Aged 12+ Reporting Alcohol Use in the Past Month, by Gender

	1979	1982	1985	1988	1990	1993	1995	1996
Monthly Use								
Males	72.4	66.8	69.2	62.3	60.5	58.7	60.1	59.4
Females	54.9	47.4	52.0	48.1	45.4	43.6	45.1	44.5
Heavy Use*								
Males			13.8	10.2	10.8	11.9	9.4	10.3
Females			3.2	1.8	2.1	2.5	2.1	2.0

Source: *Substance Abuse among Women in the United States,* 1997
* Heavy use is defined as five or more drinks at one sitting five or more times in the last month.

---

diomyopathy (disease of the heart muscle) and brain damage (Urbano-Marquez et al., 1995). Women develop many alcohol-related diseases such as fatty liver, malnutrition, and gastrointestinal hemorrhage more rapidly than men (Blume, 1997).

Compared to men, far more women who abuse alco-

hol report having been sexually or physically abused as children, and women who drink heavily are far more likely to be the victims of spousal assault and sexual abuse (Testa & Parks, 1996). Bars and fraternity parties are particularly risky situations for women, and higher rates of drinking by the victim are associated with more severe types of sexual abuse, such as rape (Testa & Parks, 1996). Sexual victimization can occur because the woman who is drinking does not perceive cues to danger as well, or because men see women who drink as being of lower status and vulnerable to attack. Three-quarters of a sample of college men, for example, admitted to getting a date high on drugs or alcohol in order to have sex, and nearly 40 percent of adolescent males reported that it was acceptable to force a girl to have sex if she is stoned or drunk.

Women drink less and are less likely than men to become alcohol abusers (Blume, 1997). Even though women's roles have changed dramatically, their rate of alcohol abuse has not. Women who are employed full-time do drink more than homemakers, but they do not have a higher incidence of alcohol-related problems. In fact, a study of attorneys showed that the presence of women attorneys in the law firm reduced overall drinking by the men (Shore, 1997). Age plays a role for women, as it does for men. Both social and heavy drinking are most common for those 18 to 25 and for those with a college education. Older women are more likely to perceive heavy drinking as harmful, and less than 1 percent of women over 50 report recent heavy alcohol use (*Substance Abuse among Women in the United States,* 1997).

Women alcohol abusers face greater stigma than men. They have to deal with the stigma of being labeled "alcoholic," like men do, but women must also face the problem that American society has always held women to a higher moral standard than men. In the nineteenth century, many states had laws that prohibited the sale of alcohol to women. When women violated liquor laws, their *husbands* were legally liable (Nicolaides, 1996). Alcohol abuse in women has traditionally been equated with sexual promiscuity. In reality, studies show that drinking does not make women less discriminating in their choice of sexual partners (Wilsnack, Wilsnack, & Hiller-Sturmhofel, 1994).

Women alcohol abusers differ from men in other ways as well. They are more likely to be married to or living with an alcoholic sexual partner, while men are more likely to be married to a nonalcoholic spouse (Blume, 1997). This can create problems when the woman stops drinking. Women are more likely to have a psychiatric problem, especially depression, and are more likely to abuse other drugs as well as alcohol. They are also more likely to drink alone. Females are more likely to seek treatment for health or family problems, while males are usually motivated to get help for legal or job problems (Blume, 1997). Fewer women than men who need alcohol treatment actually get it, but those who do are as likely to recover (*Substance Abuse among Women in the United States,* 1997; Blume, 1997).

Alcohol Abuse in Gay Men and Lesbians

Most studies report a high incidence of alcohol abuse among gay men and lesbian women. However, these data might be misleading because they sampled only self-identified gays and lesbians. Many lesbians and gay men choose not to make their orientation widely known. It might be that these individuals have low rates of alcohol abuse and the high levels of abuse are typical only of those who are "out" (Cabaj, 1997). Alcohol use seems to be an integral part of the lives of many gay men and lesbians. The use of alcohol might be associated with identity formation, coming out, and self-acceptance processes. The settings in which lesbians and gay men socialize encourages drinking and alcohol abuse. The social stigma associated with being gay might also contribute to heavy alcohol use (Cabaj, 1997).

Men who have sex with men continue to be the group most "at risk" for HIV infection. Alcohol clearly alters judgment, making it more likely that gay men who drink alcohol heavily will engage in unsafe sexual practices. Alcohol clearly affects the immune system; this can make initial infection by the virus and progression to AIDS more likely to occur. Of course, gay men who engage in unsafe sexual practices and are intravenous drug abusers have an even greater risk of infection (Cabaj, 1997).

Gay men and lesbians who recognize the need for treatment for alcohol abuse are often hard pressed to find a center or facility that is responsive to their needs and their sexual orientation. The negative attitudes that so many people have are seen as well in treatment professionals. Gay-sensitive treatment does exist, especially in large cities, but does not come close to meeting the need. Aftercare treatment can be a problem as well. The twelve-step programs (notably AA) are open to all, but the people in AA are prone to the same prejudices as everyone else. Several professional organizations focus on helping gays in recovery; these include the National Association of Lesbian and Gay Alcoholism Professionals, the National Gay and Lesbian Health Center, and National Gay Social Workers. Nevertheless, heterosexuals have a far easier time obtaining treatment and aftercare.

Alcohol Use and the Elderly

There are approximately 30 million Americans over the age of 65, with the number expected to exceed 50 million in a few decades. You have already read about some of the characteristics of alcohol use among the elderly. It is important to consider the special characteristics of the elderly and their relationship to alcohol use. The elderly experience a number of age-related physiological changes that can alter their response to alcohol. They have a slower reaction time and take longer to learn new information. They have a reduced ability to increase heart rate in response to stress. Their number of taste buds is reduced, and they have less gastric acid secretion and intestinal motility. They have diminished lean muscle mass and a reduced basal metabolic rate (Gambert, 1997).

All of these changes can mean that alcohol will have a greater effect on the elderly than when they were younger. Their loss of bone density means that if they should fall, alcohol-related injuries might be more serious. The normal loss of brain cells means that they will have a higher ratio of alcohol to brain cells and will be more vulnerable to the side effects of alcohol such as altered cognition. Many of the elderly have chronic degenerative conditions that require medication, and alcohol interacts with many of these medications and can cause an enhanced response (Gambert, 1997).

Psychological well-being can also be a factor in drinking problems. Many of the elderly have outlived their spouses, friends, and perhaps their children. In retirement their income is often reduced and they might experience depression and anxiety. When these problems lead to increased drinking, resulting in cognitive changes such as confusion and forgetting, their condition is often attributed to their age. Because some elderly alcohol abusers are "closet drinkers," their condition may be difficult to detect (Gambert, 1997).

Two types of elderly alcohol abusers have been identified: early-onset abusers and late-onset abusers. It is difficult to identify alcohol abusers among the elderly because their drinking is more likely to occur in secrecy and many of the signs of intoxication might be diagnosed as "normal" aging. Many elderly have memory deficits and are more likely to fall. Generally speaking, alcohol abuse might best be signaled by drinking daily and continuing in spite of medical advice. With all of the changes that occur in the elderly, one drink can be sufficient to interfere with their ability to function, carry on a conversation, or recall what is being discussed. Impairment, rather than amount consumed, should be the criterion for abuse.

Alcohol Use and Native Americans

Media stereotypes to the contrary, the norm for alcohol use among Native Americans is abstinence. Most Indian tribes living on reservations prohibit the sale of alcohol. Many Indians living in majority societies are social drinkers (Westermeyer,1997). If this description surprises you, consider that the caricature of the "drunken Indian" is deeply imbedded in our society. There are tribes and individuals with alcohol-related problems, and these tend to be severe. The western and northwestern Indian tribes seem to have particularly high rates of alcohol abuse, while drinking among tribes with an agricultural society is low. Another of the stereotypes is that the Native American population has a biological predisposition for alcohol abuse. However, research has failed to discover any systematic difference in alcohol metabolism among Native Americans.

Treatment for alcohol problems must include Native American staff members if it is to have any hope of success. Success rates are low because many Native Americans who come to treatment lack family support, are unemployed, and possess few job skills. Nevertheless, there are signs of improvement. Native American healing methods, including shamanic ceremonies, sweat lodges, and herbal medication, seem to hold promise. An increasing number of recovered Native Americans are also beginning to serve as resources

and models. The role of elders, especially those who are abstinent, is extremely important. It appears that a major factor in abusive drinking for Native Americans is the lack of a respected elder or parent during the drinker's youth (Watts & Guitierres, 1997).

Alcohol Use by Asian Americans

The term *Asian American* is used to refer to people whose families come from many different cultures. Asian groups include those from China, the Phillipines, Japan, India, Korea, Vietnam, Cambodia, and other countries. Therefore it is quite difficult to accurately generalize about Asian Americans. However, many of these cultures share certain attitudes and beliefs that can affect alcohol use. Many Asian societies attach personal shame to not being able to control one's behavior. In addition, an individual's alcohol abuse can be seen as a family shame as well, with the result that families might protect abusers and delay treatment. On the other hand, these cultures typically emphasize lifelong personal development, which can fit nicely into treatment (Westermeyer, 1997).

You should recall that when alcohol reaches the liver, it is converted to acetaldehyde, which is toxic. Most non-Asians have a liver enzyme that rapidly metabolizes acetaldehyde. About 45 percent of Japanese have a different form of the enzyme that permits acetaldehyde to accumulate (Ogata & Tsunoda, 1988). The flushing response, which is like the response to Antabuse, does not prevent people from drinking, however. Three-quarters of Japanese males and nearly half of Japanese females who are flushers still drink, but they do so less frequently and drink less when they do drink (Ogata & Tsunoda, 1988). Among major Asian groups, Koreans drink the most and Chinese the least. Among Koreans and educated Japanese, drinking alcohol is an important male ritual for businessmen. Rates of drinking and alcohol abuse, especially, are extremely low for women (Yamamoto, Yeh, Lee, & Lin, 1998).

Alcohol Use by Latin Americans

Just as the term *Asian* denotes many different cultures, the terms *Latino* and *Hispanic* are used to designate people from many parts of the world. People from Cuba, Puerto Rico, Mexico, South America, Central America, and even the Phillipines are considered "Latino." This term can also include American citizens whose families were living in what is now New Mexico and Arizona before the United States was a country. Add in second- and third-generation children, and you have a diverse group indeed. Keeping this in mind, Latinos as a group drink less than Anglos and Latina women drink much less than Anglo women (*National Household Survey on Drug Abuse,* 1997).

The degree of cultural identity and integration into Anglo society seem to be important factors in moderating alcohol use. Puerto Ricans who are U.S. citizens have less cultural identity and are more likely to assimilate into Anglo society. They have higher rates of alcohol use than Cuban Americans, who have maintained their cultural identity and have achieved greater economic success than other Latino groups (Ruiz & Langrod, 1997). Latino families have extensive networks, and each member plays a significant role in family dynamics. This characteristic helps buffer the influence of Anglo society (Ruiz & Langrod, 1997).

Alcohol Use in the African American Community

Alcohol abuse is one of the most serious health problems in the African American community. At the same time, the overall rate of alcohol use is considerably less than among whites. African American youth and women, in particular, drink far less than their white counterparts (*National Household Survey on Drug Abuse,* 1997). Even among men, the percentage of abstainers is higher than in the white population. Unfortunately, those who do drink, frequently drink heavily.

African Americans who do drink heavily tend to experience more negative consequences and are more likely to be solitary drinkers than whites (Neff, 1997). They are also more likely to use drugs other than alcohol, mainly cocaine (Caetano & Schafer, 1996). African American women are less likely to experience alcohol dependence than white women are (Herd, 1997), although both drinking and the number of alcohol-related problems reported have increased among African American women in the past few years (Jones-Webb, Hsiao, & Hannan, 1997).

The issue of problem drinking among African American men is closely linked to social status, unemployment, and poverty. The differences between them and white men from similar backgrounds narrows considerably when these socioeconomic factors are taken into consideration, but the differences still exist (Jones-Webb, Snowden, Herd, Short, & Hannan, 1997). What make these data puzzling are the much lower rates of drinking among middle- and upper-class African Americans compared to whites.

Alcohol Abuse among the Homeless

If the terms *homeless* and *alcohol abuser* seem to go hand in hand, you may be surprised to learn that a substantial percentage (as many as 40 percent) of the homeless and transient are abstainers. The estimates of abuse of alcohol (either alone or combined with other drugs) ranges from 20 to 40 percent. The most visible homeless, those sleeping in public places, seem to have the highest rates (up to 50 percent); those living in single-room occupancy (who are considered homeless) have much lower rates. These percentages are far higher than in more stable groups, and if other drug abuse is included the percentage comes close to 45 percent (Joseph & Paone, 1997).

The homeless include a much wider range of people than the stereotype abuser who lives on the streets. Data from the U.S. Conference of Mayors indicate that 46 percent of the homeless are men, 36.5 percent are single women accompanied by children, and 14 percent are single women without children. African Americans constitute the largest percentage (56 percent), followed by whites (29 percent), Hispanics (12 percent), and Native Americans (2 percent). As many as 20 percent are employed but unable to find affordable housing. Another group, whose numbers are unknown, are the "hidden homeless" who live in homes and apartments belonging to friends and relatives (Joseph & Paone, 1997). Should they or the people they live with experience a crisis, most will rapidly find themselves homeless. The numbers of homeless are likely to increase with the new welfare reforms that can terminate payments for those with chemical dependency after two years.

The homeless are difficult to help because they might not have the money or identification required for even minimal services, they lack a stable environment, they lack support networks, and they often have chronic health or mental problems. As a result they are the last to receive services although they are often the group most in need of them. Many people who work in direct contact with the homeless have negative attitudes toward them and see them as being difficult and hard to help (Joseph & Paone, 1997). Think how hard it would be to get together enough money to rent an apartment, buy decent clothes, pay for transportation, and buy food without a job or friends and relatives to assist. The homeless often find themselves in a hole that is virtually impossible to get out of.

Stop and Review

1. What are the social and physical consequences of heavy drinking by women?
2. Review this section and rank the special populations by their likelihood of having alcohol problems. Do the same for alcohol consumption.
3. Native Americans and the homeless are often believed to have very high rates of alcohol abuse. How accurate is this belief?

Psychological Factors in Alcohol Abuse and Recovery

Dual Diagnosis

Many, if not most, alcoholics also have other psychological problems. The concept of **dual diagnosis** is relatively new but potentially quite important. The most common psychological problem among alcohol abusers is depression, but many also have anxiety disorders, manic depressive disorders, and addiction to other drugs. Treatment for alcohol abuse and treatment for psychiatric disorders can both be costly. The cost of treating someone with a dual diagnosis can be as much as 60 percent higher (Dickey & Azeni, 1996).

Measures of Heavy Drinking

In Depth

According to Brenden Behan, the Irish poet (and alcoholic), "an alcoholic is anyone who drinks more than I do." For someone who has one drink a month, a drink a day would seem excessive. For others, one drink a day would be light drinking. Heavy drinkers in particular tend to underestimate their consumption (Conigrave, Saunders, & Whitfield, 1995). Most problem drinkers do not seek help until they have experienced serious consequences of their drinking. Some continue to deny the extent of their drinking even when the evidence is overwhelming. One study found that patients with alcoholic liver disease who had alcohol in their urine denied drinking more than half of the time they were questioned (Conigrave et al., 1995).

An objective measure of alcohol abuse or dependence would be useful in identifying problem drinkers. Unfortunately no such measure presently exists. Both the physiological tests, typically based on liver function, and the behavioral tests, of which there are many, fail to identify many problem drinkers and inaccurately label others who "fail" the tests for reasons unrelated to drinking. The most common physiological test is for the enzyme gamma-glutamyltransferase (GGT), which is induced by the presence of alcohol. GGT levels are high in about 75 percent of drinkers who are alcohol dependent. However, GGT levels are high in as few as 30 percent of problem drinkers who are healthy and not alcohol dependent (Conigrave et al., 1995). Another problem is that various medications and some liver diseases not related to alcohol abuse can also produce elevated GGT levels. Only about 50 percent of healthy people with an elevated GGT are likely to be problem drinkers.

More recently a test for *carbohydrate-deficient transferrin (CDT)* has been developed. Transferrin is involved in iron transport in the bloodstream. As a result of heavy drinking, a specific type of transferrin forms that lacks one of its carbohydrate groups. The presence of CDT is both sensitive and specific, meaning that it identifies a large percentage of heavy drinkers (sensitive) and rarely occurs except in heavy drinkers (specific). Moreover, CDT levels can discriminate between those who are alcohol dependent and those who drink less heavily (Saini, Pettinati, Semwanga, & O'Brien, 1997). However, elevated CDT levels are useful only for identifying males who are heavy drinkers; sensitivity is much lower for women.

A number of questionnaires have been developed as well. The MAST is the Michigan Alcoholism Screening Test, which consists of 25 items that can be answered yes or no (there are also 13- and 10-item versions of the test). A more recently developed questionnaire is the Alcohol Use Disorders Identification Test (AUDIT), which consists of 10 items (Flemming, 1997). Questionnaires such as these can be useful, but they often result in a large number of false positives. That is, they identify as abusers those who are not.

Even simpler tests have been developed that can be administered during an interview. The most often used is CAGE. *CAGE* is a mnemonic for four questions: Have you ever felt you should Cut down on your drinking? Have people Annoyed you by criticizing your drinking? Have you ever felt bad or Guilty about your drinking? Have you ever had a drink first thing in the morning to steady your nerves or get over a hangover (Eyeopener)? Note that the questions use the phrase *Have you ever* and ask about cutting down or feeling guilt. Many light drinkers reduce their drinking, and the word *ever* might identify individuals that have had drinking problems in the distant past. Therefore the CAGE test has relatively low sensitivity (Fleming, 1997).

A more sensitive test is known as TWEAK, which stands for Tolerance (number of drinks to feel high), Worry (about drinking), Eyeopener, Amnesia (blackouts), and Cut down on drinking. TWEAK seems to identify as many alcohol abusers, but mislabels fewer nonproblem drinkers. It also has the advantage of being useful for women as well as men. In fact it was originally developed to detect problem drinking in pregnant women (Charp et al, 1997).

No test will invariably identify a problem drinker. Not everyone who is identified on any of these tests is automatically a problem drinker. On the other hand, a positive score should be a signal to make a further evaluation.

Many people diagnosed as mentally ill have alcohol-related problems (Beeder & Millman, 1997). The question of which comes first, the psychological disorder or the alcohol abuse, is not easy to answer. Depression is particularly common during the period after withdrawal and then is probably the result of alcohol abuse (Roy, 1996). However, depression is a common psychological disorder, and alcohol abusers might suffer from depression quite independently of their abuse problem. Furthermore, recovery from alcohol abuse seems to be predictive of recovery from depression (Hasin et al., 1996).

Anxiety disorders most often seem to be the result of abusive drinking. Of course, some people drink because they are anxious, but for most the onset of drinking problems occurred before the anxiety (Krantzler, 1996). Practically speaking, no matter what the cause of the anxiety or depression is, it must be taken into consideration during the period of recovery. One reason is that many of the drugs used to treat anxiety disorders can be abused by alcoholics (Marshall, 1997). Another is that alcohol use can reduce the effectiveness of antidepressants (Worthington et al., 1996).

Depression leads to an increased risk of suicide, and alcohol impairs judgment. When a depressed person drinks heavily, the results can be tragic. One study found that 40 percent of alcoholics who were also severely depressed had attempted suicide in the week prior to coming to treatment, and 70 percent had made an attempt at suicide sometime in the past (Cornelius, Salloum, Day, Thase, & Mann, 1996). Apparently, alcohol abuse did not lead to the thoughts of suicide, but it did reduce inhibitions enough to make the attempt. The old phrase *Dutch courage* refers to taking a few drinks to build up the courage to do something daring or foolhardy.

Other psychiatric conditions have been linked to alcohol abuse, particularly post traumatic stress disorder and the eating disorders bulimia and anorexia (Sinha et al., 1996; Ouimette, Ahrens, Moos, & Finney, 1997). Many people with psychiatric disorders also have alcohol disorders, and many alcoholics have psychological problems. To further complicate the issue, those with psychiatric disorders who are not abusers, drink alcohol with about the same frequency and for the same reasons as those who do not have psychiatric problems.

The Role of the Family in Recovery

The vast majority of alcohol abusers are part of a family. Child abuse, spousal abuse, and divorce are more common when a parent is an alcoholic (Steinglass, 1994). Furthermore, the family functions in a different manner when the parent is sober than when the parent is drinking (Steinglass, 1997). Establishing a normal relationship between the husband, wife, and children is not easy. Sexual relations are often a problem, with male impotence being the major factor (O'Farrell, Choquette, Cutter, & Birchler, 1997). Children in the family frequently suffer even when there is no physical violence (Roosa, Dumka, & Tein, 1996).

Families that have been disrupted by alcohol abuse have to change when the abuser stops. Issues that must be dealt with include improving communications, changing roles in the family, and developing trust. Consider that the family has had to function with the alcoholic drinking, sober, and in between. Now the family has to learn to function with a nondrinker. Most of the strategies that were formerly used have to change (McKay, 1996). Family therapy is often recommended as a way to address these problems. Although it can take many forms, family therapy generally centers around improving communication of thoughts and feelings and discovering the interpersonal conflicts that can trigger a relapse (McKay, 1996).

Personality Traits

The search for the "alcoholic personality" has continued for many years with little success. Those undergoing treatment for alcohol abuse often show similar personality characteristics, but it seems that many of those characteristics are the result of years of alcohol abuse. Alcoholics often have less than ideal personal relationships and engage in risky behavior. Prolonged alcohol use, as you have seen, can lead to profound changes in the brain and body that can result in psychological changes. Experiencing many failed attempts to stop drinking (as most alcohol abusers have) would seem to contribute to a changed personality.

The search for the alcoholic personality has shifted to a search for a complex of psychological traits that might increase the risk of alcoholism. High sensation seekers, for example, use alcohol at an earlier age and more recklessly than most. They seem to have a need for novelty and change. This characteristic can be demonstrated in rats and has been shown to activate the same reward system in the brain as drugs and alcohol (*NIDA Notes,* 1997). Looking for new experiences (known as novelty seeking), along with the expectation that alcohol will have positive effects, seems to be a powerful predictor of drinking. In other words, someone who is restless and easily bored and has a positive attitude toward alcohol is more likely than others to drink (Galen, Henderson, & Whitman, 1997).

One "personality" trait that is clearly associated with alcohol abuse is **antisocial personality disorder.** A personality disorder is not a characteristic or a trait that a person has. It is a long-standing pattern of maladaptive behavior. People with antisocial personality disorder lack the capacity to feel sympathy for others or respect the rights of others. They do not seem to care about the consequences of their behavior. They are selfish, impetuous, and thrill seeking. Contrary to popular belief, they are not necessarily all criminals; many people with antisocial personality disorder are business leaders, politicians, and entrepreneurs. Many, if not most, were in trouble as children and adolescents. This combination of traits often leads to alcohol abuse (Millon, 1996). In fact, you should notice similarities between this disorder and the Type 2 alcoholic. Are they one and the same? Do the characteristics overlap? These and related issues are currently being hotly debated among researchers.

Psychotherapy

Along with medical treatment, behavioral treatment is also used to help the abuser maintain abstinence. Many forms of psychotherapy have been adapted for alcohol abusers. A major study recently compared three programs for alcohol recovery: an AA-based treatment method, a motivational method, and cognitive behavioral therapy. All three were equally effective, and no one method stood out (*NIDA Notes,* 1997). The success rates were not high for any method, and relapse was common. The study called Project Match then attempted to determine if a specific type of pa-

The typical alcoholic American

Doctor, age 54

Farmer, age 35

Unemployed, age 40

College student, age 19

Counselor, age 38

Retired editor, age 86

Dancer, age 22

Police officer, age 46

Military officer, age 31

Student, age 14

Executive, age 50

Taxi driver, age 61

Homemaker, age 43

Bricklayer, age 29

Computer programmer, age 25

Lawyer, age 52

There's no such thing as typical. We have all kinds.
10 million Americans are alcoholic.
It's our number one drug problem.

For information or help, contact:
National Clearinghouse for Alcohol and Drug Information, P.O. Box 2345, Rockville, MD 20852
1–800–729–6686

U.S. DEPARTMENT OF HEALTH AND HUMAN SERVICES • Public Health Service • Alcohol, Drug Abuse, and Mental Health Administration
Prepared and published by the Office for Substance Abuse Prevention

DHHS Publication No. (ADM) 91–1801

Most alcohol abusers do not fit the stereotype of the skid row bum, as this poster demonstrates.

Alcohol and Violence

Although estimates vary widely, some studies have found that as many as 80 percent of those who commit homicide 60 percent of sexual offenders and 57 percent of males involved in marital violence were drinking at the time of the offense (Roizen, 1997). The relationship between alcohol and aggression is complicated. Alcohol may release inhibitions against impulsive behavior such as violence. Alcohol may disrupt the processing of information, leading drinkers to overreact to perceived threats. Alcohol may narrow the drinkers attention and lead to an inaccurate perception of the risk involved in violence (*Alcohol, violence and aggression, 1997*).

In addition, alcohol may lead to aggression because drinkers expect it to. If men believe that they are supposed to become aggressive when drinking and if they believe that women are more sexually uninhibited when drinking, date rape may result. A person who intends to become violent may drink to bolster his or her courage. Also, intoxication is perceived by many as a "time out" from the rules of conduct that apply when sober. Violent people may be more likely than nonviolent people to choose social situations where heavy drinking is encouraged (*Alcohol, violence and aggression, 1997*).

A biochemical link between alcohol and violence might also exist. Low levels of serotonin activity is associated with increased impulsiveness, increased aggression and the development of early onset alcohol abuse in men. Other neurotransmitters may be involved as well. Dopamine and norepinephrine are closely linked to aggression, sexual behavior and alcohol consumption. Hormonal factors may contribute to the link between alcohol and aggression. In animal studies alcohol increased aggressive behavior in male monkeys who already showed high levels of aggression and testosterone compared to monkeys who displayed less aggression and had lower levels of testosterone (*Alcohol, violence and aggression, 1997*).

Keep in mind however, that drinking is a common social activity, especially among young, violence prone individuals. Drinking and violence may occur together simply because violent people also drink. Remember, too, that someone who has been drinking heavily is more likely to get caught than a more sober offender (*Alcohol, violence and aggression, 1997*). The percentages mentioned previously were based on offenders who were caught.

---

tient was best served by a particular method. However, no "match" among patient characteristics, method, and success rate could be found. The results of this study could be considered somewhat discouraging given the relatively low rate of success.

Even a short counseling session seems to help a little. **Brief intervention** is the term used to describe a short session based on motivational principles designed for people who are not yet alcohol dependent. Heavy drinkers who have a shorter problem drinking history, are relatively young, and have greater employment stability and social resources seem to be good candidates for brief intervention. The treatment goal is moderate drinking as compared to total abstinence. Compared to those who do not get counseling, problem drinkers who received a brief intervention were more likely to moderate their drinking. Incidentally, women seem to respond better than men (Wilk, Jensen, & Havighurst, 1997).

Relapse Prevention

About 75 percent of alcoholics relapse, and most of them do so within one year. Individuals who relapse do not always return to previous levels of abuse—some drink less and others more than previously (Daley & Marlatt, 1997). In addition, those who do relapse might continue the improvement they have shown in other areas of their lives despite a relapse to alcohol use or abuse. The primary reasons for relapse seem to be lack of family or peer support, negative emotional states (boredom, anger, depression), and negative life events. Among many other variables associated with relapse are lack of coping skills, impulsivity, lack of involvement in recreational or leisure activities, and self-doubt about their ability to handle high-risk situations (Daley & Marlatt, 1997).

Long-term sobriety is difficult. The following characteristics have been found to correlate with long-term abstinence: (1) the presence of a relationship with someone that focuses on rehabilitation, (2) one or more "substitute dependencies" or activities that take up the time previously spent obtaining and consuming alcohol, (3) an increase in self-esteem, and (4) knowledge that relapse will have definite and unpleasant results (physical consequences, loss of one's job, loss of a relationship). The greater the number of these elements, the better the chances of recovery (Vaillant, 1995).

Support during Recovery

Alcoholics Anonymous

The most famous support group for abusers is **Alcoholics Anonymous (AA),** which was started in1935 by two men, Bill W. and Dr. Bob S. (AA encourages members to use only their first names.) Bill W. was a stockbroker who had been hospitalized several times for alcoholism. He had a spiritual conversion and gained his first convert in Dr. Bob S., a surgeon. The two formed Alcoholics Anonymous, and it has since spread around the world. At present it has well over 250,000 members and more than 55,000 groups. Many hundreds of thousands have been helped by AA and are no longer active members. AA has helped more people gain sobriety than any other program known (Nace, 1997).

As shown in table 4.4, the famous twelve steps are deceptively simple. The twelve steps are a pathway to sobriety. The purpose of AA is to help members stay sober. What AA doesn't do is almost easier to describe than what it does do. AA doesn't try to provide motivation for users to stop, it doesn't solicit members or keep attendance records. AA doesn't follow up on its members or provide counseling, health services, or social services. It doesn't conduct research, educate about alcohol, or accept money for its services. It is a fellowship for all men and women who want to do something about their drinking. Why does it work so well?

First, keep in mind that the dropout rate is high. Studies show that perhaps 50 percent stay with AA, for more than three months (Nace, 1997). Those who do stay with it, however, succeed about as well as those who receive outpatient treatment without AA (Humphreys & Moos, 1996). The greater the involvement in AA, the greater the chance of

TABLE 4.4 The AA Twelve Steps

1. We admitted that we were powerless over alcohol, that our lives had become unmanageable.
2. We came to believe that a Power greater than ourselves could restore us to sanity.
3. We made a decision to turn our will and our lives over to the care of God as we understood Him.
4. We made a searching and fearless moral inventory of ourselves.
5. We admitted to God, to ourselves, and to another human being the exact nature of our wrongs.
6. We were entirely ready to have God remove all these defects of character.
7. We humbly asked Him to remove our shortcomings.
8. We made a list of all persons we had harmed, and became willing to make amends to them all.
9. We made direct amends to such people wherever possible, except when to do so would injure them or others.
10. We continued to take personal inventory and when we were wrong promptly admitted it.
11. We sought through prayer and meditation to improve our conscious contact with God as we understood Him, praying only for knowledge of His will for us and the power to carry that out.
12. Having had a spiritual awakening as a result of these steps, we tried to carry this message to alcoholics and to practice these principles in all our affairs.

Source: *Alcoholics Anonymous*

Most people associate Alcoholics Anonymous with the United States. However, only about half of all chapters are in the U.S. and more than a third are in Latin America. The photo was taken in a medium sized city in Mexico. AA was established in Mexico in 1947 and while U.S. citizens who are visitors and residents of Mexico make up a significant portion of the membership, a large majority are Mexicans.

success. Outcome is more favorable for those who attend more than once a week and for those who have a sponsor (Nace, 1997). Moreover, those who stick with AA tend to have experienced more serious consequences of drinking (Humphreys, Mavis, & Stofflemeyer, 1991). AA seems to do more than increase the chances for sobriety. Those who attend AA meetings report more stable social adjustment, a more active religious life, and better employment adjustment. AA helps even those who were mandated to attend and those with dual diagnosis (Ouimette, Finney, & Moos, 1997).

Just how this success is achieved is far from clear. Researchers studying AA are faced with numerous problems. AA is a voluntary organization, and members chose to belong or quit. It is impossible to take two groups of individuals and assign one to AA and the other to some other form of treatment. AA groups vary enormously, so that the "typical AA" is impossible to define. AA members themselves volunteer to participate in research, but AA itself does not. Until recently, those who studied AA were often less than objective. Researchers who rely on interviews with members do not get a complete picture of what goes on in the meetings, and researchers who attend meetings are doing so as outsiders so they still might not fully comprehend what happens.

Recognizing that generalizations are just that and do not apply to every AA member or group, recent research has indicated something of the process that takes place and the reasons for success. An important aspect is that AA members develop a **shared ideology.** As a result of personal interaction and exposure to the concepts of AA, members come to accept the basic tenets of AA (Wright, 1997). Members typically felt isolated from others because of their drinking. They found that more-experienced members of AA could explain alcoholism to them in a language they could understand. They felt that the openness and honesty of meetings were a welcome contrast to their experiences with family and friends. They recognized that life's problems were a threat to their continued sobriety (Wright, 1997).

In a very general sense, spirituality does seem to be an important factor (Nace, 1997). Most members of AA had negative attitudes toward the spiritual aspect of AA before attending meetings, but those who remained found that the flexibility with which AA talks of a "higher power" was helpful to them. (Wright, 1997). The emphasis on many meetings in the beginning of recovery (the recommendation is ninety meetings in ninety days) correlates well with the fact that relapse often occurs within the first few months.

Moderation and Abstinence

Several groups with names like **Moderation Management** exist to help those who do not find abstinence a viable option. These groups try to help abusive drinkers find ways to return to social drinking. Their concept is that abusive drinkers have either never learned or no longer know the patterns that social drinkers use to regulate their intake. They teach ways of spacing drinks and reducing the number of days of drinking. They emphasize the importance of protective factors such as drinking only with meals and never when upset, angry, or bored. These groups have not been studied sufficiently because they are so recent; therefore little can be said about their effectiveness. Their aim, a return to social drinking, seems to go strongly against what many think of as accepted wisdom, but numerous studies have shown that at least a few alcohol abusers do spontaneously return to nonproblem drinking (Sobell, Cunningham, & Sobell, 1996).

Other support groups

Other groups also exist. **Secular Organization for Sobriety (SOS)** shares a number of characteristics with AA but denies the need for a "higher power," hence the term "secular" (Christofer, 1997). **Rational Recovery** and **SMART** developed from the same organization and have diverged over a number of issues. Rational Recovery is a group that emphasizes what they call **addictive voice recognition training (AVRT).** This training teaches the alcohol abuser how to recognize and deal with the "voice" or temptation when they experience craving (Trimpey, 1992). SMART is more eclectic and actively uses professional psychologists during their sessions, something that AA distinctly rejects. Both empha-

size the importance of cognitive-behavioral methods in eliminating drinking and are basically abstinence oriented.

Women for Sobriety (WFS) emphasizes issues that they feel are of importance to women in recovery, such as positive emotions, particularly love. WFS focuses on both emotional and spiritual growth. Our discussion of these groups is shorter than our discussion of AA, not because they are less valuable but because there has been little research conducted on them. WFS has been found to be helpful for some women and seems to help them improve their self-esteem (Kaskutas, 1996). Certainly any of these groups should be explored by those finding the experience of AA unacceptable. Because such a small percentage of alcohol abusers attend and stick with AA, other self-help groups are probably essential if the dismal recovery rate for alcoholics is to improve.

Stop and Review

1. How does alcohol abuse affect family members?
2. How can family members help the alcohol abuser?
3. What personality disorder is most associated with alcohol abuse?
4. What is the role of psychological treatment in alcohol abuse recovery?
5. What are the main triggers for relapse?
6. Why is it so difficult to evaluate the impact of AA on recovery?
7. What kind of help is available for those who do not like AA?

Summary

Alcoholic beverages can be made by fermentation or distillation. Beer and wine are fermented, and liquor is distilled. A standard drink contains .60 ounce of pure alcohol, whether it is beer, wine, or a mixed drink. Most people drink, and about 10 percent are heavy drinkers. The greatest problem is with binge drinkers, those who consume five or more drinks at one sitting.

College students are the heaviest drinkers of just about any population. Binge drinking in college leads to many academic, social, and legal problems. Drinking varies among various populations. Women drink less than men, on the average, and African American women drink the least. Cultural factors seem to play a protective role for some ethnic groups.

Drinking and driving is declining in frequency but is still a major problem. Young males between 18 and 25 constitute the greatest risk group. Jail sentences do not work as a deterrent; fines and license suspensions are more effective. Multiple arrests or causing injury while drinking and driving are punished with long jail sentences.

Alcohol abuse has sociocultural, psychological, and genetic components. No clear personality type is predictive for alcohol abuse, but some personality traits, including novelty seeking, might correlate with heavy drinking. Those with a personality disorder are at particular risk, but these do not constitute a large percentage of all alcohol abusers.

Recovery can be aided by psychological treatment, and relapse prevention has a strong psychological component. Social support also plays a role. AA is the best known of all self-help groups and has helped an untold number of people. Other groups exist for those who do not find AA compatible.

Key Terms

addictive voice recognition training (AVRT) Training that teaches the alcohol abuser to recognize and deal with the "voice" or temptation of alcohol craving.

Alcoholics Anonymous (AA) A self-help group for combating alcohol abuse.

al kohl The term *alcohol* is derived from this Arabic word meaning "the essence."

antisocial personality disorder A psychological disorder in which the person has an impulsive need for instant gratification, feels no remorse, is unable to form close relationships, and fails to learn from mistakes.

binge drinking Drinking five or more drinks in one session.

blood alcohol level (BAL) The concentration of alcohol in a person's bloodstream.

brief intervention A short counseling session using motivational principles designed for people who are not yet alcohol dependent.

chicha An alcoholic drink made by chewing grain and spitting it into a vat. The enzyme in the saliva changes the starch in the grain to sugar.

consensus estimate An estimate based on the perception of what you do.

dual diagnosis Exhibiting both substance abuse and other psychological disorders.

Moderation Management A group that tries to help individuals to learn to drink socially after a period of heavy use.

per capita Per person.

proof A measure of alcohol concentration. Twice the percentage of alcohol: e.g., 100 proof is 50 percent alcohol.

Rational Recovery A self-help recovery group that emphasizes a cognitive-behavioral approach to recovery from alcohol and drug abuse.

Secular Organization for Sobriety (SOS) A self-help recovery group for alcoholics who are agnostics and atheists.

shared ideology Basic ideas shared by all members of a group.

SMART A self-help group for alcohol and other drug abusers that actively uses professional psychologists during its sessions.

Women for Sobriety (WFS) A self-help group for female alcohol abusers.

References

Abel, E. (1987). *Alcohol wordlore and folklore.* New York: Plenum Press.

Allen, C. (1995). Alcohol problems and anxiety disorders: A critical review. *Alcohol and Alcoholism, 30,* 145–151.

Allen, J., & Columbus, M. (1995). *Assessing alcohol problems* (Treatment Handbook Series 4). Washington, DC: National Institute for Alcohol Abuse and Alcoholism.

Ballard, H. S. (1997). Hematological markers of alcoholism. *Alcohol Health & Research World, 21,* 48–49.

Blocker, J. (1989). *American temperance movement: Cycles of reform.* Boston: Twayne.

Blume, S. (1997). Women: Clinical aspects. In J. Lowinson, P. Ruiz, R. Millman, & J. Langrod (Eds.), *Substance abuse: A comprehensive textbook.* Baltimore: Williams & Wilkins.

Brennan, P., & Moos, R. (1996). Late-life drinking behavior: The influence of personal characteristics, life context, and treatment. *Alcohol Health and Research World, 20,* 197–204.

Cabaj, R. (1997). Gays, lesbians, and bisexuals. In J. Lowinson, P. Ruiz, R. Millman, & J. Langrod (Eds.), *Substance abuse: A comprehensive textbook.* Baltimore: Williams & Wilkins.

Caetano, R., & Schafer, J. (1996). *DSM-IV* alcohol dependence and drug abuse/dependence in a treatment sample of whites, blacks and Mexican-Americans. *Drug and Alcohol Dependence, 43,* 93–101.

Cherpitel, C. J. (1997). Brief screening instruments for alcoholism. *Alcohol Health & Research World, 21,* 348–351.

Christopher, J. (1997). Secular Organization for Sobriety. In J. Lowinson, P. Ruiz, R. Millman, & J. Langrod (Eds.), *Substance abuse: A comprehensive textbook* (pp. 396–399). Baltimore: Williams & Wilkins.

Cornelius, J., Salloum, I., Day, N., Thase, M., & Mann, J. (1996). Patterns of suicidality and alcohol use in alcoholics with major depression. *Alcoholism: Clinical and Experimental Research, 20,* 1451–1455.

Daley, D., & Marlatt, G. (1997). Relapse prevention. In J. Lowinson, P. Ruiz, R. Millman, & J. Langrod (Eds.), *Substance abuse: A comprehensive textbook* (pp. 458–466). Baltimore: Williams & Wilkins.

Dardis, T. (1989). *The thirsty muse.* New York: Ticknor & Fields.

Dawson, B. (1996). Temporal drinking patterns and variation in social consequences. *Addiction, 91,* 1623–1635.

Dickey, B., & Azeni, H. (1996). Persons with dual diagnoses of substance abuse and major mental illness: Their excess costs of psychiatric care. *American Journal of Public Health, 86,* 973–977.

Dufour, M. (1996). Risks and benefits of alcohol use over the life span. *Alcohol Health and Research World, 20,* 145–151.

Flemming, M. F. (1997). Strategies to increase alcohol screening in health care settings. *Alcohol Health and Research World, 21,* 340–348.

French, M. T. & Zarkin, G. A. 1995. Is moderate alcohol use related to wages? Evidence from four worksites. *Journal of Health Economics, 14:* 319–344.

Galen, L. W., Henderson, M. J., & Whitman, R. D. (1997). The utility of novelty seeking, harm avoidance and expectancy in the prediction of drinking. *Addictive Behaviors, 22,* 93–106.

Gambert, S. (1997). The elderly. In J. Lowinson, P. Ruiz, R. Millman, & J. Langrod (Eds.), *Substance abuse: A comprehensive textbook* (pp. 692–697). Baltimore: Williams & Wilkins.

Goodwin, D. (1988). *Alcohol and the writer.* Kansas City: Andrews & McMeel.

Grimes, W. (1993). *Straight up or on the rocks: A cultural history of American drink.* New York: Simon & Schuster.

Hasin, D., Tsai, W., Endicott, J., Mueller, T., Coryell, W., & Keller, T. (1996). Five-year course of major depression: Effects of comorbid alcoholism. *Journal of Affective Disorders, 41,* 63–70.

Herd, D. (1997). Sex ratios of drinking patterns and problems among blacks and whites: Results of a national survey. *Journal of Alcohol Studies, 82,* 75–82.

Humphreys, K., Mavis, B., & Stofflemeyer, B. (1991). Factors predicting attendance at self-help groups after substance abuse treatment: Preliminary findings. *Journal of Consulting and Counseling Psychology, 59,* 591–593.

Humphreys, K., & Moos, R. (1996). Reduced substance abuse related health care costs among voluntary participants in Alcoholics Anonymous. *Psychiatric Services, 47,* 709–713.

Jamison, K. (1995, February). Manic-depressive illness and creativity. *Scientific American,* 63–67.

Jones-Webb, R. J., Hsiao, C., & Hannan, P. (1995). Relationships between socioeconomic status and drinking problems among black and white men. *Alcoholism: Clinical and Experimental Research, 19,* 623–627.

Jones-Webb, R., Snowden, L., Herd, D., Short, B., & Hannan, P. (1997). Alcohol-related problems among Black, Hispanic and white men: The contribution of neighborhood poverty. *Journal of Studies on Alcohol, 58,* 539–545.

Joseph, H., & Paone, D. (1997). The homeless. In J. Lowinson, P. Ruiz, R. Millman, & J. Langrod (Eds.), *Substance abuse: A comprehensive textbook* (pp. 733–743). Baltimore: Williams & Wilkins.

Kaskutas, L. (1996). Predictors of self esteem among members of Women for Sobriety. *Addiction Research, 4,* 273–281.

Keller, M., McCormick, M., & Efron, V. (1982). *A dictionary of words about alcohol.* New Brunswick, NJ: Rutgers Center of Alcohol Studies.

Kranzler, H. R. (1996). Evaluation and treatment of anxiety symptoms and disorders in alcoholics. *Journal of Clinical Psychiatry, 57* (57 (suppl. 7)), 15–21

Lemmens, P. (1994). The alcohol content of self-report and "standard" drinks. *Addiction, 89,* 593–601.

Lender, M., & Martin, J. (1987). *Drinking in America: A history* (rev. ed.). New York: Free Press.

Leonard, K., & Roberts, L. (1996). Drinking among young adults: Prevalence, patterns, and consequences. *Alcohol Health and Research World, 20,* 185–191.

Marshall, J. (1997). Alcohol and substance abuse in panic disorder. *Journal of Clinical Psychiatry, 58* (Suppl. 2), 46–49.

McKay, J. R. (1996). Family therapy techniques. In F. Rotgers, D.

S. Keller, & J. Morgenstern (Eds.), *Treating substance abuse: Theory and technique* (pp. 143–173). New York: Guilford Press.

Nace, E. (1997). Alcoholics Anonymous. In J. Lowinson, P. Ruiz, R. Millman, & J. Langrod (Eds.), *Substance abuse: A comprehensive textbook* (pp. 383–389). Baltimore: Williams & Wilkins.

Neff, J. (1997). Solitary drinking, social isolation and escape drinking motives as predictors of high quantity drinking, among Anglo, African American, and Mexican American males. *Alcohol and Alcoholism, 32,* 33–41.

Nicolaides, B. (1996). The state's "sharp line between the sexes": Women, alcohol and the law in the United States, 1850–1980. *Addiction, 91,* 1211–1229.

NIDA Notes, 10 (1997), p. 3. Washington: National Institute for Drug Abuse.

O'Farrell, T., Choquette, K., Cutter, H., & Birchler, G. (1997). Sexual satisfaction and dysfunction in marriages of male alcoholics: Comparison with nonalcoholic maritally conflicted and nonconflicted couples. *Journal of Studies on Alcohol, 58,* 91–99.

Ogata, M., & Tsunoda, T. (1988). Flushing among the Japanese. In L. Towle & T. Harford (Eds.), *Cultural influences and drinking patterns: A focus on Hispanic and Japanese populations* (pp. 179–196). *Research Monongraph 19.* Washington, DC: National Institute on Alcoholism and Alcohol Abuse.

Ouimette, P., Ahrens, C., Moos, R., & Finney, J. (1997). Posttraumatic stress disorder in substance abuse patients: Relationship to 1-year posttreatment outcomes. *Psychology of Addictive Disorders, 11,* 34–47.

Ouimette, P., Finney, J., & Moos, R. (1997). Twelve step and cognitive behavioral treatment for substance abuse: A comparison of effectiveness. *Journal of Consulting and Clinical Psychology, 65,* 230–240.

Presley, C., Meilman, P., & Lyerla, R. (1995). *Alcohol and drugs on American college campuses.* Carbondale, IL: Southern Illinois University at Carbondale, Core Institute.

Roosa, M., Dumka, L., & Tein, J. (1996). Family characteristics as mediators of the influence of problem drinking and multiple risk status on child mental health. *American Journal of Community Psychology, 24,* 607–624.

Rorabaugh, W. (1979). *The alcoholic republic: An American tradition.* New York: Oxford University Press.

Roy, A. (1996). Aetiology of secondary depression in male alcoholics. *British Journal of Psychiatry, 169,* 753–757.

Roizen, J. (1997). Epidemiological issues in alcohol-related violence. In Galanter, M. (Ed.) *Recent Developments in Alcoholism Vol 13:* New York: Plenum Press, 7–40.

Ruiz, P., & Langrod, J. (1997). Hispanic Americans. In J. Lowinson, P. Ruiz, R. Millman, & J. Langrod (Eds.), *Substance abuse: A comprehensive textbook* (pp. 705–711). Baltimore: Williams & Wilkins.

Saini, R., Pettinati, A., & O'Brien, M. (1997). Carbohydrate-deficient transferrin: An investigative biochemical marker of heavy alcohol consumption. *Psychopharmacology Bulletin, 33,* 171–175.

Shore, E. (1997). The relationship of gender balance at work, family responsibilities and workplace characteristics to drinking among male and female attorneys. *Journal of Studies of Alcohol, 58,* 297–302.

Siegal, H. A., & Inciardi, J. A. (1995). A brief history of alcohol. In J. A. Inciardi & K. McElrath (Eds.), *The American drug scene: An anthology.* Los Angeles: Roxbury.

Sinclair, A. (1962). *Prohibition: The era of excess.* Norwalk, CT: Easton Press.

Single, E. (1996). Harm reduction as an alcohol prevention strategy. *Alcohol Health and Research World, 20,* 239–243.

Sinha, R., Robinson, J., Merikangas, K., Wilson, G., Rodin, J., & O'Malley, G. (1996). Eating pathology among women with alcoholism and/or anxiety disorders. *Alcoholism: Clinical and Experimental Research, 20,* 1184–1191.

Sobell, L. C., Cunningham, J. A., & Sobell, M. (1996). Recovery from alcohol problems: With and without treatment: Prevalence in two population surveys. *American Journal of Public Health, 86,* 966–972.

———— "Alcohol, Violence, and Aggression." In *Alcohol Alert,* 1–4. Alcohol Alert, National Institute on Alcohol Abuse and Alcoholism: US Department of Health and Human Services (October 1997).

Substance Abuse among Women in the United States. (1997). Washington, DC: SAMHSA, Office of Applied Studies.

Testa, M., & Parks, K. (1996). The role of women's alcohol consumption in sexual victimization. *Aggression and Violent Behavior, 1,* 217–234.

Trimpey, J. (1992) *The small book.* New York: Delacorte Press.

U.S. Department of Health and Human Services, *Ninth Special Report to the U.S. Congress on Alcohol and Health: From the Secretary of Health and Human Services,* June 1997.

Urbano-Marquez, A., Estruch, R., Fernandez-Sola, J., Nocolas, J., Pare, J., & Rubin, E. (1995). The greater risk of alcoholic cardiomyopathy in women compared with men. *Journal of the American Medical Association, 274,* 149–154.

Vaillant, G. (1995). *The natural history of alcoholism: Revisited.* Boston: Harvard University Press.

Watts, L., & Guitierres, S. (1997). A Native American based cultural model of substance dependency and recovery. *Human Organization, 56,* 9–18.

Wechsler, H. (1995). *Binge drinking on American college campuses.* Boston: Harvard School of Public Health.

Wechsler, H. (1996, July/August). Alcohol and the college campus: A report from the Harvard School of Public Health. *Change,* 20–25, 60.

Wechsler, H., Dowdall, G., Davenport, A., & Castillo, S. (1995). Correlates of college student binge drinking. *American Journal of Public Health, 85,* 982–985.

Wechsler, H., Dowdall, G., Davenport A., & Rimm, E. (1995). A gender-specific measure of binge drinking among college students. *American Journal of Public Health, 85,* 982–985.

Wechsler, H., Kuh, G., & Davenport, A. (1996). Fraternities, sororities and binge drinking: Results from a national study of American colleges. *NASPA Journal, 33,* 260–279.

Wechsler, H., Moeykens, B., Davenport, A., Castillo, S., & Hansen, J. (1995). The adverse impact of heavy episodic drinking on other college students. *Journal of Studies on Alcohol, 56,* 628–634.

Westermeyer, J. (1997). Native Americans, Asians and new immigrants. In J. Lowinson, P. Ruiz, R. Millman, & J. Langrod (Eds.), *Substance abuse: A comprehensive textbook* (pp. 712–715). Baltimore: Williams & Wilkins.

Wilk, A., Jensen, N., & Havighurst, T. (1997). Meta-analysis of randomized control trials addressing brief interventions in heavy alcohol drinking. *Journal of General Internal Medicine, 12,* 274–283.

Wilsnack, S., Wilsnack, R., & Hiller-Sturmhofel, S. (1994). How women drink. *Alcohol Health and Research World, 18,* 173–181.

Worthington, J., Fava, M., Agustin, C., Alpert, J., Nierenberg, A., Pava, J., & Rosenbaum, J. (1996). Consumption of alcohol, nicotine, and caffeine among depressed patients. *Psychosomatics, 37,* 518–522.

Wright, K. (1997). Shared ideology in Alcoholics Anonymous: A grounded theory approach. *Journal of Health Communication, 2,* 83–99.

Yamamoto, J., Yeh, E. L., Lee, C., & Lin, K. (1988). Alcohol abuse among Koreans and Taiwanese. In L. Towle & T. Harford (Eds.), *Cultural influences and drinking patterns: A focus on Hispanic and Japanese populations* (pp. 135–178). Washington, DC: National Institute on Alcohol Abuse and Alcoholism.

Zarkin, G. A., French, M. T., Mroz, T., & Bray, J. W. 1998. Alcohol use and wages: new results from the National Household Survey on Drug Abuse. *Journal of Health Economics, 17,* 53–68.

Chapter Five

Stimulants: Cocaine, Amphetamine, and the Xanthines

Chapter Objectives

When you have finished studying this chapter, you should

1. Be able to trace the history of cocaine from the Incas to the present.
2. Know why the Incas thought coca leaf was so valuable.
3. Know how cocaine acts in the synapse.
4. Be able to list the physiological effects of cocaine.
5. Know how cocaine use produces dependence.
6. Be able to discuss what happens when someone who is using cocaine also drinks alcohol.
7. Know why crack has created so many problems.
8. Know how cocaine use can lead to depression.
9. Be able to discuss the effects of cocaine use in pregnant women.
10. Know how cocaine dependence is treated.
11. Know how amphetamine works in the brain.
12. Be able to explain the difference between crack and crank.
13. Be able to discuss the problems associated with the illegal manufacture of methamphetamine.
14. Know the physiological effects of methamphetamine abuse.
15. Know why people coming down from amphetamine can be dangerous.
16. Be able to discuss the role that adenosine plays in the effects of caffeine.
17. Understand what caffeine dependence is and how it differs from dependence on cocaine or amphetamine.
18. Be able to decide whether and to whom caffeine use is harmful.

Of cacaos 700 (beans)
Of white sugar, one pound and a halfe
Cinnamon 2 ounces
Of long red pepper 14
Of cloves, halfe an ounce (the best writers use them not)
Three Pods of the Logwood or Campeche tree. These pods are very good, and smell like fennel or instead of that the Weight of 2 Reals or a shilling of anniseeds
As much Achiote as will give it colour which is about the quantity of a hasell nut

> *[The cacao bean is the bean from which chocolate is made. A long red pepper means a cayenne or even habanero, both of which are very hot; anniseed is like licorice, fennel is similar to dill, and achiote is commonly called annato and used for food coloring]*

> *Published in 1631, this is believed to be the first recipe for drinking chocolate (Coady, 1993)*

Oh, mighty lord, son of the Sun and of the Incas,
thy fathers, thou who knoweth of the bounties
which have been granted thy people, let me recall
the blessing of the divine Coca, which thy privileged
subjects are permitted to enjoy.

> *Prayer of the royal orator of the Incas, ca. 1520 (Quoted in Mortimer, 1901)*

Almost thirty years ago, in one of the first comprehensive examinations of the impact of drugs on our society, Brecher (1972) pointed out that epidemics of cocaine and amphetamine abuse run in cycles. When amphetamine use is high, cocaine use is low, and vice versa. At the height of cocaine use in the late 1970s and early 1980s, very few people reported using amphetamine. Now that we seem to be on the downward curve of cocaine use, use of amphetamine, especially methamphetamine, is making a comeback (*Year-End Preliminary Estimates,* 1997). Methamphetamine is known by such names as *speed, crank, crystal,* and *ice,* and increases in its use have been confined mainly to the West and Southwest (*Pulse Check,* 1997). However, most experts expect that its use will spread. Meanwhile, we continue our love affair with the most common stimulant, caffeine. Why are stimulant drugs so popular? Are they all basically the same? How dangerous are they? Let's begin by examining cocaine.

Cocaine

Cocaine was one of the first anesthetics developed. It was an ingredient in a very popular wine and several soft drinks. Shortly after it became widely available, cocaine was also recognized as a drug with strong addicting properties. The story of cocaine begins with the coca plant revered by its users for thousands of years.

History of Cocaine

Coca leaves, the source of cocaine, have been used by the indigenous people of South America for thousands of years (Schultes, 1987). The cultivation of coca leaves might have been responsible for the development of culture in these societies. The coca leaves were dried and then chewed, and wood ash or lime was added to help extract the cocaine. Chewing the leaves helps reduce hunger and increase energy (Schultes, 1987). Research has indicated also that coca contains high levels of protein, calcium, phosphorus, vitamin's A and E, and riboflavin. Given the sparse diet of the Andean people in the past, coca leaves undoubtedly were essential to their survival (Davis, 1996).

The Inca revered coca above all other plants, and coca figured in every aspect of their rituals and ceremonial life. Coca allowed the runners of the Inca empire to relay messages a thousand miles in a week. Suitors gave coca leaves to the family of the bride, and at the end of initiation rites, young men were given a large bag of the finest coca leaves to symbolize their manhood. The dying believed that if coca was the last taste in a person's mouth before death, the path to paradise was assured. To this day, descendants of the Incas sprinkle a few coca leaves on the ground before eating and during almost every ritual as an offering to the gods (Davis, 1996).

When the conquistadors conquered the indigenous people of South America, they provided them with coca leaves to get them to work harder. The Catholic Church tried to outlaw the plant, but so many Spaniards were making money growing and trading coca that the laws had no effect. By the end of the sixteenth century, taxes on coca were providing the church with much of its income. The Indians, who were forced to work as slaves in mines and on plantations, would refuse to work without it (Davis, 1996).

The bowl in the hand of this pottery figure holds coca leaves. The figure's other hand holds a limestick, which helps extract the cocaine from the leaf.

During the nineteenth century, the active chemical in coca leaves, called **cocaine,** was isolated. It became widely used as a stimulant, local anesthetic, and common ingredient in many patent medicines. One "tonic" made a fortune for Angelo Mariani, who mixed an extract of coca leaf with wine to make Vin Mariani (Karch, 1997). One reason for the popularity of Vin Mariani has only recently been discovered. When cocaine is taken in combination with alcohol, the metabolite **cocaethylene** forms. Cocaethylene produces

The chuspa, a bag worn around the neck, contains coca leaves.

many of the same effects as cocaine itself (Torres & Horowitz, 1996). We will discuss cocaethylene later in this chapter.

At first cocaine was considered harmless. As its use spread, reports began to surface of deaths due to overdose and cases of people who became addicted to its use. Sigmund Freud was one of the most enthusiastic promoters of cocaine, and his reputation was damaged when reports of cocaine abuse became widespread (Karch, 1997). In the United States, cocaine use reached a peak during the 1920s and the heyday of Prohibition. It was cheap (small amounts could be obtained for as little as a nickel), widely available, and pure, since it was largely diverted from medical supplies (Courtwright, 1995). Widespread concern led to a crackdown on cocaine, and many users then turned to heroin. From the 1930s to the 1970s, cocaine use was considered a minor problem.

The Present Cocaine Epidemic

Cocaine use took off again in the late 1970s. The past having been forgotten, the prevailing view was that cocaine was

Mariani wine made Angelo a rich man. The combination of heroin and cocaine is called a "speedball," and coffee with Irish whiskey is called an "Irish coffee." Mariani wine is a combination of cocaine and alcohol. No wonder it was so popular.

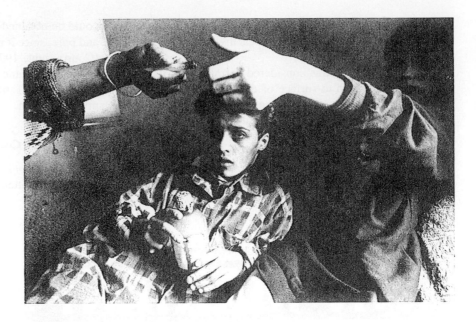
Crack is often smoked in pipes. The rapid absorption leads to strong dependency potential.

nonaddictive. Its users were mainly affluent and white. After about ten years a shift took place in the pattern of use with the introduction of **crack,** a potent smokable form of cocaine. Cocaine rapidly developed the reputation of being extremely addictive and dangerous. The increased demand led to increased production, so it became less expensive again, with the price dropping from $120 per gram in 1981 to $50 in 1988 (Courtwright, 1995). The typical user was now from the inner city, and cocaine use became associated with poverty, crime, and death.

Statistics on modern cocaine use are presented in table 5.1. Notice that cocaine use among young adults, who are the primary users of cocaine, peaked between 1979 and 1982.

Stop and Review

1. What principles of pharmacology, such as rate and quantity of drug absorption, account for the relative harmlessness of coca leaf?
2. In what form was most of cocaine consumed before the twentieth century?
3. What event coincided with the cocaine epidemic in the 1920s?

Physiology and Pharmacology of Cocaine

Cocaine was the first effective local anesthetic, and in the 1800s it was the only one. Since then numerous local anesthetics have been developed, beginning with Procaine in 1905, but imagine what a trip to the dentist was like before local anesthetics were available. All of the local anesthetics are based on cocaine, so their names all have -*caine* as a suffix. Local anesthetics work by blocking the transmission of electrical impulse down the axon (Carvey, 1998). Injected into the gum, for example, they prevent the neural firing that transmits the message of pain during dental work.

The other "-caines" are designed not to cross the blood-brain barrier, but cocaine crosses it readily. In the brain, cocaine blocks the reuptake of catecholamines into the presynaptic membrane. The result is increased amounts of dopamine, norepinephrine, and serotonin available in the synapse (Carvey, 1998). The increased amount of dopamine in the synapse is responsible for the euphoria that cocaine users experience. Cocaine blocks the **dopamine transporter** on the presynaptic membrane (figure 5.1). In the amounts that cocaine users normally take, cocaine causes an almost complete blockade of the dopamine transporter (Volkow et al., 1997). The greater the blockade, the greater the subjective "high" that users experience (Volkow et al., 1997).

TABLE 5.1 Percentage of Those Responding Who Reported Cocaine Use in the Past Year

	1976	1977	1979	1982	1985	1988	1990	1991	1992	1993	1996
Ever used	13.4	19.1	27.3	27.6	24.4	19.7	19.4	17.9	15.8	12.5	10.2
Used last year	7.0	10.2	19.5	18.2	15.6	12.1	7.5	7.7	6.3	5.0	4.7
Used last month	2.0	3.7	9.2	6.5	7.5	4.5	2.2	2.0	1.8	1.5	2.0

Source: *National Household Survey of Drug Abuse.*

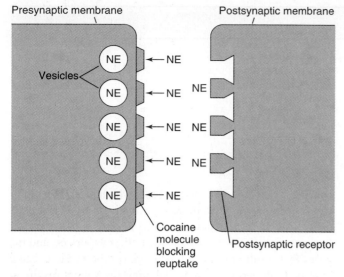

FIGURE 5.1
Cocaine (and antidepressants) prevent the reuptake of norepinephrine and dopamine into the presynaptic membrane.

With repeated use of cocaine, the brain shows adaptation. Changes take place at the level of the synapse so that more cocaine is required to have the same effect (Nestler & Aghajanian, 1997). When the user stops using, there is a sudden craving for more cocaine that is accompanied by increased activity in the prefrontal cortex (see chapter 2) for the first few days (Volkow, Ding, Fowler, & Wang, 1996). Later, there is decreased activity in this structure, which is related to feelings of depression (Volkow, et al, 1996). The term **spiralling distress** has been used to describe what the cocaine user is experiencing (Koob & LeMoal, 1997). At first, typical amounts of cocaine produce euphoria; later it takes more and more to even come close to the same feeling; and if the user stops using, craving and depression are intense. As a result, the abuser feels compelled to continue use.

Neurochemistry of Cocaine

Cocaine exerts its effects on the brain by blocking the reuptake of norepinephrine, serotonin and dopamine (Kreek, 1996; Walsh & Cunningham, 1997). Increases in norepinephrine are associated with anxiety, and serotonin affects mood. In addition, cocaine disrupts the normal endorphin system of the brain (Kreek, 1996). Because the endorphin system is also related to mood, it appears that cocaine use produces euphoria and depression through several different neural pathways. These findings might also explain why treating cocaine addiction is so difficult.

Because of its effects on several neurotransmitter systems, cocaine has widespread effects on the body as well as the brain. Cocaine causes an increase in activity of the sympathetic nervous system resulting in an increase in heart rate, blood pressure, and sweating. It causes an increase in body temperature and tremor as well. Cocaine can trigger seizures by lowering the seizure threshold (Gold & Miller,

1997). Other effects include pupil dilation and flushing. High doses can produce irregular heartbeat, nausea, agitation, respiratory depression, and chest pain. Up to 25 percent of patients who go to the emergency room with chest pains test positive for cocaine (Hollander et al., 1997).

Stop and Review

1. What effects of cocaine would be attractive to some people?
2. What neurochemical changes contribute to the effects of cocaine?

Effects of Cocaine Abuse

Overdose of cocaine can result in serious complications and even death. The pattern of overdose has three phases: (1) vomiting, headache, cold sweats, and muscle twitches; (2) convulsions, rapid and gasping breathing, and a decline in blood pressure; and (3) paralysis, fixed and dilated pupils, respiratory failure, cardiac arrest, and death. Treatment of cocaine overdose is difficult because many of the drugs normally given to treat cardiac problems are similar to cocaine and other drugs that normally are given to reduce seizures can make cocaine seizures worse (Carvey, 1998).

Prolonged use of cocaine leads to many harmful physiological effects. The user experiences insomnia and anorexia (loss of hunger) but is exhausted from the effects of cocaine. Prolonged use can cause hardening of the arteries and increased blood pressure leading to a stroke (Keller & Chappell, 1997). Sexual desire is decreased; men become impotent and women lose the ability to reach orgasm. The decrease in sexual functioning is related to the increase in dopamine and its effect on the pituitary gland (Gold, 1997). Malnutrition and serious weight loss are common (Gold & Miller, 1997). Chronic use of cocaine can lead to many health problems that might not show up for years (Chen, Sheier, & Kandel, 1996).

Cocaethylene   At the beginning of this chapter you read about the widespread use of wine and cocaine mixtures in the nineteenth century and the recent discovery of one reason for their popularity (Karch, 1997). Alcohol is metabolized in the liver into acetaldehyde, and cocaine is metabolized into two chemicals, benzoylecgonine and ecgonine. These metabolites do not affect the brain. In fact, acetaldehyde, you will remember from chapter 3, can produce serious discomfort. When someone drinks alcohol while using cocaine, however, the liver produces the metabolite **cocaethylene,** which is apparently nearly as rewarding as cocaine itself (Torres & Horowitz, 1996). It increases dopamine release in the nucleus accumbens just as alcohol and cocaine do alone. One of the enzymes that normally metabolizes cocaine combines with alcohol to produce cocaethylene.

Most cocaine users also drink alcohol (Bailey, 1996). The users seem to think that alcohol not only increases the

TABLE 5.2 Comparison of Various Forms of Cocaine Use

Route	Mode	Time to Onset	Duration
Oral	Coca leaf	5–10 minutes	45–90 minutes
Oral	Cocaine HCL	10–15 minutes	40–60 minutes
Intranasal	Snorting	2–3 minutes	20–30 minutes
Intravenous	Cocaine hcl	30–45 seconds	10–20 minutes
Smoking	Freebase or crack	8–10 seconds	5–10 minutes

effect of cocaine but also reduces some of the unpleasant side effects such as anxiety. Research indicates that in animals, at least, there is some basis for this belief. A combination of cocaine and alcohol or cocaine and cocaethylene increases the amount of time it takes for cocaine to clear the body (Parker et al., 1996). Cocaethylene also targets the part of the brain that regulates stressful events in the body (Torres, Horowitz, Lee, & Rivier, 1996). You will recall from chapter 2 that glutamate is the primary excitatory neurotransmitter in the brain. Cocaine, alcohol, and cocaethylene all increase glutamate. The net effect does seem to be an increase in the effects of cocaine. Unfortunately cocaine and alcohol in combination increase heart rate and blood pressure compared to cocaine alone, and cocaethylene has been found in the brains of a large number of people who died or were hospitalized as a result of overdose (Bailey, 1996).

Crack   The effects of cocaine depend in part on the route of administration (see table 5.2). When coca leaf is chewed, the rate of cocaine absorption is slow. Cocaine can reach high levels in the bloodstream as a result of chewing coca leaf, but the user does not experience the extreme effects that come from snorting, injecting, or smoking (Davis, 1996). Snorting cocaine (also known as insufflation) produces a faster rise in cocaine levels in the brain. In addition, because cocaine not only constricts the blood vessels in the brain but also is a local anesthetic, irritation of the septum (the membrane separating the nostrils) can occur. After prolonged snorting, the septum can become infected and even develop gangrene (Gold & Miller, 1997).

From the mid 1970s to the mid 1980s cocaine users were primarily middle-class and the drug was usually snorted. Some, but not many, people injected it intravenously. Cocaine exists normally as hydrochloride salt, meaning that the cocaine molecule (which is a base) is combined with hydrogen and choride to form a stable compound, and some individuals began to smoke "freebase" cocaine. **Freebasing** involves dissolving cocaine in a substance like ether and heating the mixture until the ether evaporates, leaving behind the pure cocaine residue, which is then smoked. Freebasing cocaine is involved, time-consuming, and dangerous.

Crack use became widespread by 1985. Crack is made by combining cocaine hydrochloride with sodium bicarbonate or ammonia and then heating it. About 90 percent of the cocaine is converted in cocaine base, which resembles waxy chunks of soap (Hatsukami & Fischman, 1996). Crack typically costs $5 to $10 and is smoked in glass pipes or modified soda cans. The crack is heated until it vaporizes, and the gases that result are inhaled. Although some of the cocaine base is destroyed by heating, inhaling the vapors results in rapid absorption.

Physiological Effects of Crack   When cocaine is smoked as crack, the peak concentration of cocaine in the arteries is reached within 15 seconds. The peak concentration for injected cocaine is reached in about 3 to 6 minutes; it takes 10 to 20 minutes for snorted cocaine to peak. The subjective "high" for snorted cocaine lasts about one hour. For injected or smoked cocaine, the subjective effects last from 30 to 45 minutes (fig. 5.2). When cocaine users were given the choice between smoking and injecting in a laboratory setting, they chose smoking even though they said they

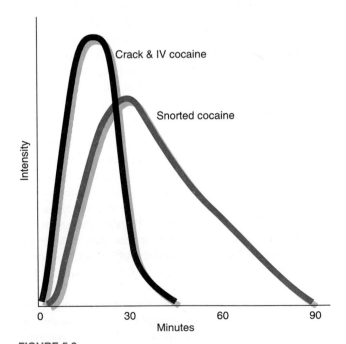

FIGURE 5.2
Crack and intravenous cocaine produce highs of nearly the same intensity. Snorting takes longer to have an effect and the peak is lower. The rapidity of onset helps explain why crack is even more readily abused than snorted cocaine.

preferred injecting cocaine on the street. They also rated smoked cocaine as producing a more pleasant experience. The reason they chose injection on the street was that they had to buy their own and they didn't like to see the cocaine "go up in smoke." In the laboratory the cocaine was free, so they chose smoking (Hatsukami & Fischman, 1996).

Smoking cocaine leads to constriction of the bronchial tubes, which can result in wheezing and asthma attacks (Tashkin, Kleerup, Koyal, Marques, & Goldman, 1996). Crack users also show other signs of lung damage (Susskind, Weber, Atkins, Francheschi, & Volkow, 1996). **Crack lung** is a condition that resembles pneumonia, with severe chest pains, breathing problems, and high body temperature. However, there is no evidence of infection and the symptoms do not respond to traditional treatment. Crack users also can develop blisters, sores, and cuts on their lips from the hot smoke, hot glass, or sharp edges of glass pipestems (Faruque et al., 1996). These open cuts increase the risk of HIV infection. Of course, the intravenous route increases the risk of HIV infection as well and can lead to hepatitis and other blood-borne diseases (DesJarlais, Hagan, & Friedman, 1997).

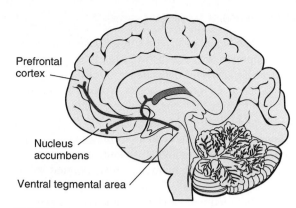

FIGURE 5.3
The reward system for cocaine and amphetamine are found in the prefrontal cortex, nucleus accumbens and ventral tegmental areas of the brain.

Stop and Review

1. What are the effects of cocaine and crack abuse?
2. What is cocaethylene and how does it contribute to the cocaine problem?
3. Why does smoking crack produce dependence?

Psychological Effects of Cocaine

The subjective effects of cocaine are listed in table 5.3. Most of the effects are the result of sympathetic nervous system arousal. The euphoria and increased self-confidence are likely the result of the effect of cocaine on dopamine in the nucleus accumbens. The reward system for cocaine (and amphetamine) is shown in figure 5.3. The effects of cocaine depend on the user's normal state of being. Individuals who are quiet or subdued are more likely to enjoy the effects of cocaine than are people who normally are quite excitable (Gold, 1997). Excitable users might feel uncomfortable as a result of increased sympathetic arousal. The alertness that users report can be seen in the electrical activity of the brain that is typical of someone who is highly aroused. The feelings of arousal and confidence are not accompanied by any real increase in mental abilities, but users misinterpret their

feelings as an indication of superior physical and mental ability. Even though prolonged cocaine use can lead to sexual dysfunction, the immediate sympathetic nervous system arousal can lead to spontaneous orgasm even without sexual stimulation.

The effects of cocaine are short-lived. Following a binge, symptoms of depression, lack of motivation, paranoia, and irritability typically occur (Gold, 1997). Cocaine makes the symptoms of depression worse, even in people who are already severely depressed (Gold, 1997). The depression that occurs during cocaine withdrawal can be very long-lasting. The depression, fatigue, low energy, and other unpleasant symptoms can lead the user to resume cocaine, and this use can become compulsive. The cycle of depression and elation following cocaine use can be very difficult to treat.

Prolonged use of cocaine can lead to psychotic symptoms including paranoia, hallucinations, and delusions (Gold, 1997). One common delusion is that insects are crawling under the user's skin. Vivid auditory and visual hallucinations occur along with repeated stereotyped behavior. The cocaine user who is paranoid, delusional, and hallucinating can be very dangerous and violent toward friends and strangers alike. The feelings of power and superiority can lead to reckless behavior as well. Occasionally cocaine-induced delusions result in violent behavior and can persist for up to a year. Chronic cocaine use can lead to panic attacks with the strong feeling of impending death (Gold, 1997).

TABLE 5.3 Psychological Effects of Cocaine

Dramatic increase in self-confidence		
Euphoria	Increased sense of energy	Enhanced thinking
Decreased appetite	Enhanced sensory awareness	Increased anxiety
Decreased need for sleep	Decreased feeling of fatigue	Increased egocentricity

Cocaine Dependence

When cocaine use began to increase in the 1970s, the standard medical opinion was that it was a relatively safe drug that did not cause physical dependence (Gold, 1997). The following quotes from popular books written during that time give some idea of how cocaine was viewed: "Cocaine use is not physiologically addicting" (Lee, 1976, p. 6). "It does not have the addictive potential of opiates and barbiturates. If a person has been enjoying cocaine on a regular basis and his supply is cut off, he may be disappointed but he won't be climbing the walls" (Gottlieb, 1976, p. 17). Comments such as these led many to believe that addiction to cocaine was impossible. However, though it is true that physical withdrawal is relatively mild and seldom requires medical treatment (Gold, 1997), the psychological dependence is extremely strong. As many as 2 million people in the U.S. have found out for themselves that it is very difficult to stop using cocaine.

Cocaine produces the typical symptoms of what in chapter 1 was labeled as behavioral addiction. Physical withdrawal is accompanied by depression, irritability, and anxiety. Sleep disturbances and agitation are common. These symptoms can last for several days and are quite unpleasant. Medical treatment is necessary if the user is experiencing symptoms of cocaine overdose such as seizures or very high body temperature. Physical withdrawal is followed by depression, sleep disturbances, and craving for cocaine (Brown et al., 1998). Relapse rates are very high, in part because of the negative feelings experienced during withdrawal (McKay, Rutherford, Alterman, Cacciola, & Kaplan, 1995).

Recent studies have indicated that the craving and negative feelings that occur when the cocaine abuser tries to stop have a biochemical basis (fig. 5.4). Prolonged use of cocaine can alter the structure of the dopamine receptors in the nucleus accumbens (Segal, Moraes, & Mash, 1997). The in-creased release of dopamine caused by cocaine leads to up regulation (an increase in the number) of the dopamine receptors. Up regulation also occurs for receptors of the endorphin system in several areas of the brain (Zubieta et al., 1996).

Cocaine abuse is also associated with changes in the serotonin system. Drugs that block the serotonin receptors seem to decrease craving for the drug, whereas drugs that increase serotonin seem to increase craving in abusers (Buydens-Branchey, Branchey, Fergeson, Hudson, & McKernin, 1997; Walsh & Cunningham, 1997). Looking at drug paraphernalia or watching a video of drug users can activate parts of the amygdala, frontal cortex, and cerebellum, all of which are involved in memory and learning (Swan, 1996). These parts of the brain appear to form a circuit that reacts to environmental cues and memories by triggering craving.

Although the description you just read is accurate for cocaine abusers, it is important to note that most users do not develop dependence. The exact percentage of cocaine users who show the symptoms just mentioned is impossible to determine precisely, but most researchers estimate that 10 to 15 percent of cocaine users who begin snorting go on to develop dependence. Estimates from the National Household Survey on Drug use indicate that more than 22 million Americans have tried cocaine at least once, so the number of U.S. abusers is obviously quite large. Because the same survey indicates that ("only") 4 million have used cocaine within the last year and 1.7 million within the last month, it is just as important to note that the vast majority of former users stopped without serious problems.

Just why some users go on to become dependent while others do not is not known. It might be that those who become abusers have different biochemical responses to cocaine (Gold, 1997). Other studies indicate differences in pathways in the brain involving the cortex and thalamus (see chapter 2) between abusers and nonabusers (Volkow et al., 1997). Research is this area is in its infancy and contradictory results are common, but it does seem clear that, at least regarding some users, the idea that cocaine does not cause physical dependence needs to be reexamined.

Treatment for Cocaine Dependence

Considering the problems facing cocaine abusers, it should not be surprising that relapse rates are high. The euphoria that occurs with cocaine use becomes conditioned to many situations. The cocaine user often has developed a lifestyle revolving around cocaine, and withdrawal, although it is not physically dangerous, leads to depression, anxiety, an inability to feel pleasure, and other symptoms. Seeing friends that are cocaine users, listening to a song that mentions cocaine, even the sight of talcum powder, can trigger urges to use. Almost any situation or stimulus previously associated with cocaine is enough to trigger craving (Childress, Ehrman, McLellan, & O'Brien, 1988).

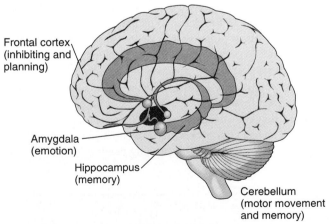

Frontal cortex
(inhibiting and
planning)

Amygdala
(emotion)

Hippocampus
(memory)

Cerebellum
(motor movement
and memory)

FIGURE 5.4
The figure shows the areas of the brain that are activated by craving for cocaine. The frontal cortex is involved in purposeful behavior and inhibition. The amygdala is involved in emotion. The cerebellum cerebellulme coordinates motor movements and is involved in memory.

Treatment for cocaine dependence requires that the user make a complete change in lifestyle. Events, objects, people, and locations associated with cocaine use can provoke urges and must be avoided. Therefore, the user needs determination and support. Inpatient treatment is not any more effective than outpatient because the hospital is an isolated environment where relapse cues are minimal. When the user leaves the hospital, the temptations return. Outpatient treatment is still needed, therefore. Successful treatment can require individual and family therapy, drug education, and support groups (Gold, 1997).

Psychological Treatment

Many, if not most, cocaine abusers have other psychological problems, and their dual diagnosis requires treatment for two conditions. Anxiety and especially depression are extremely common. Antidepressants have been used, but the results have not been especially successful. Another problem is that users report that they find it difficult to return to normal life after cocaine. They often report that life seems colorless and dull after becoming abstinent. In addition, obtaining and using cocaine, not to mention recovering from its use, takes up a great deal of time. The abuser who is trying to stop often finds that time weighs heavy. Going to support groups and therapy sessions not only helps prevent relapse, but uses up much of that time. Despite all these problems, new combined treatments have improved the rate of relapse. Previous relapse rates were 80 to 90 percent; rates have since dropped to 50 percent (Gold, 1997).

Medical Treatment

The development of medication for cocaine dependence shows promise for increasing recovery rates. Research in this area has taken two paths. One is to develop a drug that will block the dopamine receptor in the nucleus accumbens that is thought to be associated with cocaine dependence (*NIDA,* 1995). Drugs that increase firing in certain dopamine receptors seem to increase craving, at least in animals (Self, Barnhart, Lehman, & Nestler, 1996). It seems logical that drugs that block the action of these receptors would decrease craving or even the pleasurable effects of cocaine. A number of researchers are trying to develop such a drug that does not also have serious side effects in humans. No such drug is on the market, although some leads have proven promising.

Another approach is to develop a way to neutralize cocaine in the bloodstream (*NIDA,* 1995). One promising line of research has focused on developing antibodies to cocaine. Antibodies are substances that the body produces in response to many kinds of chemicals. You might think of this as a "therapeutic vaccine" (Fox et al., 1996). Motivated patients could be immunized with the vaccine as part of a comprehensive treatment program. If the user should relapse, the cocaine would be neutralized by the antibodies (Fox, 1997). Another approach under development is to administer the enzyme that metabolizes cocaine **butylcholinesterase.** The effect of cocaine would then be greatly diminished or eliminated altogether (Gorelick, 1997). Either of these methods raises various technical, ethical, and legal questions, not the least of which is whether cocaine abusers could be required to participate in such a program (Cohen, 1997).

Stop and Review

1. What physiological effects make cocaine so dangerous?
2. Why is cocaine dependence so difficult to treat?

Cocaine and Pregnancy

Early studies of infants who were exposed to cocaine prenatally have led to many media predictions of a generation of **"crack babies"** destined to have serious neurological and psychological problems throughout life. Later studies have somewhat modified this dire outlook. Cocaine use during pregnancy can lead to serious problems, including an increased risk of delivering smaller infants, premature delivery, fetal growth retardation, and early termination of pregnancy (Sprauve, Lindsay, Herbert, & Graves, 1997). In cocaine users, premature delivery is often the result of premature rupture of the chorion and amniotic sac membranes (Delaney, Larrabee, Monga, 1997). Newborns of cocaine-using mothers show problems with muscle tone and reflexes (Richardson, Hamel, Goldschmidt, & Day, 1996). They also tend to have less regular sleep and awake cycles (Delaney-Black et al., 1996).

Many of the early studies that found serious problems examined women who used many different drugs, particularly cigarettes and alcohol. Smoking cigarettes produces many of the same effects as cocaine (Delaney, Larrabee, & Monga, 1997). The studies just described controlled for use of other drugs and found that nearly all of the effects on the newborn were gone in a few days (Richardson, Hamel, Goldschnidt, & Day, 1996; Mirochnick et al., 1997). When researchers look at crack-exposed young children, they are unable to find any differences between them and other children (Hurt et al., 1996; Richardson, Conroy, & Day, 1996).

The research just reported is probably a surprise to many readers. The headlines about crack babies tend to be remembered, and contradictory studies are not given the same attention. If a baby is given such a label, parents and caretakers might expect unusual behavior in such a child and attribute all problems to the child's having been born exposed to cocaine. The result is often a self-fulfilling prophecy. None of these studies suggests that using crack is safe for a pregnant woman or her baby—heavy use, especially, can produce lasting problems (Jacobson, Jacobson, Sokol, Martier, & Chiado, 1996)—but these studies do suggest that we are not doomed to a generation of children who were physically impaired by their mother's crack use during pregnancy.

The use of crack cocaine by pregnant women can lead to serious birth defects. If they get good care after birth, however, most babies can function normally.

Amphetamine

The class of drugs that derives from **amphetamine** has been used medically (and recreationally) since the beginning of this century. Amphetamine was provided to soldiers on both sides during World War II, resulting in epidemics of amphetamine use in Japan and Scandinavia when huge quantities of the drug were dumped on the open market. In the United States, amphetamine was used by truck drivers, housewives, students, and anyone else who wanted to stay awake or lose weight. Realization of the dangers of amphetamine was not long in coming, and by the 1970s its medical use had been restricted to treatment of narcolepsy (a sleep disturbance) and attention deficit disorder.

Amphetamine accompanied marijuana and LSD use during the sixties as a favorite drug of real and would-be hippies. Individuals who injected methamphetamine, a form of amphetamine, often became violent, paranoid, and delusional as a result. Eventually such **"speed freaks"** were shunned even by those with a high tolerance for drug-taking behavior, and methamphetamine use was abandoned by most everyone except for a subculture of outlaw bikers. Recently renamed **crank,** it now has wider use again, as you will see.

Physiological and Pharmacological Effects of Amphetamine

All of the amphetamines have the same general effects. Most of the research on the pharmacology and physiology has been done using amphetamine, so this section refers to that drug. Amphetamine causes a release of dopamine, norepinephrine, and to a lesser extent serotonin into the synapse (Groves & Segal, 1984; King & Ellinwood, 1997). Although amphetamine, like cocaine, can block reuptake, its primary mode of action is to cause the release of the catecholamines into the synapse (Stone, 1995). Amphetamine also influences several other neurotransmitter systems that increase the activity in dopamine-containing neurons. Continued use of amphetamine can damage dopamine-containing neurons, especially in the area of the substantia nigra and nucleus accumbens (Villemagne et al., 1998).

Amphetamine activates the cortex and decreases the deepest stages of sleep. A major effect of amphetamine is to trigger a sympathetic nervous system arousal response resulting in the fight-or-flight syndrome. This arousal is accompanied by a massive output of adrenaline in the body. Like cocaine, amphetamine causes the pupils to dilate and increases blood pressure as well as blood supply to the muscles. It also dilates the bronchial tubes and was used for many years in the treatment of asthma. Amphetamine inhalers were available over the counter until the late 1950s (King & Ellinwood, 1997).

Amphetamine and cocaine are similar in their effects (table 5.4). They differ primarily in their mode of action at the synapse and their duration of action.

Unlike most other drugs, amphetamine is not metabolized in the liver. Amphetamine is excreted unchanged in the urine, although some is metabolized by enzymes in the bloodstream (King & Ellinwood, 1997). Because amphetamine is a base, the more acidic the urine, the faster the excretion of amphetamine. Treatment for overdose of amphetamine often includes acidifying the urine. The half-life of a therapeutic dose of amphetamine is two to four hours. The large doses taken by abusers can result in effects that last for many hours (King & Ellinwood, 1997).

TABLE 5.4 Effects of Cocaine and Amphetamine

	Cocaine	Amphetamine
Duration of action	20–40 minutes	3–4 hours
Detectable in urine	1–3 days	3–4 days
Euphoria	Strong	Moderate
Neurochemical effects	Primary action occurs by inhibiting reuptake of catecholamines	Primary action occurs by causing release of catecholamines
	Injected, smoked, snorted; oral route is uncommon	Injected, smoked, snorted, taken orally
	Seizures, paranoia, hallucinations, death	Same

Psychological Effects of Amphetamine

Laboratory studies indicate that amphetamine affects behavior in several ways. In animals, amphetamine increases locomotor activity and with chronic injections causes a stereotypy (behavior that is repeated over and over) (King & Ellinwood, 1997). Typical stereotypies include chewing on the bars of a cage, sniffing, licking, and biting. These effects are probably due to increased dopamine transmission. With continued administration, the animal shows exaggerated startle responses and assumes abnormal body postures.

Chronic doses of amphetamine disrupt social behavior in animals. Instead of interacting, they withdraw and engage in stereotopy and repeated grooming behavior (King & Ellinwood, 1997). Low doses of amphetamine increase social activity in humans, but the effect is short-lived if the amphetamine use increases ((Ward, Kelly, Foltin, & Fischman, 1997). Amphetamine use is associated with increased aggressive behavior in both humans and animals. You will read in chapter 10 about the difficulties involved in deciding how drug taking is related to aggression, but for now it appears that amphetamine use might increase aggression as a direct effect of the drug on the central nervous system (*Pulse Check,* 1997).

The best-known effect of the amphetamines is appetite suppression. In the past, amphetamine was widely prescribed for weight control. Appetite suppression comes about by the action of amphetamine in increasing dopamine transmission. The hypothalamus, a group of nuclei that regulate many behaviors, is the probable site of action (King & Ellinwood, 1997). The appetite-suppressing effects last only a week or two, so the drug is not particularly effective. Amphetamine abusers, however, often lose a great deal of weight.

Meth, Crank, Crystal, Speed

The increased use of methamphetamine has not as yet generated the kind of headlines cocaine generated twenty years ago, but many drug experts fear that **meth** abuse could become as serious a problem in the new century (*Pulse Check,* 1997). The greatest increase in methamphetamine use has occurred primarily in California and the Southwest, but increases have been reported in the Southeast and Midwest as well. Table 5.5 presents some data from various parts of the country that were compiled by the U.S. Drug Enforcement Administration (DEA).

Methamphetamine is amphetamine with a CH_3 molecule attached. Drug users prefer it to amphetamine because the methyl group apparently allows more of the drug to

TABLE 5.5 Methamphetamine Problems Noted in 1996

In Contra Costa County, near San Francisco, police have found that methamphetamine is involved in 89 percent of the reported domestic dispute cases.

In the past two years, San Diego has reported more hospital emergency room episodes for methamphetamine than for any other controlled drug, including cocaine.

In Boise, Idaho, approximately seventy pounds of methamphetamine were seized and seventeen traffickers were arrested.

In Phoenix, Arizona, police report that methamphetamine sales have become as profitable as cocaine sales.

In Polk County, Iowa, the number of drug arrests now surpasses the number of drunk driving arrests. Methamphetamine accounts for 65 percent of the drug arrests.

In Atlanta, drug treatment officials report that methamphetamine is most popular with middle-class teenagers and young adults who have no links to the crack scene.

In San Diego, methamphetamine is popular with adolescent females because it suppresses appetite and with construction workers and truck drivers who have to work long tedious hours without becoming fatigued.

In San Diego, there are more admissions to treatment facilities for methamphetamine than for alcohol.

Source: *U.S. Drug Enforcement Administration.*

cross the blood-brain barrier. Methamphetamine, like amphetamine, exists in two forms, *d-* and *l-*. The molecular structure of the two forms is identical, but they are mirror images. In the sixties and seventies, the methamphetamine called **speed** was a combination of the two: dl-amphetamine. The most popular form now is d-methamphetamine, or **crank.** Crank has become popular because it can be smoked; the dl-methamphetamine form cannot be. Since l-methamphetamine has very little central nervous system activity, it is rarely abused (*National Drug Intelligence Center, 1996*).

Ice, crystal, and **go-fast** are all forms of methamphetamine. Traditionally the outlaw drug suppliers provided dl-methamphetamine made from a precursor known as **P2P** (phenyl-2-propanol). More difficult to manufacture, dl-methamphetamine is two to three times less potent than d-methamphetamine and produces more-pronounced side effects such as tremors and stomach cramps. Organized crime groups based in Mexico revolutionized the production of crank by developing a way to make methamphetamine from **ephedrine** or **pseudoephedrine.** Figure 5.5 shows the similarites among amphetamine, methamphetamine, and ephedrine. Ephedrine is widely available and found in many over-the-counter drugs (*National Drug Intelligence Center, 1996*).

Amphetamine
Benzedrine
Dexedrine

Methamphetamine
"Speed," "Crank," "Crystal"

Ephedrine

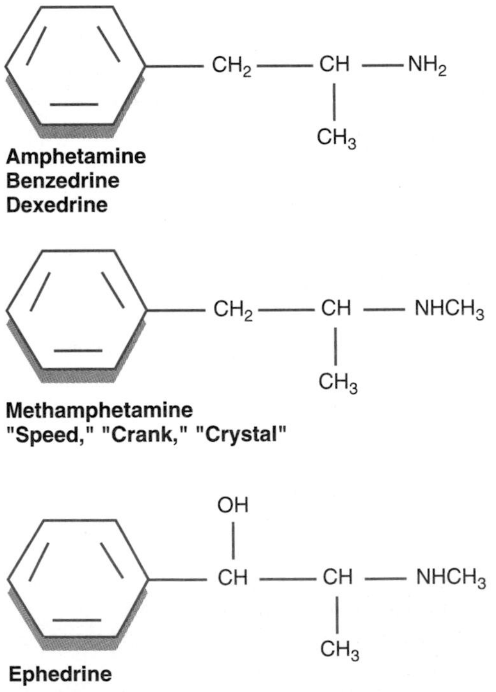

FIGURE 5.5
Notice how similar ephedrine, amphetamine, and methamphetamine are in molecular structure. Ephedrine can be purchased over the counter, while the other two are Schedule II drugs. Ephedrine is about one-tenth as effective as amphetamine in stimulating the central nervous system. The similarity in molecular structure makes it easy to manufacture methamphetamine out of ephedrine.

The manufacture of crank requires several steps involving toxic chemicals. These chemicals present a fire and exposure hazard to the people making the drug and anyone in the vicinity. Cleaning up after "cooking" crank or after the arrest of someone preparing it presents a serious problem of waste removal. Those who are "cooking" rarely worry about this and dispose of the chemicals any way they can. If the drug is being made in a remote area, they simply dump the chemicals onto the ground or into a nearby stream. In more populated areas, drain culverts or sewers are used. Some of the chemicals involved include red phosphorus, lye, hydriodic acid, and hydrogen chloride gas. Cleaning up after an arrest can cost hundreds of thousands of dollars (*National Drug Intelligence Center, 1995*).

Increases in methamphetamine use have not yet shown up in sources such as the National Household Survey of Drug Use, so nearly all data about its use come from law enforcement agencies and persons arrested for crimes. Women arrestees are more likely than men arrestees to test positive for methamphetamine, and the overwhelming majority of those testing positive on arrest are white. The peak age of use for men is 26 to 30 years old, and for women it is 21 to 25. It is not clear why women are more likely to test positive. The obvious explanation would be that more women are using the drug, but the differences could be due to different rates of metabolism, differential effects due to body size, or even different law enforcement practices toward men and women (Feucht & Kyle, 1996).

The Abuse of Methamphetamine

The physiological effects of crank are similar to those of amphetamine. In addition, chronic methamphetamine abuse seems to cause permanent damage to dopamine and serotonin systems. Abuse associated with high doses can increase the incidence of stroke and cardiovascular problems (Davis & Swalwell, 1996; King & Ellinwood, 1997). Although extensive research has not been done on fetal effects of crank, it has been implicated in fetal deaths (Stewart & Meeker, 1997).

Psychological Effects of Methamphetamine

The effects of methamphetamine depend on the way it is used. The National Drug Intelligence Center has identified three types of users. **Low-intensity users** swallow or snort the drug but are not psychologically dependent on it. Many of these users are housewives, truck drivers, and workers on overtime trying to stay awake. Others are using it to lose weight (*Pulse Check,* 1997). **Bingers** and **high-intensity users** smoke or inject methamphetamine and are clearly psychologically dependent. They differ in that bingers use large quantities occasionally, while high-intensity users use even larger amounts more frequently.

When bingers smoke or inject a large amount of crank, the effects follow a typical pattern. The user first experiences a rush that lasts 5 to 30 minutes. This stage is followed by a feeling of being high during which the user feels aggressively smarter, and becomes assertive or argumentative. This high can last 4 to 16 hours. The abuser can continue to smoke or inject after the high wears off, but each dose produces less and less euphoria. This phase, called the binge, can last 3 to 15 days, after which the user is tweaking. The user is now feeling very bad and no amount of crank will relieve the emptiness. The user will sometimes use depressants such as alcohol to deal with the bad feelings. Finally, in the crash stage the user is nearly comatose for 1 to 3 days. During this time the body tries to replenish its supply of dopamine and adrenaline (NDIC, 1997).

Someone abusing crank is most dangerous to others when **tweaking.** Tweaking occurs on the downward side of a crank run. The abuser has probably not slept in 3 to 5 days and will be extremely irritable. The user who is also drinking alcohol is even more likely to be dangerous. The tweaker can appear normal, with clear eyes, concise speech, and brisk movements—but the tweaker's eyes are moving rapidly, and bodily movements are often exaggerated because the tweaker is overstimulated and usually delusional and paranoid. Because the delusions and hallucinations seem very real, the tweaker can act irrationally. A friend or complete stranger might be viewed as a danger to the tweaker's life, and acts of violence are common. From what you learned in chapters 3 and 4, you know that alcohol would make the situation worse. Table 5.6 shows some of the characteristics of heavy use over a prolonged period of time (NDIC, 1997).

High-intensity users focus their entire existence around avoiding the crash and seeking the experience of the first rush. However, each successive rush becomes less euphoric, and it takes more crank to produce it. Their run might continue until they are completely physiologically exhausted, which could take many days. With effort they can

TABLE 5.6 Indications of High-Intensity Abuse of Crank

Weight loss	High-intensity abusers can lose 50 to 100 pounds.
Pale facial skin	Crank constricts blood vessels, especially in the face.
Sweating	Crank increases body temperature. Abusers sweat, especially on upper lip and brows.
Body odor	Abusers lose interest in personal hygiene. The drug causes an odor resembling that of glue and mayonnaise.
Bad teeth	Teeth turn gray and then black. Abusers grind their teeth continuously. May be related to drug use.
Scars, open sores	An indication of "crank bugs." Users feel and see bugs on their skin, and scratch and dig at the skin to remove them.

appear rational and even "normal," but they cannot maintain the effort for long (*Pulse Check,* 1997).

Treatment for Methamphetamine Abuse

The most recent wave of methamphetamine abuse has not yet generated a corresponding increase in programs to deal with abusers who want to stop. Very few studies have dealt exclusively with treatment for crank users. However, because most of the effects of meth are the same as for cocaine, it is probably safe to conclude that the prognosis is the same: Treatment for methamphetamine abuse will be difficult, and relapse rates will be high. In the past, as you have read, crank users were unlikely to have either the money or the insurance to pay for treatment. Now that use has moved into the middle class, expect to see an increasing number of

What Do You Think?

Why Don't We Hear More About Crank Therapy?

Both cocaine and methamphetamine produce strong psychological dependence and serious physical problems. Although treatment has been developed for cocaine abusers, none has been developed for methamphetamine abusers who are considered criminals. Crank abuse has long been a problem, but formerly the people who were abusing it were usually not considered part of mainstream American society. Crank it is now becoming popular with college students and middle-class young adults, so its dangers are becoming better known. If a treatment for methamphetamine abuse is developed—and it will be if abuse continues—it will undoubtedly be available primarily to those who can afford it, namely college students and the middle class. Why has it taken so long to develop treatments? Is it because there was no demand? Was it because crank users typically didn't have insurance? Or was it because no one really cared what happened to those who were previously abusing it?

What Do You Think?

treatment programs. Perhaps they will find a way of treating the abuse that is more successful than current methods, but don't bet your paycheck on it.

Stop and Review

1. What are the similarities and differences between cocaine and amphetamine?
2. Why might some people prefer amphetamine to cocaine?
3. How might crank use contribute to crime?

The Xanthines

The **xanthines** are a class of drugs that include caffeine, **theophylline,** and **theobromine** (fig. 5.6). Caffeine is found in coffee, tea, and chocolate and is added to innumerable other products and drinks. Table 5.7 lists some of the medications that contain caffeine. Theophylline is found in tea and has medical use in the treatment of asthma. Theobromine, found in chocolate, has few stimulating properties and no medical use (Ott, 1985). Of the three xanthines, caffeine is the most widely used and has been the most widely studied, so it will be the topic of our discussion.

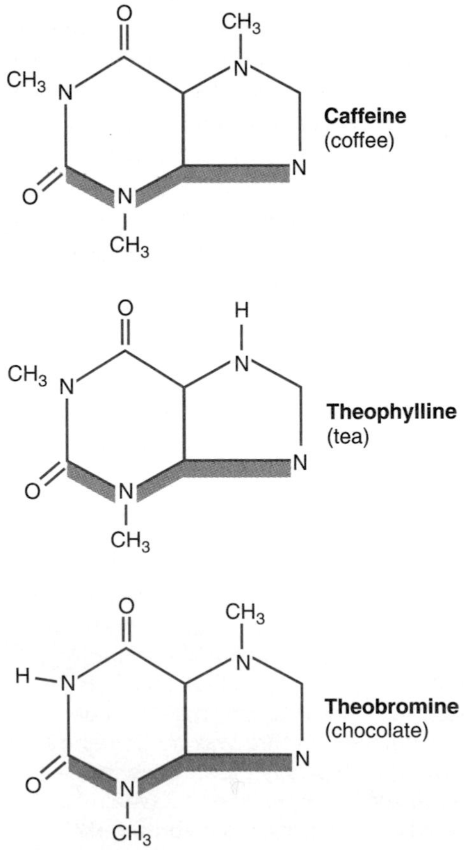

Caffeine
(coffee)

Theophylline
(tea)

Theobromine
(chocolate)

FIGURE 5.6
Notice how similar the three xanthines are, yet they have very different effects.

TABLE 5.7 Caffeine Content of Nonprescription Drugs

Product	Average (mg)	Range (mg)
Weight loss pills	200	100–200
Stimulants		
NoDoz	100	
Vivarin	200	
Analgesics		
Anacin	32	
Excedrin	65	
Midol	32	
Vanquish	33	
Cold tablets		
Dristan	16	
Triaminicin	30	

Source: *Food and Drug Administration*

Coffee and Soft Drinks

Coffee was first domesticated in Ethiopia about A.D. 1000. The world's first coffeehouse opened in Constantinople in 1475. The Turkish became so fond of coffee that they made it legal for a wife to divorce her husband if he did not provide her with an adequate supply. Coffee use spread rapidly throughout the world, and coffeehouses opened up all over Europe and Great Britain. Captain John Smith of Pocahontas fame is credited with introducing coffee to North America. Coffee shops were often a base for political turmoil and they were periodically closed in many countries, but the demand for coffee was so strong that they invariably reopened almost immediately. In fact, when a governor of Mecca, the sacred home of Muhammad, tried to ban coffee, the Sultan had him executed!

Coffee use in the United States is undergoing a revival. In the 1970s, multinational companies took over the coffee industry. They processed and shipped huge quantities of coffee and made sure that the coffee sold in New York tasted the same as the coffee sold in Alaska. Unfortunately, the taste did not please many coffee drinkers and coffee drinking declined. The Pacific Northwest came to the rescue. Coffeehouses run by several coffee producers became popular again. The coffee or espresso bars have trendy decor and offer a wide variety of choices in order to attract a wide variety of customers. They are now found in almost every town and city in America.

Part of the reason for the widespread use of caffeine is the popularity of cola-type soft drinks. Caffeine was first added to soft drinks in the early 1900s to replace cocaine. Guess where it comes from? The companies that decaffeinate coffee. The amount of caffeine in soft drinks varies, but most contain about 35 milligrams—except, of course, for the one that advertises itself as having "twice the caffeine." By now, you are probably aware that you can skip all the tasty but unnecessary ingredients of soda and buy pure water with caffeine added. Sold under various names, these

Tea, Opium, Coffee, and the American Revolution

Tea, coffee, and chocolate became extremely popular in the eighteenth and nineteenth centuries. Most drinking water was unsafe back then, and these beverages provided a tasty way to drink boiled water. Virtually all of the tea that was imported to England and the American colonies came from China. As a result there was a tremendous balance-of-payment problem because the Chinese, who considered Westerners to be barbarians, did not want anything that Westerners had. So an enormous quantity of British wealth ended up in Chinese hands. To balance the payments, the British smuggled opium from India into China and sold it there. The Chinese, outraged, tried to stop its importation. The ensuing war between Great Britain and China ended with the Chinese ceding Hong Kong and other ports to the British. Control of Hong Kong, now a major economic power, reverted to China in the summer of 1997.

Even though the American colonists loved tea, they resented buying it from the British. The British tried to regain some of the money that they had spent defending the colonies against the French and Indians by imposing a small tax on tea. The American colonists, who had been smuggling tea for many years, felt this was an inexcusable intrusion upon their rights. So colonists threw the Boston Tea Party, sacking ships in several harbors and throwing the tea overboard. From that time on, Americans demonstrated their allegiance to the new republic by drinking coffee. Coffee moved with the colonists as they settled the West and has become our staple legal stimulant. The British remain loyal to tea.

---

drinks are nothing more than plain water with about 75 milligrams of caffeine. Undoubtedly more than one person in need of a caffeine fix has thought of making coffee with "caffeine water."

Incidentally, cola (originally spelled *kola*) is an important caffeine-containing berry in Africa. It was introduced into the United States as a health tonic. At the time when cola drinks were becoming popular, cola was well known so its name was added. These drinks contained cola when they were health drinks but dropped the substance and kept the name when they became a popular beverage for everyday use (Lovejoy, 1995). It is interesting that there is neither cocaine nor kola in the drink known by that name.

Physiology and Pharmacology of Caffeine

Several billion pounds of caffeine are consumed annually worldwide. Per capita intake for the entire world is about 70 milligrams per day. In the United States, we average about 240 milligrams per day for every man, woman, child, and baby (Gilbert, 1984). Considering how few young children drink coffee, some people must be consuming several times that amount. In fact, some people have reported consuming as much as 5,000 milligrams of caffeine a day (Molde, 1975). That much caffeine is the equivalent of more than fifty cups of coffee, and they claim no ill effects! Given the enormous consumption of caffeine, it should be comforting to know that most researchers view caffeine as a safe drug. Of course, no drug is completely safe, so let's look at the research.

The average cup of coffee contains about 100 milligrams of caffeine. Caffeine is rapidly absorbed from the gastrointestinal tract, and peak caffeine levels are reached in 30 to 45 minutes. The half-life is roughly 3.5 to 5 hours, and caffeine is metabolized in the liver. Caffeine has numerous actions in the nervous system; it increases norepinephrine and also affects acetylcholine and serotonin transmission. The most important action seems to be on the neuromodulator **adenosine,** which you read about in chapter 2 (Greden & Walters, 1997).

Adenosine-containing neurons are found in various parts of the brain. When adenosine is released from these neurons, it binds to cell membranes and has an inhibitory effect. Adenosine dilates arteries in the brain and seems to produce a calming effect (Snyder, 1984). Caffeine is an adenosine antagonist, so caffeine consumption can produce anxiety and is considered a stimulant. Because it reverses the effect of adenosine, it is often used to treat migraine headaches, which are thought to be caused by dilation of the arteries in the brain. The effect of caffeine on adenosine does not entirely explain its actions, and some of the effects are due to increases in the other neurotransmitters just mentioned.

Caffeine increases heart rate as well as the force of heart contraction. The increased heart rate can present problems for people whose heart rhythm is not normal (von Borstel & Wurtman, 1984). Caffeine is a powerful diuretic and increases urination (along with urgency) one or two hours after intake (Victor, Lubetsky, & Greden, 1981). Caffeine also increases gastric secretions, which often causes an upset stomach. Death from caffeine overdose has been reported, but the amount necessary is in excess of 5,000 milligrams at one sitting.

This drive-up coffee shop is an indication of the popularity of caffeinated beverages in the U.S.

Caffeinism is a fairly common problem that typically is ignored (Greden & Walters, 1997). The term is used in many different ways; it can refer to the effects of too much caffeine taken suddenly, or to caffeine withdrawal and dependence. The *DSM-IV* distinguishes *caffeine intoxication* and *caffeine withdrawal.* Caffeine intoxication is defined as the consumption of more than 250 milligrams of caffeine (about 2 to 3 cups) and symptoms such as restlessness, nervousness, insomnia, flushed face, muscle twitching, gastrointestinal disturbance, and cardiac arrythmia. Most coffee drinkers develop tolerance, so the dose required to produce caffeine intoxication is typically much higher.

Withdrawal from caffeine results in headache, fatigue, and drowsiness and begins about18 to 24 hours after the last dose (Greden & Walters, 1997). It begins to taper off after the first week. Withdrawal has been reported from consumption of as little as 100 milligrams a day, but it is far more common in those consuming about 300 milligrams or more (Strain, Mumford, Silverman, & Griffiths, 1994). In one controlled study, subjects consumed 300 milligrams of caffeine daily and then underwent withdrawal. They reported headache and other subjective symptoms, but withdrawal did not affect their performance on tasks requiring vigilance (Comer, Haney, Foltin, & Fischman, 1997).

The realization that caffeine withdrawal can result in headaches has changed postoperative care in many hospitals. Anyone who has ever undergone surgery (or what many physicians now call "a procedure") knows the rule "nothing by mouth after midnight." It is usually afternoon or later by the time the "procedure" is completed and the patient comes out of anesthesia. The regular coffee drinker by now has a caffeine withdrawal headache in addition to all the other pains. In one study, patients were given either a placebo or caffeine tablets equal to their usual average consumption. Fifty percent of patients receiving the placebo reported a headache, compared to none of the patients receiving caffeine (Fenelly, Galletly, & Purdie, 1991).

Is it reasonable to talk as if caffeine dependence is the same thing as alcohol or cocaine dependence? Using a strict interpretation of the criteria for dependence, one survey found that 44 percent of caffeine users could be classified as dependent (Griffiths et al., 1990). They reported being tolerant to the drug, had a desire to reduce use, and had been unsuccessful in doing so. Is it reasonable to claim that 44 percent of coffee drinkers are caffeine dependent in the same way as alcohol abusers are dependent? Caffeine causes few health problems and does not impair normal functioning. Although one should never say never, no one is referred for inpatient or outpatient caffeine dependence.

The criteria for caffeine withdrawal that were used in the research just mentioned are listed in table 5.8. These were only research criteria, and will not be added to the *DSM* unless sufficient evidence is found to warrant their inclusion.

Caffeine and Health

If studies were to demonstrate that caffeine causes serious health problems, hundreds of millions of people would have to change their habits. The popular media regularly report research findings that coffee drinkers have higher rates of one disease or another. A few months later another study is said to show that there is no such correlation. These studies are extremely difficult to do, for many reasons. The differences, while statistically significant, are typically small or involve conditions that rarely occur.

Caffeine does have a significant effect on the two most common anxiety disorders, generalized anxiety disorder and panic disorder (Charney, Heninger, & Jatlow, 1985; Bruce, Scott, Shine, & Lader, 1992). People with these disorders seem to be more sensitive to the effects of caffeine. In fact, caffeine can trigger panic attacks in those who have panic disorder. In persons with either condition, caffeine seems to produce greater increases in blood pressure, sweating, and skin conductance than it does in normal control subjects. It is easy to see how this increase in sympathetic nervous system

---

TABLE 5.8 Research Criteria for Caffeine Withdrawal

A. Prolonged use of caffeine
B. Abrupt cessation of caffeine use, or reduction in the amount of caffeine used, closely followed by headache and one (or more) of the following symptoms:
  1. Marked fatigue or drowsiness
  2. Marked anxiety or depression
  3. Nausea or vomiting
C. The symptoms in Criterion B cause clinically significant distress or impairment in social, occupational, or other important areas of functioning.
D. The symptoms are not due to the direct physiological effects of a general medical condition and are not better accounted for by another mental disorder.

Source: *DSM-IV.* Appendix B

arousal could be interpreted as a worsening of symptoms by persons with these disorders. Caffeine use is also high among individuals with eating disorders and might contribute to their common symptoms of anxiety and even depression (Krahn, Hasse, Ray, Gosnell, & Drenowski, 1991). Cardiologists routinely warn patients with heart conditions to be careful about caffeine intake because it can cause arrythmia and increase blood pressure (Lovallo et al., 1991).

For the rest of us, caffeine seems to be a relatively safe drug. Earlier studies seemed to link caffeine intake to several conditions, but the studies had serious flaws. Studies that were alleged to show that coffee drinkers have higher rates of cancer failed to control for alcohol intake and cigarette smoking. When these factors were controlled, no increased risk was seen (Vecchia, 1993). Although women who develop fibrous breast tumors are often advised to avoid caffeine, recent studies failed to show a relationship (Heyden, 1993). Caffeine does not increase the overall risk of heart disease even at large doses (four or more cups a day), nor does it seem to increase cholesterol (Grobbee, Rimm, & Giovannucci, 1990; Thelle, 1993). Pregnant women might want to be careful about caffeine use, because heavy use has been associated with a small but significant increase in spontaneous abortion (Infante-Rivard, Fernandez, Gauthier, David, & Rivard, 1993).

Tea

Although it is widely consumed throughout the world, tea has not been as extensively studied as coffee. Recently, however, some studies have suggested that tea drinking can result in a lower incidence of cancer (Blot, McLaughlin, & Chow, 1997). Tea contains several antioxidants that might be responsible. Animals studies have supported this possibility, but in humans the relationship remains unclear (Dreosti, Wargovich, & Yang, 1997). There is no way to test the effect directly, so researchers must look for groups in which tea drinking is common and groups in which tea drinking is rare, and compare cancer rates in those groups. The available data suggest a very modest effect that is clearest when looking at the relationship between green tea and digestive cancers (Blot, Chow, & McLaughlin, 1996), although black tea might also be effective (Blot, McLaughlin & Chow, 1997).

Summary

The coca leaf played an essential role in the lives of the indigenous people of South America for centuries before the Spaniards arrived. Cocaine was also an important drug used for medicinal purposes throughout the nineteenth century. Cocaine epidemics have come and gone in the United States and elsewhere. The most recent epidemic seems to be waning, although cocaine abuse remains a serious problem. Crack, the smokable form of cocaine, has caused more problems than any other form of cocaine.

Cocaine abuse can lead to short-term as well as long-term problems. Strokes, heart attacks, seizures, and paranoid behavior occur among abusers of cocaine. Long-term problems include depression. Cocaine abuse is difficult, but not impossible, to treat, and new methods are presently being introduced.

Amphetamines have also had a long history and were used and abused during the 1950s and 1960s. The advent of speed, or, as it was later called, crank, became a problem because of the method of administration. Methamphetamine can be snorted, smoked, or taken orally. Its use by middle-class individuals is increasing, and it might be the next big wave of stimulant abuse. Of particular concern is the fact that methamphetamine can be made in the United States from readily available chemicals. Methamphetamine abuse can lead to many of the same problems as cocaine abuse. Treatment for methamphetamine abuse has not taken on the urgency that cocaine abuse treatment has.

The xanthines are stimulants that affect behavior by means of a different system than cocaine and amphetamine. Although physical dependence as measured by withdrawal is common, the xanthines do not produce the same problems, physiologically or economically. Overall, caffeine is a relatively harmless stimulant, although it can cause problems for some people.

Key Terms

adenosine An inhibitory neuromodulator found in many parts of the brain. Caffeine exerts part of its effect by altering adenosine metabolism.

amphetamine A stimulant drug used medically for the treatment of attention deficit disorder and narcolepsy.

bingers Users who take large quantities of methamphetamine for several days and then abstain for a period of time.

butylcholinesterase An enzyme that metabolizes cocaine.

caffeinism Irritability, rapid heart rate, and other symptoms that arise after the ingestion of excess amounts of caffeine.

cocaethylene The metabolite formed in the liver when cocaine and alcohol are used together.

cocaine The active ingredient isolated from the leaves of coca plants.

coca leaves The leaves of the plant from which cocaine is derived.

crack A potent form of cocaine that is easily smoked.

crack babies Infants who were exposed to cocaine in utero.

crack lung A condition resembling pneumonia, involving severe chest pains, breathing problems, and high temperature, due to smoking crack.

crank Methamphetamine sulfate.

crystal A form of methamphetamine.

dopamine transporter The structure on the presynaptic

neuron that enables the neuron to reabsorb dopamine from the synapse.

ephedrine   A peripherally acting antiasthmatic drug that closely resembles methamphetamine.

freebasing   Smoking the pure cocaine residue that remains after dissolving cocaine in a substance like ether and heating the mixture.

go-fast   A street name for methamphetamine.

high-intensity users   People who smoke or inject methamphetamine and are psychologically dependent on it.

ice   A form of methamphetamine that can be absorbed quickly by means of inhalation.

low-intensity users   People who swallow or snort methamphetamine but are not psychologically dependent on it.

meth   A street name for methamphetamine, a form of amphetamine with a methyl group added.

P2P   Phenyl-2-propanol.

pseudoephedrine   A form of ephedrine used in over-the-counter medications as a bronchodilator. It resembles methamphetamine.

speed   A slang term for methamphetamine that was popular in the 1960s and 1970s.

speed freaks   A term used in the 1960s and 1970s to refer to methamphetamine abusers.

spiralling distress   The steady progress of deeper despair and depression brought on by abuse of cocaine.

theobromine   A mild stimulant similar to caffeine and found in chocolate.

theophylline   A mild stimulant similar to caffeine and found in tea.

tweaking   The downward side of a crank run. The abuser is low on sleep, is very irritable, has rapid eye movement, and can become quite violent.

xanthines   A class of stimulant drugs that includes caffeine, theophylline, and theobromine.

References

Bailey, D. N. (1996). Comprehensive review of cocaethylene and cocaine concentrations in patients. *American Journal of Clinical Pathology, 106,* 701–704.

Blot, W. J., Chow, W. H., & McLaughlin, J. K. (1996). Tea and cancer: A review of the epidemiological evidence. *European Journal of Cancer Prevention, 5,* 425–428.

Blot, W. J., McLaughlin, J. K., & Chow, W. H. (1997). Cancer rates among drinkers of black tea. *Critical Reviews in Food Science and Nutrition, 37,* 739–780.

Brecher, E. M. (1972). *Licit and illicit drugs.* Boston: Little, Brown.

Brown, R. A., Monti, P. M., Myers, M. G., Martin, R. A., Rivinus, T., Dubreuil, M. E., & Rohsenow, D. J. (1998). Depression among cocaine abusers in treatment: Relation to cocaine and alcohol use and treatment outcome. *The American Journal of Psychiatry, 155,* 220–225.

Bruce, M., Scott, N., Shine, P., & Lader, M. (1992). Anxiogenic effects of caffeine in patients with anxiety disorders. *Archives of General Psychiatry, 49,* 867–869.

Buydens-Branchey, L., Branchey, M., Fergeson, P., Hudson, J., & McKernin, C. (1997). The meta-chlorophenylpiperazine challenge test in cocaine addicts: Hormonal and psychological responses. *Biological Psychiatry, 41,* 1071–1086.

Buydens-Branchey, L., Branchey, M., Fergeson, P. H., & McKernin, C. (1997). Craving for cocaine in addicted users. *American Academy of Addiction Psychiatry, 6,* 65–73.

Carvey, P. M. (1998). *Drug action in the central nervous system.* New York: Oxford University Press.

Charney, D. S., Heninger, G. R., & Jatlow, P. I. (1985). Increased anxiogenic effects of caffeine in panic disorders. *Archives of General Psychiatry, 42,* 233–242.

Chen, K., Scheier, L. M., & Kandel, D. B. (1996). Effects of chronic cocaine use on physical health: A prospective study in a general population sample. *Drug and Alcohol Dependence, 43,* 23–27.

Childress, A., Ehrman, R., McLellan, A. T., & O'Brien, C. (1988). Conditioned craving and arousal in cocaine addiction: A preliminary report. *NIDA Research Monographs, 81,* 74–80.

Coady, C. (1993). *Chocolate: The food of the gods.* San Francisco. Chronicle Books.

Cohen, R. J. (1997). Immunization for prevention and treatment of cocaine abuse: Legal and ethical implications. *Drug and Alcohol Dependence, 48,* 167–174.

Comer, S. D., Haney, M., Foltin, R. W., & Fischman, M. W. (1997). Effects of caffeine withdrawal on humans living in a residential laboratory. *Experimental and Clinical Psychopharmacology, 5,* 399–403.

Courtwright, H. T. (1995). The rise and fall of cocaine in the United States. In J. Goodman, P. E. Lovejoy, & S. Sherratt (Eds.), *Consuming habits: Drugs in history and anthropology* (pp. 206–228). London: Routledge.

Davis, D. D., & Swalwell, C. I. (1996). The incidence of acute cocaine or methamphetamine intoxication in deaths due to ruptured cerebral (berry) aneurysms. *Journal of Forensic Sciences, 41,* 626–628.

Davis, W. (1996). *One river: Explorations and discoveries in the Amazon rain forest.* New York: Simon & Schuster.

Delaney, D. B., Larrabee, K. D., & Monga, M. (1997). Preterm premature rupture of the membranes associated with recent cocaine use. *American Journal of Perinatology, 14,* 285–288.

Delaney-Black, V., Covington, C., Ostrea, E., Romero, A., Baker, D., Tagle, M., & Nordstrom-Klee, B. (1996). Prenatal cocaine and neonatal outcome: Evaluation of dose-response relationship. *Pediatrics, 98,* 735–740.

DesJarlais, D. C., Hagan, H., & Friedman, S. R. (1997). Epidemiology and emerging public health perspectives. In J. H. Lowinson, P. Ruiz, R. B. Millman, & J. G. Langrod (Eds.), *Substance abuse: A comprehensive textbook* (pp. 591–596). Baltimore: Williams & Wilkins.

Dreosti, I. E., Wargovich, M. J., & Yan, C. S. (1997). Inhibition of carcinogenesis by tea: The evidence from experimental studies. *Critical Reviews in Food Science and Nutrition, 37,* 761–770.

Faruque, S., Edlin, B. R., McCoy, C. B., Word, C. O., Larsen, S. A., Schmid, D. S., Von Bargen, J. C., & Serrano, Y. (1996). Crack cocaine smoking and oral sores in three inner-city neighborhoods. *Journal of Acquired Immune Deficiency Syndromes and Human Retrovirology, 13,* 87–92.

Fenelly, M., Galletly, D. C., & Purdie, G. I. (1991). Is caffeine withdrawal the mechanism of postoperative headache. *Anesthesia and Analgesia, 72,* 449–453.

Feucht, T. E., & Kyle, G. M. (1996). *Methamphetamine use among adult arrestees: Findings from the drug use forecasting (DUF) program.* Washington, D.C.: National Institute of Justice.

Foltin, R. W., Fischman, M. W., & Levin, F. R. (1995). Cardiovascular effects of cocaine in humans: Laboratory studies. *Drug and Alcohol Dependence, 37,* 193–210.

Fox, B. S. (1997). Development of a therapeutic vaccine for the treatment of cocaine addiction. *Drug and Alcohol Dependence, 48,* 149–151.

Fox, B. S., Kantak, K. M., Edwards, M. A., Black, K. M., Bollinger, B. K., Botka, A. J., French, T. L., Thompson, T. L., Schad, V. C., Greenstein, J. L., Gefter, M. L., Exley, M. A., Swain, P. A., & Briner, T. J. (1996). Efficacy of a therapeutic cocaine vaccine in rodent models. *Nature Medicine, 2,* 1129–1132.

Gilbert, R. M. (1984). Caffeine consumption. In G. A. Spiller (Ed.), *The methylxanthine beverages and foods: Consumption and health effects* (pp. 185–213). New York: Alan R. Liss.

Gold, M. S. (1997). Cocaine (and crack): Clinical aspects. In J. H. Lowinson, P. Ruiz, R. B. Millman, & J. G. Langrod (Eds.), *Substance abuse: A comprehensive textbook* (pp. 181–198). Baltimore: Williams & Wilkins.

Gold, M. S., & Miller, N. S. (1997). Cocaine (and crack): Neurobiology. In J. H. Lowinson, P. Ruiz, R. B. Millman, & J. G. Langrod (Eds.), *Substance abuse: A comprehensive textbook* (pp. 166–180). Baltimore: Williams & Wilkins.

Gorelick, D. A. (1997). Enchancing cocaine metabolism with butylcholinesterase. *Drug and Alcohol Dependence, 48,* 159–165.

Gottlieb, A. (1976). *The pleasures of cocaine.* Berkeley, CA: And/Or Press.

Greden, J. F., & Walters, A. (1997). Caffeine. In J. H. Lowinson, P. Ruiz, R. B. Millman, & J. G. Langrod (Eds.), *Substance abuse: A comprehensive textbook* (pp. 294–306). Baltimore: Williams & Wilkins.

Greenblatt, J. C. & Gfroerer, J. C. (1997). *Methamphetamine Abuse in the United States.* OAS Working Paper from the Substance Abuse and Mental Health Services Administration, Center for Substance Abuse Prevention: RP0906.

Griffiths, R. R., Evans, S. M., Heishman, S. J., Preston, K. L., Sannerud, C. A., & Wolf, B., et al. (1990). Low dose caffeine dependence in humans. *Journal of Pharmacology and Experimental Therapeutics, 255,* 1123–1132.

Grobbee, D., Rimm, E., & Giovannucci, E. (1990). Coffee, caffeine and cardiovascular disease in men. *New England Journal of Medicine, 323,* 1026–1032.

Groves, P. M., & Segal, D. S. (1984). Psychobiological foundations of behavior induced by amphetamines. In C. M. Sharp (Ed.), *Mechanisms of tolerance and dependence.* National Insitutue of Drug Abuse Monograph No. 54. Washington, DC: U.S. Department of Health and Human Services.

Hatsukami, D. K., & Fischman, M. W. (1996). Crack cocaine and cocaine hydrochloride. *Journal of the American Medical Association, 276,* 1580–1588.

Heyden, S. (1993). Coffee and cardiovascular diseases. In S. Garattini (Ed.), *Caffeine, coffee and health.* New York: Raven Press.

Hollander, J. E., Shih, R. D., Hoffman, R. S., Harchelroad, F. P., Phillips, S., Brent, J., Kulig, K., & Thode, H. C. (1997). Predictors of coronary artery disease in patients with cocaine associated myocardial infarction. *American Journal of Medicine, 102,* 158–163.

Hurt, H., Brodsky, N. L., Betancourt, L., Braitman, L. E., Belsky, J., & Gianetta, J. (1996). Play behavior in toddlers with in utero cocaine exposure: A prospective, masked, controlled study. *Developmental and Behavioral Pediatrics, 17,* 372–379.

Infante-Rivard, K., Fernandez, A., Gauthier, R., David, M., & Rivard, G. (1993). Fetal loss associated with caffeine intake before and after pregnancy. *Journal of the American Medical Association, 270,* 2940–2943.

Jacobson, S. W., Jacobson, J. L., Sokol, R. J., Martier, S. S., & Chiado, L. M. (1996). New evidence for neurobehavioral effects of in utero cocaine exposure. *Journal of Pediatrics, 129,* 581–590.

Karch, S. B. (1997). *A brief history of cocaine.* Boca Raton, FL: CRC Press.

Keller, T. M., & Chappell, E. T. (1997). Spontaneous acute subdural hematoma precipitated by cocaine abuse: Case report. *Surgery and Neurology, 47,* 12–15.

King, G. R., & Ellinwood, E. H. (1997). Amphetamine and other stimulants. In J. H. Lowinson, P. Ruiz, R. B. Millman, & J. G. Langrod (Eds.), *Substance abuse: A comprehensive textbook* (pp. 207–222). Baltimore: Williams & Wilkins.

Koob, G. F., & LeMoal, M. L. (1997). Drug abuse: Hedonic homeostatic dysregulation. *Science, 278,* 52–57.

Krahn, D. D., Hasse, S., Ray, A., Gosnell, B., & Drenowski, A. (1991). Caffeine consumption in patients with eating disorders. *Hospital and Community Psychiatry, 42,* 313–315.

Kreek, M. J. (1996). Cocaine, dopamine and the endogenous opioid system. *Journal of Addictive Diseases, 15,* 73–96.

Lee, D. (1976). *Cocaine: Consumer's handbook.* Berkeley, CA: And/Or Press.

Lovallo, W. R., Pincomb, G. A., Sung, B. H., Everson, S. A., Passey, R. B., & Wilson, M. F. (1991). Hypertension risk and caffeine's effect on cardiovascular activity during mental stress in young men. *Health Psychology, 10,* 236–243.

Lovejoy, P. E. (1995). Kola nuts: The "coffee" of Central Sudan. In J. Goodman, P. E. Lovejoy, & A. Sherratt (Eds.), *Consuming habits: Drugs in history and anthropology* (pp. 103–125). London: Routledge.

McKay, J. R., Rutherford, M. J., Alterman, A. I., Cacciola, J. S., & Kaplan, M. R. (1995). An examination of the cocaine relapse process. *Drug and Alcohol Dependence, 38,* 35–43.

Mirochnick, M., Meyer, J., Frank, D., Cabral, H., Tronick, E. Z., & Zuckerman, B. (1997). Elevated plasma norepinephrine after in utero exposure to cocaine and marijuana. *Pediatrics, 99,* 555–559.

Molde, D. A. (1975). Diagnosing caffeinism. *American Journal of Psychiatry, 132,* 202.

Mortmer, W. G. (1901). *Peru: History of Cocoa.* New York. J. H.

Vail & Co. Quoted in G. Andrews and D. Solomon, *The Coca Leaf and Cocaine Papers* (New York: Harcourt Brace and Javonovich, 1975), 50–238.

Nestler, E., & Aghajanian, G. K. (1997). Molecular and cellular basis of addiction. *Science, 278,* 58–64.

NIDA Capsules (1995). Methamphetamine Abuse. *Press Office of the National Institute on Drug Abuse.* U.S. Department of Health and Human Services, Public Health Service, National Institutes of Health, 1–2.

Ott, J. (1985). *The cacahuatl eater: Ruminations of an unabashed chocolate addict.* Vashon, WA: Natural Products Company.

Parker, R. B., Williams, C. L., Laizure, S. C., Mandrell, T. D., Labranche, G. S., & Lima, J. J. (1996). Effects of ethanol and cocaethylene on cocaine pharmacokinetics in conscious dogs. *Drug Metabolism and Disposition, 24,* 850–853.

Polter, M. J., & Kolbye, K. F. (1996). *Effects of Methamphetamine.* U.S. Department of Justice National Drug Intelligence Center. 96-C0109-003.

Pulse Check: National trends in drug abuse. (1997). Washington, DC: Office of National Drug Control Policy.

Richardson, G. A., Conroy, M. L., & Day, N. L. (1996). Prenatal cocaine exposure: Effects on the development of school age children. *Neurotoxicology and Teratology, 18,* 627–634.

Richardson, G. A., Hamel, S. C., Goldschmidt, L., & Day, N. L. (1996). The effects of prenatal cocaine use on neonatal neurobehavioral status. *Neurotoxicology and Teratology, 18,* 519–528.

Schultes, R. E. (1987). Coca and other psychoactive plants: Magicoreligious roles in primitive societies in the New World. In S. Fisher, A. Raskin, & K. Uhlenhuth (Eds.), *Cocaine: Clinical and biobehavioral aspects.* New York: Oxford University Press.

Segal, D. M., Moraes, C. T., & Mash, D. C. (1997). Up-regulation of D3 dopamine receptor mRNA in the nucleus accumbens of human cocaine fatalities. *Molecular Brain Research, 45,* 335–339.

Self, D. W., Barnhart, W. J., Lehman, D. A., & Nestler, E. J. (1996). Opposite modulation of cocaine seeking behavior by D1 and D2-like dopamine receptor agonists. *Science, 271,* 1586–1589.

Snyder, S. H. (1984). Adenosine as a mediator of the behavioral effects of caffeine. In P. B. Dews (Ed.), *Caffeine* (pp. 129–152). New York: Springer-Verlag.

Sprauve, M. E., Lindsay, M. K., Herbert, S., & Graves, W. (1997). Adverse perinatal outcome in parturients who use crack cocaine. *Obstetrics and Gynecology, 89,* 674–678.

Stewart, J. L., & Meeker, J. E. (1997). Fetal and infant deaths associated with maternal methamphetamine use. *Journal of Analytical Toxicology, 21,* 515–518.

Stone, T. W. (1995). *Neuropharmacology.* Oxford: W. H. Freeman Spektrum.

Strain, E. C., Mumford, G. K., Silverman, K., & Griffiths, R. R. (1994). Caffeine dependence syndrome: Evidence from case histories and experimental evaluations. *Journal of the American Medical Association, 272,* 1043–1048.

Susskind, H., Weber, D. A., Atkins, D., Francheschi, D., & Volkow, N. D. (1996). Does detoxification reverse the acute lung injury of crack smokers? *Nuclear Medicine Communications, 17,* 963–970.

Swan, N. (1996). Response to Escalating Methamphetamine Abuse Builds on NIDA Funded Research. *National Institute of Drug Abuse Notes. Volume II,* 1, 5–6, 18.

Tashkin, D. P., Kleerup, E. C., Koyal, S. N., Marques, J. A., & Goldman, M. D. (1996). Acute effects of inhaled and IV cocaine on airway dynamics. *Chest, 110,* 904–910.

Thelle, D. (1993). Metabolic effects of coffee and caffeine intake on the cardiovascular system. In S. Garrattini (Ed.), *Caffeine, coffee and health* (pp. 151–165). New York: Raven Press.

Torres, G., & Horowitz, J. (1996). Individual and combined effects of ethanol and cocaine on intracellular signals and gene expression. *Progress in Neuropsychopharmacology and Biological Psychiatry, 20,* 561–595.

Torres, G., Horowitz, J. M., Lee, S., & Rivier, C. (1996). Cocaethylene stimulates the secretion of ACTH and corticosterone and the transcriptional activation of hypothalamic NGFI-B. *Molecular Brain Research, 43,* 225–232.

Vecchia, L. (1993). Caffeine and cancer epidemiology. In S. Garratini (Ed.), *Caffeine, coffee and health* (pp. 379–392). New York: Raven Press.

Victor, B. S., Lubetsky, M., & Greden, J. F. (1981). Somatic manifestations of caffeinism. *Journal of Clinical Psychiatry, 42,* 185.

Villemagne, V., Yuan, J., Wong, D. F., Dannals, R. F., Hatzidimitriou, G., Mathews, W. B., Ravert, H. T., Musachio, J., McCann, U. D., & Ricaurte, G. A. (1998). Brain dopamine neurotoxicity in baboons treated with doses of methamphetamine comparable to those recreationally abused by humans. Evidence from C-11 Win-35, 428 positron emission tomography studies and direct in vitro determinations. *Journal of Neuroscience, 18,* 419–427.

Volkow, N. D., Ding, Y., Fowler, J. S., & Wang, G. (1996). Cocaine addiction: Hypothesis derived from imaging studies with PET. *Journal of Addictive Diseases, 15,* 55–71.

Volkow, N. D., et al. (1997). Relationship between subjective effects of cocaine and dopamine transporter occupancy. *Nature, 386,* 827–830.

von Borstel, R. W., & Wurtman, R. J. (1984). Caffeine and the cardiovascular effects of physiological levels of adenosine. In P. B. Dews (Ed.), *Caffeine* (pp. 142–152). New York: Springer-Verlag.

Walsh, S. L., & Cunningham, K. A. (1997). Serotonergic mechanisms involved in the discriminative stimulus, reinforcing and subjective effects of cocaine. *Psychopharmacology, 130,* 41–58.

Ward, A. S., Kelly, T. H., Foltin, R. W., & Fischman, M. W. (1997). Effects of d-amphetamine on task performance and social behavior of humans in a residential laboratory. *Experimental and Clinical Psychopharmacology, 5,* 130–136.

Year-end preliminary estimates from the 1996 Drug Abuse Warning Network. (1997). Washington, DC: Substance Abuse and Mental Health Services Administration.

Zubieta, J., Gorelick, D. A., Stauffer, R., Ravert, J. T., Dannals, R. F., & Frost, J. J. (1996). Increased mu opioid receptor binding detected by PET in cocaine-dependent men is associated with cocaine craving. *Nature Medicine, 2,* 1225–1229.

Chapter Six

Marijuana

Chapter Objectives

When you have finished studying this chapter, you should

1. Be able to trace the use of marijuana from its earliest use to the present.
2. Know the various types of cannabis and how marijuana is used.
3. Know how THC is absorbed, metabolized, and eliminated.
4. Understand the difference between testing positive for THC and being under the influence of THC.
5. Know the physiological effects of THC.
6. Know what anandamide is and how it is related to marijuana.
7. Understand how the distribution of anandamide in the brain helps explain the effects of marijuana.
8. Be able to decide whether marijuana produces dependence as serious as the dependence produced by other drugs of abuse.
9. Be able to discuss the ways in which marijuana use harms the body.
10. Understand the controversy over medical use of marijuana.
11. Be able to decide whether marijuana could have any valid medical use.
12. Know how hemp and marijuana are related.

Del Rio, Texas, 1940. One Eleutero G., while under the influence of marijuana, shot to death two women and then committed suicide by literally slicing himself to bits about the abdomen, heart and throat. G. had wandered around in the fields for hours after the killing and his self-mutilation.

(Quoted in Anslinger & Tompkins, 1953)

Marijuana is one of the safest therapeutically active substances known to man.

Frances Young, administrative law judge, Drug Enforcement Administration, 1988

There is not a shred of scientific evidence that shows that smoked marijuana is useful or needed.

Barry McCaffrey, White House Drug Policy Director, 1996

A pipe of kif (marijuana) before breakfast gives a man the strength of a hundred camels in the courtyard.

Nchaioui proverb quoted in Bowles (1962)

The controversy over marijuana use has been raging for more than three decades. In fact, the adolescents that grew up during the period of greatest marijuana use now have to deal with marijuana use by their children. Discoveries about marijuana in the past ten years have opened avenues of research with the potential to develop new drugs. At the same time, the illegal use of marijuana continues to cause concern. The controversy over marijuana often generates more heat than light. After reading this chapter, you should be able to draw your own conclusions.

History of Marijuana Use

The plant that we call marijuana, *Cannabis sativa,* has been recognized and used throughout history. The first mention is found in medical texts in China, India, and Assyria, some of which go back almost five thousand years. Herodotus, writing in the fifth century B.C.E., mentions smoking cannabis (Conrad, 1997). Large quantities of it were found on a Carthagian ship sunk sometime near the end of the First Punic War (264–241 B.C.E.). The manner of storage indicated that it was there for the enjoyment of the crew (Frost, 1987). The epic Indian poem *The Mahabharta* dates back to 1300 B.C.E. and contains a warning against what we would now call amotivational syndrome. In addition to its use as medicine and for enjoyment, cannabis (known as **hemp**) was a widely grown crop used to make clothing (Morningstar, 1985).

Marijuana was very familiar to the Muslim world during the Middle Ages. Its stronger form, hashish, gave its name to a group of fanatics who were followers of a certain Sheik Hasan Ibn-Sabah. The **hashishiyya,** as they were called, were responsible for political assassinations and other forms of mayhem. Depending on whose story you believe, they either smoked hashish to get the courage to go out and kill, or were given the name because they smoked to relax after committing their nefarious deeds (Abel, 1980). According to Muslim sources of the time, marijuana made you crave sweets, made you high, improved sex, and stimulated creativity. On the other hand, it was also supposed to make men effeminate, decrease sex drive, and destroy motivation (Rosenthal, 1971). Marijuana and hashish were briefly popular in Europe in the1800s. Noted writers such as Dumas and Baudelaire used it, although they later opposed it (Kusinitz, 1987).

We grew hemp throughout the colonies, and George Washington mentions it several times in his diaries. It was used to make rope, clothing, and sails. Its use continued through the end of World War II, although by the middle of the eighteenth century most hemp was being imported. Smoking marijuana for enjoyment did not seem to catch on until Mexican laborers immigrated to the United States to escape political upheaval following the Mexican Revolution of 1910 (Musto, 1987). They had used marijuana recreationally at home, and they did the same in the United States. Just as now, there was widespread prejudice against legal and illegal laborers, and their marijuana smoking set them further apart (Schlosser, 1994). During the Great Depression, the "marijuana menace" was invented. Smoking marijuana was said to lead normal young men and women into a life of crime and depravity. According to the lurid reports of the day, several people were supposed to have committed multiple murders after smoking marijuana (Inciardi, 1986).

In 1936, Harry Anslinger, who made a career out of warning Americans about the dangers of marijuana, called it the "foremost menace to life, health and morals in the list of drugs used in America" (Anslinger & Cooper, 1937). Because he was chief of the Bureau of Narcotics at the time, many people believed him. The Marijuana Tax Act of 1937 was supposed to end the menace by placing marijuana in the same category as the opiates. Thirty years later, marijuana made a comeback and, along with LSD, became a drug of middle-class youth. In the 1960s, hippies, psychedelic music, and marijuana helped define an entire era in our history. After a gradual decline in use, marijuana is becoming more popular again and the medical marijuana movement is pushing to make the drug legal for medical purposes.

For all of the publicity that marijuana receives, you might think that its attributes and effects would have been determined by numerous definitive medical studies. In real-

Marijuana was widely grown in many parts of the world as a source of plant material for clothing and rope.

This photo was taken in the late sixties near Aspen, Colorado. One may wonder what this individual looks like today.

ity, we know only a little more about it than we did when the Marijuana Tax Act was passed. We are basically still in the dark about its potential long-term effects. We don't know what percentage of people who use it become dependent. We don't know if the supposed medical benefits outweigh the supposed dangers. Finally, we still know very little about it effects on the brain and the body. We know that there are more than sixty chemicals known as **cannabinoids** found in marijuana, and that the most active in producing the behavioral effects of marijuana is **delta-9-tetrahydrocannabinol (THC)** (Grinspoon & Bakalar, 1997).

Types of Marijuana

The confusion concerning marijuana begins with it botanical status. The commonest form of the plant is *Cannabis sativa.* Two other forms exist: *Cannabis indica,* which originated in India and *Cannabis ruderalis,* which originated in

northern Europe and Eurasia. Sativa is a tall, woody plant, indica is shorter and has a higher THC content. Ruderalis has little THC but has a very short growing season, as befits its origins in the far northern hemisphere (Stafford, 1992). Most botanists believe that these three types are subspecies of the same genus rather than different species. Selective breeding has led to plants with a high THC content, strong compact growth, and a short growing season.

Hashish is made from the resin of the cannabis plant. It can have a THC content of up to 40 percent. **Hash oil** is the result of extracting THC from the marijuana plant and concentrating the resulting solution. Its concentration of THC can also reach 40 percent (DEA, 1994). **Sinsemilla** is Spanish for "without seeds" and refers to the buds and leaves of the female cannabis plant that has not been fertilized. Sinsemilla has a higher THC content than ordinary cannabis, though differences vary from year to year (see table 6.1). **Thai sticks** are bamboo shoots that have buds

TABLE 6.1 THC Content (Percentage) of Confiscated Marijuana

	1988	1989	1990	1991	1992	1993	1994	1995
Commercial	3.82	3.46	3.61	3.26	3.84	5.43	4.06	3.33
Sinsemilla	7.62	6.96	10.10	10.53	8.57	6.03	7.29	6.66

Source: *U.S. Department of Justice.*

from the plant glued to them. A rich colloquial vocabulary has developed to describe marijuana.

Current Patterns of Marijuana Use

Table 6.2 shows marijuana use among various age groups for the period 1976 to 1996. As with cocaine, the highest use rates were in 1979 to 1982. As you can see, the percentages of use declined in the early 1990s, then began to increase again. The reason for this increase is unclear. The younger age groups have typically had a number of antidrug programs in school, so the decline might be expected to continue. Some feel that the increase is the result of the movement to make marijuana available for medical purposes and to a general decrease in the intensity of antidrug messages in our culture. The percentage who think that marijuana is harmful has decreased, which might account for the change.

Stop and Review

1. Why was marijuana considered an important product in the past?
2. When did the current increase in marijuana use begin?
3. What changes have taken place in marijuana use in the last thirty years?

Pharmacology of Marijuana

In the United States, marijuana is usually smoked, and so absorption is quite rapid. About one-quarter of the THC in a marijuana cigarette appears in the mainstream smoke (the smoke inhaled directly in the cigarette). The rest is destroyed by burning or lost in sidestream smoke, which is the smoke that is not inhaled (Huestis, Sampson, Holicky, Henningfield, & Cone, 1992). The amount the smoker actually receives with each puff depends on the percentage of THC found in the cigarette. Many claims have been made that the potency of marijuana has increased in recent years. Judging from the figures for marijuana seized in the United States, the potency of most forms has remained about the same for the last ten years. Table 6.1 shows that there is more THC in sinsemilla than in commercial grade marijuana.

In controlled laboratory studies, peak THC levels are reached 10 minutes after smoking first begins. By 2 hours after smoking, THC levels are negligible, although some can be detected for up to 12 hours. When the subjects in the study were asked for their experience of "liking" and whether they "felt" the drug, responses peaked at about 30 minutes and were gone by 12 hours (Huestis, et al., 1992). The amount of THC absorbed and the psychological effects can be increased by holding the smoke in the lungs longer, although there is some debate about this (Zacny & Chait, 1989; Block, Erwin, Farinpour, & Braverman, 1998).

In the 1998 Olympics, a Canadian athlete was stripped of his medal because he tested positive for marijuana. He was given it back on a technicality, but he claimed that he had not smoked marijuana. According to him, he had been at a party where others were smoking, and he inhaled enough secondhand smoke to test positive. According to one study it is possible to test positive after exposure to secondhand marijuana smoke. However, in that study the "room" was unventilated and a mere 4 by 4 by 8 feet. The subjects were exposed to the equivalent of 16 marijuana cigarettes for one hour a day for six days. Exposure to only 4 marijuana cigarettes in the same situation did not result in positive urine tests (Cone et al., 1987). Unless his party lasted a long time and he partied with sixteen smokers in a small closet, there is a good chance the athlete was lying.

Once THC is in the bloodstream, it is distributed to all parts of the body. Being fat soluble, it is readily absorbed in fatty tissue and released slowly back into the bloodstream and metabolized (Grinspoon & Bakalar, 1997). The primary metabolites are called 11-nor-delta-9- and 11-nor-delta-8-TCH-9-carboxylic acid. In one study, peak concentration of the primary metabolite tested (11-nor-delta-9-TCH-9-carboxylic acid), was reached 8 to 13 hours after smoking a cigarette either high or low in THC content. The metabolite could be detected up to 88 hours later (Huestis, Mitchell, & Cone, 1996). With higher doses, detectable amounts of THC metabolite were found after two to three weeks, and one study reported a positive result 95 days after use (Mirin & Weiss, 1983; Johansson & Halldin, 1989).

The fact that trace amounts of the metabolite can be detected in the urine days and weeks after use does not necessarily mean that someone who smoked marijuana would fail a typical urine test. The most commonly used urine test (called **EMIT**) has a cutoff point for detection of THC

TABLE 6.2 Trends in Use of Marijuana within the Last Year by Various Age Groups (Percentage Using)

Age	1976	1977	1979	1982	1985	1988	1990	1991	1992	1993	1996	1997
12–17	18.4	22.3	24.8	20.7	19.4	12.6	11.3	10.1	8.1	10.1	13.0	15.8
18–25	35.0	38.7	46.9	40.1	36.3	27.9	24.6	24.5	22.7	22.9	23.8	22.3
26 + older	5.4	6.4	9.2	10.8	9.3	6.9	7.3	6.6	6.0	6.3	7.0	7.2

Source: *National Household Survey of Drug Abuse*

metabolite. The cutoff point can be set at either 20 or 40 nanograms. Unless a urine sample shows *more* than the specified cutoff value, the test will be reported as negative, even if detectable THC metabolite is present. As you can guess, the number of positive urine samples can be affected by the choice of cutoff. One large-scale study showed that lowering the cutoff from 40 to 20 nanograms, would result in a 150 percent increase in positive samples (Wingert, 1997). As you will read in chapter 10, interpreting results from urine samples can be difficult. Similar problems exist with hair sampling, an alternative measure of drug use. Marijuana use can be detected in the hair of regular users, but **false negatives** and **false positives** are common (Wilkins et al., 1995). False negatives occur when use of the drug is not detected, and false positives occur when a sample is reported to be positive even though no use occurred.

The presence of the metabolites for marijuana in urine or hair samples tells us only that the person has probably used marijuana. The more important questions concern the possible harm from such use. Some researchers claim that marijuana causes birth defects, fetal damage, lung cancer, long-term impairment of memory, schizophrenia, suppression of the immune system, and leukemia (in the children of mothers who smoke marijuana) (Nahas & Latour, 1992). Others maintain that there is no evidence that marijuana does anything of the sort, and that "marijuana is relatively safe, even when used as an intoxicant" (Grinspoon & Bakalar, 1997). How can researchers come to such opposite conclusions? As you read the next few pages, you should be able to form your own opinion.

Physiological Effects of Marijuana

The short-term physiological effects of smoking marijuana are not very remarkable. Smoking marijuana results in an increase in alpha-wave activity in the brain during periods of marijuana-induced euphoria (Lukas, Mendelson, & Benedikt, 1995). These changes are similar to those seen during meditation and hypnosis. Marijuana use causes an increase in the heart rate, an increase in appetite, and a reddening of the eyes (Grinspoon & Bakalar, 1997). Blood pressure increases, and skin temperature decreases (Benedikt, Cristofaro, Mendelson, & Mello, 1986; Huestis et al., 1992). Blood flow through the main artery in the brain, the middle cerebral artery, is increased (Mathew, Wilson, Humphreys, Lowe, & Wiethe, 1992). Marijuana use also seems to interfere with REM (or dream) sleep, and a rebound occurs when the user stops (Jones, 1980).

Marijuana and the CNS: The Role of Anandamide

The real breakthrough in understanding how marijuana affects the brain came with the discovery of a receptor on neurons that responds to THC. Because a THC receptor exists, a neurotransmitter similar to THC must exist in the brain.

The neurotransmitter has been identified and named **anandamide.** The chemical structures for THC and anandamide are shown in figure 6.1. One of the privileges of discovering a neurotransmitter is the opportunity to name it. The researchers who discovered it named it after the Sanskrit word for "bliss," *ananda* (DeVane, Hanus, & Breuer, 1992). The formal name is arachidonylethanolamine. Anandamide works on the second messenger system, which you read about in chapter 2 (Felder et al., 1993). Since the discovery of the receptor for THC and the naturally occurring anandamide, synthetic compounds have been created that have a potency hundreds of times that of THC (Budney et al., 1997).

There are two separate types of anandamide receptors, one affecting the brain and the other affecting peripheral systems such as the spleen, lymph nodes, testes, and ovaries (DeVane, 1994; Adams & Martin, 1996). In the brain, anandamide is found in large amounts in the basal ganglia, hippocampus, and cerebellum. These parts of the brain are involved in the reward system, memory, and motor coordination (Matsuda, Bonner, & Lolait, 1993). Marijuana clearly affects memory, and difficulties with motor coordination are among the most prominent signs of THC intoxication in animals.

In contrast to the large number of sites for anandamide in these areas, very low levels are found in the brain stem areas controlling cardiovascular and respiratory functions (Adams & Martin, 1996). Although marijuana does increase heartbeat, the effect is due to the peripheral rather than the central receptor. These findings might explain why the lethal dose of THC is extraordinarily high (Adams & Martin, 1996). In fact, there has never been a substantiated case of death due to marijuana overdose. One study reports the case of a body packer who was smuggling hashish oil with a

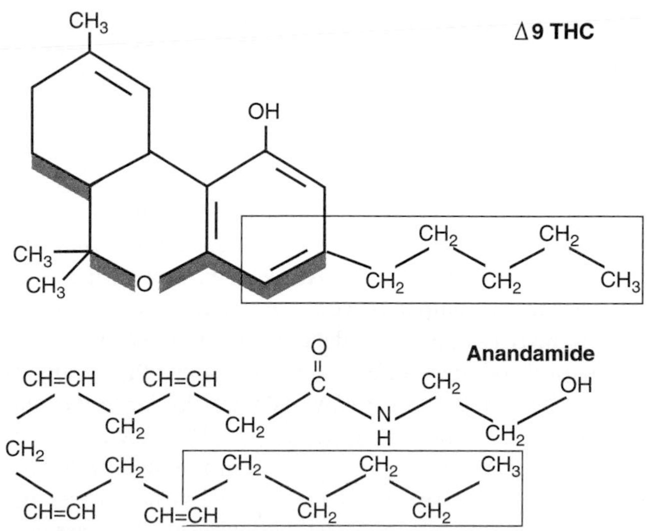

FIGURE 6.1
THC and anandamide are both complex molecularly, and they do not resemble each other. However, the areas indicated by the rectangles are thought to be the parts of the molecules that bind to the postsynaptic receptor.

THC content of 24 percent. Apparently he had swallowed a large number of condoms containing the hashish. Some must have broken, because his urine showed approximately 11,000 nanograms/milliliter of THC metabolite. A typical smoker might show 100 nanograms/milliliter after one joint. Apparently he ingested the equivalent of more than one hundred joints. He reported feeling "high" since swallowing the balloons, but all medical tests were normal (Meatherall & Warren, 1993)!

Marijuana and the Reward System

The question of whether THC causes the same effects on the reward system of the brain as other drugs of abuse is still being debated. Recently two studies have provided evidence that THC does share many properties with drugs like heroin. In one study, researchers measured the output of dopamine in the shell of the nucleus accumbens. You should remember from chapter 2 that dopamine release in the nucleus accumbens is associated with reward. The increase in dopamine as a result of THC was similar to that caused by injections of heroin. The recent development of an antagonist to THC has enabled researchers to demonstrate more clearly that THC works directly on specific receptors (Budney et al., 1997). Antagonists work by occupying receptor sites. If giving THC increases dopamine and the antagonist blocks the release, it is strong evidence that THC is acting as a neurotransmitter agonist.

THC-specific antagonists (antagonists that block only the THC receptor) blocked the release of dopamine, as did the injection of naloxone, an endorphin antagonist (Tanda, Pontieri, & DiChiara, 1997). This is the first study to show clearly that THC produces many of the changes in the brain that are seen with other drugs of abuse. The study further indicates that the endorphin system is involved in the effects of THC, since blocking that system prevents the release of dopamine. The finding that the THC receptor system involves the endorphins might help explain marijuana's effect on pain.

In the other study, rats injected daily for two weeks with a THC-like compound showed signs of withdrawal when a cannabinoid antagonist was administered (de Fonseca, Carrera, Navarro, Koob, & Weiss, 1997). Behavioral withdrawal was seen, and its existence was supported by an increase in the output of stress hormones as well as increased activity in the amygdala, the emotional center of the brain. Both of these effects are seen with other drugs of abuse. The changes in the amygdala are similar to the neuroadaptation you read about in chapter 2. Behavioral withdrawal was measured by increases in grooming, scratching, teeth chattering, "wet dog shakes," and diarrhea. These behaviors are also typical of opiate withdrawal (de Fonseca et al., 1997).

Not everyone accepts these findings as proof that the effects of THC are identical to those of other drugs of abuse. First, animals will learn to self-administer most drugs of abuse. Monkeys will learn to press a bar to receive an intravenous injection of cocaine, for example. No one has been able to train any animal to self-administer THC or its synthetic relatives (Adams & Martin, 1996). The technique of suddenly inducing withdrawal by administration of a cannabinoid antagonist is not characteristic of the experience of most marijuana users. THC, as you have seen, takes a long time to leave the body, so it is reasonable to assume that THC leaves the receptors slowly as well. Withdrawal symptoms have been seen in a small percentage (16 percent) of heavy users (daily use for up to six years), but they are relatively mild and include nervousness, sleep disturbance, and appetite change. More moderate use was not associated with withdrawal (Weisbeck et al., 1996).

Stop and Review

1. What are the characteristics of marijuana absorption and metabolism?
2. What is anandamide, and how does it help explain the effects of marijuana?
3. What evidence suggests that marijuana should be classified as similar to heroin and other illegal drugs?

Tolerance and Dependence on Marijuana

Tolerance to the effects of marijuana is clearly seen in laboratory studies with animals (Adams & Martin, 1996). Humans develop tolerance to most of the physiological effects of THC such as changes in heart rate, interocular pressure, and sleep disturbances (Jones & Benowitz, 1976). In fairness, however, it should be pointed out that large doses must be taken over a prolonged period of time before tolerance is seen. When doses are small and infrequent, little tolerance develops to behavioral effects (Adams & Martin, 1996).

The question of dependence on marijuana is crucial to understanding the possible dangers of the drug. Data from the most recent National Household Survey on Drug Use indicate that more than 32 million people in the United States have used marijuana and about 5 million admit to having used it within the last month (*National Household Survey,* 1997). The National Comorbidity Study found that 9.2 percent of those who reported any lifetime use of marijuana developed dependence (Budney et al., 1997). Physical dependence seems relatively mild. However, some users find it difficult to stop or cut down when they want to. You will recall from chapter 1 that difficulty in stopping or cutting down is characteristic of what we called behavioral addiction. The percentage of those who become dependent on marijuana is lower than for cocaine, alcohol, or tobacco (Grinspoon & Bakalar, 1997).

Marijuana use peaks at ages 19 to 23 for both males and females. Dependence occurs more frequently among younger users. Oddly, adolescents use marijuana less heavily than older populations and yet are more likely to become dependent. Adolescents seem to be at greater risk, therefore, for developing dependence, because they seem to be more sensitive to its effects. The relapse rate for those who seek treatment is similar to the relapse rate for cigarette smokers, alcohol abusers, and heroin addicts. The main reasons for wanting to stop seem to be the desire to regain self-control and health concerns (Weisbeck et al., 1996; Budney et al., 1997). Users also report financial difficulties, feelings of procrastination about life goals because of use, family complaints, inability to stop, loss of self-confidence, and memory loss.

Treatment for Marijuana Dependence

There have only been a few studies of the effectiveness of treatment for marijuana dependence. The studies used a variety of methods, including brief intervention, relapse prevention, social support, and twelve-step programs. For those that were motivated to quit, the success rate was comparable to rates for other drugs of abuse. As is the case with the stimulants, narcotics, alcohol, and cigarettes, relapse rates were high (Budney et al., 1997). One reason for the lack of studies stems from the small number of people seeking such treatment. The lack of demand for treatment might indicate that most users do not feel that marijuana interferes significantly with their lives (Grinspoon & Bakalar, 1997).

Negative Effects of Marijuana

It is abundantly clear that marijuana smoking can damage the lungs. Some studies have even linked marijuana use to lung cancer (Sridhar et al., 1994). One joint is approximately equivalent to 5 tobacco cigarettes in terms of carbon monoxide intake, 4 cigarettes in terms of tar intake, and 10 cigarettes in terms of damage to cell linings in the lungs (Sussman, Stacey, Dent, Simon, & Johnson, 1996). Those in favor of the medical use of marijuana (or its legalization) point out that use of a water pipe is likely to reduce the harm of inhaled smoke. Nevertheless, there is little question that inhaling the smoke of burning leaves, be they tobacco or marijuana, is bad for the lungs.

Marijuana use has been linked to reduced effectiveness of the immune system (Sussman et al., 1996), and cannabinoid receptors have been found on the cells of the immune system (Kaminski, 1996). However, most evidence suggests that this reduction is temporary and might not be of medical concern (Sussman et al., 1996). Smoking marijuana during pregnancy has been linked to low birth weight and prematurity, and fetal exposure has been associated with later problems in thinking and attention (Hatch & Bracken, 1986; Swan, 1994; Fried, 1995). Furthermore, receptors for anandamide have been found in the cells of the uterus of mice and rats (Paria, Deutsch, & Day, 1996).

Although rare, high doses can produce a toxic delirium or psychosis, the symptoms of which include confusion, agitation, disorientation, and even hallucinations (Sussman et al., 1996; Grinspoon & Bakalar, 1997). Short-term memory deficits exist during the period of intoxication. Time estimation is particularly affected, and time seems to pass much more slowly than normal. Several studies have concluded that, for heavy users, memory deficits continue even after abstinence (Schwartz, Gruenewald, Klitzner, & Fedio, 1989; Mathias, 1996).

Amotivational syndrome is a term used to describe a lack of desire to accomplish goals. Some studies of marijuana use have reported such effects, others have not. In general it is difficult to conclude whether people who are lacking in motivation are more likely to choose marijuana or whether marijuana causes people to lose motivation (Sussman, et al., 1996; Grinspoon & Bakalar, 1997).

You have undoubtedly heard of the concept stepping stone drugs or gateway drugs. Marijuana use is supposed to lead to the use of other, more dangerous drugs. Marijuana users are at relatively high risk for use of other drugs, but 40 percent of marijuana users do not use other drugs and users of other drugs sometimes switch to marijuana. Because marijuana is illegal, those who purchase it probably have access to other drugs from the dealer. Rather than there being a direct biochemical or physiological connection between marijuana use and use of other drugs, it might be that use of one pleasurable drug reinforces the tendency to try other drugs as well (Grinspoon & Bakalar, 1997).

Marijuana can cause panic attacks, and even though such attacks are rare, they are frightening to the sufferer. In high doses, marijuana can cause a short-acting psychotic-like reaction, although the balance of evidence suggests that this breakdown occurs only in users who are already susceptible. Marijuana has been linked to schizophrenia (Andreasson, Allebeck, Engstrom, & Rydberg, 1987), although susceptibility is also a factor in this study (Grinspoon & Bakalar, 1997). Flashbacks have been linked to marijuana although they are rare. Curiously, many users find the flashback enjoyable (Sussman et al., 1996; Grinspoon & Bakalar, 1997).

Stop and Review

1. To what extent does tolerance develop to the use of marijuana?
2. What is the evidence for marijuana dependence?
3. What are some potentially harmful effects of marijuana?

Marijuana and Medicine

Marijuana is classified as a Schedule I drug, meaning that it is classified as having no medical use and as having a high potential for abuse. As of this writing, the voters of two states, California and Arizona, have passed referenda permitting compassionate use of marijuana for patients with medical problems. In California, state and local law en-

The Dutch Experiment

In 1976, the Dutch legalized the possession of small amounts of marijuana. In Amsterdam it is possible to go to a "coffee shop" and legally purchase marijuana. What has happened as a result, and what can it teach us about our own problems with marijuana and other drugs? Keep in mind as you read this that the Netherlands is a small country with a much more homogeneous population than ours, where crime is rare and tolerance is high.

Prior to 1976, about 3 percent of the Dutch people had used marijuana at least once. In 1998, the best estimate is about 14 percent. Keep in mind that these are cumulative figures, so that those who had tried it in 1970, for example, are still around and those who began to use it subsequently are added to them. The data from adolescents is similar, however. In 1970, 20 percent of Dutch youth had used marijuana at least once. The figure dropped to 15 percent in 1980, after legalization. It has risen to about 30 percent at present. The 1996 figure for the United States, by the way, was 32 percent. More than half of those who said they had used marijuana used it only a couple of dozen times or less. It appears that legalization ultimately leads to an increase in marijuana use, but data from Germany, where marijuana is prohibited, show virtually the same trends.

Marijuana has been considered a gateway drug leading to harder drugs. The Netherlands has fewer addicts per capita than Italy, Spain, Switzerland, France, Britain, or the United States. The number of hard-drug addicts has been the same for the last ten years and the average age is 44, indicating that few young people in the Netherlands are becoming addicts. Only 0.3 percent of users seek treatment for marijuana dependence, and nearly half of those are having trouble with alcohol and other drugs as well. It seems that most of those who use drugs in the Netherlands use marijuana, try it a few times, and then stop without going on to other drugs. Finally, Dutch teenagers get among the highest scores in the world on international science and mathematic tests!

Source: Adapted from *New Scientist* (1998).

forcement agencies are nevertheless arresting people who sell marijuana to others (presumably for "compassionate use") and people who are growing large numbers of plants. The state courts have not yet made a definite ruling about whether someone can sell marijuana or how much an individual can grow for "personal use." As you might expect, arrests are made selectively and confusion is rampant. In Arizona, the legislature refused to pass the legislation necessary to enable the referendum. Even though marijuana might be legal in California for medical purposes, it is still illegal under federal statutes. The states cannot pass a law superseding federal law. Therefore, someone could be arrested in California and prosecuted in federal court for possession of marijuana even if it were legal in California.

The issue of marijuana as medicine is not simply a scientific question. Marijuana use has been a symbol of youthful rebellion and a major problem for law enforcement. Ever since the first "war on drugs," politicians have vowed to eradicate the drug problem in the United States. It would be extremely difficult for most politicians to admit that they had been wrong all along about marijuana and that it has a legitimate use rather than being the scourge of humankind. By the same token, some of those who are advocating medical marijuana have a not-so-hidden agenda: the legalization of marijuana for everyone. Others feel strongly that physicians should be able to prescribe whatever drugs they believe will help their patients and that the government has no right to interfere in such medical decisions.

The federal government also maintains that the primary active ingredient in marijuana, THC, is already available in the form of a synthetic compound used in pill form. Medical THC is called dronabinol and the trade name is Marinol. Marinol has generally been found to be effective for treating nausea that occurs as a result of chemotherapy (Voth & Schwartz, 1997). Those who support the use of marijuana claim that the pill causes unwanted side effects and that smoking marijuana would be better because a pill can be difficult to swallow for some patients, especially those with nausea (Conrad, 1997).

The advocates of medical marijuana often ignore the fact that, regardless of the reason, there really have not been any controlled studies demonstrating its effectiveness. The studies that have been done have yielded mixed results. Smoking marijuana does reduce nausea, but many patients cannot or will not smoke it (Voth & Schwartz, 1997). The positive reports of marijuana come mainly from personal testimony. History is replete with drugs that have seemed to be useful based on the testimonies of patients only to prove ineffective when carefully studied. On the other hand, the federal government seems to have done all it can to prevent controlled studies from being conducted. Until 1998, they refused to provide marijuana to researchers who were interested in studying the subject, and without federally supplied marijuana, good research cannot be done.

The controversy may have reached such an impasse that the necessary studies will be done. The Federation of American Scientists, the American Medical Association, and the British Medical Association have to varying degrees called for definitive research on the subject. But, even if studies show a clear effect one way or the other, the controversy is not likely to go away. Both sides will undoubtedly do all they can to maintain their positions.

Possible Medical Benefits

Smoking marijuana seems to increase one's appetite for food—especially between-meal snacks (Foltin, Brady, & Fishman, 1986), although it has no appetite-enhancing effects in animal studies (Graceffo & Robinson, 1998). Marijuana smokers often describe the "munchies" they get when they are stoned. Several medical conditions, including cancer and AIDS wasting syndrome, have as a common element a loss of appetite with resultant weight loss. Marijuana is reported to help these patients regain their appetite and zest for eating. On the other hand, AIDS patients have an impaired immune system. Even though the effect of marijuana on the immune system might not cause medical problems in healthy individuals, AIDS patients might be a different story (Adams & Martin, 1996).

Glaucoma is the leading cause of blindness in the United States, affecting 2 to 4 million people every year. It is caused by the buildup of pressure inside the eye. The eye is filled with vitreous humor, a thick fluid that is continuously produced and drained from the eye. In glaucoma the vitreous humor builds up and the pressure damages the optic nerve, resulting in blindness. Marijuana (or more correctly, THC) lowers the intraocular pressure although it does not cure the disease (Grinspoon & Bakalar, 1997).

Smoking marijuana also leads to relief of pain. The pharmaceutical industry has been very active in developing THC-like compounds that might be useful as analgesics without the "side effects" that constitute being stoned. The market for such a drug would be enormous if, as the companies apparently believe, the risk of addiction is low. Assuming that the drug is similar to THC in other respects, an overdose would be virtually impossible, and it might have the additional advantage of reducing nausea. Some promising advances have been made in developing drugs that are based on THC, but they are still in the research and development stage (Rowen, Embry, Moore, & Welch, 1998).

The Legal Issues of Medical Marijuana

None of the propositions that have been passed or are pending permit casual use of marijuana. Proposition 215, passed in California in 1996, is a case in point. Under the law it is legal to possess and use medical marijuana with the consent of one's physician. Growing it and selling it are still illegal. This raises the obvious question of where to obtain it.

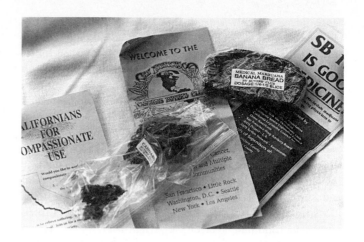

Legally, giving it away is the same as selling, and marijuana does not fall from the sky in smokable form. The federal government has threatened to continue prosecuting those who grow or sell it, and in several cases have carried out the threat. At this writing the cases are winding their way through the court system.

The most blatant example of providing marijuana is the case of the various buyers clubs. In California, a buyers club has existed under various names for several years. Originally it was called the California Buyers Club but has switched names each time it has been raided and closed. The original owner of the club is awaiting trial on felony charges of selling marijuana. Until the raid, the club existed more or less openly and was supported by the board of supervisors and tolerated by local law enforcement. Even the U.S. Drug Enforcement Administration, which had targeted the group, eventually decided to stay out of the issue. During this period several people were arrested for growing thousands of marijuana plants and claimed immunity under Proposition 215. However, even the most ardent advocate of medical marijuana would probably find it hard to believe that anyone could need two or three tons of marijuana for medical purposes!

Marijuana and Hemp

Hemp products are being widely promoted in catalogs and by some major retailers. Hemp oil and hemp seed are available as "food supplements" or "dietary aids." *Cannabis sativa* grown for hemp (the fiber) is the same as *Cannabis sativa* grown for marijuana (the drug). Advocates claim that the variety grown as hemp has virtually no THC and so is somehow different (Conrad, 1997). Legally, however, *Cannabis sativa* is either legal or illegal and there is no easy way to discriminate on the basis of THC content. A similar issue exists regarding the opium poppy. Some seed companies sell opium poppy seeds, and it is technically legal to grow poppies in your garden. However, you can be prosecuted if you extract the opium. In fact there are a number of plants with psychoactive properties that are perfectly legal to grow and possess. It would be impossibly cumbersome to devise laws that would allow law enforcement to determine whether you intend to grow a plant for its beauty in your garden or because you intended to get high from it.

You can buy shoes, backpacks, clothing, and many other items made from hemp. You won't get high from smoking them, however. When grown as hemp, the plant actually does have a very low THC content because it is grown to produce fiber, not leaves and flowers. The same is not true for the other legal hemp products, however. Both **hemp oil** and **hemp seed** can produce a positive urine test for marijuana (Costantino, Schwartz, & Kaplan, 1997; Fortner, Fogerson, Lindman, Iversen, & Armbruster, 1997). Hemp seeds are sterilized and are legal and approved for use in food by the U.S. Food and Drug Administration (FDA). Hempseed oil is also legal and is reported to be replete with important health-maintaining essential fatty acids (Conrad, 1997). Eating hemp seed cakes resulted in a positive urine test using the most common FDA-approved method. A more sophisticated test, called a GC-MS, was able to distinguish hemp seed from marijuana (Fortner et al., 1997). However, even this test resulted in positive values when hempseed oil was ingested (Costantino et al., 1997).

The fact that these products can produce a positive urine test could mean significant trouble for some people. In some cases, employers are required to follow-up a positive urine sample that uses the most inexpensive method with the more expensive GC-MS. Such a follow-up is not typically required in many other circumstances such as preemployment screening. You will read in chapter 10 about the legal aspects of testing, but here you should realize that the potential employer does not have to inform the applicant of the reason why he or she was not hired and is under no obligation to reveal a positive urine test. The case of hempseed oil is even more serious because it will fool even the more sophisticated test and the federal government has ruled that a claim of ingestion of hemp food products can never be accepted as a defense. The only acceptable reasons for a positive urine test is a prescription for dronabinol (Costantino et al., 1997; Fortner et al., 1997).

Stop and Review

1. What are some of the problems associated with doing research on the medical effects of marijuana?
2. What is the evidence that marijuana might be useful as a medicine?
3. What effect might the increased popularity of hemp have on laws regarding marijuana?

Summary

Like cocaine, marijuana has had a long history of use. Marijuana use was not recognized as a problem in the United States until the 1930s and did not become a major problem until the 1960s. Recently its use has begun to increase again.

THC, the primary active drug found in marijuana, affects a neural receptor for which there is a naturally occurring neurotransmitter in the brain. This neurotransmitter, anandamide, is found in various parts of the brain and the body, although its function is not well understood.

The harmful effects of marijuana have been overestimated by some and underestimated by others. It probably does not produce a strong physical dependence, but the psychological dependence is real. Smoking is harmful to your health regardless of what you smoke. There is evidence that marijuana can cause memory problems, at least temporarily.

The medical marijuana movement wants to make marijuana available for those who find it helpful in managing their medical condition. Some who are part of the movement want marijuana to be legalized altogether. The sudden popularity of hemp is curious because hemp is a form of marijuana and yet clothing and other objects made from it are legal to obtain.

Key Terms

amotivational syndrome   A condition characterized by a lack of ambition or desire to succeed, presumed to be the result of smoking marijuana.

anandamide   A neurotransmitter that occupies the same receptors in the brain as THC.

California Buyers Club   A buyers club in California for marijuana.

cannabinoids   A class of chemical compounds found in marijuana.

Cannabis indica   A kind of marijuana that originated in India.

Cannabis ruderalis   A kind of marijuana that originated in northern Europe and Eurasia.

Cannabis sativa   The most common form of the marijuana plant.

delta-9-tetrahydrocannabinol (THC)   The most psychoactive cannabinoid.

EMIT   A method of drug testing that tests for the presence of metabolites of drugs in the urine by measuring the response to antibodies to the drugs in question.

false negative   In the context of alcohol and other drug abuse, a report that a person has not used a drug when in fact they have.

false positive   In the context of alcohol and other drug abuse, a report that a person has used a drug when in fact they have not.

hashish   The resin of the marijuana plant.

hashishiyya   A group of fanatics who followed Sheik Hasan Ibn-Sabah and were responsible for political assassinations during the Middle Ages in various Arab countries.

hash oil A slang term for oil of cannabis, a liquid extracted from the marijuana plant.

hemp Cannabis, widely used to make clothing.

hemp oil Oil from the cannabis plant. Hemp oil is legal and reported to contain substances (essential fatty acids) that are important to maintaining health.

hemp seed Sterilized seeds from the cannabis plant; they are legal and approved for use in food in the United States.

The Mahabharta Epic Indian poem from 1300 B.C.E.

sinsemilla Marijuana from female plants that have not been fertilized. The name means "without seeds."

Thai sticks Bamboo shoots that have buds from the marijuana plant glued to them.

References

(1998, 21 February). Vraag een politieagent. *New Scientist,* 30–31.

Abel, E. I. (1980). *Marijuana: The first twelve thousand years.* New York: Plenum Press.

Adams, I. B., & Martin, B. J. (1996). Cannabis: Pharmacology and toxicology in animals and humans. *Addiction, 91,* 1585–1614.

Andreasson, S., Allebeck, P., Engstrom, A., & Rydberg, U. (1987). Cannabis and schizophrenia: A longitudinal study of Swedish conscripts. *Lancet, 2,* 1483–1486.

Anslinger, H., & Cooper, C. R. (1937). Marijuana: Assassin of youth. *American Magazine, 24,* 153.

Anslinger, H. J., & Tompkins, W. F. (1953). *The traffic in narcotics.* New York: Funk and Wagnalls.

Benedikt, R. A., Cristofaro, P., Mendelson, J. H., & Mello, N. K. (1986). Effects of acute marijuana smoking in post-menopausal women. *Psychopharmacology, 90,* 14–17.

Block, R. I., Erwin, W. J., Farinpour, R., & Braverman, K. (1998). Sedative, stimulant and other subjective effects of marijuana: Relationship to smoking techniques. *Pharmacology, Biochemistry and Behavior, 59,* 405–412.

Bowles, P. (1962). *A hundred camels in the courtyard.* San Francisco: City Lights Books.

Budney, A. J., Kandel, D. B., Cherek, D. R., Martin, B. R., Stephens, R. S., & Roffman, R. (1997). Marijuana use and dependence. *Drug and Alcohol Dependence, 45,* 1–11.

Cone, E. J., Johnson, R. E., Darwin, W. D., Yousernejad, D., Mell, L. D., Paul, B. D., & Mitchell, J. (1987). Passive inhalation of marijuana smoke: Urinalysis and room air levels of delta-9-tetrahydrocannabinol. *Journal of Analytical Toxicology, 11,* 89–96.

Conrad, C. (1997). *Hemp for health.* Rochester, VT: Healing Arts Press.

Costantino, A., Schwartz, R. H., & Kaplan, P. (1997). Hemp oil ingestion causes positive urine tests for delta 9 tetrahydrocannabinol carboxylic acid. *Journal of Analytical Toxicology, 21,* 482–486.

de Fonseca, F. R., Carrera, M. R., Navarro, M., Koob, G. F., & Weiss, F. (1997). Activation of coticolimbic-releasing factor in the limbic system during cannabis withdrawal. *Science, 276,* 250–254.

DeVane, W. (1994). New dawn of cannabinoid pharmacology. *Trends in Pharmaceutical Sciences, 15,* 40–41.

Felder, C. C., Briley, E. M., Axelrod, J., Simpson, J. T., Mackie, K., & Devane, W. A. (1993). Anandamide, an endogenous cannabimimetic eicosanoid binds to the cloned human cannabinoid receptor and stimulates receptor mediated signal transduction. *Proceedings of the National Academy of Sciences, 90,* 7656–7660.

Foltin, R. W., Brady, J. V., & Fishman, M. W. (1986). Behavioral analysis of marijuana effect on food intake in humans. *Pharmacology, Biochemistry and Behavior, 25,* 577–586.

Fortner, N., Fogerson, R., Lindman, D., Iversen, T., & Armbruster, D. (1997). Marijuana-positive urine test results from consumption of hemp seeds in food products. *Journal of Analytical Toxicology, 21,* 476–481.

Fried, P. A. (1995). Prenatal exposure to marijuana and tobacco during infancy, early, and middle childhood: Effects and an attempt at synthesis. *Archives of Toxicology-Supplement, 17,* 233–260.

Frost, H. (1987). How Carthage lost the sea. *Natural History, 96,* 67–68.

Gattey, C. N. (1986). *Excess in food, drink, and sex.* London: Harrap.

Gessa, G., Melis, M., Muntoni, A., & Diana, M. (1998). Cannabinoids activate mesolimbic dopamine neurons by an action on the cannabinoid CB1 receptors. *European Journal of Pharmacology, 341,* 39–44.

Gong, H., Fligiel, D. P., Tashkin, D. P., & Barbers, R. G. (1987). Tracheobronchial changes in habitual, heavy smokers of marijuana with and without tobacco. *American Review of Respiratory Diseases, 136,* 142–149.

Graceffo, T. J., & Robinson, J. K. (1998). Delta-9-tetrahydrocannabinol (THC) fails to stimulate consumption of highly palatable food in the rat. *Life Sciences, 62,* 85–88.

Grinspoon, L., & Bakalar, J. B. (1997). Marihuana. In J. H. Lowinson, P. Ruiz, R. B. Millman, & J. G. Langrod (Eds.), *Substance abuse: A comprehensive textbook* (pp. 199–206). Baltimore: Williams & Wilkins.

Hatch, E. E., & Bracken, M. B. (1986). Effect of marijuana use in pregnancy on fetal growth. *American Journal of Epidemiology, 124,* 986–994.

Huestis, M. A., Mitchell, J. M., & Cone, E. J. (1996). Urinary excretion profiles of 11-nor-9-carboxy-delta 9-tetrahydrocannabinol in humans after single smoked doses of marijuana. *Journal of Analytical Toxicology, 20,* 441–444.

Huestis, M., Sampson, A., Holicky, B., Henningfield, J., & Cone, E. (1992). Characterization of the absorption phase of marijuana smoking. *Clinical Pharmacology and Therapeutics, 52,* 31–41.

Inciardi, J. A. (1986). *The war on drugs: Heroin, cocaine, crime and public policy.* Palo Alto, CA: Mayfield.

Johansson, E., & Halldin, H. (1989). Urinary excretion half life of delta-9-tetrahydrocannabinol in heavy users after smoking. *Journal of Analytical Toxicology, 13,* 213–222.

Jones, R. T. (1980). Human effects: An overview. In R. C. Petersen (Ed.), *Marijuana research findings.* 1980 National Institute of Drug Abuse Monograph No. 31. Washington, DC: U.S. Department of Health and Human Services.

Jones, R. T., & Benowitz, N. L. (1976). The 30-day trip: Clinical studies of cannabis tolerance and dependence. In M. C. Brande & T. Szara (Eds.), *Pharmacology of marijuana* (pp. 627–642). New York: Raven Press.

Kaminski, N. E. (1996). Immune regulation by cannabinoid compounds through the inhibition of the cyclic AMP signaling cascade and altered gene expression. *Biochemical Pharmacology, 52,* 1133–1140.

Kirk, J. M., Doty, P., & deWit, H. (1998). Effects of expectancies on subjective responses to oral delta (9) -tetrahydrocannabinol. *Pharmacology, Biochemistry and Behavior, 59,* 287–293.

Kusinitz, M. (1987). *Drugs and the arts.* New York: Chelsea Press.

Linszen, D. H., Dingemans, P. M., & Lenior, M. E. (1994). Cannabis abuse and the course of recent-onset schizophrenic disorders. *Archives of General Psychiatry, 51,* 273–279.

Lukas, S. E., Mendelson, J. H., & Benedikt, R. (1997). Electroencephalographic correlates of marihuana-induced euphoria. *Drug and Alcohol Dependence, 37,* 131–140.

Mathew, R. J., Wilson, W. H., Humphreys, D. F., Lowe, J. V., & Wiethe, K. E. (1992). Changes in middle cerebral artery velocity after marijuana. *Biological Psychiatry, 32,* 164–169.

Mathias, R. (1996). Studies show cognitive impairments linger in heavy marijuana users. *NIDA Notes, 11,* 1,4.

Matsuda, L. A., Bonner, T. I., & Lolait, S. J. (1993). Localization of cannabinoid receptor mRNA in rat brain. *The Journal of Comparative Neurology, 327,* 535–550.

Matsuda, R., & Warren, R. (1993). Localization of cannabinoid receptor mRNA in rat brain. *Journal of Comparative Neurology, 327,* 535–550.

Meatherall, R., & Warren, R. (1993). High urinary cannabinoids from a hashish body packer. *Journal of Analytical Toxicology, 17,* 439–440.

Mirin, S. M., & Weiss, R. L. (1983). Substance abuse. In E. L. Bassok, S. C. Sclevonne, & A. J. Gelenberg (Eds.), *The practitioner's guide to psychoactive drugs* (2nd ed.). New York: Plenum Press.

Morningstar. (1985). Thandai and chilam: Traditional Hindu beliefs about the proper uses of cannabis. *Journal of Psychoactive Drugs, 17,* 141–165.

Musto, D. (1987). *The American disease: Origins of narcotic control.* New York: Oxford University Press.

Nahas, G. G., & Latour, C. (1992). The human toxicity of marijuana. *Medical Journal of Australia, 156,* 495–497.

National Institute on Drug Abuse. 1995. *Marijuana: Facts Parents Need to Know.* NIH Publication 95-4036.

Paria, B., Deutsch, D. D., & Key, S. K. (1996). The uterus is a potential site for anandamide synthesis and hydrolysis: Differential profiles of anandamide synthase and hydrolase activities in the mouse uterus during the periimplantation period. *Molecular Reproduction and Development, 45,* 183–192.

Pettit, D. A. D., Harrison, M. P., Olson, J. M., Spencer, R. H., & Cabral, G. A. (1998). Immunohistochemical localization of the neural cannabinoid receptor in rat brain. *Journal of Neuroscience Research, 51,* 391–402.

Rosenthal, F. (1971). *The herb: Hashish versus medieval Muslim society.* Leiden: E.J. Brill.

Rowen, D. W., Embrey, J. P., Moore, C. H., & Welch, S. P. (1998).

Antisense oligodeoxynucleotides to the kappa(1) receptor enhance delta(9) -THC-induced antinociceptive tolerance. *Pharmacology, Biochemistry and Behavior, 59,* 399–404.

Schlosser, E. (1994). Reefer madness. *Atlantic Monthly,* February 45–63.

Schmid, P. C. (1997). Changes in anandamide levels in mouse uterus are associated with uterine receptivity for embryo implantation. *Proceedings of the National Academy of Sciences, 94,* 4188–4192.

Schwartz, R. H., Gruenewald, P. J., Klitzner, M., & Fedio, P. (1989). Short-term memory impairment in cannabis-dependent adolescents. *American Journal of Diseases of Children, 143,* 1214–1219.

Shafer, R. P. 1972. Forward to *Marihuana: A Signal of Misunderstanding,* the official report of The National Commission on Marihuana and Drug Abuse. New York: The New American Library.

Sridhar, K. S., Raub, W. A., Weatherby, N. L., Metsch, L. R., Surratt, H. L., Inciardi, J. A., Duncan, R. C., Anwyl, R. S., & McCoy, C. B. (1994). Possible role of marijuana smoking as a carcinogen in the development of lung cancer at a young age. *Journal of Psychoactive Drugs, 26,* 285–288.

Stafford, P. (1992). *Psychedelics encyclopedia* (3rd ed.). Berkeley, CA: Ronin.

Struve, F. A., Patrick, G., Straumanis, J. J., Fitz-Gerald, M. J., & Manno, M. (1998). Possible EEG sequelae of very long duration marijuana use: Pilot findings from topographic quantatitive EEG analyses of subjects with 15–24 years of cumulative daily exposure to THC. *Clinical Electroencephalography, 29,* 31–36.

Sussman, S., Stacy, A. W., Dent, C. W., Simon, T. R., & Johnson, C. A. (1996). Marijuana use: Current issues and new research directions. *Journal of Drug Issues, 26,* 695–733.

Swan, N. (1994). A look at marijuana's harmful effects. *NIDA Notes: National Institute on Drug Abuse, 10,* 8–9.

Tanda, G., Pontieri, F. E., & DiChiara, G. D. (1997). Cannabinoid and heroin activation of mesolimbic dopamine transmission by a common mu-1 opioid receptor mechanism. *Science, 276,* 2048–2049.

Voth, E. A., & Schwartz, R. H. (1997). Medicinal applications of delta-9-tetrahydrocannabinol and marijuana. *Annals of Internal Medicine, 126,* 791–798.

Walton, R. P. (1938). *Marihuana: America's new drug problem.* Philadelphia: J. B. Lippincott.

Weisbeck, G. A., Schuckit, M. A., Kalmijn, J. A., Tipp, J. E., Bucholz, K. K., & Smith, T. L. (1996). An evaluation of the history of a marijuana withdrawal syndrome in a large population. *Addiction, 91,* 1469–1478.

Wilkins, D., Haughey, H., Cone, E., Huestis, M., Foltz, R., & Rollins, D. (1995). Quantitative analysis of THC 11-OH-THC and THCCOOH in human hair by negative ion chemical ionization mass spectrometry. *Journal of Analytic Toxicology, 19,* 483–491.

Wingert, W. E. (1997). Lowering cutoffs for initial and confirmation testing for cocaine and marijuana: Large-scale study of effects on the rates of drug-positive results. *Clinical Chemistry, 43,* 100–103.

Zacny, J., & Chait, l. (1989). Breathold duration and response to marijuana smoke. *Biochemistry and Behavior, 33,* 481–484.

Chapter Seven

Nicotine

Chapter Objectives

When you have finished studying this chapter, you should

1. Be able to trace the history of tobacco use from the time of Columbus to the present.
2. Be able to describe how the modern cigarette is designed to deliver nicotine.
3. Know how cigarettes, smokeless tobacco, and cigars differ.
4. Know the different trends of cigarette use for males and females.
5. Know how nicotine affects the body.
6. Know why nicotine is addicting.
7. Be able to discuss the rewarding effects of cigarette smoking.
8. Be able to list the three main ways in which cigarette smoking harms the body.
9. Know the role cigarette smoking plays in heart disease, COPD, and cancer.
10. Know how nicotine and cigarette smoking affect pregnancy and the developing fetus.
11. Be able to discuss the link between nicotine and psychological disorders.
12. Understand what the controversy over environmental tobacco smoke is all about.
13. Be able to discuss why addiction is not the only reason smoking is difficult to stop.
14. Be able to define nicotine replacement therapy.
15. Understand the role nicotine replacement therapy plays in smoking cessation.
16. Be able to list the health benefits of smoking cessation.

The General Court forbid any person to use tobacco publicly, on fine of 2 shillings 6 pence, or privately in his own dwelling, or dwelling of another, before strangers, and they also forbid two or more to use it in any place together.

Prince's Annals of New England, 1634
(Quoted in Lander, 1886)

A visitor from another planet would probably find it difficult to understand the popularity of tobacco. What pleasure, they might ask, can humans receive from inhaling the smoke of burning, dried leaves? Part of the answer, of course, is nicotine. Just as THC is the psychoactive product in marijuana, nicotine is the psychoactive chemical found in tobacco leaves. Nicotine use does not impair the ability to think, it doesn't cause hallucinations, or cause euphoria, and it doesn't affect gross motor behavior. Since the psychoactive effects are not obvious, nonsmokers might have the same questions as the visitors from another planet. Tobacco smoking is responsible for the death of millions of people worldwide every year. Nearly everyone who smokes knows it is harmful, and few can explain why they continue to smoke. An anonymous poem (undoubtedly written by a smoker) recognizes the paradox. It begins: "Tobacco is a filthy weed, I like it. It satisfies no human need, I like it." In this chapter we will explore why tobacco which seems to "satisfy no human need" is so popular.

History of Tobacco

When Christopher Columbus landed on the shores of San Salvador in the West Indies on 12 October 1492, the "Indians" presented him with gifts of fruit, other valuables, and some dried leaves. He was confused as to the purpose of the leaves, but saw that the Indians held them in high esteem. To avoid offending them, he ordered the gifts taken on board,

Sketch of a Mayan smoking what seems to be a cigar. The lack of ritual figures indicates that the cigar was in everyday use.

Although this picture was taken quite recently, the early European explorers probably saw exactly the same scene. Look at figure 8.1 for comparison.

but he threw away the leaves (Corti, 1931/1996). After a four-day trip in present-day Cuba, two men of Columbus's crew—Luis de Torres and Rodrigo de Jerez—were the first to witness the custom of smoking tobacco (Wilbert, 1987). Since then tobacco use has spread worldwide. No society that has adopted its use has ever given it up. Customs change and the way tobacco is used changes, but by means of a pipe, cigar, cigarette, snuff, a chaw in the jaw, or a dip in the lip, tobacco use remains with us.

How Tobacco Is Used

Various societies have developed many different means of absorbing nicotine from tobacco. In the colonies that became the United States, pipe smoking was the most popular. Later came chewing tobacco (now called smokeless tobacco), cigars and finally cigarettes. Each of these kinds of tobacco delivers nicotine to the blood stream. Cigarettes, as you will see, were the ultimate development.

The indigenous people of North and South America used pipes, cigars, cigarettes, snuff, and chewing tobacco (Heiman, 1960). Some societies licked a paste made of tobacco plants, others rubbed tobacco juice on the skin or into wounds. Some even used tobacco enemas as a cure for constipation or a treatment for worms. Drinking tobacco was popular. Tobacco leaves were steeped or boiled in water and the fluid was then drunk. Sometimes other plants were added and the concoction was consumed along with alcoholic beverages or hallucinogenic substances. Tobacco was used for social and religious occasions, to seal bargains, and in ceremonies to predict the future (Kiernan, 1991).

High doses were taken to induce a trance and for spiritual purposes such as consulting with the spirit gods. Some cultures gave young men such quantities of tobacco that they were brought to the brink of death and experienced comas and seizures (Wilbert, 1987). In present-day Afro-Caribbean and Brazilian cults, strong tobacco is taken during religious rituals. Tobacco has been grown for thousands of years in places like the state of Chiapas, Mexico.

In Europe, tobacco was first considered a medicine and was prescribed for many conditions, including intestinal problems (Goodman, 1993). One theory held that tobacco smoke blown into the rectum would revive a drowning victim. The transition from tobacco as medicine to tobacco as a recreational drug was swift. Even though the recreational use of tobacco has been condemned by legal, medical, and moral authorities since its introduction, use has flourished. From colonial days in the United States, tobacco has been a major crop, and it was one of the main sources of revenue for the Revolutionary Army. George Washington was a leading tobacco grower and one of the richest men in the fledgling country (Heiman, 1960). At one point 50 percent of all the British colonists gained their living from tobacco production. In 1775, tobacco exported from the American colonies totaled 55 million pounds.

Stop and Review

1. How was tobacco used by the indigenous people of the Americas?
2. What role did tobacco play during early years of this country?

History of Cigarettes

Cigarette smoking is a twentieth-century phenomenon (Burns, Garfinkel, & Samet, 1997). Until just after World War I, the most popular way to take tobacco was the cigar. In 1915, 6.5 billion cigars were produced; in 1980, 700 billion cigarettes were smoked. The change to cigarettes was partly due to the development of a milder form of tobacco and mechanical cigarette-rolling machines that greatly reduced the cost of the cigarette (Burns et al., 1997). Another reason was that clever advertising preyed upon fears of disease and dislike of foreigners to discredit the cigar, which was hand-rolled. The crowded conditions in the undeniably filthy slums where cigars typically were rolled were portrayed as breeding grounds of tuberculosis and worse.

The middle part of the century was the heyday of cigarette smoking in the United States. Tobacco companies gave away cigarettes on street corners and in college dormitories. Lucky Strike "patriotically" donated three packs of cigarettes apiece to the brave fighting men during World War II. In 1946, the makers of Camels reported that, according to their survey of 113,597 physicians, "more doctors smoke Camels than any other cigarette." The company did not report how many doctors didn't smoke at all. Until fairly recently, smoking was common in college classrooms, airplanes, offices, and restaurants. The changes have come about swiftly; in California smoking is even banned in bars and jails.

The cigarette is as perfect a drug delivery system as modern technology can provide. Nearly everything that can be done, has been done to make the modern cigarette "milder," meaning easier to inhale. There are several different kinds of tobacco, and several different means of curing them—yielding tobacco that is either mild or strong tasting and high or low in nicotine and tar. In addition, various additives are mixed with the tobacco to make it burn smoother and taste better. Cigarette paper is designed to burn slowly at an even temperature and not go out when the cigarette is put down. The vast majority of cigarettes sold today are filtered. The filter further controls the temperature and absorbs some of the nicotine. The tobacco used is freeze dried and "fluffed" so the cells of the leaf can absorb more additives.

Until 1994, the additives in cigarettes were considered trade secrets. Under pressure from the U.S. Food and Drug Administration, the ingredients were finally disclosed. The

Do you think that the increase in cigarette smoking in the United States in the fifties had anything to do with the free cigarettes that soldiers received during World War II?

According to a recent Nationwide survey:

MORE DOCTORS SMOKE CAMELS THAN ANY OTHER CIGARETTE

YOUR "T-ZONE" WILL TELL YOU...

T for Taste...
T for Throat...

that's your proving ground for any cigarette. See if Camels don't suit your "T-Zone" to a "T."

CAMELS

Physicians did smoke more when this ad first appeared than they do now, but the copy suggests that over 113,000 smoked.

manufacturers claim that these are added as flavoring and to reduce tar and nicotine, replace moisuture, add taste, and make the smoke smoother. Some of the ingredients are listed in table 7.1. More than 98 percent of the additives are considered safe when used as directed. Overall, the six major American cigarette companies put nearly 500 additives into their tobacco.

The tobacco industry has been accused of secretly growing high-nicotine tobacco to add to the cigarette. There is no doubt that the industry carefully monitors the amount of nicotine delivered. In fact, the tobacco used in low-tar, low-nicotine cigarettes is actually *higher* in nicotine than the tobacco in unfiltered cigarettes—the reduction in nicotine comes from the filter (Benowitz, 1986). The industry claims that nicotine is essential for "taste" and that growing the high-nicotine tobacco was an attempt to reduce costs. Regardless of the rationale, each puff of a cigarette (as determined by a standard smoking machine) delivers the same amount of nicotine. The problem is that people aren't machines and don't smoke like them.

If a smoker takes ten puffs from the cigarette and smokes regularly during the day, the smoker can maintain a very consistent level of nicotine with little effort or discomfort. The tar and nicotine content of cigarettes varies (hence the labels "light" and "ultralight"), but smokers compensate by varying the number of puffs, holding the smoke in their

TABLE 7.1 You Are What You Smoke
Some of the More Recognizable of the 499 Ingredients the Six Major American Cigarette Companies Add to Their Product. None of the Additives have been Proven Harmful in the Amounts Used.
Acetic acid (vinegar)
Allspice
Ammonia
Anise
Apple juice concentrate
Basil oil
Caffeine
Chocolate
Corn silk
Fig juice concentrate
Molasses
Pine needle oil
Rum
Spearmint oil
Vanilla
Wine and sherry
Yeast

Source: *Food and Drug Administration*

lungs, and smoking the cigarette farther down (Woodman, Newman, & Pavia, 1987). As a result nearly every smoker obtains roughly 1 milligram of nicotine from each cigarette.

Clove cigarettes contain 60 percent strong tobacco and 40 percent ground cloves, which contain **eugenol.** Eugenol is similar to the menthol in mentholated cigarettes—it anesthetizes the back of the throat, making it easier to inhale the smoke. Clove cigarettes can also trigger a spasm of the bronchial tubes and have been linked to several deaths. As a result they are banned in several states.

Smokeless Tobacco

Smokeless tobacco includes chewing tobacco, moist snuff, and pouch tobacco. Chewing tobacco was popular in the United States until the advent of cigarettes. In the rural areas and particularly in the West, chewing tobacco, spitting, and spittoons were so common that they were the source of endless comment by visitors (Kiernan, 1991). Its unsanitary and unaesthetic nature led to the decline of spitting.

Moist snuff and pouch tobacco are still widely used, however. With both, a small amount of tobacco is placed between the cheek and gum. Absorption occurs through the mucous lining of the mouth. Blood levels of nicotine can reach the same peak as for cigarette smokers, although the rate of absorption is much slower for smokeless tobacco. Blood nicotine levels of smokers, chewers, and oral snuff users show similar changes during the day, with peak nicotine levels being reached about noon. Levels stay high until about midnight and are lowest in the early morning (Hatsukami, Nelson, & Jenson, 1991). The nicotine content of smokeless tobacco varies. The best-selling moist snuff contains 3.35 percent nicotine, while other brands contain slightly less. Chewing tobacco typically contains less than 1 percent nicotine.

Advertisements for smokeless tobacco feature athletes and run in adventure and sport magazines that appeal to adolescents. Not surprisingly, therefore, smokeless tobacco use is most common among males 18 to 30 years old. It is most prevalent in the South and least common in the Northeast. Persons of lower socioeconomic status are more likely to use it. Young women, African Americans, and Asian Americans are rarely users, but it is very common among Native Americans (Glover & Glover, 1992). Users typically "graduate" to cigarette use; a switch in the opposite direction is rarely reported (Hatsukami et al., 1991).

Cigars

The increase in cigar smoking has caught nearly everyone by surprise. From 1964 until 1993, cigar consumption declined by 66 percent in the United States. Between 1993 and 1997 it increased 50 percent. In 1997, more than 5 billion cigars were consumed in the U.S. (Gerlach, et al, 1998). Media spending on cigar advertising has increased more than four times since 1994 and a one time full color full page advertisement in the most popular magazine devoted to cigars was $18,360 in December 1996 (Slade, 1998). Cigars are advertised as lavish, but affordable luxuries. Until recently most people associated cigar smoking with older males. The advertisements attempt to legitimize new users and new settings for cigars. Many advertisements are aimed at a target

"ANOTHER CIVIL-SERVICE OUTRAGE."
Less Smoke and More Fire.

To counteract advertising, the National Cancer Institute provides these posters that emphasize the short-term effects of using snuff and the long-term dangers.

group of young, affluent males. Others encourage women to smoke (Slade, 1998).

Cigar-centered evenings of dining and entertainment are becoming popular. Sometimes the events are linked to charities so those attending can feel that they are participating in a good cause. Social clubs organized around cigars have appeared on many college campuses. Cigar clubs and cigar bars are appearing in many communities. In a New York city cigar club, patrons can attend a cigar school to learn the ritual of smoking (Slade, 1998).

Cigars differ from cigarettes in several ways. Cigar tobacco is aged differently and allowed to ferment for a year or more. Unlike cigarettes, no flavoring is added to cigars, the taste and aroma are the result of the fermentation process (Hoffman & Hoffman, 1998). The nicotine in cigar smoke is "free" meaning that it is not bound to other compounds and the smoke has a high ph meaning that it is basic. In cigarettes, the nicotine is combined with compounds that render it acidic, as is the smoke. The difference is that nicotine in cigar smoke can be absorbed in the mouth. Cigarette smoke must be inhaled (Gerlach, et al, 1998).

Despite these differences, cigar smoke contains the same toxic and carcinogenic compounds as cigarette smoke and animal studies indicate that the tar in cigar smoke is as carcinogenic as the tar in cigarette smoke. While cigar smokers have a lower risk of some forms of cancer and of chronic obstructive pulmonary disease, the difference is due primarily to the pattern of use. Cigar smokers do not smoke as frequently as cigarette smokers and they are less likely to inhale. Those who are exsmokers of cigarettes or who are cigar and cigarette smokers, usually do inhale and their risk is similar to cigarette smokers (Shanks & Burns, 1998). Cigar smokers are at equal risk as cigarette smokers for cancer of the mouth and cancer of the esophagus (Burns, 1998). Considering mortality from all smoking related conditions, cigarette smokers run the greatest risk, with combined cigarette and cigar smokers close behind. Those who smoke only cigars are at greater risk than nonsmokers but less than the other two groups (Shanks & Burns, 1998).

Because cigars are larger than cigarettes, they are smoked for a longer period of time. A single cigar produces far more environmental tobacco smoke than does a single cigarette. Measures of carbon monoxide (a component of cigar and cigarette smoke) at a cigar party showed carbon monoxide levels comparable to those on a crowded freeway. Smoke from a single cigar smoked in a typical home can require 5 hours to dissipate exposing everyone present to known carcinogens (Repace, Ott, & Klepeis, 1998).

Stop and Review

1. List the ways that cigarettes have been designed to increase the absorption of nicotine in the lungs.
2. How does absorption of nicotine from smokeless tobacco and from cigars differ from absorption from cigarettes?

Trends in Cigarette Use

Cigarette prices affect smoking rates. As prices increase, smoking rates decrease (Cavin & Pierce, 1996). The tobacco industry has responded to these findings by introducing **generic,** or off-brand, cigarettes and offering what are called **"branded discounts."** Discount premium brands and generics account for about one-third of the market. Adults and adolescents who switch to the cheaper brands tend to be lower-income, non-Hispanic whites and rural residents. Heavy smokers are also likely to smoke generics. Women (especially those over 45) tend to purchase generics more than men do. Adolescents remain brand conscious—Marlboro and Camels are the preferred brand of more than three-quarters of young smokers (Cavin & Pierce, 1996).

Cigarette smoking is related to both gender and occupational status. Women who smoke are workers in transportation, management, the crafts, the service industry, administration, and sales; the women least likely to smoke are professionals. Males are most likely to be transportation workers, unemployed, laborers, craft workers, service workers, and technicians; professionals again are the least likely to smoke. Other women with high rates of smoking include waitresses, telephone operators, and cosmetologists. For men, specific occupations with high rates of smokers were water-transportation workers, roofers, foresters, and loggers. Teachers were among the least likely of any group to smoke (Leigh, 1996). Findings like these might help target specific groups for intensive intervention. As you can see in

TABLE 7.2 Percentage of Those Who Have Used Cigarettes in the Past Month, by Gender and Age

Age	Males	Females
12–17	17.8	18.7
18–25	43.2	33.3
26–34	38.5	31.5
35 +	28.8	25.4

Of those that reported smoking within the last month, 47 percent smoke a pack or more a day.

Source: *National Household Survey on Drug Abuse, 1997.*

table 7.2, young females are as likely to be smokers as young males, although male smokers still outnumber female smokers in all other age groups (USDHHS, 1997).

Despite the very clear evidence (to be discussed below) that nicotine is addicting, not everyone seems to be vulnerable. One study showed that about 20 percent of all smokers do not smoke daily (Gilpin, Cavin, & Pierce, 1997), and that this occasional smoking is a stable pattern for long periods. In addition, more than a third of smokers who used to smoke daily report smoking less than every other day, consuming about four or five cigarettes per smoking day. Two characteristics mark occasional smokers—they are far more likely to have gone to college, and nearly half began smoking after age 20. In contrast, regular smokers tend to be less well educated and begin smoking as early as 12 or 13. Occasional smokers typically have no plans to quit, but they are sure that they could quit if they wanted to. They don't perceive themselves as addicted, don't worry about the cost, and are less likely to smoke in their homes (Gilpin et al., 1997). What prevents these smokers from smoking more, and what keeps them smoking as little as they do?

Pharmacology of Nicotine

Nicotine is a toxic substance widely used as an insecticide. Fatalities have been reported after as little as 40 milligrams taken orally (Leiken & Paloucek, 1995). Cigarettes contain 10 to 25 milligrams of nicotine, but most of the nicotine in a cigarette is not absorbed. Measured in terms of blood level, fatalities are found with about 5 milligrams/milliliter. One cigarette results in a nicotine level of about .05 milligrams/milliliter (Leiken & Paloucek, 1995). Overdoses result in seizures, and death is by cardiac arrest and respiratory failure. Toxic but nonfatal doses are associated with sweating, nausea, and tremors (Carvey, 1998).

Absorption and Metabolism of Nicotine

Nicotine is rapidly absorbed from the lungs, mucous membranes, and gastrointestinal tract. In the lungs, nicotine is absorbed from the droplets of tar in cigarette smoke. The curing process used in the United States changes nicotine ions, typically basic, to an acidic form (Schmitz, Schneider, & Jarvik, 1997). The acidic form is not readily absorbed in the mouth, so the smoke must be drawn into the lungs for absorption to take place. Cigars, pipe tobacco, and some European cigarettes deliver the nicotine in its basic form so that inhalation is not necessary. Smokeless tobacco is likewise alkaline, and hence nicotine is readily absorbed in the mouth (Schmitz et al., 1997).

Behavioral Effects of Smoking

When inhaled, nicotine reaches the brain within ten seconds. Nicotine is an agonist for **acetylcholine** in the neuromuscular junction, which is the reason that overdose is associated with seizures. Nicotine also increases heart muscle tone through its effect on the acetylcholine receptor and increases heart rate because it releases **epinephrine** through the sympathetic nervous system. It directly stimulates the **chemical trigger zone** in the medulla to produce nausea and vomiting. The increase in muscle tone and the release of epinephrine lead to an increased metabolic rate (Carvey, 1998). Other effects include increased blood pressure, constriction of peripheral blood vessels, and changes in levels of hormones, including those associated with stress (Schmitz et al., 1997).

Metabolism of nicotine occurs primarily in the liver. The metabolite is **cotinine.** The half-life of nicotine is approximately two hours, but cotinine has a half-life of twenty hours and can be detected in the urine for several days (Gourlay, Benowitz, Forbes, & McNeill, 1997). Any exposure to nicotine results in a positive value for cotinine. Studies have shown that levels of this metabolite are four times higher among young children living with smokers than in children who do not live with smokers. The presence of cotinine can also be used to identify smokers who do not wish to reveal their habit. Cotinine levels can be used to verify non-smoking status for life insurance applications and employment. It is also a useful means of identifying those who relapse after smoking cessation programs (Gourlay et al., 1997).

The average smoker adjusts his or her intake of cigarette smoke to maintain a relatively constant level of nicotine in the bloodstream. Most smokers increase their rate of smoking during the day to ensure that nicotine levels build up by nighttime. This buildup is enough to keep the smoker's level of nicotine above zero during a night's sleep. It also means that the regular cigarette smoker is exposed to nicotine twenty-four hours a day (Benowitz, 1996). The average smoker's nicotine level is lowest upon awakening, and the first cigarette of the morning is usually smoked as soon as possible. In table 7.3 you should note that smoking within five minutes of awakening receives as many points toward dependence as any other indicator. For most smokers, the first cigarette of the day also produces stronger subjective

TABLE 7.3 Are You a Nicotine Addict?	
The Fagerstrom Test for Nicotine Dependence	**Points**
1. How soon after you wake up do you smoke your first cigarette?	3
Within 5 minutes	2
6–30 minutes	2
31–60 minutes	1
More than 60 minutes	0
2. Do you find it difficult to refrain from smoking in places where it is forbidden (e.g., in church, at the library, in the cinema)?	
Yes	1
No	0
3. Which cigarette would you hate most to give up?	
The first one in the morning	1
All others	0
4. How many cigarettes do you smoke a day?	
10 or less	0
11–20	1
21–30	2
31 or more	3
5. Do you smoke more frequently during the first hours after waking than during the rest of the day?	
Yes	1
No	2
6. Do you smoke if you are so ill that you are in bed most of the day?	
Yes	1
No	0

Scores over three indicate some kind of dependence.

Source: *Faberstrom & Schneider,* 1989.

and cardiovascular effects, compared with cigarettes later in the day (Schmitz et al., 1997).

Stop and Review

1. What are the primary effects of nicotine on the body?
3. How do smokers adjust their intake to the known characteristics of the absorption and metabolism of nicotine?

Nicotine Dependence and Withdrawal

Nicotine increases dopamine levels in the reward pathway of the **nucleus accumbens,** placing it in the same category as drugs such as cocaine, heroin, and alcohol. Tolerance certainly occurs to most of the effects of nicotine, especially the cardiovascular and behavioral effects. Indications of physical withdrawal begin within twenty-four hours after the last cigarette and include depressed mood, insomnia, anxiety, difficulty concentrating, and restlessness. Impaired cognitive functioning and decreased heart rate are also seen. These symptoms can be relieved by nicotine replacement therapy such as nicotine gum (Schmitz et al., 1997).

TABLE 7.4 Symptoms of Nicotine Withdrawal

Irritability	Difficulty concentrating	Sleep disturbances
Anxiety	Increased peripheral circulation	Sweating
Depression	Craving for cigarettes	Constipation
Drowsiness	Weight gain	Hunger
Restlessness	Decrease in heart rate	Headaches

Adapted from *Schmitz et al, 1997.*

Withdrawal and craving are more severe for some people than for others, and theories have been developed that account for this. It might be that some people are less sensitive to the unpleasant effects of nicotine and thus they can smoke more and develop stronger dependence. Another theory suggests that some people are more sensitive to both the rewarding and the unpleasant effects (Schmitz et al., 1997). Both theories can be supported by experimental evidence, so the jury is still out, but it is clear that nicotine leads to physical tolerance and physical dependence as indicated by physical withdrawal signs. Table 7.4 lists some of the recognized withdrawal symptoms.

The brain is the primary site for the rewarding action of nicotine. Nicotine reaches the brain within ten seconds after a cigarette is inhaled. There are specific nicotinic cholinergic receptors in the brain. Upon prolonged exposure, the receptors become desensitized to nicotine and **up regulation** of the postsynaptic receptors occurs, probably in order to compensate for the desensitization. Nicotinic receptors are found in the limbic system and in the thalmus and cerebral cortex. The phenomenon of tolerance might be explained in part by the action of nicotinic receptors on glutamate neurotransmission. **Glutamate,** the primary excitatory neurotransmitter in the brain, is also believed to be involved in the development of tolerance to alcohol (Schmitz et al., 1997).

Behavioral Consequences of Smoking

Smokers typically report that smoking helps them concentrate. Injections of nicotine in animals result in improved learning. It is difficult to demonstrate enhanced performance in humans who are nonsmokers, but nicotine clearly improves function in smokers after they have been deprived of nicotine (Henningfield & Schuh, 1996). Smokers also reported increases in positive mood states after smoking. As with enhanced cognitive performance, this improvement seems due to the fact that nicotine deprivation produces negative mood states—in contrast, mood feels positive when nicotine is restored. Ironically, smokers also report that smoking calms them in stressful situations (Henningfield & Schuh, 1996).

Nicotine reduces hunger, and cigarette smokers typically weigh six to ten pounds less than nonsmokers. Smokers usually gain weight when they stop smoking. Smokers

trying to stop typically report increased hunger and eating, but these symptoms seem to decline with length of abstinence. The weight gain by smokers who have quit is difficult to prevent and is often viewed as a reason for relapse. Smoking cessation programs have been largely unsuccessful in preventing weight gain, although the reasons are not clear (Schmitz et al., 1997).

The rewarding effects of nicotine are readily conditioned to environmental cues. Smokers who typically smoked after a meal or while drinking coffee or alcohol typically report craving during these times when they are trying to stop. Being around other smokers, smelling the smoke, and seeing others smoking are also powerful cues that result in craving. One goal of smoking cessation programs is to break the association between certain activities and smoking (Schmitz et al., 1997). From a vast number of psychological experiments we know that if the stimuli that cause craving are presented often enough, their strength diminishes (assuming, of course, that the smoker does not relapse).

Harmful Effects of Tobacco Use

Cigarettes, smokeless tobacco, pipes, and cigars are all nicotine delivery systems. But the effects of nicotine are not the only problems associated with tobacco use. Smoke consists of the burned residue of organic matter and the four hundred chemicals that are added to the cigarette. Pipes, cigars, and cigarettes also increase the amounts of carbon dioxide, carbon monoxide, and tars, which contain carcinogens. Smokeless tobacco is treated with numerous chemicals, and these are constantly in contact with the mucous membranes of the mouth (Harris, 1996). Figure 7.1 shows the chances of dying from a smoking-related illness. In all, tobacco use is responsible for more than 430,000 deaths each year and the cost of illnesses related to tobacco use is staggering. Let's see how this damage occurs.

Smoking and Cancer

Lung cancer used to be extremely rare—it is now the leading cause of death by cancer for both men and women. Smoking is responsible for 95 percent of all lung cancers and plays a role in the development of cancer in just about every other part of the body as well (Greenwald, 1997). To-

The Economic Cost of Smoking versus the Rights of Smokers

Many smokers maintain that because they know the risks involved in smoking and still choose to smoke, they are not "addicted" or pawns of the tobacco industry. They claim that they are harming only themselves and that the government has no more right to interfere with their smoking behavior than it has to restrict fats in their diet or even prevent people from drinking themselves to death. However, as you can see below, society pays a tremendous cost for smoking, and it is not limited to treating diseases caused directly by cancer. The federal government and the individual states have sued the tobacco companies to recover some of the costs to society incurred by smokers.

Should society restrict smoking due to the cost? Should smokers pay a premium to continue to smoke (beyond the taxes on cigarettes)? Will cigarettes ever be declared illegal?

What do you think?

Reason	Cost
Excess medical costs incurred by smokers	$6,000 lifetime
Financial cost of smoking	$1,000 a year
Excess work absence	6.5 days/year
Excess visits to physicians	6 times/year
Excess visits to physicians by dependents	4 times/year
Lost productivity due to smoking	$47 billion/year
Lost productivity due to passive smoking	$8.6 billion/year
Fires caused by smoking	$552 million/year
Deaths due to fires caused by smoking	2300 people/year
Injuries due to fires caused by smoking	5000 people/year

Source: *Data from McKenzie, et al, 1994.*

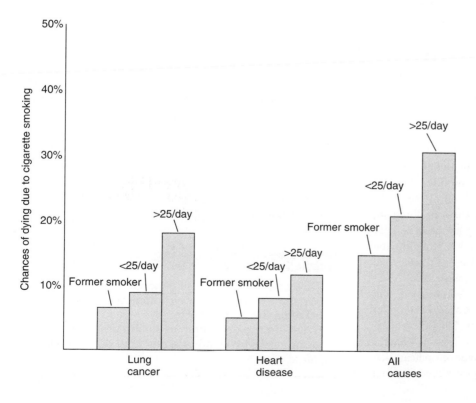

FIGURE 7.1

Chances of dying of a smoking-related illness by the age of 85. Remember that these are excess deaths that would not have happened if the person was a nonsmoker.

bacco use is responsible for 93 percent of oral cancers, 80 percent of cancers of the esophagus, 30 percent of cervical cancers, and 14 percent of all leukemias. When increased rates for bladder, pancreas, and kidney cancer are included, tobacco use is responsible for more than 30 percent of all cancer deaths (Greenwald, 1997). Those who drink and smoke (and most smokers do drink) are at even greater risk, especially for cancers of the mouth, esophagus, small intestine, and pancreas (Morse et al., 1996; Zhang et al., 1996; Muscat, Stellman, Hoffman, & Wynder, 1997; Wu, Yu, & Mack, 1997).

Another way of looking at the relationship between cancer and smoking is to examine **relative risk ratios,** which compare the increased risk of various conditions for different groups. For example, according to one study, the relative risk ratio for lung cancer is 23.2 for males and 12.8 for females. This means that, compared to people who have never smoked, male smokers have 23 times the chance of dying of lung cancer and women smokers have almost 13 times the chance (Greenwald, 1997). Male smokers are 3.5 times as likely to die of all cancers, and female smokers are 2.6 times as likely (Greenwald, 1997). The lower percentages of women who develop cancer is not due to some protective factor, but instead are most likely due to the fact that women start smoking later than men.

The **tars** in tobacco smoke carry at least forty known or suspected carcinogens (Harris, 1996). The carcinogens are carried in the bloodstream from the lungs to all other parts of the body. Chemicals thought to be particularly carcinogenic are **nitrosamines, formaldehyde,** and **benzene** (Harris, 1996). One cigarette is not going to increase cancer rates; it takes several decades of smoking before cancer rates start to increase. Furthermore, not every smoker gets cancer. Just why long exposure is necessary and why only some people get cancer is still an open question. Diet, genetics, and the environment probably play important roles.

Smoking and the Cardiovascular System

In addition to causing cancer, smoking increases the rates of many types of heart disease. Smoking increases heart rate and the volume of blood the heart pumps. Over time this strains the heart, and cardiac output begins to decline. Cigarette smoke contains **carbon monoxide.** Carbon monoxide binds with hemoglobin, the portion of the blood responsible for carrying oxygen to the tissues. In doing so, it displaces oxygen, and smokers have only about 85 percent of normal oxygen-carrying capacity, further straining the heart (USDHHS, 1988). Nicotine increases LDL, the bad cholesterol, and decreases HDL, the good cholesterol (Harris, 1996). Nicotine speeds the formation of blood clots, and it can trigger cardiac arrythmias in some people. No wonder smoking-related heart diseases kill nearly 200,000 Americans every year (Bartecchi, MacKenzie, & Schrier, 1994).

Men are more likely than women to develop heart disease, but women who take oral contraceptives are at special risk. The risk of one kind of heart disease, myocardial infarct, is ten times greater for women who smoke and take the pill compared to women who do neither. The woman who is a pack-a-day smoker has four times the risk of developing a stroke, especially if she is over 35 (Barrett et al., 1994). The increasing frequency of strokes, heart attacks, and cancer in women smokers makes it clear: smoke like a man, die like a man.

Smoking and Chronic Obstructive Pulmonary Disease

Chronic obstructive pulmonary disease (COPD) is a combination of **chronic bronchitis** and **emphysema** that is seen almost exclusively in smokers. More than 90 percent of all cases of COPD can be attributed to smoking, and COPD kills more than 60,000 people a year (Thun et al., 1997). Emphysema decreases the ability of the air sacs in the lungs to hold oxygen. The chest cavity expands and the diaphragm stretches, with the result that each breath becomes shorter and shallower. The concentration of oxygen in the blood decreases, and the heart must beat faster and faster to get less and less oxygen to the rest of the body.

The expanded chest cavity and weakened diaphragm mean that the person with COPD cannot let all the air out of their lungs. As a result, the lungs fill with mucus and breathing becomes even more difficult. Try taking the deepest breath possible, and then let out as little air as you can. Your rate of breathing will increase. Now try to cough without letting out air. The experience that you are having is even worse in the person with COPD. After all, you can breathe normally when this becomes uncomfortable, the COPD sufferer cannot—ever.

The mucus collects in the lungs because the **cilia,** or hairlike cells, that normally protect the lung from dust are damaged by cigarette smoke. The irritation of the smoke itself causes more mucus to be formed. The result is chronic bronchitis and a hacking cough that can never clear the lungs. The person with COPD usually has to breathe pure oxygen. You have seen people with a container of oxygen, a mask strapped over their nose and mouth, or breathing tubes in their nostrils. More than 90 percent of them have been smokers. Sadly, many still are. The COPD sufferer dies as a result of pneumonia, as a result of a heart attack brought on by the strain, or from suffocation. Figure 7.2 depicts some of these damaging effects of smoking.

Stop and Review

1. How does nicotine cause dependence?
2. What are some of the psychological effects of nicotine that make it attractive?
3. What are the three primary health problems associated with cigarettes, and how does smoking cause them?

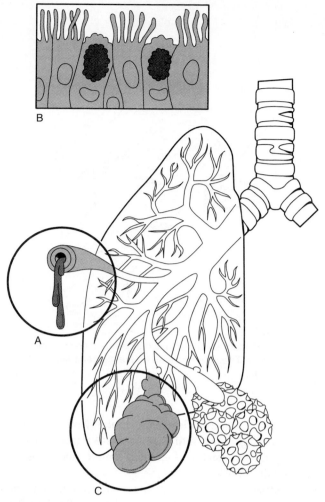

FIGURE 7.2

Effects of smoking: (A) airways are narrowed and production of mucus that leads to smoker's cough is increased; (B) cilia are killed and the ability to clear the lungs of mucus and other secretions is impaired; (C) inflammatory cells increase and these release a substance that impairs the lung's ability to expand and contract, leading to emphysema.

Smoking and Pregnancy

Smoking has a negative impact on various aspects of conception and pregnancy. In men, smoking is associated with decreased sperm motility and increased impotence (Harris, 1996). In pregnant women, smoking is associated with an increased risk of spontaneous abortion, premature birth, and abnormalities of fetal growth. Taken together, women who smoke are one and a half times more likely to experience loss of the fetus. Smoking is also thought to be responsible for 15 percent of all premature births (Andres & Larrabee, 1996). Babies born to women who smoke tend to be smaller, and smoking is estimated to be responsible for 20 to 30 percent of all low-birth-weight babies.

The two primary culprits for these fetal effects are nicotine and carbon monoxide. Nicotine crosses the placenta, and the level found in the fetus is higher than in the mother. Nicotine decreases the blood flow from the uterus, alters the blood flow in the umbilical arteries, and reduces the oxygen supply to the fetus (Andres & Larrabee, 1996). Carbon monoxide, as you read earlier, binds to hemoglobin. It crosses the placenta rapidly, and levels of carbon monoxide are about 15 percent higher in the fetus than in the mother. The result is a decreased oxygen supply to the fetus (Andres & Larrabee, 1996). Most studies have found dose-related effects, meaning that fetuses whose mothers smoke the most have the most likelihood of problems. Dose-related effects are strong indicators that smoking, and not some other co-factor, is the actual cause of the problems.

Another indicator that smoking is the cause of fetal harm and deaths is that mothers who stop smoking during pregnancy have a lower rate of fetal difficulties (Andres & Larrabee, 1996). Unfortunately, women who smoked before pregnancy and stop until the baby is born are very likely to be smoking again within a year. One study showed that the relapse rate was nearly two-thirds (Mullen, Richardson, Quinn, & Ershoff, 1997). As you might expect, relapse rates increase if the husband and friends remain smokers. Of course, you don't have to be a smoker to be exposed to cigarette smoke. Later you will read about environmental tobacco smoke (ETS) and its effects on young children. The studies of ETS on fetal growth are not conclusive. Some have found decreased body weight and other problems, but other studies have not. It appears that the risk is relatively small (Andres & Larrabee, 1996; Witorsch & Witorsch, 1996 [funded in part by Phillip Morris]).

Babies born to mothers who smoke (and continue to smoke) are more likely to experience sudden infant death syndrome (SIDS), a poorly understood condition in which the baby dies suddenly in its sleep with no prior indication of any health problems (Golding, 1986). Some babies born to mothers who smoke show difficulties in thinking and might have lower IQ scores as children. In addition, the mother's smoking during and after pregnancy is associated with the child's increased risk of allergies, impaired lung function, mental retardation, and leukemia (Martinez, Wright, & Taussig, 1994). Fathers are also culprits. Paternal smoking has been associated with many of the same conditions that occur when the mother smokes (Martinez et al., 1994).

Smoking and Psychiatric Disorders

A substantial number of those who smoke have psychological problems, including attention deficit disorder, anxiety disorders, anorexia/bulimia, and especially depression (Pomerleau, 1997). It seems that individuals with psychological problems find it more difficult to quit. And there is some evidence that smokers at risk for depression are more likely to become depressed after they stop smoking. The relationship between smoking and depression is particularly strong for women. Adolescents seem at risk as well; regular adolescent smokers are twice as likely as occasional smokers to report high levels of depression and anxiety (Patton et al., 1996).

Smoking and alcohol use and abuse are closely related. Overall, 61 percent of smokers drink at least occasionally (within the last month), compared to only 45 percent of nonsmokers. Nearly 20 percent of heavy smokers are alcohol abusers, and 80 percent of alcohol abusers in treatment are smokers (Hughes, 1996). Smokers who are alcohol abusers are far less likely to quit smoking, and treatment for alcohol abuse greatly increases the likelihood of smoking cessation. In fact, one study showed that successful treatment for alcohol abuse was associated with a threefold increase in smoking cessation (Breslau, Peterson, Schultz, Andreski, & Chilcoat, 1996).

The most severe form of mental illness is schizophrenia. This disorder is characterized by hallucinations, delusions, and thought disturbances. Schizophrenics are at risk to use and abuse many drugs, including alcohol, but the relationship between the disorder and nicotine seems particularly important (Taiminen et al., 1998). Studies have shown that schizophrenics might self-medicate themselves and that nicotine might somehow reduce the severity of their symptoms (Taiminen et al., 1998). The relationship between nicotine and schizophrenia is far from clear, but dopamine plays a role in the expression of schizophrenia and nicotine might alter dopamine levels in a way that schizophrenics find helpful (Le Hourzek, 1998).

The idea that some people with psychological problems might smoke as a form of self-medication is intriguing. Nicotine enhances activity in parts of the brain thought to be associated with conditions such as obsessive compulsive disorder, depression, and schizophrenia. Nicotine might also inhibit pain (Jamner, Dirdler, Shapiro, & Jarvik, 1998). Characteristics of depression include low self-esteem and a feeling of failure. People with a history of depression and a number of failed attempts to stop smoking seem to have more severe depressive symptoms than others who either have not tried to quit or who were successful (Borelli et al., 1996).

Environmental Tobacco Smoke

To most nonsmokers, tobacco smoke is offensive. King James I of England was particularly eloquent about the subject when he wrote: "A custome loathsome to the eye, harmful to the nose, harmful to the brain, dangerous to the lungs, and in the black, stinking fume thereof, nearest resembling the horrible Stygian smoke of the pit that is bottomless" (quoted in Corti, 1931/1996). Even the king of England could do little about it, however, and until recently, nonroyal nonsmokers have been in the same boat (or pit). Within the last few years, however, enough evidence has accumulated to label secondhand smoke an environmental pollutant (Maskin, Connolly, & Noonan, 1993). The term *secondhand smoke* is familiar but somewhat inaccurate. The more correct term is **environmental tobacco smoke (ETS).** The difference is that the word *secondhand* implies that this smoke is somehow less potent than inhaled smoke. *ETS* refers to

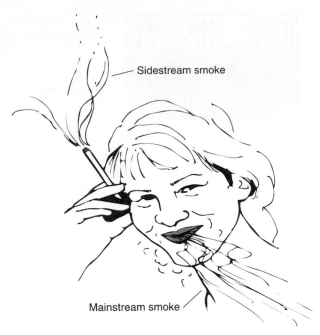

FIGURE 8.6
Exhaled mainstream smoke is less dangerous than sidestream smoke because it has been filtered by the cigarette filter and the smoker's lungs.

three kinds of smoke: **sidestream smoke** (from the burning end of the cigarette), **mainstream smoke** (the smoke inhaled by the smoker), and **exhaled smoke** (the smoke exhaled by the smoker).

Sidestream smoke contains more carcinogens than mainstream smoke, because it is not filtered (fig. 7.3). Nine out of ten Americans have positive levels of cotinine, meaning that they have been exposed to environmental tobacco smoke (Centers for Disease Control and Prevention, 1996). Cotinine levels of nonsmokers who live with active smokers are simlar to those found in light smokers. "Passive smoking" (inhalation of ETS) is estimated to cause more deaths per year than any other environmental pollutant. Specific health problems associated with environmental tobacco smoke include lung problems, cardiovascular problems, and effects on children living with smokers (USDHHS, 1993).

The Environmental Protection Agency published a report in 1993 and drew the following conclusions. ETS causes lung cancer and is responsible for approximately 3,000 lung cancer deaths annually in the U.S. in otherwise healthy nonsmokers. ETS causes reduced lung function as well as increased coughing, phlegm production, and chest discomfort. In the U.S., as many as 300,000 cases of respiratory infection in infants and young children up to 18 months can be traced to ETS. In addition, ETS has been causally linked to an increase in frequency and severity of asthma attacks in children affecting as many as 1,000,000 asthmatic children. Finally, ETS is a risk factor for asthma in children who had not previously displayed symptoms (Environmental Protection Agency, 1993). These findings are particularly troublesome in light of research indicating that half of all children have at least one parent who smokes (Huang, et al. 1998).

The evidence for a link between ETS and heart disease is not as clear, but studies have shown that exposure to ETS results in faster clotting and a decrease in the oxygen supply to the heart. The increased rate of clotting can lead to stroke as well as hardening of the arteries. A decrease in the oxygen supply can lead to damage to the muscles of the heart (Glantz & Parmley, 1995). Combining all of the risks, ETS may be responsible for as many as 50,000 deaths a year in the United States (Wells, 1994).

Children of parents who smoke have more respiratory infections and show reduced lung function as they mature. As many as 300,000 cases of bronchitis and pneumonia can be attributed to ETS. ETS increases the risk of middle-ear infection in children. Asthma has become more common, and it appears that ETS can aggravate its severity and even cause asthma in otherwise healthy children (USDHHS, 1993). The health effects of ETS have been the basis for custody disputes in which one parent (a nonsmoker) has claimed that the other (a smoker) is harming the child.

Treatment for Nicotine Dependence

The fact that nicotine is addicting is one reason smoking is hard to give up. Smokers also enjoy sensorimotor aspects of smoking—lighting the cigarette, holding the cigarette, see-

ing and smelling the cigarette smoke. Smokers are reinforced by every puff they take, and a pack-a-day smoker gets several hundred reinforcements a day. All of these factors and others mean that the relapse rate is high and that some smokers cannot quit even if they are dying of a smoking-related illness. **Nicotine replacement therapy** has been developed to help the smoker separate the various factors that make stopping so difficult. The concept is to prevent withdrawal while breaking the habit of smoking itself. Later, then, nicotine withdrawal should be less likely to precipitate relapse.

Nicotine Replacement Therapy

The first form of nicotine replacement therapy was **nicotine polacrilex,** which was introduced in 1984 (Schmitz et al., 1997). The nicotine is incorporated into a gum, such as Nicorette, and is released and absorbed in the mouth. Usually called nicotine chewing gum, it is not meant to be chewed in the same way as regular chewing gum, and unless the smokers follow the appropriate instructions they could underdose and experience withdrawal. In 1991 a stronger version was approved for use (4 milligrams vs. 2 milligrams of nicotine) and there is some evidence that it is more effective, especially for women. Nicotine gum prevents withdrawal when properly used and improves smoking cessation outcomes (see fig. 7.4). Support in the form of a smoking clinic further enhances the chances of success. As you might suspect, heavier smokers seem to benefit more from the

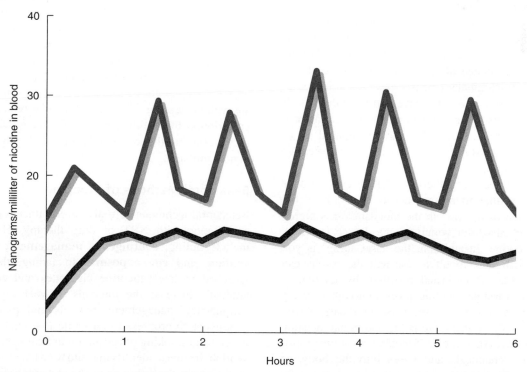

FIGURE 7.4
Changes in blood nicotine levels after smoking one cigarette per hour (top line) and using 4 mg of Nicorette per hour. As you can see, the blood nicotine levels after Nicorette are lower and do not show the "spike" indicated after cigarette smoking.

higher- rather than the lower-dose gum. Nicotine gum was a prescription drug until 1996, when it became available over the counter (Schmitz et al., 1997).

The nicotine patch has been in use since 1992 and has been available over the counter since 1996. The patch provides a steady dose and is easier to use. The patches are available in 16- and 24-hour versions. The 24-hour patch produces nicotine levels during sleep and prevents withdrawal symptoms on awakening. However, it also is more likely to cause sleep disturbance and is more irritating to the skin. Studies indicate that the two versions are equally effective (Schmitz et al., 1997). Like nicotine gum, the patch is most effective when combined with behavioral therapy, although it is also effective alone. Overall, it seems that the patch might be slightly more effective than nicotine gum, probably because its easier use increases compliance.

Two new techniques attempt to mimic the fast rise of nicotine in the bloodstream caused by smoking. The rationale is that fast absorption will speed relief from withdrawal and will make quitting easier. The first method is a **nicotine nasal spray.** A small bottle is inserted into the nostril, and a pump mechanism is pressed to deliver a squirt of a mist consisting of nicotine and water. Nicotine nasal spray is easier to use than nicotine gum and provides more precise dosing for relief from withdrawal and craving (Schmitz et al., 1997). The few studies that have evaluated the nasal spray indicate that it is an effective method of smoking cessation when combined with behavioral therapy. Like all systems, the nasal spray does have side effects, including nasal irritation, sneezing, runny nose, watery eyes, and coughing, which might be deterrents to its use.

The second method is the **nicotine inhaler.** Ironically, the nicotine inhaler originated with the noncombustible cigarette called "Favor." The cigarette never caught on, but the inhaler has the advantage of satisfying smokers' oral and handling needs. Each inhaler consists of a mouthpiece with a quantity of nicotine and can deliver up to 400 puffs. It takes at least 80 puffs to receive the amount of nicotine provided by one cigarette. No studies have compared all of these methods, so we don't know which is most effective (Schmitz et al., 1997).

Nicotine replacement therapy (NRT) can produce nicotine levels similar to those reached by smokers, but the actual amount of nicotine in the bloodstream is highly variable. Individuals differ widely in the degree to which they absorb nicotine. In addition, the nasal spray, as you might expect, can be difficult to use and the results can be highly variable. Transdermal nicotine, by its nature, produces a less variable nicotine level, although it rarely reaches the levels common in smokers (Benowitz, Zevin, & Jacobs, 1997). Of course there is the additional question of the health effects of nicotine. Smoking cigarettes introduces numerous chemicals and gases into the body, as you have read. Nicotine alone, however, also causes problems. Nicotine can contribute to cardiovascular disease in particular. However, the available evidence suggests that the risks of NRT for those trying to stop are minimal compared with the risks of continuing smoking (Benowitz & Gourlay, 1997).

Nicotine does produce dependence, so you might have wondered whether nicotine replacement therapy itself might lead to dependence. NRT is available over the counter, and it is certainly possible that a smoker could switch from cigarettes to gum or the patch and maintain dependence. On the other hand, the smoker who chooses NRT is presumably motivated to stop smoking and nicotine replacement is supposed to be used for a relatively short period of time. Also, the gum and the patch have a slow onset of action and do not deliver the spike of nicotine that smoking provides. The nasal spray and the inhaler might have a higher risk of maintaining dependence, because they do provide a rapid onset, but these methods are still available only by prescription and some control can be maintained. There is simply not enough evidence available to indicate whether the patch, gum, spray, or inhaler can be addicting (Schmitz et al., 1997).

Drug Treatment for Nicotine Dependence

In 1998 a new treatment became available for smoking cessation that does not involve nicotine replacement. The drug is marketed under the name Zyban. Its chemical name is bupropion, and it is also marketed under the name Wellbutrin as a drug for depression. You have read that depression and smoking are related. Does Zyban help people stop smoking by relieving depression? Studies have shown that depressed smokers are more likely to quit when taking either Wellbutrin or Prozac, but there is almost no research to indicate whether it is helpful in nondepressed smokers. You might wonder why the same drug is marketed under two different names. Some stigma attaches to having a psychological disorder (at least for some people). Smokers who are trying to stop might be reluctant to take a drug they associate with depression. They might also be reluctant to give a prescription for Wellbutrin to a pharmacy where they are known, for fear that others might think they have a psychological problem.

Behavioral Methods of Stopping

Behavioral techniques are also used either separately or in conjunction with NRT or drug therapy. The techniques include **fading, contingency management, relapse prevention,** and **cue exposure.** In fading, the smoker is switched to lower-nicotine cigarettes and encouraged to gradually increase the intervals between cigarettes. With contingency management, rewards and punishments are contingent on progress toward a desired goal such as abstinence from smoking or remaining in treatment. Relapse prevention involves identifying situations and emotions that might trigger the desire to smoke and emphasizes the development of coping mechanisms. Cue exposure is based on principles of classical conditioning. Certain cues in the environment become associated with (conditions of) smoking. Classical conditioning theory predicts that experiencing these environmental cues without the reward of smoking will reduce the cue's ability to cause craving. Behavioral methods are useful as adjuncts to other methods, but none have been shown to be very effective when used by themselves.

Health Benefits of Smoking Cessation

With all the negative health consequences of smoking, it should not be surprising that your health will improve if you stop smoking. What might be surprising, however, is how much healthier you are likely to be. Overall, smokers who quit before 50 years of age are only half as likely to die in the next fifteen years as are those who continue (USDHHS, 1990). The risks for lung cancer and COPD are both slightly higher for former smokers than for people who have never smoked, but they are still much lower than if the person had continued smoking. Fifteen years after quitting, the risk for increased coronary disease is essentially the same as a nonsmoker's. Heavier smokers, of course, are at greatest risk even after they stop, but they also have the most to gain (Greenwald, 1997). Table 7.5 shows the short-term and

---

TABLE 7.5 Health Benefits of Stopping Smoking

According to the American Cancer Society and the Centers for Disease Control and Prevention, snuff out your last cigarette and:

Within 20 minutes your blood pressure and pulse rate drop to normal and your hands and feet return to their normal temperature.

Within 8 hours your carbon monoxide level drops to normal and your oxygen level increases to normal. Smoker's breath disappears.

Within 24 hours your chance of a heart attack decreases.

Within 48 hours your nerve endings start to regrow, and your ability to smell and taste increases.

Within 3 days you'll breathe easier.

Within 2 weeks to 3 months your circulation improves, walking becomes easier, and lung function improves 30 percent.

Within 1 to 9 months you'll cough less, sinus congestion and shortness of breath decrease, and the cilia in your lungs will grow back.

Within 1 year your risk of heart disease is half that of a smoker.

Within 2 years your risk of heart attack is near normal.

Within 5 years your risk of lung cancer, stroke, and cancer of the mouth, throat, and esophagus are half that of a smoker.

Within 10 years your risk of lung cancer is the same as a nonsmoker's.

Within 15 years your risk of heart disease is the same as a nonsmoker's.

Source: *American Cancer Society*

---

long-term effects of smoking cessation. The message should be clear: if you don't smoke, don't start. If you do smoke, stop.

Stop and Review

1. How does smoking during pregnancy affect the fetus?
2. What are some of the psychological disorders associated with cigarette smoking?
3. Why is environmental tobacco smoke dangerous and what are its effects?
4. How is nicotine dependence treated physiologically and psychologically?

Summary

Nicotine is an addictive drug when measured by the standards used for illegal drugs, yet its use remains legal. The problems associated with nicotine addiction stem from the manner in which it is administered, primarily by cigarette smoking. Pipes, cigars, and smokeless tobacco also contribute to tobacco-related deaths.

Cigarette smoking is harmful because the smoke contains carcinogens and carbon monoxide in addition to nicotine. Although we have come a long way in reducing cigarette use, many people still smoke and some find it almost impossible to stop. Cigarettes are legal, so smokers aren't sent to jail. Nevertheless, society pays an enormous price for their smoking.

Smoking cessation can be difficult, but it is not impossible. Recognition of the addictive characteristics of nicotine has led to treatments based on the physiological and psychological characteristics of addiction. These include nicotine replacement and behavioral techniques, which can help the user stop.

Even though cigarette smoking can result in death from cardiovascular problems, emphysema, and cancer, nearly every smoker who stops has a rapid improvement in health. Cigarette smoking is far less acceptable socially than it used to be. Its future is unclear.

Key Terms

acetylcholine A neurotransmitter in the brain and the peripheral nervous system. In the brain it is involved in memory and other behaviors; in the peripheral nervous system it operates at the junction between the neuron and the muscle.

benzene A harmful chemical linked to liver and kidney problems and used in the manufacture of cigarettes.

branded discounts Discounted premium brands.

carbon monoxide A colorless, odorless gas that combines with hemoglobin in the bloodstream to reduce the availability of oxygen.

chemical trigger zone The part of the brain stem that initiates vomiting.

chronic bronchitis Inflammation and infection of the lungs, specifically the bronchial tubes.

chronic obstructive pulmonary disease (COPD) A disease involving emphysema and bronchitis that is seen almost exclusively in smokers.

cilia Hairlike cells that protect the lung from dust.

clove cigarettes Cigarettes imported from Indonesia that contain strong tobacco and ground cloves, which contain eugenol, a local anesthetic similar to menthol.

cotinine The major metabolite of nicotine.

contingency management A behavioral technique that uses reward and punishment to work toward abstaining from smoking.

cue exposure A behavioral technique, based on principles of classical conditioning, used to weaken the association between cues in the environment and smoking.

emphysema A disease characterized by enlargement of the air sacs and spaces in the lungs, and decreased ability of the sacs to hold oxygen.

environmental tobacco smoke A combination of sidestream, mainstream, and exhaled smoke.

epinephrine Another term for adrenaline, the substance that activates the sympathetic nervous system.

eugenol A local anesthetic found in cloves and clove cigarettes.

exhaled smoke Smoke exhaled by the smoker.

fading A behavioral technique where the smoker switches to lower-nicotine cigarettes and progressively increases the interval between cigarettes.

formaldehyde A toxic chemical used as an additive in cigarettes.

generic Off-brand cigarettes.

glutamate The primary excitatory neurotransmitter in the brain.

lung cancer The leading cause of death in men and women.

mainstream smoke The smoke that is inhaled by the smoker from the unlit end of the cigarette.

nicotine A very toxic chemical substance found in tobacco and used in insecticides. It has a high dependence potential and can cause seizures, coma, and death.

nicotine inhaler A nicotine replacement device that satisfies the smoker's oral and handling needs.

nicotine nasal spray A mixture of nicotine and water that is sprayed into the nostril as nicotine replacement therapy.

nicotine polacrilex A gum that releases nicotine into the mucous membranes, of the mouth as nicotine replacement therapy.

nicotine replacement therapy Therapies that treat nicotine withdrawal while the user is breaking the habit of smoking.

nitrosamines Some of the most potent of all cancer-causing agents, found in tobacco.

nucleus accumbens A structure in the brain involved in feelings of euphoria and hence in the reward system.

relapse prevention A behavioral technique that involves identifying situations and emotions that trigger the desire to smoke and developing coping mechanisms to handle them.

relative risk ratios Comparative measures of the increased risk of various conditions (such as cancers) for different groups.

sidestream smoke The smoke escaping from the burning end of a cigarette.

smokeless tobacco A euphemism for chewing tobacco, dip, and snuff.

tar The component of cigarette smoke that transports carcinogenic chemicals.

up regulation An increase in the number of postsynaptic receptors, brought on by an increase in neurotransmitter release.

References

The health benefits of smoking cessation: A report of the Surgeon General (1990). Washington, DC: United States Department of Health and Human Services.

The health consequences of smoking: Nicotine addiction. A report of the Surgeon General (1998). Washington, DC: Office on Smoking and Health.

Respiratory health effects of passive smoking, lung cancer and other disorders: The report of the U.S. Environmental Protection Agency (1993). Washington, DC: National Cancer institute, 1993.

Substance use among women in the United States (1997). Washington, DC: Office of Applied Studies; Substance Abuse and Mental Health Services Administration.

Andres, R. L., & Larrabee, K. (1996). The perinatal consequences of smoking and alcohol use. *Current Problems in Obsetrics, Gynecology and Fertility, 19,* 167–206.

Barrett, D., Anda, R., Escobedo, L., Croft, J., Williamson, D., & Marks, J. (1994). Trends in oral contraceptive use and cigarette smoking. *Archives of Family Medicine, 3,* 438–443.

Bartecchi, C., MacKenzie, T., & Schrier, T. (1994). The human costs of tobacco use. *New England Journal of Medicine,* 438–443.

Benowitz, N. L. (1986). The human pharmacology of nicotine. *Research Advances in Alcohol and Drug Problems, 9,* 1–53.

Benowitz, N. L. (1996). Biomarkers of cigarette smoking. In *The FTC cigarette test method for determining tar, nicotine, and carbon monoxide yields of U.S. cigarettes: Monograph 7* (pp. 93–111). Washington, DC: National Insitutues of Health.

Benowitz, N. L., & Gourlay, S. B. (1997). Cardiovascular toxicity of nictoine: Implications for nictoine replacement therapy. *Journal of the American College of Cardiology, 29,* 1422–1431.

Benowitz, N. L., Zevin, S., & Jacobs, P. (1997). Sources of variability in nicotine and cotinine levels with use of nicotine nasal spray, transdermal nicotine and cigarette smoking. *British Journal of Clinical Pharmacology, 43,* 259–267.

Borrelli, B., Niaura, R., Keuthen, N. J., Goldstein, M. G., DePue, J. D., Murphy, C., & Abrams, D. B. (1996). Development of major depressive disorder during smoking cessation treatment. *Journal of Clinical Psychiatry, 57,* 534–538.

Breslau, N., Peterson, E., Schultz, L., Andreski, P., & Chilcoat, H. (1996). Are smokers with alcohol disorders less likely to quit? *American Journal of Public Health, 86,* 985–990.

Burns, D. M. (1998). Cigar smoking: Overview and current state of the science. *Cigars: Health Effects and Trends,* 1–20. Washington, DC: U.S. Department of Health and Human Services.

Burns, D. M., Garfinkel, L., & Samet, J. M. (1997). Introduction, summary, and conclusions. In D. M. Burns, L. Garfinkel, & J. M. Samet (Eds.), *Changes in cigarette related disease risks and their implications for prevention and control.* Washington, DC: National Cancer Institue.

Carvey, P. M. (1998). *Drug action in the nervous system.* New York: Oxford University Press.

Cavin, S. W., & Pierce, J. P. (1996). Low cost cigarettes and smoking behavior in California, 1990–1993. *American Journal of Preventive Medicine, 12,* 17–21.

Corti, C. (1931/1996). *A history of smoking.* London: Bracken Books.

Escobedo, L. G., & Peddicord, J. P. (1997). Long-term trends in cigarette smoking among young U.S. adults. *Addictive Behaviors, 22,* 427–430.

Exposure to second-hand smoke widespread. (1996). Press release. Atlanta: Centers for Disease Control and Prevention.

Fagerstrom, K., & Schneider, N. G. (1989). Measuring nicotine dependence: A review of the Fagerstrom Tolerance Questionnaire. *Journal of Behavioral Medicine, 12,* 159–182.

Gerlach, K. K., Cummings, K. M., Hyland, A., Gilpin, E. A., Johnson, M. D., and Pierce, J. P. (1998). Trends in cigar consumption and smoking prevalence. In *Cigars, Health Effects and Trends,* 21–54. Washington, DC: U.S. Department of Health and Human Services.

Gilpin, E., Cavin, S. W., & Pierce, J. P. (1997). Adult smokers who do not smoke daily. *Addiction, 92,* 473–480.

Glantz, K., & Parmley, W. (1995). Passive smoking and heart disease. *Journal of the American Medical Association, 273,* 1047–1053.

Glover, E., & Glover, P. (1992). Smokeless tobacco or health. In *Smokeless tobacco or health: An international perspective: Research monograph No. 2* (pp. 3–10). Washington, DC: U.S. Department of Health and Human Services.

Golding, J. (1986). Child health and the environment. *British Medical Bulletin, 46,* 204–211.

Goodman, J. (1993). *Tobacco in history: The cultures of dependence.* London: Routledge.

Gourlay, S. B., Benowitz, N. L., Forbes, A., & McNeill, J. J. (1997). Determinants of plama concentrations of nicotine and cotinine during cigarette smoking and transdermal nicotine treatment. *European Journal of Clinical Pharmacology, 51,* 407–414.

Greenwald, P. G. (1997). *Preface: Changes in cigarette-related disease risks and their implication for prevention and control.* Washington, DC: National Cancer Institute.

Harris, J. E. (1996). Cigarette smoke components and disease: Cigarette smoking is more than a triad of tar, nicotine and carbon monoxide. In *The FTC cigarette test method for determining tar, nicotine, and carbon monoxoide yields of U.S. cigarettes: Monograph 7* (pp. 59–75). Washington, DC: National Institutes of Health.

Hatsukami, D., Nelson, R., & Jensen, J. (1991). Smokeless tobacco: Current status and future directions. *British Journal of Addiction, 86,* 559–563.

Heiman, R. K. (1960). *Tobacco and Americans.* New York: McGraw-Hill.

Henningfield, J. E., & Schuh, L. M. (1996). Pharmacology and markers: Nicotine pharmacology and addictive effects. In *The FTC cigarette test method for determining tar, nicotine, and carbon monoxoide yields of U.S. cigarettes: Monograph 7* (pp. 113–126). Washington, DC: National Institutes of Health.

Hoffman, D., & Hoffman, I. (1998). "Chemistry and toxicology." *Cigars: Health Effects and Trends,* 55–104. Washington, DC: U.S. Department of Health and Human Services.

Huang, L. X., Cerbone, F. G., & Gfroerer, J. C. (1998). *Children at risk because of parental substance abuse.* Washington, DC: Office of Applied Studies; Substance Abuse and Mental Health Services Administration.

Hughes, J. R. (1996). Treating smokers with current or past alcohol dependence. *American Journal of Health Behavior 20:* 86–290.

Jamner, L. D., Dirdler, S. S., Shapiro, D., & Jarvik, M. E. (1998). Pain inhibition, nicotine and gender. *Experimental and Clinical Psychopharmacology, 6,* 96–106.

Kiernan, V. G. (1991). *Tobacco: A history.* London: Hutchinson Radius.

Lander, M. (1886). *The tobacco problem.* Boston: Cupples, Upham, & Company.

Le Hourzec, J. (1998). Nicotine: Abused substance and therapeutic agent. *Journal of Psychiatry and Neuroscience, 23,* 95–108.

Leigh, J. P. (1996). Occupations, cigarette smoking, and lung cancer in the epidemiological follow-up to the NHANES I and the California Occupational mortality study. *Bulletin of the New York Academy of Medicine, 73,* 370–397.

Leiken, J. B., & Paloucek, F. P. (1995). *Poisoning and toxicology handbook.* Cleveland: Lexi-Comp.

MacKenzie, T., Bartecchi, C., & Schrier, R. The human cost of tobacco use. *New England Journal of Medicine 330:* 975–980.

Martinez, K., Wright, A., & Taussig, L. (1994). The effect of paternal smoking on the birthweight of newborns whose mothers did not smoke. *American Journal of Public Health, 84,* 1489–1491.

Maskin, A., Connolly, A., & Noonan, E. (1993). Environmental tobacco smoke: Implications for the workplace. *Occupational Safety and Health Reporter,* 1663–1667.

Morse, D. E., Katz, R. V., Pendryx, D. G., Holford, T. R., Krutchkoff, D. J., Eisenberg, E., Kosis, D., & Mayne, S. T. (1996). Smoking and drinking in relation to oral epithelial dysplasia. *Cancer Epidemiology, Biomarkers and Prevention, 5,* 769–777.

Mullen, P. D., Richardson, M. A., Quinn, V. P., & Ershoff, D. H. (1997). Postpartum return to smoking: who is at risk and when. *American Journal of Health Promotion, 11,* 323–330.

Muscat, J. E., Stellman, S. D., Hoffman, D., & Wynder, E. L. (1997). Smoking and pancreatic cancer in men and women. *Cancer Epidemiology, Biomarkers and Prevention, 6,* 15–19.

Patton, G. C., Hibbert, M., Rosier, M. J., Carlin, J. B., Caust, J., & Bowes, G. (1996). Is smoking associated with depression and anxiety in teenagers? *American Journal of Public Health, 86,* 225–230.

Pomerleau, C. S. (1997). Co-factors for smoking and evolutionary psychobiology. *Addiction, 92,* 397–408.

Repace, J. L., Ott, W. R., & Klepies, M. S. (1998). Indoor air pollution and cigarette smoke. *Cigars: Health effects and trends,* 161–180. Washington, DC: U.S. Department of Health and Human Services.

Schmitz, J. M., Schneider, N. G., & Jarvik, M. E. (1997). Nicotine. In J. H. Lowinson, P. Ruiz, R. B. Millman, & J. G. Langrod (Eds.), *Substance abuse: A comprehensive textbook* (3rd ed., pp. 276–294). Baltimore: Williams & Wilkins.

Shanks, T. G., & Burns, D. M. (1998). Disease consequences of cigar smoking. *Cigars: Health Effects and Trends,* 105–160. Washington, DC: U.S. Department of Health and Human Services.

Slade, J. (1998). Marketing and promotion of cigars. *Cigars: Health Effects and Trends,* 191–220. Washington, DC: U.S. Department of Health and Human Services.

Taiminen, T. J., Salokangas, R. K. R., Saarijarvi, S., Niemi, H., Lehto, H., Ahola, V., & Syvalahti, E. (1998). Smoking and cognivitive deficits in schizophrenia: A pilot study. *Addictive Behaviors, 23,* 263–266.

Thun, M. J., Myers, D. J., Day-Lally, C., Namboodiri, M. M., Calle, E. E., Flanders, W. D., Adams, S. L., & Heath, C. W. (1997). *Changes in cigarette-related disease risks and their implications for prevention and control.* Washington, DC: National Cancer Institute.

Wells, A. (1994). Passive smoking as a cause of heart disease. *Journal of the American College of Cardiology, 24,* 546–554.

Wilbert, J. (1987). *Tobacco and shamanism in South America.* New Haven: Yale University Press.

Witorsch, R. J., & Witorsch, P. (1996). Environmental tobacco smoke and birthweight of offspring. *Indoor Built Environments, 5,* 219–231.

Woodman, G., Newman, S. P., & Pavia, D. (1987). Response and acclimatization of symptomless smokers on changing to low tar, low nicotine cigarettes. *Thorax, 42,* 336–341.

Wu, A. H., Yu, M. C., & Mack, T. M. (1997). Smoking, alcohol use, dietary factors and risk of small intestinal adenocarcinoma. *International Journal of Cancer, 70,* 512–517.

Zhang, Z., Kurtz, R. C., Sun, M., Karpeh, M., Yu, G., Gargon, N., Fein, J. S., Georgopoulus, S. K., & Harkap, S. (1996). Adenocarcinomas of the esophagus and gastric cardia: Medical conditions, tobacco, alcohol, and socieconomic factors. *Cancer Epidemiology: Biomarkers and Prevention, 5,* 761–768.

Chapter Eight

Hallucinogens and Inhalants

Chapter Objectives

When you have finished studying this chapter, you should

1. Understand the role hallucinogens have played in history.
2. Be able to distinguish the two major types of hallucinogens.
3. Be able to trace the history of LSD.
4. Understand the relationship between LSD and serotonin.
5. Be able to discuss the reasons why LSD does not produce physical tolerance.
6. Be able to decide whether the dangers of LSD have been overstated.
7. Know the psychological effects of LSD.
8. Know how peyote is used and why.
9. Be able to discuss the similarities and differences among MDMA, mescaline, and amphetamine.
10. Be able to discuss the possibility that MDMA produces brain damage.
11. Know who uses inhalants.
12. Be able to list the four main classes of inhalants.
13. Know the dangers of inhalant use.

Coming at the very first, at the time of feasting, they ate mushrooms; they drank only chocolate during the night. And they ate mushrooms with honey. When the mushrooms were taking effect there was dancing, there was weeping. Some saw in a vision they would die in war. Some saw in a vision that they would perish in water. Some saw in a vision that they would become rich, wealthy.

Description of a hallucinogenic mushroom ceremony conducted by Aztec merchants, by Bernardino de Sahagún Ca. 1520
(Quoted in Hoffman, 1983)

In this chapter you will read about a wide range of substances. Despite their differences in chemical structure and effects on the brain, they have one thing in common, they are taken primarily to alter the user's consciousness. You might not put LSD, airplane glue, angel dust, and Ecstasy into the same category, yet their effects are surprisingly similar. Some of these substances have gained a dubious reputation while others are known only to a small number of users. All of them produce a feeling of disorientation that some people seem to enjoy. This chapter begins with the only group of drugs that seems to have had as long a history of human use as alcohol—the hallucinogens.

History of Hallucinogens

In 1975, the skeleton of a Neanderthal man was discovered in a cave and was estimated to be 60,000 years old. Among his possessions was a quantity of a plant containing ephedrine, a psychostimulant (Devereux, 1997). Neanderthals, who became extinct as *Homo sapiens* (present-day humans) emerged, apparently knew about mind-altering drugs. In cave paintings that date back 40,000 years or more, strange geometric figures abound. The same kinds of shapes are commonly experienced by people who take hallucinogenic drugs. Given this and other evidence, it appears that the use of plants with psychoactive properties began at least as early as the human species itself (Devereux, 1997).

You can see in figure 8.1 that hallucinogenic drugs are used worldwide. More than half a million species of plants exist, but only 150 or so are believed to be hallucinogenic. Mentions of hallucinogenic drugs are found in the first written records. In the Rig Veda, a collection of hymns from India thought to be over 3,500 years old, there are references to what is probably fly agaric. This fungus, whose botanical name is *Amanita muscaria,* has potent hallucinogenic properties that have been exploited wherever the fungus is found. The natives of Siberia use fly agaric and report visions and mood disturbances under its influence (Wasson, 1968). The active chemicals in this fungus, ibotenic acid and muscimol, are excreted unchanged in the urine. Some reports maintain that users collect their urine and pass it along to others to drink (Dobkin de Rios, 1984). The urine is believed to be effective through five filterings (Ott, 1993).

Various cultures have developed equally ingenious drug-ingestion methods that demonstrate a sophisticated understanding of pharmacology. Bushmen of South Africa rub the bulb of the kasi plant on incisions on their scalps. Absorbing a chemical through the scalp eliminates first-pass metabolism by the liver. Some cultures use water lilies and tobacco as enemas, which also avoids first-pass metabolism. The Yanomami and other tribes in South America take epena by blowing it into each other's nostrils through long tubes. This method also avoids (you guessed it) first-pass metabolism (Ott, 1993).

Plants are not the only source of chemicals used to alter consciousness. More than two hundred species of toads from the family *Bufo* have glands on their backs that secrete various biolologically active substances. Some of these sub-stances appear to have mind-altering characteristics. The rarest is **bufotenine,** found in only one toad species, *Bufo alvairus.* This toad species and all of the others produce several other substances that are poorly understood but largely toxic. The belief that toads secrete hallucinogenic substances has led to newspaper reports of people licking toads or smoking their venom. There is probably as much myth as reality in many stories of the psychogenic properties of toads. Little scientific evidence exists to either refute or confirm the reports (Lyttle, Goldstein, & Gartz, 1996). In all probability—toad licking is a media invention. Someone, somewhere may have tried it, but there are no verified reports in the scientific literature that *Bufo* venom is currently used at all, not to mention by that method.

Perhaps the most unusual method of altering consciousness was employed by some indigenous groups in what is now southern and south-central California. Reliable reports indicate that they would swallow red harvester ants as part of their vision-inducing ceremonies. Even though the harvester ants cause painful stings, the person (always a male) who was seeking the visions would ingest huge quantities of the ants over a period of several days. The toxic effects of the ants would induce a coma during which the seeker would find his visions (Groark, 1996).

Why was the use of hallucinogens virtually universal? Why has their use largely been discontinued by so-called civilized societies? Why did the "hippies" of the 1960s embrace them so avidly? These plants and their chemical constituents have been lost to modern society for so long that we do not even have an adequate vocabulary to describe them. Consider the thousands of terms we all know for drinking, getting drunk, and having a hangover. Then consider that not a single English word for hallucinogens existed until fifty years ago. Even the term *hallucinogen* itself is inaccurate

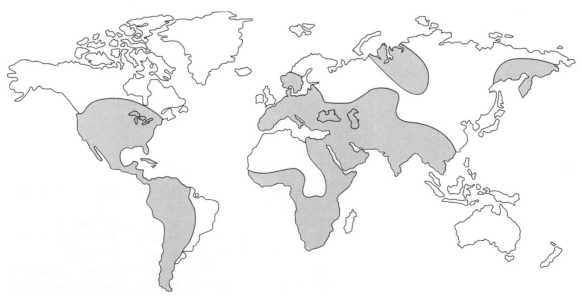

FIGURE 8.1
Areas in which hallucinogenic drugs are widely used.

and inadequate. Except at high doses, most of these drugs do not cause hallucinations in the technical sense.

Significant differences exist between the effects of these drugs and hallucinations in the psychchiatric sense. They profoundly alter our perceptions of reality, but distorted visions of something that already exists are not hallucinations. Furthermore, the drugs typically distort visual perceptions, and most true hallucinations are auditory. Other terms such as *psychedelic, psychotomimetic, deliriants,* and *misperceptogen* have been suggested, but they are even worse. Recently the term **entheogen** has come into use. *Entheogen* means "caused from within" and better describes the effects of these drugs (Szara, 1994). This term has not been widely adopted, however, so we seem stuck with *hallucinogen* for the present.

One effect of these drugs could, with a considerable stretch, be considered hallucinogenic. Most of these drugs cause the user to see geometric forms and shapes. Just how they are formed is unclear, but they seem to be innate characteristics of our visual system. Migraine sufferers experience a similar visual phenomenon if they have auras. These geometric figures have been found on pottery, wall paintings, and statues since the beginning of humankind. Their occurrence throughout human history suggests strongly that early people were quite familiar with the "hallucinogenic drugs" (Devereux, 1997).

Stop and Review

1. What are the differences in motivation for people who use hallucinogens at present compared to users in older cultures?
2. If hallucinogens aren't hallucinogenic. What are they?

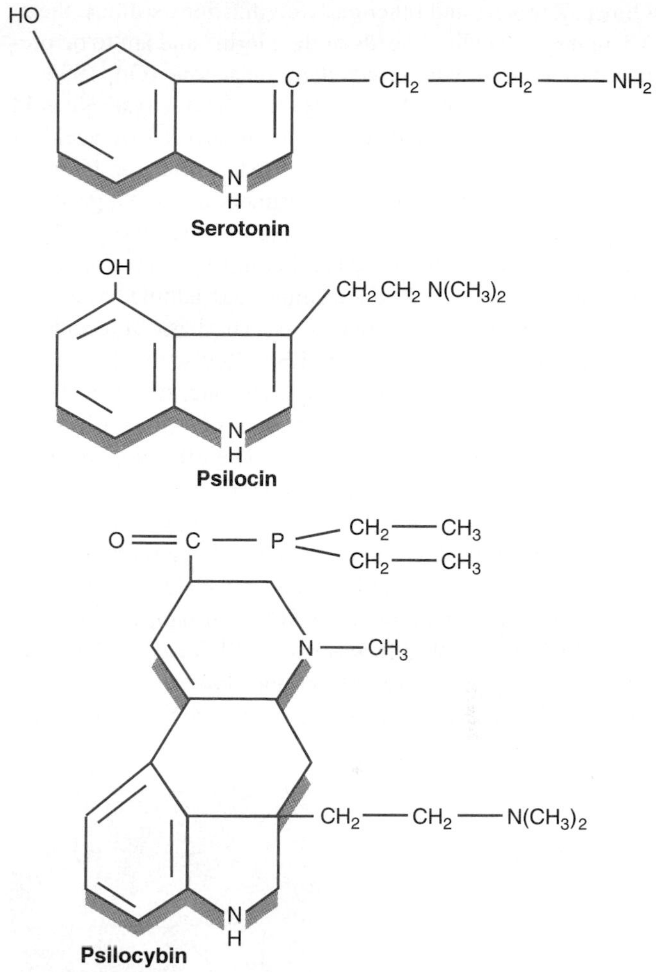

Types of Hallucinogens

Most of the hallucinogenic drugs fall into two groups. In figure 8.2 you can see that hallucinogens like LSD and psilocybin resemble the neurotransmitter serotonin. Because serotonin is know chemically as an indoleamine, these hallucinogens are called indole-like. The second group, which includes mescaline and MDMA (Ecstasy), resembles norepinephrine and dopamine. You already learned that these neurotransmitters are called catecholamines, but a more general term is *phenethylamine,* so these are called phenethylamine-like. There are other hallucinogens of minor importance, such as the tryptamines (**DMT** and **epena**), betacarbolines (**ayahuasca**), and isoxasoles (**fly agaric**).

Classification of Hallucinogens

The hallucinogens can be categorized many ways. The most common method is to describe them in terms of their chemical structure. Drugs like LSD and psilocybin resemble sero-

FIGURE 8.2

The conversion of psilocybin to psilocin takes place very rapidly once psilocybin is absorbed into the bloodstream. So psilocybin reaches its peak effect as quickly as LSD does. Notice how psilocin, the active metabolite of psilocybin, resembles serotonin.

tonin while drugs like mescaline and Ecstasy resemble norepinephrine. Others hallucinogens resemble neither of these neurotransmitters. Since these other hallucinogens, DMT, epena, ayahuasca and fly agaric, are of minor importance we will focus on the four above that have had the greatest impact on our culture.

Lysergic Acid Diethylamide

Lysergic acid is one of the constituents of the ergot fungus that grows on rye. There have been many reports of fungus-infected bread being eaten with bizarre results. Ergot-infected bread has been implicated in a scourge during the Middle Ages called St. Anthony's fire, in the Salem Witchcraft episode, and in other, more recent events (Fuller, 1968). Lysergic acid and some of its derivatives are found in the seeds of the common morning glory vine. These seeds were used by the Aztecs, who called them *oloiuqui,* which means "round things." Indian descendants of the Maya,

Olmec, Zapotec, and other early civilizations still use them. There they are called "seeds of the virgin" and are to be prepared by a virgin who grinds them on a stone (Ott, 1993).

The best-known form of lysergic acid is **lysergic acid diethylamide (LSD-25).** LSD was discovered by accident when a chemist named Albert Hoffman of Sandoz Pharmaceuticals in Switzerland was experimenting with a group of drugs that were thought to stimulate the circulatory system (Hoffman, 1983). Pharmaceutical companies develop drugs by beginning with a basic formula and adding molecular groups, hoping to find a new drug. The basic molecule in this case was lysergic acid, and LSD-25 was the 25th in the series of compounds to be tested. No one, not even Hoffman, knows exactly what happened on 16 April 1943. Somehow he absorbed some LSD. The effects were quite spectacular and included rapidly changing imagery and visions of billiant colors. The effects subsided after about three hours. Three days later Hoffman intentionally ingested 250 micrograms, with similar results thus becoming the first person ever to knowingly take LSD (Hoffman, 1983).

After World War II was over, LSD research began in earnest, and by 1968 over a thousand studies had been published (Bliss, 1988). Researchers tested LSD as a model for

(a)

(b)

(a) This common garden flower has hallucinogenic properties. The seeds contain an LSD-like substance. (b) The Psilocybin mushroom has been used for hundreds of years in Central and South America and similar mushrooms are found throughout much of the United States.

Timothy Leary

schizophrenia, as an adjunct to therapy, and as a treatment for alcoholism. Studies indicated that it might have some usefulness in psychotherapy as a means to help patients gain insight into their problems. Other studies found that it helped alcohol abusers, and when given to the terminally ill made their last days more comfortable. By 1965, over 40,000 patients had received LSD as part of their psychiatric treatment (Henderson & Glass, 1994). One of the most famous early users was Cary Grant, who took LSD as part of his psychotherapy.

Use of LSD for other than psychiatric purposes began in 1962. In 1965 the drug was outlawed in the United States. Use expanded as a result, and LSD captured the imagination of a nation, attracting some and terrifying others. Some people who took it experienced what they described as visions of heaven; others found themselves descending into what seemed like hell. By the 1980s, LSD use had largely disappeared, and public attention shifted to cocaine, heroin, and crack. LSD did not entirely vanish, and use of LSD has remained at a low but stable rate for many years (Henderson & Glass, 1994). Every few years there is a new wave of adolescent and young adult users in various areas of the country. Curiously, there are very few reports of LSD use by older adults. The "aging hippies" who never seemed to let go of their idealism did seem to let go of their LSD.

The most famous figure associated with LSD was Timothy Leary. In 1961, Leary was on the faculty of Harvard University. He and a colleague, Richard Alpert, began research with psilocybin and then switched to LSD. Leary felt that the scientific laboratory approach did not lend itself to finding out what these drugs did and began giving them out in social situations and doing rather casual research without medical supervision. One thing led to another, and both Leary and Alpert had the distinction in 1963 of being the first two tenured faculty members to be fired from Harvard. Alpert turned to Eastern mysticism and has long been involved with foundations trying to alleviate suffering in third-world countries. Leary took another path (Lee & Schlain, 1985).

After his firing, Leary was in and out of jails on various charges for the next few years. His fame and notoriety made him both a target and a hero during the psychedelic period of the late 1960s. His message was far less radical than his followers assumed, and he felt that the enlightenment from LSD came about as a result of hard work and preparation. As early as 1964 he was saying that LSD was only one path to enlightenment Nevertheless, for most Americans he epitomizes the drug scene of the sixties (Stevens, 1987).

For a period of time, hallucinogenic drugs played an important role in a political and social movement that had an enormous impact on society that is still being felt today. The movement fizzled out, public outcry made LSD illegal, and publicity about its dangers led to a decrease in its popularity. Many bad experiences were not the fault of LSD, but much of the mythology surrounding its use still exists.

Physiology and Pharmacology of LSD

LSD is absorbed readily through the gastrointestinal tract and is the most powerful of the known hallucinogenic drugs. As little as 20 micrograms can affect mood and perception. This amount is equivalent to the amount of ink in the period at the end of this sentence. It is distributed throughout the body and less than 1 percent reaches the brain. The half-life of LSD is about 3 to 5 hours, although the behavioral effects persist for a longer period of time. Symptoms begin about an hour after ingestion and peak at 2 to 4 hours, and the user returns to normal in 10 to 12 hours. For the next day or so, users might report a letdown or a feeling of fatique (Pechnick & Ungerleider, 1997).

LSD is metabolized in the liver, and the metabolic products are excreted through the small intestine. Only about 1 percent is excreted unchanged in the urine, making detection very difficult (Henderson & Glass, 1994).

Unless you are an elephant, LSD has extremely low toxicity for you. Researchers gave an elephant 297 milligrams of LSD by means of intramuscular injection. The elephant promptly began to trumpet, went into seizures, and died (West, Pierce, & Thomas, 1962). The dosage given the elephant was about 6,000 times the dose required to produce psychological effects in humans. Even so, the researchers were unable to determine whether LSD was the reason for the elephant's death. Needless to say, this experiment was never repeated. Are you wondering why someone would inject an elephant with LSD? The rationale was that male elephants experience something called "musth" around the time when female elephants become sexually receptive. Male elephants in musth act in a bizarre manner. The researchers felt that the LSD might trigger musth behavior.

In humans, the fatal dose is unknown, as there are no unequivocal cases of fatal overdoses in the medical literature. One case is reported of eight people inhaling "milligram amounts" of LSD thinking it was cocaine. Five were taken to the hospital in a coma, two others walked in themselves and left several hours later. Those who had been comatose were able to talk within five hours and were normal within twelve. No effects were noted in a follow-up exam

one year later and most of the five continued to use LSD (Henderson & Glass, 1994).

Most of the effects seem to be caused by the action of the drug on serotonin receptors. Specifically, LSD primarily acts as an agonist on the 5-HT2 receptor subtype. LSD acts as an agonist on these receptor, which are found in various areas of the brain. Figure 8.3 highlights the 5-HT2 pathway. As you can see, these receptors are found in the cortex and the limbic system. In addition to the 5-HT2 receptor, LSD binds to most of the other serotonin receptors, as well as dopamine and norepinephrine receptors (Watts et al., 1995; Fiorella, Rabin, & Winter, 1995).

Most users self-limit their LSD experiences, and very few, if any, go on to be chronic users, so the effects of long-term use are not clear. LSD does not seem to cause brain damage or permanently alter cognitive functioning (Henderson & Glass, 1994). LSD can alter chromosomes in the bloodstream but does not cause changes in the sperm or ova, so there is no evidence that it can cause birth defects. Occassionally there are reports of eye damage from sun-gazing while under the influence of LSD. Eye damage occurs to many sun-gazing people, whether or not they take LSD. Sunbathers and those who watch solar eclipses without eye protection are particularly prone to eye problems. Of the few published reports attributing eye damage to LSD use, no permanent damage occurred (Henderson & Glass, 1994).

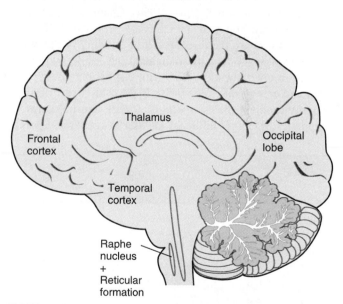

FIGURE 8.3
Location of the 5-HT2 receptors sites for LSD. The frontal cortex controls our ability to plan ahead, to consider several courses of action at once and to put a series of thoughts together. The temporal cortex is involved in hearing. The thalamus and the occipital lobes comprise the primary visual pathway. The optic nerve connects to the thalamus. The raphé nucleus is involved in sleep and dreaming. The reticular formation filters out distracting stimuli and arouses the cortex to important incoming sensory messages. LSD affects visual and auditory perception as well as disrupting thinking. It also causes distorted perception which may stem from the effect of LSD on the raphé nucleus and reticular formation.

Table 8.1 shows LSD use for 1976–1996 for persons 18 to 25 years of age. If you compare this table with those in the chapters on marijuana and cocaine, you can see that the peak of drug use occurred in 1979 for all three drugs. For the last ten years, use of LSD has remained about the same.

Psychological Effects of LSD

The effects of LSD are dose related. At low doses, **synesthesia** and time distortion are the most common reports. Synesthesia refers to "seeing sounds" or "hearing colors." Time distortion results in the feeling that seconds pass as minutes and minutes as hours. At higher doses, some users experience a distortion of body image and a loss of boundary between the self and the environment. Even higher doses can lead to a resurfacing of memories and mystical or religious experiences. Higher doses also are more likely to result in adverse reactions (Pechnick & Ungerleider, 1997).

Paranoia, true hallucinations, and psychotic reactions can develop, although these are rare. It does not seem that LSD can "cause" long-term psychosis, it is more likely to trigger it in someone who is otherwise susceptible. Most of the cases in which a user has had a long-term psychotic break as a result of using LSD involve individuals with a past psychiatric history, but it is important to note that serious consequences have occurred in individuals without such a history (Henderson & Glass, 1994). Changes in personality have been reported in cases of repeated LSD use. Whether these are the direct result of the drug or the result of the experience that the individual has while taking the drug is an open question. LSD trips can be extremely powerful and emotional experiences. If the user is part of a social environment that supports or fosters unusual ways of thinking, LSD might influence the user to adopt these points of view (Henderson & Glass, 1994; Pechnick & Underleider, 1997).

If talking the person down doesn't work, several drugs can be given to reduce the symptoms. The antianxiety drugs such as Valium and Xanax are usually effective and quite safe. If the person is extremely agitated, a drug such as Thorazine (an antipsychotic) may be needed. However, drug treatment is rarely necessary (Pechnick & Ungeleider, 1998).

LSD can produce very negative experiences, widely known as "bad trips." Bad trips were much more common in the 1970s when the street dose was 150 to 200 micrograms, compared to 50 to 75 micrograms at present (Pechnick & Underleider, 1997). Medical treatment for bad trips is available and successful, but it is rarely needed.

One of the most common beliefs about LSD is that it can cause **flashbacks,** or short-lived recurrences of the LSD experience. Flashbacks can happen days, weeks, or months after the last use of LSD and are not related to dosage or frequency of use. The *DSM-IV* categorizes flashbacks as **post hallucinogenic perceptual disorders.** The percentage of people who experience flashbacks is low, and most flashbacks are mild. Very little is known about what causes them, and they tend to decrease in frequency with time. Unless they are particularly disturbing, no treatment is necessary. Sometimes antianxiety drugs are prescribed, but most often reassurance is all that is necessary (Abraham & Aldridge, 1993).

Tolerance to both the physiological and psychological effects of LSD develops very rapidly. After two or three days of regular use, when almost no amount of LSD will produce any effects. Regular LSD users typically limit themselves to taking the drug once or twice weekly. Animal studies indicate that physical dependence does not seem to occur, because no withdrawal symptoms are seen even when large doses are given over a long period of time (Pechnick & Underleider, 1997).

Stop and Review

1. If no one ever died of an LSD overdose and dependence does not occur, why is LSD a Schedule I drug?
2. What are the primary physical and psychological effects of a street dose of LSD?
3. What possible harmful effects can occur with LSD?

Psilocybin

Evidence suggests that the psilocybin mushroom was the most important hallucinogen among the Aztec and the Maya before the Spanish Conquest. The Aztec name for them was **teonanacatl,** "God's flesh." The indigenous people of the region never stopped using the mushrooms; they merely hid their use from their conquerors. They were so successful that it wasn't until 1953 that Western society learned of their

TABLE 8.1 Percentage Reporting Use of LSD within the Last Year, Ages 18 to 25

Drug	LSD
1976	6.0
1977	6.4
1979	9.9
1982	6.6
1985	4.0
1988	5.6
1990	3.9
1991	4.7
1992	4.8
1993	4.9
1995	3.8
1996	4.6

Source: National Household Survey on Drug Use (1997).

existence. By this time the descendants of the Maya and Aztecs had incorporated worship of the mushroom into the dominant Catholic faith (Wasson et al, 1986).

Once thought to exist only in Southern Mexico, mushrooms containing psilocybin grow throughout the continental United States, Hawaii, Mexico, and Europe. People who collect them in the wild run a considerable risk of poisoning from deadly varieties that resemble the "magic mushrooms." Mushroom poisoning results in liver damage that can be fatal. If a large enough quantity is taken, the only treatment is a liver transplant within a few days of the onset of symptoms.

Psilocybin is an example of a **prodrug**—a chemical that is inactive itself but is converted in the body to an active substance, in this case psilocin. Psilocin is unstable and so it cannot be taken directly. Heroin, or diacetylmorphine, is another example of a prodrug; it is converted into morphine once it reaches the brain. Psilocybin has effects similar to LSD although less intense and shorter acting. It is an agonist at the 5HT2 and 5HT1 receptors. Taking psilocybin results in faster glucose use in the brain, particularly in the frontal cortex and temporal cortex. Smaller increases in brain activity are seen in the basal ganglia, sensorimotor cortex, and occipital lobes. The frontal cortex is particularly rich in 5HT2 receptors, which suggests that psilocybin acts through these receptors in the cortex to produce its effects (Pechnick & Underleider, 1997).

Phenethylamines

In a series of studies that will almost certainly never be repeated, researcher Alex Schulgin, along with a small group of his friends, systematically experimented with virtually every possible combination of chemicals known as **phenethylamines.** The best known of these is **mescaline,** the active compound in **peyote.** Over the course of thirty years, Schulgin developed nearly two hundred compounds based on the phenethylamine (catecholamine) molecule. Any drug similar to LSD or psilocybin is automatically a Schedule I drug. As a result, Schulgin was threatened with legal sanctions several times, some of which were carried out. Nevertheless he persisted in synthesizing, ingesting, and rating these compounds. The title of the book he wrote about his research and legal adventures gives an insight into his point of view. The book is titled *PIHKAL,* which stands for *Phenethylamines I Have Known And Loved* (Schulgin & Schulgin, 1991).

Outside of Shulgin and his small circle of friends, the only drugs in this class that have been carefully studied are mescaline and **methylenedioxymethamphetamine,** better known as **MDMA** or **Ecstasy.** These two drugs are quite similar, and both are similar to methamphetamine. But the three drugs have quite different effects, as you will see. Other phenethylamines that have had some brief period of

What Do You Think?

What Do You Think?

Why Does Western Society Use Alcohol and Not Hallucinogens?

You read in chapter 3 that fermented alcoholic beverages such as beer and wine are mentioned in the first written historical records, dating back five thousand years. There is evidence that the use of mind-altering plants is even more ancient. These plants that we refer to as hallucinogenic might have played a role in the development of moral, ethical, and religious systems (Dobkin de Rios, 1984; Wasson, Kramrisch, Ott, & Ruck, 1986). Why does our culture view the use of alcohol as acceptable but make the use of hallucinogens illegal?

The question becomes even more complicated when we consider Mayan and Aztec cultures in what is now Latin American. Being highly sophisticated societies, they had both alcoholic beverages and hallucinogenic substances. The hallucinogenic substances were revered and considered holy, alcohol was not (Devereaux, 1997). Although the dangers of excessive drinking have been recognized in every culture that has learned to ferment alcohol, there is no evidence of abuse of hallucinogenic substances in any of the cultures that have been studied (Dobkin de Rios, 1984).

Many theories have been proposed to explain how our culture came to use alcohol to the virtual exclusion of hallucinogenic substances (McKenna, 1992; Devereaux, 1997). Both alcohol and mind-altering plants were known to Western society, and evidence suggests that mind-altering plants were used before alcohol (Devereaux, 1997). What factors do you think might be responsible for alcohol becoming the predominant drug of our culture? Here are some ideas to consider:

1. Alcohol in the form of wine has symbolic significance in our predominant religious system, Christianity.
2. Greek society, which was familiar with both alcohol and mind-altering plants, was supplanted by the Romans, whose overwhelmingly favorite drink was wine.
3. Alcohol kills bacteria, and wine and beer are much safer drinks when the only alternative is contaminated water.
4. Beer and (to a lesser extent) wine contain nutrients and vitamins that could have supplemented a meager diet.

popularity are **MDE** (methylenedioxyethamphetamine), **MDA** (methylenedioxyamphetamine), and **DOM** (dimethoxymethamphetamine). MDE is known as **Eve,** MDA was known as "businessman's LSD" because of its short action, and DOM was known in the 1960s as **STP** (Pechnick & Undgerleider, 1997). Since the Controlled Substance Analog Act, none of these drugs has been widely distributed. Mescaline and MDMA, however, are a different story.

Figure 8.4 shows the structures of various phenethylamines as well as the structure of amphetamines.

Mescaline

Mescaline is the most important hallucinogen found in peyote and the first naturally occurring hallucinogen to be synthesized (Kluver, 1966). The peyote cactus, whose scientific name is *Lophophora williamsii,* grows in parts of Texas and Mexico and was widely used by the Aztec Indians. The cactus is portrayed in Aztec sculpture and pottery (Devereaux, 1997). The Tarahumara and Huichol Indians of Mexico were identified by the Spanish after the conquest as the primary users of peyote (Stewart, 1987). The use of peyote spread to other Indian tribes in the Southwest, including the Kiowa, who developed a religion surronding the use of peyote; this religion eventually developed into the Native American Church (Stewart, 1987).

Several North American Indian tribes have adopted some of the peyote ritual and formed the **Native American Church.** The Native American Church uses peyote as a sacrament in its religious ceremonies, and its members may legally possess and use peyote buttons. Membership in this church is estimated at more than 200,000. Members of the church have run into problems when their use of peyote has conflicted with the requirements of their jobs. The U.S.

Supreme Court has ruled that church members have a right to use peyote. What happens when the use of peyote is prohibited by job requirements is still an issue. Several recent rulings have first permitted job discrimination, then reversed the decision.

Taking peyote requires more than a little dedication. Peyote has a bitter taste and causes nausea, vomiting, and diarrhea. These symptoms can last for several hours. A typical peyote ceremony involves chanting, incense, and repetitive drumming, which serve to accentuate the effects of the drug. The unpleasant gastrointestinal experiences are followed by vivid images of intense color and a sense of depersonalization. Mescaline, like LSD, acts on the serotonin-containing neurons, although which receptors are activated is not clear (Pechnick & Ungerleider, 1997). The visual experiences typically last for about two hours and the drug remains in the system for ten hours. Peyote ceremonies usually begin late at night and the visual experiences usually coincide with the appearance of dawn (LaBarre, 1989).

MDMA

Ecstasy is the street name for methylenedioxymethamphetamine, also known as MDMA and **Adam.** It was patented in 1914 as an appetite suppressant, but failed to catch on. In the late 1970s, MDMA was used by psychiatrists who felt that it helped their patients gain insight into their problems and facilitated communication between patient and therapist. Word of its characteristics leaked out and MDMA use became popular, in part because it was legal. It wasn't long before the U.S. Drug Enforcement Administration got wind of it, and in 1988 it was declared a Schedule I drug despite protests by many psychiatrists (Cohen, 1998).

Peyote cactus

A painting representing a vision experienced under the influence of peyote.

MDMA causes nausea, increased heart rate, tight jaw muscles, and headache. Its effects begin about half an hour after taking it orally and last several hours. MDMA is supposed to induce a sense of "closeness" with others and a sensual feeling that is difficult to describe. The earliest published work described the drug as producing an "altered state of consciousness with emotional and sensual overtones" (Schulgin & Nichols, 1978). Its effects are different from those of either mescaline or amphetamine, both of which it resembles (Cohen, 1998). MDMA is not a potent stimulant like methamphetamine, and hallucinations have rarely been reported. According to users it produces effects halfway between those of amphetamine and LSD, with unique properties of its own (Parrott & Stuart, 1997).

MDMA acts as a serotonin agonist by causing the release of serotonin and blocking its uptake (Cohen, 1998). Other serotonin agonists do not produce the same effects as MDMA, so it appears that part of the uniqueness of the drug is due to the fact that it also acts on the dopamine and norepinephrine systems (Obradovic, Imel, & White, 1996; White, Obradovic, Imel, & Wheaton, 1996; Koch & Galloway, 1997). The serotonin agonist effects appear to cause damage to serotonin nerve terminals, mainly the loss of reuptake sites (Cohen, 1998). Degeneration of nerve terminals for serotonin have been demonstrated in rats, mice, guinea pigs, monkeys, and baboons (Grob & Poland, 1997). The doses given to animals are higher than doses normally taken by humans and are administered over a longer period of time.

No one knows whether MDMA is as toxic in humans as it is in animals, although there is little evidence for neurotoxicity in humans (Grob & Poland, 1997; Morgan, 1997). Given that MDMA is a Schedule I drug, it is interesting that the drug with the greatest similarity regarding serotonin

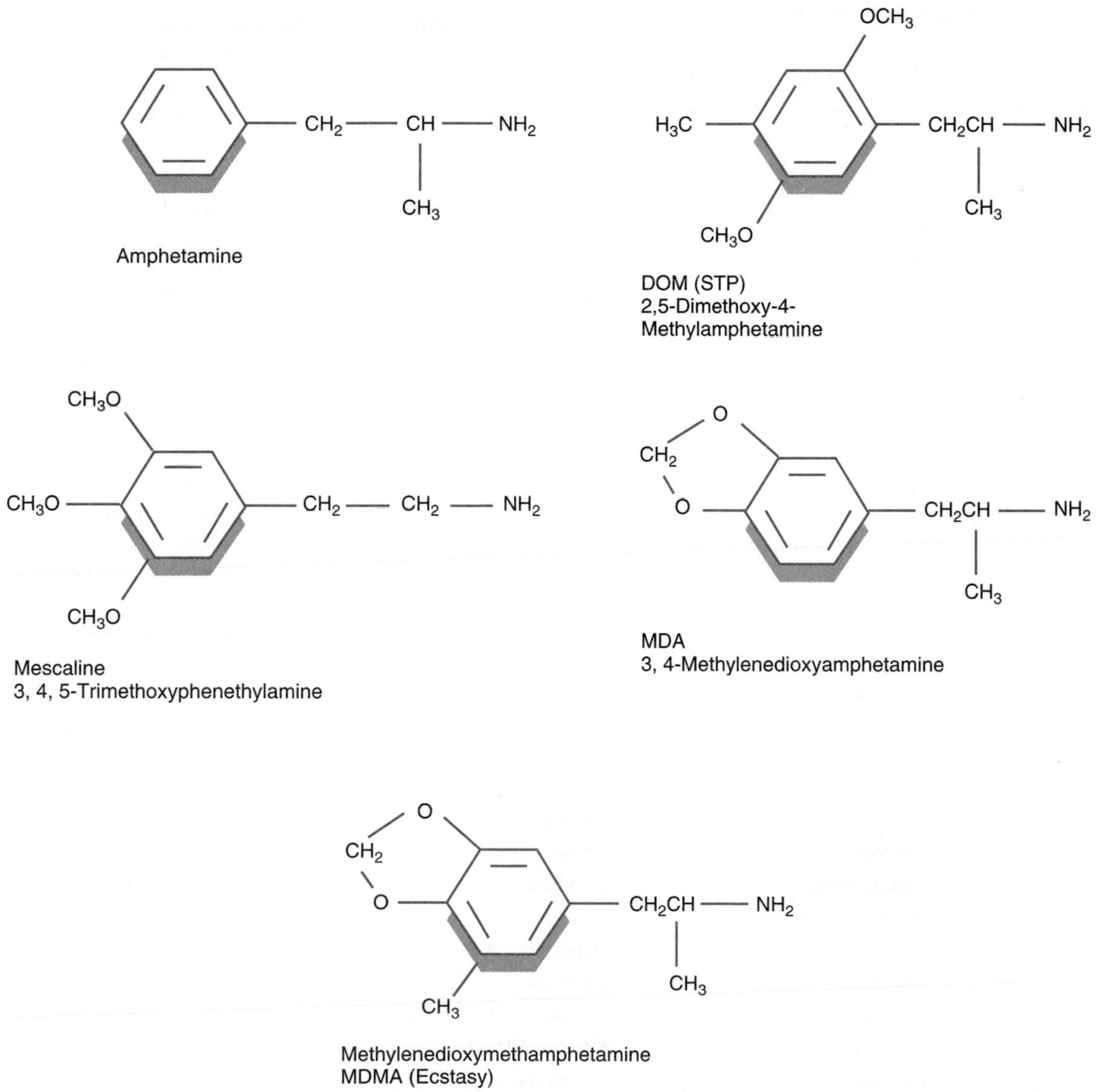

FIGURE 8.4
Notice how similar all of these "hallucinogens" are to each other and how similar each is to amphetamine.

damage is **fenfluramine,** a drug used to reduce appetite (Grob & Poland, 1997). Fenfluramine has been administered to 50 million people worldwide in the last 25 years with no evidence of long-term neurological damage.

Given that millions of doses of MDMA have been taken worldwide, it is not surprising that some serious reactions have been reported, including fatalities due to heart attack, stroke, and malignant hyperthermia (a sudden and nearly irreversible rise in body temperature) (Lapostolle et al., 1997; Mallick & Bodenham, 1997). Liver damage has also been attributed to MDMA use (Grob & Poland, 1997). Some researchers have found evidence that MDMA can induce a long-lasting psychotic state in some users (Cohen & Cocores, 1997).

MDMA use is common at **raves,** all-night dance parties in which people gather at a pre-planned destination such as an empty warehouse or an open field. Strobe lighting and techno and house music contribute to the setting, as does the expectation that hundreds of people will dance, hug, and sway to the beat of the music. Raves began in England and quickly spread to the United States. MDMA use is virtually synonymous with raves, and participants wear clothing and pendants identifying their allegiance to the drug (Eisner, 1989; Beck & Rosenberg, 1994). Not all experiences are positive, of course, and adverse experiences such as those listed in table 8.2 are fairly common. Some users will bring pacifiers to suck on to prevent injuring their teeth and gums, because MDMA causes teeth grinding.

The Unusual Drugs

The use of these two drugs is not common. They do not resemble the more traditional "hallucinogens" and in high doses can produce serious neurological damage and death. Low doses, however, have psychological effects that some people find rewarding. In addition, both of these drugs have developed a reputation that needs to be examined objectively.

Phencyclidine

Phencyclidine was first introduced as an anesthetic and showed unusual properties. Unlike other anesthetics, PCP does not depress respiration or cardiovascular functioning. Instead of falling asleep, patients injected with PCP remained conscious (although they appeared catatonic) yet reported no feelings of pain. Unfortunately, about half of the time they also became agitated and developed hallucinations. Many of the patients developed psychotic symptoms that persisted for several days. PCP was taken off the market in 1965 but veterinary use was still allowed (Zukin, Sloboda, & Javitt, 1997). Somehow it made its way to the street, where it was often sold as LSD, THC, mescaline, and even cocaine. PCP can be taken orally or smoked by mixing it with tobacco or marijuana. On the street PCP is known as **angel dust** or **peace pill.**

Use of PCP (phencyclidine) seems to occur in waves. There were peaks between 1973 and 1979 and again between 1981 and 1984. Among high school seniors, use has declined from a peak in 1979 of 12.8 percent to less than 3 percent recently (Zukin et al., 1997). Use also varies by gender (males are twice as likely to use), race (whites are more likely to use), and geography (use is higher in the West). Several cities, such as Denver, Los Angeles, and Washington, D.C., seem to have the greatest problem; PCP use is rarely seen in Miami (Zukin et al., 1997).

Both the neurochemical and the behavioral effects of PCP are extremely complex. In the brain, PCP seems to bind to receptors for **glutamate,** the primary excitatory amino acid neurotransmitter (see chapter 2) as well as many other sites. As a result, use of PCP results in a wide range of behavior. The most striking effect of small to moderate amounts of PCP is a condition that almost exactly duplicates schizophrenia, the most severe form of mental illness. Users become withdrawn and negative, and their thinking processes are severely impaired. In persons who have recovered

TABLE 8.2 Common Effects of MDMA

Physiological Effects	Psychological Effects	Medical Problems
Headache	Anxiety	Kidney failure
High blood pressure	Disorientation	Convulsions
Nausea, vomiting	Depression	Coma
Rapid heartbeat	Mood swings	Hepatitis
Clenching of jaw	Depersonalization	Stroke
Sweating	Insomnia	Hyperthermia
Tremors	Psychosis	Jaundice
Blurred vision	Memory loss	Incontinence
Muscle spasms	Flashbacks	Intracranial hemorrhage
Backache	Panic attacks	Cerebral edema

Source: Adapted from Cohen, 1998.

from a schizophrenic episode, PCP can trigger a long-lasting psychosis (Zukin et al., 1997).

Users of PCP almost always show nystagmus (exaggerated eye movement), which can be vertical, horizontal, or even circular. PCP can cause a life-threatening increase in body temperature. Users often experience anxiety, panic, rage, and aggression. They often show exaggerated responses to environmental stimuli such as lights and sounds and are difficult to control. Higher doses can lead to delirium and seizures. Long-term use has been linked to brain damage in animals and indications of damage in humans. Because they have a reduced sensitivity to pain and an increased response to the environment, and are confused and sometimes hostile, PCP users can be extremely dangerous to themselves and others (Zukin et al., 1997).

You are probably familiar with PCP as a drug that is supposed to make you supernaturally strong. Depending on the personality characteristics of the user, it can cause withdrawal or violence. Those who believe its reputation and are hostile and aggressive to begin with can become violent

In Depth

In Depth

Other Hallucinogens

As you have read, more than a hundred hallucinogenic plants have been discovered and thousands more have been synthesized. A few of these are of suffcent importance that you should know a little about them. **Belladonna** (*Atrop belladonna*) is a plant known as "deadly nightshade." The word *belladonna* is Italian for "beautiful women." Belladonna contains atropine and scopolamine, which are anticholinergic and dilate the pupils. When this plant was named, women with dilated pupils were considered especially beautiful. **Datura** also contains atropine and scopolamine. Known as **jimson weed,** datura grows wild just about everywhere. These anticholinergics produce

This plant, Datura stramonium, known in the U.S. as Jimson Weed, grows in profusion in Mexico where this picture was taken. The leaves and seeds are hallucinogenic and the plant has played an important role among the shamans of Latin America. The hallucinogenic properties are the result of the plant's anticholinergic properties and are accompanied by delirium, coma, and sometimes death. It is a very dangerous plant if ingested.

very unpleasant "hallucinations" that are more like a toxic delirium.

There are various **harmala alkaloids** that are widely employed in South America although rarely found in the United States. Shrubs and trees known as **Banisteriopsis** contain harmala alkaloids such as harmine and harmaline. In South America the bark is made into a drink known as **ayahuasca** or **yage**. *Peganum harmala* is known as Syrian rue and is found in the United States, often sold in gardening stores. It is reported to have both stimulating and hallucinogenic properties. Both **mace** and **nutmeg,** found in most spice cabinets, are hallucinogenics in high doses. They also result in nausea, severe headache, and a terrible hangover. Very few people try nutmeg or mace more than once. These spices come from the same East Indian shrub. Mace is the outercovering, nutmeg is the meat or nut. They contain myristicin, a cousin of mescaline (Leiken & Paloucek, 1996).

The **acacia** shrub and tree have been found to contain the hallucinogen dimethyltryptamine (DMT). The leaves can be taken orally, dried and smoked, or brewed into a tea. **Desmanthus,** also known as bundleweed, Illinois bundleflower, and prairie mimosa, grows wild throughout the United States. The root bark and root contain DMT. **Ipomoea** is the morning glory, referred to in this chapter. In addition to visual and auditory distortions, users experience nausea, vomiting, sweating, and diarrhea. *Lactuca virosa* is known as lettuce opium. It was widely promoted in the 1970s as a legal opium. Lettuce opium grows wild and has a milky sap, but most users do not find that it has any psychoactive properties. **Lobelia** is a common garden plant. The leaves contain lobeline, and smoking it is supposed to result in a mild marijuana-like high. **Mimosa** is reported to be used as a marijuana substitute in Mexico. Some varieties contain DMT. *Stirpa robusta* is found in many parts of the United States and is known as "sleepy grass." It contains several LSD-like substances.

when they take it. Because it also causes anesthesia, the user feels no pain and is more likely continue an attack despite being injured. PCP does not make you supernaturally strong, just supernaturally stupid.

Gamma-hydroxy-butyrate (GHB)

Gamma-hydroxybutyrate (GHB) is known on the street as **GBH** or **Grievous Bodily Harm** and as **liquid ecstasy.** It is a naturally occurring substance in the brain, similar to GABA, and might function as a neurotransmitter (Beardsley, Balster, & Harris, 1996). Originally developed for surgical anesthesia, GHB subsequently was given to alcoholics to help them through withdrawal. Its use as an anesthetic is limited by the fact that it is not very effective at blocking pain and can cause seizures when the patient is going under (Galloway et al., 1997). GHB is not available as a prescription drug in the United States but was, until recently, available in health food stores where it was considered an amino acid.

GHB has been used by bodybuilders to increase muscle mass in the belief that it increases the amount of deep sleep (it does) and therefore should increase the amount of human growth factor. Human growth factor is secreted in the pituitary during stage 4 or deep sleep. There is no clear evidence that GHB has any anabolic or muscle-building effects (Galloway et al., 1997). Many users have found that it causes euphoria and others have found it useful as a sedative.

GHB first decreases then increases dopamine in the reward center in the brain. It is a potentially dangerous drug because there is only a small difference between the dose required to have an effect and the toxic dose. GHB is no longer legal, and street versions of the drug are of unknown purity and strength, increasing the possibility of overdose. High doses of GHB can cause vomiting, respiratory depression, seizures, and coma. GHB is often combined with alcohol, which potentiates its sedative effects, or amphetamine, which increases the likelihood of seizures (Galloway et al., 1997).

GHB does cause dependence and users increase their dose, indicating that it is pharmacologically addictive. Withdrawal symptoms include insomnia, anxiety, and tremor and can last for several days (Galloway et al., 1997). GHB use is not widespread, although this drug is quite popular in some areas of the country, notably southern California.

Stop and Review

1. What are the major classes of hallucinogenics?
2. How does LSD affect the brain?
3. What is one serious danger associated with magic mushrooms?
4. What is the relationship between mescaline and MDMA?
5. What are the primary dangers associated with MDMA?
6. Why are phencyclidine users potentially dangerous?

7. What characteristics of GHB make it attractive to some people?

Inhalants

Inhalants are readily available, inexpensive, and legal. This combination almost guarantees that they will be used. The term *inhalant* covers a wide variety of compounds with many different effects. About the only thing they have in common is that they are all volatile, meaning that they exist in a form that can be inhaled. Users talk of huffing or sniffing inhalants (Maniscalco & Sinclair, 1998). The extent of inhalant use, as measured by standard surveys, is not great. The National Household Survey, for example, estimates that 5.6 percent of the population, or 12 million people, have used an inhalant (USDHHS, 1997). Use of inhalants seems to be on the rise; first-time use has increased from 400,000 in 1991 to almost 700,000 at present.

As is the case with other drugs, inhalant use begins in the early teen years. Unlike most other drugs, however, use rapidly drops off after a few years. The peak of use is eighth and ninth grade, with roughly half a million children experimenting with or using inhalants. Some go on to become chronic users. Abusers are often delinquents and have numerous medical, psychological, and social problems stemming from use of inhalants.They are often lethargic, physically weakened, and confused. Detoxification can take 20 to 30 days because the inhalants are stored in fatty tissue in the body. The neurological damage is usually reversible, with time (*National Inhalant Prevention Coalition,* 1998). Needless to say, inhalant abusers are not popular in the managed care system where inpatient treatment rarely lasts more than a few days.

More than a thousand household items are capable of being used as inhalants, and just about every possible in-

NOTICE!

State law prohibits the sale of spray paint cans or any product containing Toluene to anyone under 18 years of age.

STATE OF CALIFORNIA BILL AB-797

FIGURE 8.5
The awareness of the effects of toluene and other inhalants has led some states to issue warnings such as this.

halant seems to be used by someone somewhere (Miniscalco & Sinclair, 1998). Some of the more unusual inhalants are transmission fluid, rocket fuel, and wax stripper. However, inhalant users rarely confine themselves to one type of inhalant, and many inhalants do not fully list all of their ingredients. This can have serious consequences should the inhalant user need hospitalization (Sharp & Rosenberg, 1997). Furthermore, the various chemicals can interact with each other to increase the dangers of use.

Inhalant use can be thought of as a "quick drunk." Many of the symptoms resemble alcohol intoxication. They included drowsiness, loss of inhibition, lighted-headedness, and agitation. Higher doses lead to difficulty in moving and disorientation. Deaths are relatively rare, but they do occur—probably due to loss of oxygen or cardiac arrythmias. Ironically, the federal government does not collect data on inhalant-related deaths. Prolonged use can lead to serious consequences that are difficult, if not impossible, to treat. Prolonged use of **toluene,** for example, can produce effects resembling the symptoms of multiple sclerosis or diffuse brain damage. Toluene is one of the most commonly abused inhalants, found in gasoline, airplane glue, rubber cement, and paint remover (Dinwiddie, 1994).

Inhalants can be divided into four main classes: (1) **volatile solvents,** such as glue, gasoline, and paint thinner; (2) **aerosols,** such as hair spray and spray paint; (3) **anesthetics,** such as **ether** and **nitrous oxide;** and (4) **volatile nitrites,** such as amyl nitrate and butyl nitrite (Maniscalco & Sinclair, 1998). Choice of inhalant varies with age. Young adolescents prefer glue and toluene, older adolescents use nitrous oxide, gasoline, and amyl nitrite. Amyl nitrite and nitrous oxide are the preferred inhalants of young adults (26 to 35) and older abusers (Sharp & Rosenberg, 1997).

Volatile Solvents

The most common component of volatile solvents is toluene. In addition to brain damage, toluene abuse can lead to hallucinations, kidney damage, and liver problems. Several states have laws prohibiting the purchase of toluene-containing substances like airplane glue by anyone under 18. Restriction of other toluene-containing substances, such as gasoline and paint thinner, is almost impossible. Other substances such as hexane and lead are often found in toluene-containing fluids. These compounds can cause damage by themselves or in combination with toluene (Sharp & Rosenberg, 1997).

Aerosols

Aerosols typically contain **butane** and propane. The aerosols most commonly abused are found in paint sprays, hair sprays, room fresheners, and even cigarette lighters. Use of butane and propane leads to dizziness but otherwise it is difficult to understand the attraction of these toxic substances. Deaths have been reported from the use of aerosols. Fatalities can be the result of asphyxia, cardiac arrythmias,

buildup of fluid in the lungs and brain, and other causes (Sharp & Rosenberg, 1997).

Anesthetics

Nitrous oxide is a well-known anesthetic that is sometimes abused. The nitrous oxide found in the dentist's office is mixed with 25 percent oxygen. Nitrous oxide causes lightheadedness and giddiness and is commonly known as laughing gas (Sharp & Rosenberg, 1997). The attractiveness of nitrous oxide is something of a mystery. Its effects begin within thirty seconds and are over in five minutes (Zacny et al., 1994). It can cause dizziness and mild euphoria (Matthews, Wilson, Humphreys, & Lowe, 1997) and reduce the sensation of pain, but very few users in laboratory studies reported the experience as particularly positive. The exception apparently is those who are normally consumers of alcohol (Zacny, Cho, et al., 1996; Zacny, Klafta et al., 1996; Cho et al., 1997).

Although rare, several cases have been reported of people stealing canisters of nitrous oxide, breathing the gas without proper ventilation, and dying of asphyxiation (Wagner, Wesche, Clark, Doedens, & Lloyd, 1992). Nitrous oxide affects the endorphine receptors, where it acts as a partial agonist, meaning that high doses can result in negative effects (Gillman, 1992). Tolerance develops rapidly to the euphoric effects (Gillman, 1992), which, as you just read, last only a few minutes. Inhaling large quantities over a long period of time would require carrying about special equipment and a heavy cylinder, so the inconvenience alone would seem to be a strong deterrent (Gillman, 1992).

Volatile Nitrites

Amyl nitrite is a prescription drug used to treat the pain of angina (insufficient blood supply to the heart muscle) and cyanide poisoning. Butyl nitrite is a similar drug that is not currently available from legal sources, although it is still a fairly common street drug. Both of these drugs cause peripheral vasodilation leading to flushing and fainting, relaxation of smooth muscle tissue, feelings of warmth, and a throbbing sensation. These effects are very short-lived and often followed by a severe headache and chills. Other effects include ringing in the ears, abdominal cramps, and diarrhea.

While most of these effects would seem rather unpleasant, some users find that these drugs increase the intensity of orgasm. In addition, because nitrites relax smooth muscle, they are reported to make anal sex more pleasant. Some studies have linked nitrite use with the development of Kaposi's sarcoma, an otherwise rare form of cancer seen with uncommon frequency in males with AIDS. Another concern about nitrites has to do with their effect on the oxygen-carrying capacity of the blood. Use can lead to abnormal hemoglobin formation that can have serious consequences for individuals with heart problems (Sharp & Rosenberg, 1997).

1. How do inhalant users, beer drinkers, and marijuana smokers compare, agewise?
2. What are the primary short-term health problems associated with inhalants?
3. Why do most users seem to grow out of inhalants?

Summary

The term *hallucinogen* covers a wide variety of drugs, most of which do not produce hallucinations at all. Hallucinogens may have been, along with alcohol, the earliest drugs developed in preliterate cultures. Most Americans did not become aware of their existence until the 1960s.

The hallucinogens are not like most other drugs, in that they do not produce physical or psychological dependence. Huge doses can be taken with no apparent short-term or long-term dependence effects in most people. Tolerance occurs very rapidly, and it is imossible to use the drugs for more than a day or so a time.

Even though there was some evidence for their usefulness as drug treatment in the 1960s, possession of LSD and other similar drugs was made illegal because of their widespread street use. They played an important role in the social movements of the 1960s and have not dropped completely out of sight. The main problem with their use seems to be the intense experiences they produce. Users who have existing psychological problems can be overwhelmed, and even users who do not can harm themselves while under their influence.

Inhalant use is a serious problem that has remained more or less hidden. Inhalants are used primarily by users who cannot get other drugs. Some go on to become abusers and can suffer serious psychological and physical consequences. The problem is difficult to control because the active substances are found in so many common products that have legitimate uses. Those who use them are liable to long-term health problems or sudden death.

Key Terms

acacia   A type of shrub and tree containing the hallucinogen dimethyltryptamine (DMT).

Adam   Methylenedioxymethamphetamine, or MDMA or Ecstasy.

aerosols   Inhalants, such as hexane or butane, that are used to alter consciousness.

anesthetics   Drugs that reduce the sensation of pain; examples are ether and nitrous oxide.

angel dust   A street name for phencyclidine, or PCP.

ARRRT   Acceptance, Reduction of stimuli, Reassurance, Rest, Talk down. Guidelines for helping a person who is having a bad trip from LSD.

ayahuasca   A hallucinogenic South American drink made from the bark of the Banisteriopsis.

Banisteriopsis   A type of shrub and tree containing harmala alkoids such as harmine and harmaline.

belladonna   A plant that contains atropine-like chemicals. It has been used in the past as a poison and as a means of dilating pupils.

bufotenine   A biologically active substance found in the toad species *Bufo alvairus.*

butane   A flammable gas used in cigarette lighters and occasionally abused.

datura   Jimson weed, a toxic plant that causes a serious reaction when ingested.

desmanthus   A plant that contains DMT in its root and root bark. Also known as bundleweed, Illinois bundleflower, and prairie mimosa.

DOM   Dimethoxymethamphetamine.

DMT   Dimethyltryptamine, a hallucinogenic compound found in various plants used throughout the world. DMT was briefly popular in the 1960s.

Ecstasy   Methylenedioxymethamphetamine, (MDMA), a drug with effects similar to those of both mescaline and methamphetamine. It is classified as a hallucinogenic, but it rarely produces hallucinations.

entheogen   A term, meaning "caused from within," that could be used instead of *hallucinogen.*

epena   A snuff used by South American Indians to induce visions and hallucinations.

ether   An anesthetic gas sometimes abused for recreational purposes.

Eve   A slang term for MDA, or methlyenedioxyamphetamine.

fenfluramine   A drug used to reduce appetite.

flashbacks   A short-lived recurrence of an LSD experience.

fly agaric   *Amanita muscaria,* a hallucinogenic mushroom.

gamma-hydroxybutyrate (GHB)   A naturally occurring substance in the brain similar to GABA. It may function as a neurotransmitter. It is also used to stimulate muscle growth and alter consciousness.

GBH (Grievous Bodily Harm)   A street name for gamma-hydroxybutyrate (GHB).

glutamate   The primary excitatory neurotransmitter in the brain.

harmala alkoids   A group of chemical compounds with hallucinogenic properties similar to LSD found in various plants.

ipomoea   The common morning glory, which can cause visual and auditory distortions.

jimson weed   A toxic plant that causes a serious reaction when ingested.

Lactuca virosa   Lettuce opium. It is reputed to have psychoactive properties, although this is doubtful.

liquid ecstasy   A street term for gamma-hydroxybutyrate (GHB).

lobelia   A common garden plant whose leaves contain lobeline. Smoking the leaves is supposed to result in a mild marijuana-like high.

lysergic acid diethylamide (LSD-25)   An extremely potent hallucinogenic drug still widely used by young adults.

mace   The outer shell of nutmeg.

MDMA   Methylenedioxyamphetamine. A hallucinogenic drug that was popular in the 1960s because it has a short duration of action.

MDE   Methylenedioxyethamphetamine.

mescaline   The psychoactive chemical found in peyote.

methylenedioxymethamphetamine (MDMA or Ecstasy) A hallucinogenic drug.

mimosa   A marijuana substitute in Mexico.

Native American Church   A church composed of North American Indians who use peyote in religious rituals.

nitrous oxide   An anesthetic gas occasionally used nonmedically for its euphoric properties.

nutmeg   A spice containing myristicin, a mildly hallucinogenic substance.

peace pill   A street name for phencyclidine, or PCP.

Peganum harmala   Syrian rue. Found in gardening stores, it contains stimulating and hallucinogenic properties.

peyote   A cactus found in the southwestern United States and in Mexico.

phencyclidine (PCP)   An anesthetic that reduces the sensation of pain without causing unconsciousness. Also can cause disorientation, emotional changes, and, in high doses, rigidity and stupor.

phenethylamine   A chemical structure that is the basis of many hallucinogenic drugs.

post hallucinogenic perceptual disorders   Flashbacks of an LSD trip.

prodrug   A chemical that is inactive itself but is converted in the body into an active substance.

psilocybin   The psychoactive substance found in many mushrooms.

raves   All-night parties in empty warehouses or open fields. Use of MDMA is widespread at the parties.

Stirpa robusta   A plant that contains several LSD-like substances; known as "sleepy grass" in the United States.

STP   A term in the 1960s for dimethoxymethamphetamine (DOM).

synesthesia   Seeing sounds or hearing colors while on an LSD trip.

teonanacatl   The Aztec name for the psilocybin mushroom; meaning "God's flesh."

toluene   The psychoactive substance in solvents.

volatile nitrites   Inhalants such as amyl nitrite and butyl nitrite.

volatile solvents   Inhalants such as glue, gasoline, and paint thinner.

yage   A South American drink made from the bark of the Banisteriopsis.

References

Abraham, H., & Aldridge, A. (1993). Adverse consequences of lysergic acid diethylamide. *Addiction, 88,* 1327–1334.

Beardsley, P. M., Balster, R. L., & Harris, L. S. (1996). Evaluation of the discriminative stimulus and reinforcing effects of gammahydroxybutyrate (GHB). *Psychopharmacology, 127,* 315–322.

Beck, J., & Rosenbaum, M. (1994). *Pursuit of Ecstasy.* Albany: State University of New York Press.

Bliss, K. (1988). LSD and psychotherapy. *Contemporary Drug Problems, 3,* 519–563.

Cohen, R. (1998). *The love drug: Marching to the beat of Ecstasy.* New York: The Haworth Medical Press.

Cohen, R. S., & Cocores, J. (1997). Neuropsychiatric manifestations following the use of 3, 4-methylenedioxymethamphetamine (MDMA, "Ecstasy"). *Progress in Neuropsychopharmacology and Biological Psychiatry, 21,* 727–734.

Devereux, K. (1997). *The long trip: A prehistory of psychedelia.* New York: Peguin Arkana.

Dinwiddie, S. (1994). Abuse of inhalants; A review. *Addictions, 89,* 925–939.

Dobkin de Rios, M. (1984). *Hallucinogens cross cultural perspectives.* Albuquerque: University of New Mexico Press.

Eisner, B. (1989). *Ecstasy: The MDMA story.* Berkeley, CA: Ronin Press.

Fiorella, D., Rabin, R. A., & Winter, J. C. (1995). The role of 5HT-2A and 5-HT-2C receptors in the stimulus effects of hallucinogenic drugs: I. Antagonist correlation analysis. *Psychopharmacology, 121,* 347–356.

Fuller, J. G. (1968). *The day of St. Anthony's fire.* New York: Macmillan.

Galloway, G. P., Frederick, S. L., Staggers, F. E., Gonzales, M., Stalcup, S. A., & Smith, D. E. (1997). Gammahydroxybutyrate: An emerging drug of abuse that causes physical dependence. *Addiction, 92,* 89–96.

Gillman, M. A. (1992). Nitrous oxide abuse in perspective. *Clinical Neuropharmacology, 15,* 297–306.

Groark, K. P. (1996). Ritual and therapeutic use of "hallucinogenic" harvester ants (*Pogomyrmex*) in native south-central California. *Journal of Ethnobiology, 16,* 1–29.

Grob, C. S., & Poland, R. E. (1997). MDMA. In J. H. Lowinson, P. Ruiz, R. B. Millman, & J. G. Langrod (Eds.), *Substance abuse: A comprehensive textbook* (pp. 269–275). Baltimore: Williams & Wilkins.

Henderson, L. A., & Glass, W. J. (1994). *LSD: Still with us after all these years.* New York: Lexington Books.

Hoffmann, A. (1983). *LSD, my problem child.* Los Angeles: Tarcher.

Kluver, H. (1966). *Mescal and mechanisms of hallucinations.* Chicago: University of Chicago Press.

Koch, S., & Galloway, M. P. (1997). MDMA induced dopamine release in vivo: Role of endogenous serotonin. *Journal of Neural Transmission, 104,* 135–146.

LaBarre, W. (1989). *The peyote cult* (5th ed.). Oklahoma City: University of Oklahoma Press.

Lapostolle, F., Eliez, C. A., El Massioui, Y., Adnet, F., Leclrec, G., Efthymiou, M. L., & Baud, F. (1997). Toxic effect of Ecstasy. *Presse Medicale, 26,* 1881–1884.

Lee, M. A., & Schlain, B. (1985). *Acid dreams: The CIA, LSD and the sixties rebellion.* New York: Grove Press.

Leiken, J. B., & Paloucek, F. P. (1996). *Poisoning and toxicology handbook.* Hudson (Cleveland): Lexi-Comp Inc.

Lyttle, T., Goldstein, D., & Gartz, J. (1996). Bufo toads and bufotenine: Facts and fiction surrounding an alleged psychedelic. *Journal of Psychoactive Drugs, 28,* 267–289.

Mallick, A., & Bodenham, A. R. (1997). MDMA induced hyperthermia: A survivor with an initial body temperature of 42.9 degrees C. *Journal of Accident and Emergency Medicine, 14,* 336–338.

Maniscalco, P. M., & Sinclair, J. D. (1998). *Inhalant abuse: The cocaine of the 90s?* (Vol.7, pp. 2-3). Austin, TX: National Inhalant Prevention Coalition.

Mathew, R. J., Wilson, W. H., Humphreys, D., & Lowe, J. V. (1997). Effect of nitrous oxide on cerebral blood velocity while reclining and standing. *Biological Psychiatry, 41,* 979–984.

Morgan, J. P. (1997). Designer drugs. In J. H. Lowinson, P. Ruiz, R. B. Millman, & J. G. Langrod (Eds.), *Substance abuse: A comprehensive textbook* (pp. 264–268). Baltimore: Williams & Wilkins.

McKenna, T. (1992). *Food of the gods: The search for the original tree of knowledge.* New York: Bantam Books.

Obradovic, T., Imel, K. M., & White, S. R. (1996). Methylenedioxymethamphetamine-induced inhibition of neuronal firing in the nucleus accumbens is mediated by both serotonin and dopamine. *Neuroscience, 74,* 469–481.

Ott, J. (1993). *Pharmacotheon: Entheogenic drugs, their plant sources and history.* Kenniwick, WA: Natural Products.

Pechnick, R. N., & Underleider, J. T. (1997). Hallucinogens. In J. H. Lowinson, P. Ruiz, R. B. Millman, & J. G. Langrod (Eds.), *Substance abuse: A comprehensive textbook* (pp. 230–237). Baltimore: Williams & Wilkins.

Schulgin, A. T., & Nichols, D. (1978). Characterization of three new psychotomimetics. In R. C. Stillman & R. E. Willette (Eds.), *The psychopharmacology of hallucinogens.* New York: Pergamon Press.

Schulgin, A., & Schulgin, A. (1991). *PIHKAL: A chemical love story.* Berkeley, CA: Transform Press.

Sharp, C. W., & Rosenberg, N. L. (1997). Inhalants. In J. H. Lowinson, P. Ruiz, R. B. Millman, & J. G. Langrod (Eds.), *Substance abuse: A comprehensive textbook* (pp. 246–263). Baltimore: Williams & Wilkins.

Stevens, J. (1987). *Storming heaven: LSD and the American dream.* New York: Atlantic Monthly Press.

Stewart, O. C. (1987). *Peyote religion.* Oklahoma City: University of Oklahoma Press.

Wagner, S., Wesche, D., Clark, M., Doedens, D., & Lloyd, A. (1992). Asphyxial deaths from the recreational use of nitrous oxide. *Journal of Forensic Medicine, 37,* 1018–1015.

Wasson, R. G. (1958). The divine mushroom: Primitive religion and hallucinatory agents. *Proceedings of the American Philosophical Society, 102,* 221–223.

Wasson, R. G. (1968). *Soma: Divine mushroom of immortality.* New York: Harcourt Brace Jovanovich.

Wasson, R. G., Kramrisch, S., Ott, J., & Ruck, C. A., (1986). *Persephony's quest: Entheogens and the origins of religion.* New Haven: Yale University Press.

Watts, V., Lawler, C. P., Fox, D. R., Neve, K. A., Nichols, D. E., & Mailman, R. B. (1995). LSD and structural analogs: Pharmacological evaluation at D-1 receptors. *Psychopharmacology, 118,* 401–409.

West, J. L., Pierce, C. M., & Thomas, W. D. (1962). Lysergic acid diethylamide: Its effects on a male Asiatic elephant. *Science, 138,* 1100–1102.

White, S. R., Obradovic, T., Imel, K. M., & Wheaton, M. J. (1996). The effects of methylenedioxymethamphetamine (MDMA, "Ecstasy") on monoaminergic neurotransmission in the central nervous system. *Progress in Neurobiology, 49,* 455–479.

Zacny, J. P., Cho, A. M., Coalson, D. W., Rupani, G., Young, C. J., Klafta, J. M., Klock, P. A., & Apfelbaum, J. L. (1996). Differential acute tolerance development to effects of nitrous oxide in humans. *Neuroscience Letters, 209,* 73–76.

Zacny, J. P., Klafta, J. M., Coalson, D. W., Marks, S., Young, C. J., Klock, A., Toledano, A. Y., Jordan, N., & Apfelbaum, J. L. (1996). The reinforcing effects of brief exposures to nitrous oxide in healthy volunteers. *Drug and Alcohol Dependence, 42,* 197–200.

Zacny, J. P., Lichtor, J. L., Coalson, D. W., Apfelbaum, J. L., Flemming, D., & Voster, V. (1994). Time course of effects of brief inhalations of nitrous oxide in normal volunteers. *Addiction, 89,* 831–839.

Zukin, S. R., Sloboda, Z., & Javitt, D. C. (1997). Phencyclidine. In J. H. Lowinson, P. Ruiz, R. B. Millman, & J. G. Langrod (Eds.), *Substance abuse: A comprehensive textbook* (pp.238–245). Baltimore: Williams & Wilkins.

Chapter Nine

Use and Abuse of Prescription Drugs

Chapter Objectives

When you have finished studying this chapter, you should

1. Be able to describe the path from opium use to heroin addiction.
2. Know the two primary components of opium and how they differ.
3. Know how heroin is related to morphine.
4. Be able to describe the how narcotic drugs interact with the endorphin system.
5. Be able to discuss how management of pain with narcotics is changing.
6. Be able to discuss neurochemical and psychological theories of narcotic addiction.
7. Know how heroin withdrawal is managed.
8. Be able to discuss the role of methadone and other drugs that are used to treat addiction.
9. Know what therapeutic communities are and how they work.
10. Know how heroin use has changed.
11. Be able to describe how aspirin relieves pain and how its alternatives work.
12. Be able to list the three main types of antidepressants and discuss how they differ.
13. Know the role of benzodiazepines in managing anxiety and insomnia.
14. Be able to discuss the controversy over the use of fen-phen.
15. Understand what ergogenic aids are and how they work.

Dr. Tufts states that after forty years study, he hath discovered Several strange Diseases as yet unknown to the world for which hath infallible cures. *Now the names of these new Distempers are:*
THE STRONG FIVES, THE MOON PALL,
THE MARTHAMBLES AND THE HOCKOGROCLE.

Advertisement of a "doctor" about 1670
(Quoted in Thompson, 1993)

For most of recorded history, there were very few drugs that were actually effective. Foremost among these was **opium,** whose first use is lost in antiquity. It was already widely used and known by the ancient Egyptians, Greeks, Romans, and Arabs (Inciardi, 1992). Galen, the last great physician of ancient Greece, considered it a cure for everything from asthma to depression to leprosy and snakebite. When Greek and Roman civilizations declined about A.D. 400, Arab countries became the storehouses of accumulated knowledge. Wherever they went, opium was sure to follow (Owen, 1968). In China, opium was widely used as medicine, but also widely smoked for its pleasurable effects (Scott, 1969).

Until the beginning of the twentieth century, about the only other effective drugs were an aspirin-like drug, quinine to treat malaria, and mercury (now known to be very poisonous) for syphilis. The thousands of other medicines that had been used and highly regarded throughout history were basically placebos (Shapiro & Shapiro, 1997). Not even these three medicines cured any conditions, but they did relieve symptoms. In the nineteenth century, physicians, druggists, and just about anyone else could put virtually anything on the market and tout it as a cure or treatment. "Remedies" called patent medicines could be purchased through the mail and were widely advertised in magazines. Nearly all were useless and some caused great harm. The few that did pro-

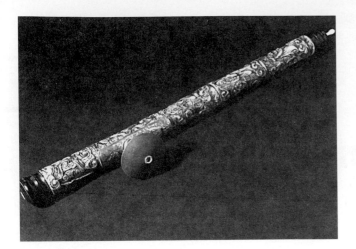

An opium pipe.

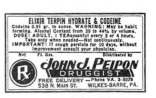

Notice that all of these patent medicines contain either opium or morphine.

vide some relief contained opium, alcohol, and sometimes cocaine.

Our present pharmaceutical system originated early in this century, as a result of expanding medical knowledge and federal legislation. One law led to the system of prescriptions that we have today. The **Harrison Narcotic Act of 1914** required doctors and druggists to keep records of the prescriptions they wrote. We now have two categories of drugs, over-the-counter (OTC) drugs, for which no prescription is necessary, and prescription drugs, for which various requirements exist. **Herbal remedies** are not required to meet the same standards because they are not advertised as treating or curing disease. Legislation is introduced almost every year to change the situation, but so far the herbal remedy lobbyists have prevailed.

In this chapter we will look at the following kinds of legal drugs with psychoactive properties: (1) analgesics, (2) drugs used to treat mood disorders, (3) antianxiety drugs, (4) drugs used to treat obesity, and (5) ergogenic aids.

Analgesics

As you just read, opium has been an extraordinarily useful drug for thousands of years. As you can read in the In Depth box on opiate users, it also played a significant role in world history. Opium comes from the poppy **Papaver somniferum,** called the Oriental or opium poppy. For about a week after the poppy flower fades, the seed pod will ooze a tarlike substance when cut. The substance is collected and refined into opium. Opium contains several compounds, including **morphine** and **codeine.**

Narcotic Analgesics

Morphine was isolated from opium by a pharmacist's apprentice named Serturner in 1806. Researchers at that time typically experimented on themselves, and Serturner was no exception. As a result he nearly died of an overdose (Hollinger, 1997). Morphine is named after Morpheus, the

Greek god of dreams and sleep. Morphine use did not really take off until the hypodermic syringe was perfected. Now there was not only a powerful drug but a means of delivering it almost immediately to the brain (Courtwright, 1982). Injecting morphine was so common that the Sears Roebuck catalog of 1897 offered hypodermic kits, including a syringe, two needles, and a carry case, for $1.50 (Inciardi, 1992).

In the nineteenth century, doctors would usually leave a prescription for morphine along with a hypodermic syringe at the bedside of many of their patients. The prescription could be filled endlessly and the syringe belonged to the patient (Courtwright, 1982). When the inevitable happened and patients became dependent on morphine, the withdrawal symptoms they experienced were seen as an illness for which there existed a wonderful remedy—more morphine. If morphine wasn't available from the druggist, the now-dependent patient could find a substitute quite easily—morphine in patent medicines. While taking "hair of the dog that bit you" (i.e., more morphine to treat morphine dependence), the patient became even more dependent.

Types of Narcotics and Pain

Morphine primarily affects the central nervous system and the gastrointestinal tract. In the CNS, morphine reduces pain, depresses respiration, suppresses cough, and causes

Herbal Remedies

Most of the world's population relies on herbal remedies to treat illnesses, so you might expect to find
some that really work. Many of the herbs have been
promoted on the basis of anecdotal accounts or personal testimony. The problem with anecdotal accounts
is that there isn't any way to determine what would
have happened if a person hadn't tried the remedy.
Most problems are self-limiting, and the remedy a
person takes when the body is curing itself is given
the credit. Another reason herbal "remedies" work is
the power of suggestion, which can be quite powerful. Nevertheless, there is reasonably good evidence
that the following remedies might have beneficial effects.

Chamomile: The flower heads of this herb are
made into a tea and taken for indigestion, muscle
spasms, and inflammation of the gastrointestinal
tract. As an oil it is applied to the skin and mucous
membranes to reduce inflammation. To be effective
the tea should be brewed using fresh chamomile. People who are allergic to ragweed or flowers from the
daisy family might have an allergic reaction to
chamomile.

Feverfew: The leaves, or capsules that contain the
leaves, help reduce the incidence of migraines if taken
daily.

Garlic: Hung around the neck, garlic is supposed
to repel vampires. It must work, because no one wear-
ing garlic has ever seen a vampires, right. Aside from
folk myths, one-half to one whole clove can lower
cholesterol. Eating a clove of garlic can keep away
people as well as vampires, so a capsule that dissolves
in the intestine has been marketed. It works even better than eating the clove and reduces mouth odor. It
is also effective in slowing blood clotting, which can
be a problem for some people.

Ginger: This familiar spice is used for nausea. It
can prevent motion sickness when taken before a trip.

It might also be effective against other kinds of nausea. Like garlic, it slows clotting time. The candied
form, called crystallized ginger, also seems to work
and tastes better.

Gingko biloba: This remedy is derived from the
gingko tree, which is believed to be one of the oldest
tree species in existence. It has been found to improve
circulation, enhance blood flow in the brain, and relieve painful cramps in the legs.

Milk thistle: The small hard fruits of the milk thistle contain silymarin, which prevents toxins from
entering the membrane of undamaged liver cells and
so protects against further damage. It seems to be
useful for treating hepatitis and cirrhosis. This remedy
should not be taken without consulting a doctor.

St. John's wort: This plant begins to bloom by 24
June, which Catholics and the Eastern Orthodox consider the birthday of John the Baptist, hence the
name. It is effective in treating mild to moderate depression and has fewer side effects than prescription
antidepressants. Since no one is quite sure how it
works, anyone already taking an antidepressant
should be very cautious and consult a doctor before
trying St. John's wort because of the slight possibility
that it might interact with the prescription antidepressant.

Saw palmetto: This plant is regularly used for
problems of the urinary tract. It can improve urinary
flow in men with benign prostate enlargement (a very
common ailment of middle-aged and elderly men). It
might also reduce inflammation.

Valerian: This plant is more frequently prescribed
in Europe than any other sleeping aid. It helps promote restful sleep. The tea made from valerian smells
and tastes very bad to some people, so valerian is also
available in a capsule, which also works and is not
nearly so odorus.

---

nausea. In the GI tract, morphine decreases intestinal motility and thus decreases diarrhea. For many individuals, even
those in severe pain, the effects of morphine are quite unpleasant and include vomiting, anxiety, sweating, and general depression. For others, morphine reduces the emotional
component of pain as well as the pain itself, and the effects
are experienced as quite pleasant indeed.

Codeine is also found in opium. Its chemical name is
methylmorphine, and it is more lipid soluble than morphine.
However, it must be converted into morphine to be effective.
Only about 10 percent of codeine taken into the body is converted (Carvey, 1998). Therefore codeine is only about one-

tenth as potent in relieving pain. Codeine is more effective
than morphine as a cough suppressant, however, and is more
easily absorbed orally (Carvey, 1998). Codeine is extremely
constipating and so is useful in treating people with serious
bowel problems. Dependence does occur, but it seems that
withdrawal is considerably milder than for morphine or
heroin (Stimmel, 1997).

Heroin is diacetylmorphine, morphine with two other
molecules added. In the body it is converted into morphine.
Heroin is a more lipid soluble than morphine and is three to
four times more potent, although in clinical studies it is not
a noticeably better analgesic; when addicts are given both

Three Famous Opiate Users

With morphine addiction common among the educated and well-to-do, it is not surprising that some famous people of the nineteenth century were addicted. In most cases their addiction had harmful effects on their productivity, but in one case there seemed to be no effect at all.

William Halsted was one of the great physicians of the century, a founder of Johns Hopkins Medical School, a brilliant surgeon, a devoted husband—and a morphine addict for thirty-six years. He was one of the first medical researchers to experiment with cocaine, and he became dependent on it. After several unsuccessful attempts to stop using cocaine he "cured" his problem by becoming a morphine addict. In fact, he did his most brilliant work while addicted to morphine and managed to keep his secret from his friends, his family, and all but one of his professional colleagues.

Thomas DeQuincy became addicted to laudanum (a mixture of alcohol and opium). If he had been born in 1950 instead of 1785, DeQuincy would have been a hippie. He ran away from his middle-class parents at age 17 and went to London. At first he refused to accept money from his family, but he finally gave in when he realized he would otherwise have to go to work, an occupation unfit for a gentleman. During his career as a professional student, he cultivated the friendship of the major artists of the day.

His experience with opium is supposed to have begun one Sunday afternoon when he had a toothache. He went to a druggist who suggested laudanum. He loved the experience he got from laudanum, from the very first time he took it. Although he tried to regulate his use of it, he began taking more and more until he was essentially nonfunctional as a writer. It appears that he finally either reduced or gave up his opiate addiction and became able to write once again. His most famous work, *Confessions of an English Opium Eater,* is a description of his experience with the drug. An inability to work while taking opium is far more common than the sorts of successes Halsted achieved while addicted.

Samuel Taylor Coleridge wrote *The Rime of the Ancient Mariner* and *Kubla Kahn.* Coleridge freely admitted that an opium-induced dream was the source of *Kubla Kahn* (remember that opium was not illegal), and internal evidence, plus what is known of his life, suggests that *The Ancient Mariner* was written while he was in a similar condition. At one point in his life, Coleridge was taking half a gallon of laudanum a week! He spent most of his life dependent on his friends who recognized his genius, especially William Wordsworth (Hayter, 1988). In the nineteenth century, opium was not illegal or even disapproved of, and its use was widespread among both the famous and the common people. Others who were widely considered to be opium users, for medical or other reasons, include Edgar Allen Poe, Charles Dickens, and John Keats.

---

morphine and heroin, they prefer morphine and rate the "high" as equivalent (Stimmel, 1997). Nevertheless, heroin is the preferred narcotic drug for addicts in the United States. **Dilaudid** (hydromorphone) and **Numorphan** (ozymorphone) are drugs that are similar in structure to morphine and heroin and are legal analgesics in this country. Dilaudid (called "Blues" on the street) is so similar to heroin that addicts cannot tell them apart. It is often the target of drugstore robberies for this reason. **Darvon** (propoxyphene) is less potent than codeine and is extremely irritating when injected. High doses taken orally produce unpleasant symptoms. Because of these two deterrent characteristics, it is widely prescribed.

Other narcotic analgesics have been developed that are completely synthetic. **Methadone** is very similar to morphine but is more readily absorbed orally and has a slow onset of action. Its analgesic effects last about six hours. Although it is increasingly being prescribed for long-term treatment of chronic pain, it has been more widely used as a substitute for heroin in those who are addicted. When given orally, it occupies the same receptor sites as heroin, so someone who takes methadone and then injects heroin will experience virtually no effects from the heroin. Methadone can block the effects of heroin for more than 24 hours. As you will read later, it is just as addicting as heroin, so its primary advantage is that it does not produce euphoria and can help heroin addicts to function more or less normally (Jaffee, Knapp, & Ciraulo, 1997).

Demerol (meperidine) is another widely used wholly synthetic narcotic drug. It is somewhat more effective as a pain reliever than codeine but less so than morphine or heroin. It can be converted into a popular street drug called MPPP or China White. **MPPP** does produce euphoria when injected and has been a widely sought after drug by addicts. Fentanyl and sufentanyl are much more potent than morphine or heroin. They are rarely diverted to illegal use because of very close monitoring in hospitals and pharmacies, and because they are difficult for street chemists to synthesis. Rarely does not mean ever, though, since there have been reports of fentanyl patches stolen from deceased patients who had been using them for pain relief (Flannagan, Butts, & Anderson, 1996). Only a few micrograms of sufentanyl are sufficient to produce profound analgesia, and it is widely used in surgery. Fenatanyl is also available in a patch that can be worn by patients who are in chronic pain. Delivered this way, fentanyl is maintained at a steady level in the bloodstream and so provides superior pain relief with less sedation and nausea (Stimmel, 1997).

Figure 9.1 shows some of the common opioids and their relative potentials for abuse.

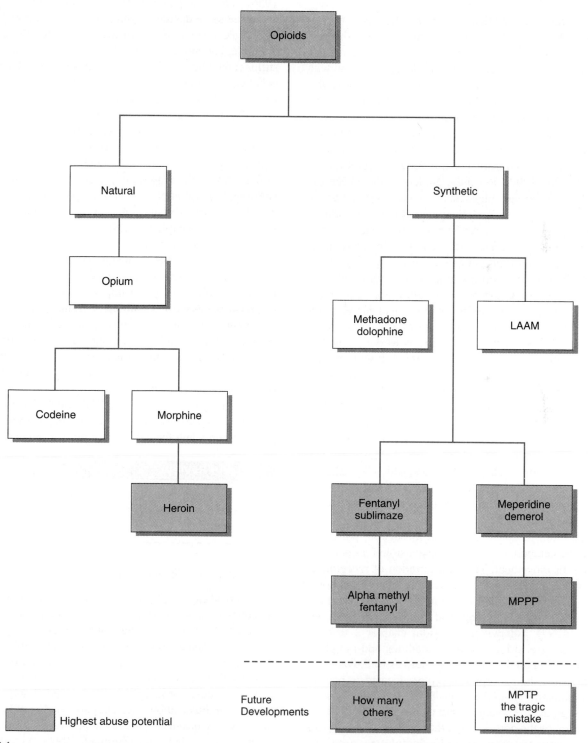

FIGURE 9.1

The diagram shows some common opioids. There are many more, both natural and synthetic. The shaded boxes indicate the drugs that have, for various reasons, the highest abuse potential.

Stop and Review

1. Many types of narcotic drugs are used to relieve pain. Some of them have high abuse potential and some do not—why do you think this is?

Narcotics and Acute Pain

Narcotics rarely cause addiction in users who take them for severe pain. They can readily produce dependence, however. Virtually anyone taking the stronger narcotics for more than two weeks or so will develop physical dependence and will experience withdrawal (Stimmel, 1997). Fortunately, the withdrawal from even high doses of narcotics is seen by patients as being relatively mild (Stimmel, 1997).

In the past the fear of causing "addiction" deterred many physicians from prescribing adequate doses of pain-relieving narcotics, and many patients suffered needless pain (Jaffe & Martin, 1997). Recently, guidelines have been established to encourage physicians to prescribe whatever dosages are necessary to keep the pain-sufferer comfortable (Portnoy & Payne, 1997). An important element of these guidelines is that the *patient's* self-report is the determining factor in prescribing. The guidelines make it clear that the *patient* is the source of information about pain relief. The physician is to respect the patient's self-assessment of the pain. If you have recently been injured or had surgery, you probably remember being asked to rate your pain on a scale of 0 to 10. The purpose of the rating is to determine the strength and effectiveness of the analgesic you will receive.

All of the opiates and their synthetic cousins act in similar fashion to relieve pain. You will recall from chapter 2 that endorphin is the naturally occurring morphine-like substance in the brain and body. There are at least five separate endorphin receptor types: *mu* (μ), *delta* (δ), *sigma* (σ), *kappa* (κ), and *epsilon* (ϵ) (Carvey, 1998). Morphine acts primarily on the mu and kappa receptors, which are believed to affect analgesia, respiratory depression, and euphoria. The other narcotics bind to receptors in a different pattern and have different effects.

Endorphin receptors are found throughout the brain, except in the cerebellum, which is responsible for coordination of motor movement. The concentration of receptors is highest in the **amygdala,** the area responsible for emotional expression, and is also high in the **medulla,** the area of the brain that controls breathing and other basic functions (Stimmel, 1997). You will recall from chapter 2 that the emesis center is also located in the medulla, and morphine has a direct effect on this area of the brain as well. Narcotics are agonists for the endorphin receptors located in both of the two pain pathways in the brain. The first pathway carries pain messages up the spinal cord to the thalamus and then to various areas of the cortex. The other carries messages to a part of the brain called the **periaqueductal gray area,** and to the limbic system (Carvey, 1998). The first pathway is responsible for the dull chronic pain that morphine relieves so well. The second pathway carries messages that control the emotional content of pain (Stimmel, 1997).

Severe pain is nearly always accompanied by distress and anxiety. There are exceptions, though. For example, soldiers whose wounds mean that they will be leaving the battle zone and going home require less morphine than patients who have suffered similar wounds in accidents (Beecher, 1956). The first pathway (to the thalamus) is signalling about the same degree of pain, but the second pathway (to the limbic system) seems to make the soldier's pain more tolerable. Patients given morphine typically report that they still feel pain but that it doesn't seem to matter. Therefore, it is believed that morphine affects the limbic system pathway more than the thalamic pathway.

We have seen, then, that morphine relieves pain, depresses respiration, causes nausea and vomiting, and affects emotions. Morphine also can cause either euphoria or dysphoria, depending on the individual, the dose, and the purpose for taking the drug (Zacny, Conley, & Marks, 1997). In addition, because of effects on other parts of the central and peripheral nervous systems as well as on various hormones, morphine causes pupil contraction, constipation, and urinary retention (Stimmel, 1997).

In addition to being an agonist at the endorphin receptor, opiates also activate a serotonin pathway that plays a prominent role in pain. An important part of the analgesic response is caused by a norepinephrine pathway as well. Morphine causes a release of dopamine in the nucleus accumbens, and this release is assumed to be responsible for the euphoria and craving addicts experience. Because pain is mediated by numerous neurotransmitter systems, physicians often prescribe antidepressants along with the opiates, not because the patient is depressed (although that is certainly possible) but because most of the antidepressants increase both serotonin and the catecholamines (Stimmel, 1997).

Stop and Review

1. Pain is a very complex process. What are the anatomical pathways and the neurochemical systems involved?

Narcotics and Chronic Pain

As you read earlier, physicians are often wary of prescribing narcotics because of concern that the patient might become addicted. You will remember from chapter 1 that pharmacological and behavioral addiction are quite different. Even though the use of narcotics to relieve pain can result in dependence, most pain specialists no longer see this as a problem. If the doses of morphine are reduced slowly and other appropriate medication is given, patients do not have to experience any physical withdrawal and rarely report craving or drug-seeking behavior (Stimmel, 1997). Why those who use narcotics for nonmedical reasons find it so difficult to stop remains a considerable enigma.

In the last few years, pain specialists have begun to prescribe narcotics for prolonged periods of time to treat patients with chronic pain such as severe headache and lower back pain (Ziegler, 1994; Brown, Fleming, & Patterson, 1996). Even though doses of narcotics given to relieve acute pain result impaired coordination and thinking, chronic users seem to be able to function normally, even when taking high doses of narcotics (Zacny,1995). Chronic pain patients have difficulty functioning with pain, so it is likely that the patient taking opiates on a long-term basis might actually show improvement in overall functioning.

Long-term use of narcotics does lead to side effects such as constipation, impaired sexual functioning, and increased sweating. Some hormonal changes also seem to accompany such treatment, but they do not seem to cause any significant problems and most patients probably feel that chronic constipation (the most common side effect) is worth the benefit of being relatively pain-free (Zacny, 1995). Unlike with alcohol and almost any other drug, long-term use of narcotics does not seem to be associated with harm to any of the major organ systems. Addicts on methadone maintenance (described below) for twenty or more years are essentially as healthy as nonusers of opiates. (Stimmel, 1997)

Narcotic Addiction

It is not particularly easy to become a heroin addict, any more than it is easy to become dependent on morphine. The potential addict has to take heroin several times a day for a week or two before addiction becomes apparent. When first beginning heroin use, the most common response is nausea and vomiting. Why would anyone use a drug several times a day that causes nausea ? Depending on dose and route of administration, the nausea and vomiting are followed by a wave of pleasurable feeling. This euphoria is followed by a sudden relief of anxiety and tension, and this **rush** is followed by several hours of feelings of being relaxed, peaceful, and drowsy. The user might doze off in a twilight state between sleep and wakefulness often accompanied by vivid dreams—**on the nod,** the user can be aroused but is lethargic and has difficulty paying attention (Inciardi, 1992).

Heroine Overdose + Withdrawal

Once addiction has occurred, the addict must take heroine to avoid withdrawal. Withdrawal from heroin begins about 6–8 hours after last use, peaks at 2–3 days and is usually resolved within a week. Withdrawal is characterized by nausea, vomiting, runny nose, muscle aches, diarrhea, yawning and insomnia (Banbery, 1998). Notwithstanding the television programs and movies you have seen, heroin addicts themselves describe withdrawal as being similar to a bad case of the flu (Inciardi, 1992). When in custody or around medical personnel, withdrawing addicts will often exaggerate their condition to get attention and perhaps even narcotics, and this probably accounts for the common misconception. The unpleasant aspects of withdrawal can be eliminated altogether by a combination of two drugs, **clonidine** and **naloxone** (Stimmel, 1997). Clonidine was developed originally to treat high blood pressure. It blocks the action of norepinephrine. Naloxone occupies the receptor sites for the endorphins and displaces the heroin molecule. This technique is known as **rapid detoxification.**

Recently, a new treatment has been developed that involves giving addicts drugs that induce a profound sleep for several days and administering clonidine and naloxone during that time. This **ultrarapid detoxification** allows detoxification to occur when the patient is unconscious. After two or three days, they can awake and be virtually symptom free (Tretter et al., 1998). Whether this method will result in lower relapse rates remains to be seen. Neither rapid nor ultrarapid detoxification has been used in controlled studies for a long enough period of time to permit conclusions to be drawn (O'Connor & Kosten, 1998).

Heroin overdose is always a risk for addicts. Since the heroin content of the drug sold on the street varies widely, addicts can never be sure how much heroin they are taking. Overdose causes death by respiratory depression. Pulmonary edema (fluid buildup in the lungs) is common, and there can be changes in heart rate and blood pressure. An overdose can be easily reversed by injections of naloxone, provided it is given promptly. Unfortunately, addicts seldom overdose near hospitals, so several thousand deaths per year are attributed to heroin overdose. Nearly all could have been prevented (Best, Oliveto, & Kosten, 1996; Hung & Hoffman, 1997).

Neurochemical and Psychological Theories

Despite many years of research, it is still not clear why a small percentage of people who use narcotics increase their drug use and show signs of severe craving when trying to stop, whereas others simply taper off with few problems. Attempts to explain narcotic addiction at the neurochemical level are numerous, but none has been clearly proven. Perhaps addicts have fewer endorphin receptors even before they try narcotics and thus are more sensitive to physical and emotional pain. For them opiates might be seen as correcting a preexisting condition. Another theory suggests that only some people (for unknown reasons) experience euphoria when they take narcotics and it is these who become addicted. Maybe chronic use produces different neurochemical changes in some users than in others. In animals at least, chronic injection of narcotics produces physical changes in the neurons composing the dopamine reward system from the substantia nigra to the nucleus accumbens (Sklair-Tavron et al., 1996).

Psychological theories are numerous as well. Research indicates that narcotic addicts are more likely than nonaddicts to have experienced family problems as young children (Nurco, Kinlock, O'Grady, & Hanlon, 1996). Some studies have suggested that substance abuse is more likely when the mother is the one experiencing the problems, while others indicate that the father is more important (Nurco, Blatchley, Hanlon, O'Grady, & McCarren, 1998; Gabel et al., 1998). A substantial percentage of narcotic addicts have symptoms of **psychopathic personality disorder** (Dinwiddie, Cottler, Compton, & Abdallah, 1996; Jaffe, Knapp, & Ciraulo, 1997). Psychopaths exhibit a wide range of characteristics including risk taking, need for immediate gratification, and lack of remorse. These characteristics might predispose the individual to find heroin and the heroin lifestyle particularly attractive. You will recall that the Type 2 alcohol abuser shows many of the same characteristics.

Stop and Review

1. How have doctors changed their minds about prescribing narcotics, and why?
2. What are the characteristics of narcotic withdrawal, and how can they be treated?
3. What theories have been proposed to account for narcotic addiction?

Treatment for Narcotic Addiction

Relapse rates for narcotic addicts are extremely high—so high, in fact, that the preferred treatment at this time is to substitute another, safer narcotic for the one the addict was using (Lowinson et al., 1997).

Methadone

Methadone is a synthetic narcotic that is very effective taken orally and has a duration of effect of more than 24 hours. If an addict takes heroin while on methadone maintenance, no euphoria is felt (Knight, et al, 1996). Since methadone also relieves craving, there is very little incentive to continue heroin use. Typically, addicts on methadone maintenance take the drug under supervision once a day, usually mixed with orange juice. Methadone maintenance is usually chosen after a number of attempts to abstain from narcotics using other means. After they have a chance to stabilize their lives, addicts may choose withdrawal from methadone as well. Those that do rarely return to heroin use (Knight et al., 1996). Table 9.1 compares heroin addiction and methadone maintenance.

In 1997, the National Institute of Drug Abuse released the findings from the Drug Abuse Treatment Outcome Study (DATOS), which collected data on more than 10,000 heroin addicts (Mathias, 1997). A follow-up study was conducted one year later on a sample of about 3,000 of them. The follow-up study indicated that methadone maintenance was successful in more than 70 percent of the addicts. The National Institutes of Health released recommendations based on the DATOS survey. The NIH called opiate addiction a medical disorder that can be treated effectively with methadone maintenance. They urged that government regu-

TABLE 9.1 Comparison of Illicit Heroin Addiction and Methadone Maintenance

Characteristics	Illicit Heroin	Methadone Maintenance
Duration of action	4–6 hours	24–36 hours
Routes of administration	Injection, snorting, smoking several times a day	Orally administered once a day
Overall safety	Potentially lethal	Medically safe
Withdrawal	Can be severe	Less severe but lasts longer
Euphoric effects	Approximately 2 hours duration	None
Narcotic craving	Recurring and high	Relieved and blocked
HIV transmission risk	Risk very high	None
Mood alteration	Constant swings	None
Sexual functioning	Impaired	Normalized during treatment
Emotional and intellectual functioning	Impaired	Normal
Employment	Virtually impossible	Functioning has been demonstrated at every level of occupation
Criminal activity	Constant high level	Greatly reduced
Personal relationships and social functioning	Greatly impaired	Normal with counseling
Cost to society	Estimated cost to the addict as much as $40,000/year. Est. cost as a result of crime to maintain addiction as much as $40,000/year. Est. cost for incarceration $30,000. Hospital costs for final stages of AIDS at least $100,000	$3,000/year

Sources: *Regan (1995), Woods (1994), Joseph (1994), and others.*

lation of methadone programs be reduced or eliminated and that methadone be made available to all who need it. They also found that psychological counseling, social skills training, and other services are helpful to recovering addicts (Mathias, 1997).

On the surface it might not seem logical to "treat" addiction to one narcotic by causing addiction to another narcotic. Keep in mind, however, that heroin is illegal and expensive. The ups and downs associated with heroin use and the hustle and bustle required to get money to pay for the habit are not conducive to normal functioning. Methadone, on the other hand, does not cause euphoria when taken orally, lasts for a long time, and is provided free to addicts (Lowinson et al, 1997). If addicts are motivated to change their lifestyle (and this is a big "if"), they now have the ideal opportunity. Also consider that if the neurochemical theories are correct, the endorphin system of addicts is not functioning normally, and thus addicts have a disease, like diabetes. From this viewpoint, they are taking medication to relieve the symptoms of a medical disease (Lowinson et al., 1997).

Alternatives to Methadone

Not everyone agrees with the methadone maintenance approach. Opposition comes from substance-abuse treatment specialists, public officials, the medical profession, and the public at large. The criticisms are many. Objections are raised to the idea of using public funds to support drug habits. Others seem to feel that heroin addicts are criminals (which most of them are) who should be punished, not treated. Still others feel that it is morally or ethically wrong to be addicted to a substance, even one that is medically indicated. The underlying issue is that heroin addiction is seen as somehow different from other chronic diseases that require medications for management (Lowinson et al., 1997).

Methadone maintenance is not a perfect solution by any means. There is no established protocol for administering the drug, and the many programs take a number of different approaches. Some approaches are more effective than others, and outcomes vary widely. Methadone maintenance does nothing more than relieve craving, it does not provide motivation to change or relief from poverty, homelessless, abuse of other drugs, or other social ills (Lowinson et al., 1997). There is a strong economic rationale for methadone maintenance. As you can see in table 9.1, the cost of methadone maintenance is minuscule compared to the cost to society of heroin addiction.

Many addicts on methadone maintenance continue to use other drugs such as cocaine, and a large percentage are heavy drinkers (Chatham, Rowan-Szal, Joe, Brown, & Simpson, 1995). Oddly enough, those who are the heaviest drinkers seem to benefit most from treatment (Chatham, Rowan-Szal, Joe, & Simpson, 1997). Cocaine use seems to be more difficult than alcohol to treat in methadone users (Chatham et al., 1997). Methadone users are also likely to abuse benzodiazepines (drugs used to treat anxiety). Even though we normally think of heroin addiction as being associated with inner-city neighborhoods, a substantial number of addicts hold responsible positions and many more are gainfully employed (Lowinson et al., 1997).

Other methods of drug treatment for addicts have been developed. One that shows considerable promise is levo-alpha-acetylmethadol (**LAAM**). LAAM, like methadone, is an agonist at the endorphin receptors and like methadone does not produce euphoria. The major advantage of LAAM is that it needs to be taken only three times a week (Greenstein, Fudala, & O'Brien, 1997). Methadone must be taken every day. Since clinics are not usually set up to provide services seven days a week, patients are often given "take home" doses, and some sell these doses on the street to heroine addicts who find methadone desirable when there is a heroin shortage. LAAM was approved for use in1993, and recent studies have shown that it is as effective as methadone (Jaffe, Knapp, & Ciraulo,1997).

Other drugs that have been or are being considered include **naltrexone,** which is like naloxone except that it has a longer duration of action. **Buprenorphine** is a new compound currently undergoing intensive study. It is administered sublingually and absorbed rapidly. Significant blood levels are reached in three to five minutes (Mendelson, Upton, Everhart, Jacob, & Jones, 1997). It is a partial agonist, meaning that it has both agonistic and antagonist actions on different receptors. Buprenorphine can be given three times a week and will block euphoria. The major advantage of buprenorphine over methadone is a lower risk of narcotic overdose. A major disadvantage is that it can produce euphoria and dependence when injected (Jaffe, Knapp, & Ciraulo, 1997).

Even if there were a perfect treatment for heroin addiction, addicts would still have problems. Most heroin addicts have a spotty employment history, a criminal record, and a difficult time adjusting to "straight" society. **Community outreach programs** and **therapeutic communities** are designed to help deal with these issues. Community outreach programs provide psychological and job counseling, social skills training, and medical treatment for the many health problems addicts are likely to have acquired as a result of their addiction. They employ both professional counselors and ex-addicts and seem to reduce the rate of relapse (O'Brien & Devlin, 1997). They are expensive to run, however, and funding is often difficult to obtain.

Therapeutic communities are highly structured environments in which addicts learn the skills necessary to make it in a straight world while learning to get off drugs. These are residential programs and typically insist on strict abstinence from all drugs. The addict lives in the community, gradually takes on increasing responsibility in the programs, and learns to reenter normal society while continuing contact with the therapeutic community (O'Brien & Devlin, 1997).

Recent Changes in Heroine Use

No one knows how many people are addicted to heroin in the United States. Estimates vary between 400,000 and 600,000 although the number might be much larger (Epstein & Gfroerer, 1997). Until a few years ago, most heroin users injected the drug. The purity of the bags of heroin was low (about 5 percent) and the risk of becoming HIV-positive was high (Mathias, 1997). As many as half of the addicts in New York City are believed to be HIV-positive. Partly as a result of the AIDS epidemic, users have begun to smoke or snort the drug (Cone, Holicky, Grant, Darwin, & Goldberger, 1993). Snorting and smoking reduce the transmission of the HIV virus but are less efficient than an intravenous injection. As a result, heroin users require a stronger bag of heroin, and the purity of heroin sold on the street is as high as 80 percent. Some users see snorting and smoking as being "different" from injecting, and incorrectly believe they cannot become addicted with these methods (Mathias, 1997).

Partly as a result of the switch to snorting and smoking, heroin use has made inroads with young people, especially those 12 to 26 years old (Mathias, 1997). In several parts of the country there have been outbreaks of heroin use (and fatal overdose) among high school students in middle-class, suburban areas. A type of look popular for fashion models for a while was "heroin chic"—gaunt, haggard, and anorexically thin. The number of people going to emergency rooms with heroin-related problems has increased as well (Epstein & Gfroerer, 1997). It remains to be seen whether this trend will continue. The allure of heroin is difficult for most people to understand, and the lifestyle that often accompanies it is less than attractive. On the other hand, the author has heard former addicts say, "It's so good, you don't even want to try it once."

Stop and Review

1. What is the basis for shifting heroin addicts to methadone maintenance?
2. Why is heroin addiction so difficult to treat?
3. What are the advantages of methods of treatment other than methadone maintenance?

Over-the-Counter Analgesics

The most familiar over-the-counter (OTC) drug is **aspirin.** Aspirin was first developed in Germany in 1853, but it did not come into wide use until many years later (Stimmel, 1997). Although we don't generally think of lowly aspirin as being a wonder drug, it probably has more beneficial properties with fewer harmful side effects than any other drug. It reduces fever, inflammation, and pain. Recent studies have shown that it can reduce the risk of a first heart attack by as much as 40 percent when taken daily (Verheugt, 1998). It also reduces the risk of a second heart attack (Stimmel, 1997).

Aspirin has very little effect on the central nervous system. It inhibits **prostaglandins,** which are produced by virtually every cell and are released when the cell is damaged. Prostaglandins make pain more noticeable, increase inflammation, and increase temperature by means of the hypothalamus. Because aspirin blocks prostaglandins, it relieves pain, inflammation, and fever (Stimmel, 1997; Lacey, Armstrong, Ingrim, & Lance, 1997). It helps reduce clotting which can lead to a stroke or heart attack. Hemophiliacs never take aspirin.

Under most circumstances, aspirin is a remarkably safe drug. However, it can cause light stomach bleeding and minor gastrointestinal problems, and some people manage to take far too many aspirin. Side effects of aspirin related to a mild overdose include blood loss, ringing in the ears, headache, sweating, and vomiting (Stimmel, 1997). The lethal dose of aspirin in adults is approximately 40 extra-strength tablets (Leiken & Paloucek, 1995). Children and the elderly have serious symptoms at much lower doses (Stimmel, 1997). In addition, children and teenagers taking aspirin run the risk of Reye's syndrome (Zamula, 1990). Reye's syndrome can result in coma, brain damage, and death; milder cases are characterized by vomiting and major personality changes.

Other OTC analgesics include, **acetaminophen, ibuprofen,** and **naproxen;** their brand names include Tylenol, Advil, and Aleve. They all relieve fever and are analgesics, and all work on the prostaglandin system (Lacey et al., 1997). They all have side effects as well. Ibuprofen can cause stomach upset and can trigger asthma and hives. It blunts the effects of diuretics and in high does can damage the liver and kidneys. Naproxen can cause kidney problems as well as ulcers and other gastrointestinal problems. Acetaminophen relieves fever and pain but does not affect inflammation. It can cause serious liver damage, especially in heavy drinkers. Liver damage has been reported after use of 10 to 15 tablets a day for several months (Lacey et al., 1997).

Stop and Review

1. How do the OTC pain relievers differ from narcotics?
2. What are some of their side effects?

Antidepressants and Antimanic Drugs

It is likely that you know someone (perhaps yourself) who is or has been depressed. Depression is often called the "common cold" of psychological disorders because it is so common (Comer, 1998). Hopefully, you have also seen how effective antidepressants are in treating this condition. The basic *DSM-IV* definition of depression can be found in table 9.2. Some cases of depression are very mild and some are devastatingly severe. Depression can lead to suicide, as many as 15% of depressed patients take their own life (Simon & Vonkorff, 1998). Because depression is so common, many drugs have been marketed to treat this condition. All

TABLE 9.2 The Characteristics of Depression

The following are basic criteria for depression:

A. Five or more of the following symptoms. They must have been present for two weeks and must represent a change from previous functioning.
   1. Depressed mood most of the day, nearly every day.
   2. Markedly diminished interest or pleasure in all, or almost all, activities most of the day, every day.
   3. Significant weight loss (more than 5 percent in a month) or decrease or increase in appetite.
   4. Insomnia or hypersomnia nearly every day.
   5. Psychomotor agitation or retardation.
   6. Fatigue or loss of energy nearly every day.
   7. Feelings of worthlessness or excessive guilt nearly every day.
   8. Diminished ability to think or concentrate, or indecisiveness, nearly every day.
   9. Recurrent thoughts of death, recurrent suicidal thinking, or a suicide attempt.

B. The symptoms cause clinically significant distress or impairment in social, occupational, or other important areas of functioning.

Note: This definition has been adapted from the *DSM-IV* (APA, 1994). There are other criteria that have not been included. In addition there are several other types of mood disorders. *No one should every try to diagnose any psychological condition without consulting a professional.*

TABLE 9.3 Antidepressant Medications

Brand Name	Generic Name
Adapin, Sinequan	doxepin
Anafranil	clomipramine
Asendin	amoxapine
Desyrel	trazodone
Effexor	venlafaxine
Elavil	amitriptyline
Ludiolmil	maprotiline
Nardil	phenelzine
Norpramin	desipramine
Pamelor	nortriptyline
Parnate	tranylcypromine
Paxil	paroxetine
Prozac	fluoxetine
Remeron	mirtazapine
Serzone	nefazodone
Surmontil	trimipramine
Tofranil	imipramine
Vivactil	protriptyline
Wellbutrin	bupropion
Zoloft	sertraline

of the prescription drugs work by altering either the catecholamine system or the serotonin system or both (Comer, 1998). The antidepressants alter catecholamine and/or serotonin levels in different ways and have different kinds of side effects. Table 9.3 shows the available prescription antidepressant drugs. Drug companies are always coming up with new antidepressants. There will undoubtedly be additions to this list in the next few years.

Note that *a substance-induced mood disorder* is considered different from a major depressive disorder. The difference is that the substance-induced mood disorder is diagnosed by considering the onset, time course, and other factors. The mood disorder should occur only after a period of substance abuse and not at other times.

MAO Inhibitors (MAOIs)

MAOIs were the first antidepressants developed. They act by blocking the enzyme monoamine oxidase, which, as the name suggests, breaks down monoamines (norepinephrine, dopamine, and serotonin). Monoamine oxidase is found in the presypnaptic neuron and helps to regulate the monoamines. Though MAOIs are effective, they can have serious side effects. Monoamine oxidase is found in various parts of the body as well as the brain, and it regulates the production of adrenaline (Carvey, 1998). A person taking an MAOI must be very careful not to eat foods that contain high levels of tyrosine, such as red wine and aged cheese and meat. Such foods can trigger severe high blood pressure when

taken in combination with MAOIs (Preston, O'Neal, & Talaya, 1998).

Tricyclic Antidepressants

The second class of antidepressants to come along, the **tricyclic antidepressants,** block the reuptake of catecholamines and serotonin (Carvey, 1998). The down regulation that occurs as a result of the increase in neurotransmitter is believed to be one of the mechanisms by which the antidepressants relieve depression. Reuptake inhibition means that more catecholamines and serotonin will be available in the synapse. As a result, down regulation is believed to occur in the postsynaptic neuron (fig. 9.2). Down regulation can take several weeks, so the antidepressant effect might not be noted for up to two months (Carvey, 1998). The drugs have numerous side effects, such as drowsiness, altered heartbeat, dry mouth, and urine retention. Other side effects include sedation, nausea, heartburn, and diminished sex drive (Lacey et al., 1997).

Selective Serotonin Reuptake Inhibitors (SSRIs)

By far the most commonly prescribed antidepressants, the **SSRIs**—fluoxetine **(Prozac),** sertraline **(Zoloft),** and paroxetine **(Paxil)**—work by inhibiting the reuptake of serotonin (Lacey et al., 1997). Since 1988, millions of people have taken these drugs and their safety is quite remarkable. Despite early reports that they led to an increase in suicide and aggressive behavior, the scientific evidence indicates that they do neither, have fewer side effects than the tricyclic antidepressants, and are useful in treating conditions such as obsessive compulsive behavior and depression (Carvey, 1998).

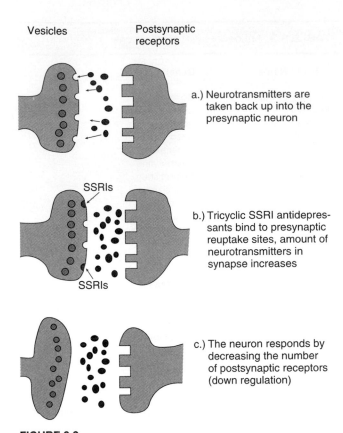

Vesicles   Postsynaptic receptors

a.) Neurotransmitters are taken back up into the presynaptic neuron

SSRIs

SSRIs

b.) Tricyclic SSRI antidepressants bind to presynaptic reuptake sites, amount of neurotransmitters in synapse increases

c.) The neuron responds by decreasing the number of postsynaptic receptors (down regulation)

FIGURE 9.2
Most antidepressants inhibit the reuptake of neurotransmitters into the presynaptic membrane, increasing the amount of neurotransmitter available in the synapse. The postsynaptic neuron responds by decreasing the number of receptors. The decrease is called "down regulation."

The SSRIs are not without side effects, of course. For males, the most troublesome side effects are decreased sex drive, impotence, and delayed orgasm (Hsu & Shen, 1995). Women sometimes experience a decrease in sex drive as well as delayed orgasm (Shen & Hsu, 1995). In one study, nearly three-quarters of those interviewed experienced some sexual side effects (Modell, Katholi, Modell, & DePalma, 1997). In a study that is remarkable for its thoroughness, men were instructed to engage in their normal sexual activity while their wives timed them with a stop watch. Paxil interfered least, while Zoloft produced an eightfold increase in time to orgasm (Kim & Seo, 1998).

Sexual dysfunction can lead patients to stop taking medication. Psychiatrists have tried using other medications to counteract these effects. One report suggests using a drug normally taken for chemotherapy-induced nausea. This drug blocks one of the serotonin receptors, and animals studies have shown that blocking this receptor leads to an increase in sexual activity. The drug seems to work, but there is one drawback—the drug costs $42 *per pill, wholesale!* Low doses of other antidepressants, especially bupropion (Wellbutrin) have also been suggested (Soorani & DeVincent, 1997). Antihistamines are reported to work, and some have even suggested amphetamine. The idea of taking a pill to

counteract another pill does not make sense to many people, however. Some antidepressants are less likely to cause sexual dysfunction, and switching to one of those might help (*Psychopharmacology Update,* 1998).

Even though the reported effects are not severe, withdrawal symptoms have been reported with the SSRIs. The symptoms include dizziness, numbness and tingling, vivid dreams, irritability, and a return of depression. The symptoms are more pronounced in men and in those who have been taking them for more than several months. These effects are seen in those who are tapered off the drugs as well as in those who stop abruptly (Roy-Byrne, 1996). The presence of withdrawal symptoms is not the same as the presence of addiction. Unfortunately, many people are reluctant to take antidepressants for fear they will become addicted. Even if they might experience withdrawal symptoms when they stop, individuals taking antidepressants do not experience craving, increase their dose, take the medications for nonmedical purposes, or use them in spite of negative consequences. In short, they are not addicted (Preston et al., 1998).

Other Antidepressants

Several new drugs have been marketed in the last few years and more are being developed. **Effexor** (venlafaxine), **Remeron** (mirtazepine), and **Serzone** (nefazodone) are similar to the tricyclic antidepressants—they inhibit the reuptake of norepinephrine and serotonin. They seem to be more specific, however, and have fewer side effects (Preston et al., 1998). Unlike the SSRIs, they do not appear to decrease sexual desire or performance. **Wellbutrin** (bupropion) does not fit into the other categories mentioned. It is considered an "atypical" antidepressant because its chemical formula does not resemble any of the other antidepressants. It affects norepinephrine, but not serotonin. Uniquely among the antidepressants, it appears to increase sexual desire (*Psychopharmcology update,* 1998). Under a different name, Zyban, bupropion is available in a sustained-release formula marketed to help smokers stop smoking. If you are confused about the rationale behind prescribing an antidepressant for smoking cessation, you are not alone. Just how it helps some people stop smoking is anyone's guess, but evidence suggests that it does.

Stop and Review

1. How do the various types of antidepressants produce their effects?
2. What are some side effects of each?

Antimanic Drugs

People with a **bipolar disorder** (more commonly known as manic depression) have wide mood swings. In the manic phase the person "can do no wrong," is euphoric, hardly ever sleeps, and often gets into trouble because of impulsiveness.

The depressive phase is similar to clinical depression. Manic depression has a definite genetic component. About 25 percent of individuals with a positive family history for bipolar disorder will become manic-depressive themselves (Comer, 1998). The cause of this disorder is unknown, as are the underlying neurochemical changes that accompany it.

Drugs used to treat bipolar or manic-depressive disorder include **lithium** (a metal salt), carbamazepine (**Tegretol),** and valproic acid (**Depakote). ** Lithium is effective in about 80 percent of cases and is the preferred treatment. No one knows how it works, although theories abound. Lithium has significant side effects that can be deterrents to compliance. These include nausea and vomiting, diarrhea and abdominal cramps, slowed reaction time, impaired thinking, and frequent urination. Depakote and Tegretol do not produce as wide a range of side effects, but they are less effective (Carvey, 1998). No one knows how they work either.

Antianxiety Drugs

Most readers will be familiar with the term *mild tranquilizer.* This term is no longer used because the drugs in question are not really tranquilizers. The preferred terms are *sedative hypnotic* or *antianxiety drug.* With two exceptions, all are members of a family known as **benzodiazepines.** Benzodiazepines are prescribed for insomnia and as muscle relaxants as well as to treat anxiety (Wesson, Smith, Ling, & Seymour, 1997). Benzodiazepines are lipid soluble and have a long duration of action (Carvey, 1998). In fact, duration of action is the primary difference among the various drugs. In table 9.4 you can see the duration of action of the most common benzodiazepines.

Benzodiazepines

Benzodiazepines operate on the GABA receptor and facilitate its inhibitory effects (Carvey, 1998). Therefore they are considered agonists. Because GABA is the primary inhibitory neurotransmitter in the brain (see chapter 2), drugs that act upon the GABA receptor, such as alcohol and the benzodiazepines will affect a wide range of behavior (Wesson et al., 1997).

Most people find the benzodiazepines useful to reduce anxiety and induce sleep. They have a low abuse potential because high doses produce unpleasant side effects including light-headedness, dry mouth, amnesia, nausea, vomiting, and diarrhea (Carvey, 1998). A few groups of people are at risk, however. Methadone maintenance patients and present or former alcohol abusers often find the effects of benzodiazepines desirable. Methadone maintenance patients in particular are at risk. The benzodiazepines are widely used to reduce the symptoms of alcohol withdrawal, so physicians must be careful not to substitute dependence on the benzodiazepines for dependence on alcohol (Wesson et al., 1997).

Withdrawal from benzodiazepines can occur after long periods of taking therapeutic doses. Not every user experiences withdrawal, and for most who do, the symptoms are relatively mild. The symptoms are the intensified return of the symptoms that first prompted drug use. Rebound anxiety and insomnia are therefore the primary signs of withdrawal, as they are the primary reasons for taking the benzodiazepines in the first place. A small percentage of patients experience a severe withdrawal syndrome that can include hallucinations (Wesson et al., 1997).

For those who are severely dependent on benzodiazepines, meaning that they have been taking the drug at high, nontherapeutic levels, withdrawal can be much more serious. Common signs include anxiety, tremors, nightmares, insomnia, seizures, and delirium. The user might become disoriented for time and place. The length of time the withdrawal lasts and the time to appearance of the symptoms depend on the drug being used (Carvey, 1998). Although these drugs are useful in managing short-term anxiety or insomnia, it is clear that they should not be taken for long periods of time.

Non-Benzodiazepines

Two relatively new drugs have effects similar to the benzodiazepines. Buspirone, or **Buspar,** is used to treat anxiety disorders. It does not work on the GABA receptors, although it does affect serotonin metabolism (Lacey et al., 1997). Buspar is considered a safe drug for those who might abuse benzodiazepines. Like antidepressants, it can take two weeks before its effects are felt and so is most useful in the long-term treatment of anxiety. Another non-benzodiazepine is zolpidem (**Ambien),** which is used for short-term treatment of insomnia. It works primarily on the same GABA receptors in the brain stem as benzodiazepines. Although it is generally assumed that it does not produce dependence, both animal studies and case reports with humans indicated that tolerance and dependence are possible (Wesson et al., 1997).

TABLE 9.4 Duration of Action of Common Benzodiazepines

Short Acting (3–8 hours)
  Triazolam (Halcion)**
  Oxazepam (Serax)*

Intermediate Acting (10–20 hours)
  Lorazepam (Ativan)*
  Temazepam (Restoril)**

Long Acting (1–3 days)
  Diazepam (Valium)*
  Chlorazepate (Tranxene)*
  Chlordiazepoxide (Librium)*
  Flurazepam (Dalmane)*

---

*Typically prescribed for anxiety.
**Typically prescribed to induce sleep.
Source: *Adapted from Carvey, 1998.*

The Date Rape Drug

In the last few years there have been sensational media reports of a drug that can be slipped into someone's drink to render them either unconscious or unable to defend themselves. The drug also is supposed to cause amnesia (Wesson, Smith, Ling, & Seymour, 1997). It is said to be odorless, tasteless, and easily dissolved in water and alcohol, and does not color the drink. With low doses of alcohol, it is supposed to reduce inhibitions. The reports claim that use of this drug—**Rohypnol**—is becoming widespread, and many warnings have been issued to be on the lookout for someone putting something in your drink (Wesson, et al., 1997). Are these accounts accurate, or are they another example of media hype?

Rohypnol is a product of Hoffman-LaRoche pharmaceutical company and is the trade name for flunitrazepam. It is a benzodiazepine similar to Valium, Xanax, and Ativan, among others. It is not legally available in the United States but is widely prescribed in other parts of the world. On the street Rohypnol is called, among other things, roofies, roach, R2, Mexican Valium, Rib, and Rope (Rohypnol, Flunitrazepam, 1997). It is about ten times stronger than Valium. It comes in 1- and 2-milligram tablets, while Valium is available in 2-, 5-, and 10-milligram tablets, so a 1-milligram tablet of Rohypnol is the same strength as a 10-milligram tablet of Valium (Lacey et al., 1997). Contrary to media reports, it is not soluble in water and only poorly soluble in alcohol, which means that if Rohypnol were slipped into a drink, a substantial part of the drug would not dissolve (Woods & Winger, 1997).

Any of the benzodiazepines can cause amnesia for events that occur while the drug is in the body (Woods & Winger, 1997). This kind of amnesia is called **anterograde amnesia.** In fact, one of the benzodiazepines, Versed, is used surgically for the *purpose of causing* anterograde amnesia. Some procedures, such as cardiac catherization or colonoscopy, require the patient to be conscious but can be extremely uncomfortable. Versed calms the patient, who has very little memory of the procedure after the drug wears off. As the author can attest, however, the amnesia is sometimes not complete and might not occur at all in some people.

A study of the effects of Rohypnol in countries where it is legal indicate that it is not associated with any greater incidence of abuse than several of the other benzodiazepines (Woods & Winger, 1997). In another study, subjects who said they had used Rohypnol were asked to pick out a tablet of Rohypnol from a group of drugs. Many of them misidentified Rohypnol and confused it with a drug available in the United States called Clonipin. Others were asked to describe the pill and described one of several other benzodiazepines instead. Of those who said they had used it, most said its effect was unappealing to them (Calhoun, Wesson, Galloway, & Smith, 1996).

Date rape is a serious and complex, social issue (Woods & Winger, 1997). Many drugs, including alcohol, have been used for the purpose of having sex with someone who is unwilling. Rohypnol is not available legally in the United States and is considered a Schedule I drug. Therefore, it must be obtained illegally and other drugs are frequently substituted. Few would-be users know what Rohypnol looks like: the tablets are round, white, and have the word Roche and a 1 or 2 inside a small circle. Several other benzodiazepines are marketed in Mexico and Latin America with the word Roche stamped on them (Calhoun et al 1996). It seems likely, therefore, that someone purchasing "roofies" is getting something else.

Stop and Review

1. How do the benzodiazepines relieve anxiety?
2. How serious is the problem of dependence?

Antiobesity Drugs

Any drug company that could come up with a drug that would cause weight loss with no side effects would see its profits soar. The drug combination called **fen-phen** was wildly popular for a short time. The "fen" stood for dexfenfluramine and the "phen" for phentermine. Although the chemical structures of these two compounds resemble amphetamine, the primary effect as an appetite suppressant was supposed to be on serotonin. In late 1996, dexfenfluramine was first associated with pulmonary hypertension, a potentially fatal condition. In 1997, fen-phen was associated with numerous cases of heart valve disease in persons who had been taking the drug for ten months or more. Nearly a third of patients taking fen-phen showed signs of abnormal cardiac valves (Schwenk, 1998). Fen-phen was pulled from the market and warnings were issued for persons who were considered to be at risk.

Hot on the heels of fen-phen came another drug, sibutramine (**Meridia**). Meridia is a reuptake inhibitor like the tricyclic antidepressants you read about earlier, and it increases the activity of norepinephrine and serotonin. It has many of the side effects of the tricyclic antidepressants, including dry mouth and constipation, and is not recommended for individuals who have a history of stroke, coronary heart disease, or other cardiovascular problems. Meridia is approved for use in treating severe obesity, not as a way to lose a few pounds (Schwenk, 1998).

Fen-phen was widely prescribed by weight clinics and was often taken inappropriately. Like Meridia, fen-phen was supposed to be reserved for those who were at least 20 percent overweight or who had excess body fat (30 percent for women, 25 percent for men) (*Psychopharmacology Update,* 1998). Physicians specializing in treating obesity knew that the drugs have to be used in combination with diet and exercise. What often happened was that patients took the drug *instead* (Dubovsky, 1997). Dieting and exercise are not nearly as easy as popping a pill, and with our culture's emphasis on thinness, it seems likely that there will always be a market for a pill that is supposed to produce weight loss. In fact, in 1998, Redux (fenfluramine) was reintroduced as a short-term treatment for obesity, meaning that it should only be prescribed for a few weeks (*Psychopharmacology Update,* 1998).

OTC drugs to treat obesity are also available. They contain 75 milligrams of **phenylpropanolamine** (PPA), another drug that resembles amphetamine (fig. 9.3). The appetite suppressant effects of PPA are mild. Studies show that dieters who take PPA lose more weight than dieters who take a placebo, but the difference is only four or five pounds (Griboff, Berman, & Silverman, 1975; Altshuler, Conte, Sebok, Marline, & Winick, 1982). At the doses recommended, PPA does not have amphetamine-like behavioral effects, and side effects are minimal. Herbal variations on fen-phen have also been marketed. They contain **ephedra,** which contains ephedrine. These widely available ephedra-containing pills have been linked to cardiovascular problems and cannot be recommended. The "secret" to losing weight is to burn more calories than you take in. No diet aids are going to provide the will power necessary to remain on a diet or cause you to exercise more. The most they can do is temporarily dull your appetite (Schuckit, 1995).

Ergogenic Aids

As long as split seconds separate winners from losers, and as long as society rewards only the winners, athletes will go to incredible lengths to gain that slight edge. **Ergogenic aids** are drugs used to enhance athletic performance. Ergogenic aids that have been used include (1) anabolic steroids; (2) beta-blockers, drugs used to treat high blood pressure that slow the heartbeat; (3) amphetamines, which are no longer widely used because they are easy to detect; (4) caffeine, be-

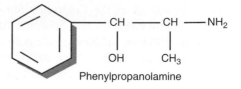

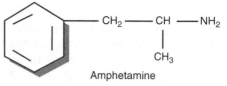

FIGURE 9.3

Note how similar phenylpropanolamine (used in appetite suppressants) is to amphetamine.

cause of its stimulant properties; (5) diuretics, for weight loss; and (6) growth hormone, to increase body size and strength. The two most widely used are anabolic steroids and growth hormones (Segura, 1998).

Anabolic Steroids

Two groups of people are the most likely users of steroids—bodybuilders and athletes (Catlin, 1998). Bodybuilders are seeking the psychological rewards of a muscular physique. Athletes, including wrestlers and football linebackers, are seeking to increase muscle mass. Even some law enforcement officers use steroids to obtain an intimidating physique and fighting prowess (Galloway, 1997). Studies suggest that some personality characteristics are seen more often in users than nonusers. Antisocial and narcissistic personality disorders are especially common in users (Galloway,1997). You have read about antisocial personality elsewhere. Narcissistic personalities are convinced of their own superiority, feel that because of their superior ability they deserve special treatment, and are extremely sensitive to criticism. It is not difficult to see why these personality characteristics might predispose someone to use steroids.

Testosterone is responsible for the greater muscle strength and lung capacity, of males. Testosterone and other sex hormones also are responsible for the secondary male sex characteristics, including deeper voice, more body hair, and the male distribution of body fat. The effects of the male sex hormones, therefore, include greater overall strength and size as well as male sexual functioning and appearance (Catlin, 1998). **Anabolic steroids** are created by adding a molecule to testosterone to produce a drug that is supposed to have only muscle-building (anabolic) properties. However, at high doses the brain responds to anabolic steroids in the same way as it responds to testosterone (Hoberman & Yesalis, 1995).

Because of widespread abuse of steroids, Congress passed the Anabolic Steroids Control Act of 1990 placing these drugs in Schedule III of the Controlled Substances Act. You will recall from chapter 1 that Schedule III drugs have medical use but also have moderate abuse potential. As a result, legal sources of steroids have been difficult to come by and most steroids are purchased on the street. Some are smuggled in from Mexico and others are fakes.

Using a principle called "stacking," athletes will take several kinds of steroids and then taper off just prior to a performance where they know they will be tested. Anabolic steroids increase weight and muscle mass, but they have significant harmful side effects as well (fig 9.4). Some of the circulating steroids are converted to estrogen, leading to **gynecomastia** (male breast development), testicular atrophy (a decrease in size of the testes), and a decrease in sperm production (Pope & Katz, 1994; Bickelman, Ferries, & Eaton, 1995). Cysts of blood can form in the liver, which could rupture and cause hemorrhage. Jaundice and liver cancer have also been reported (Lukas, 1993). Steroids have psychological effects as well, with many users reporting feelings of well-being and an increase in sexual desire. Unfortunately, there are also reports of increased aggression ("'roid rage"), sleep disturbances, frightening dreams, and even hallucinations (Su et al., 1993).

Women athletes also take steroids, and their problems can be equally grim. Steroids can increase body hair, increase the size of the clitoris, and disrupt menstruation (Catlin, 1998). Changes in body hair and the growth of the clitoris appear to be irreversible. However, many women athletes seem to find these changes acceptable when weighed against the benefits (Strauss, Mariah, & Liggett, 1985). In fact, although the use of steroids by men has leveled off in the last few years, steroid use by women has increased (Dershewitz, 1998).

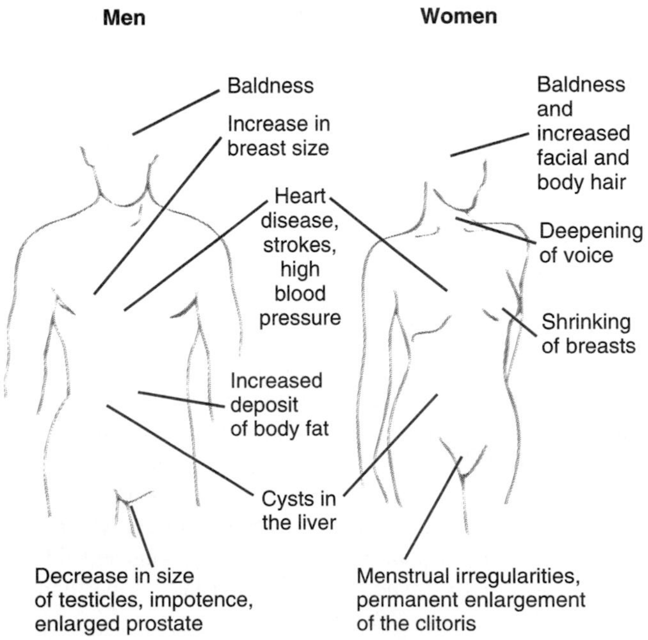

Growth Hormone

Human pituitary factor, or human growth hormone, is secreted in the pituitary and is responsible for the rapid growth of babies and adolescents. Use of growth hormones by athletes has become an issue because it is impossible to detect (Cuneo, Wallace, & Sonsken, 1998). Its only recognized medical use is to treat those who are extremely small for their age. Nevertheless there are widespread reports of its use by athletes (Cuneo et al., 1998). Increased secretion of growth hormone after sexual maturity results in a condition known as acromegaly, which involves enlargement of the tendons and connective tissue as well as high blood pressure and diabetes (Wadler & Hainline, 1989, Cuneo et al., 1998).

Stop and Review

1. How do antiobesity drugs work?
2. Why is it unlikely that they will solve the problem of obesity?
3. How do the two primary types of ergogenic aids differ?
4. What are their primary disadvantages?

Summary

Prescription drugs have legitimate uses to relieve suffering and treat numerous conditions. Many also have the potential to be abused. Narcotic and antianxiety drugs can produce dependence but their use rarely results in addiction.

The narcotics are essential for the management of pain, even if they do cause dependence. Over the counter analgesics are less effective but have no abuse potential. Nonmedical use of heroin does lead to addiction which is difficult to treat. At present the most successful treatment involves substitution of a safer narcotic, methadone.

The antianxiety drug, which work on the GABA system, can be abused and addiction is possible. However, they are also valuable when used properly. Although withdrawal symptoms can occur when patients stop taking antidepressants, they are not addicting. They are useful in treating depression and other conditions. Antiobesity drugs do not compensate for lack of willpower and can have serious side effects. They should be prescribed only for those whose obesity is life threatening.

The steroids have limited medical use but are widely abused by athletes and others. When used to enhance performance or appearance they can produce serious side effects. Use of most steroids is not difficult to detect. Use of growth factor, however, is very difficult to detect. Like the steroids, its use can lead to serious problems.

Men   **Women**

Baldness

Increase in breast size

Heart disease, strokes, high blood pressure

Increased deposit of body fat

Cysts in the liver

Decrease in size of testicles, impotence, enlarged prostate

Baldness and increased facial and body hair

Deepening of voice

Shrinking of breasts

Menstrual irregularities, permanent enlargement of the clitoris

FIGURE 9.4
Effects of steroids. Most of these changes are permanent.

Key Terms

acetaminophen An analgesic that relieves pain and fever. Can cause liver damage especially in heavy drinkers.

ambien Zolpidem, a non-benzodiazepine used for short-term treatment of insomnia.

amygdala A structure in the limbic system believed to be involved in the expression and perception of emotion.

anabolic steroids A drug for building muscle, derived from testosterone.

anterograde amnesia Amnesia for events that occur while a drug is in the body; caused by benzodiazepines, alcohol, and other drugs.

aspirin A white crystalline drug used to relieve pain and fever.

benzodiazepines Sedative or antianxiety drugs, prescribed for insomnia and as muscle relaxants.

bipolar disorder Manic depression, characterized by wide mood swings.

buprenorphine A drug used to treat withdrawal from heroin.

Buspar Buspirone, a drug used to treat anxiety disorders.

clonidine A drug originally developed to treat high blood pressure. Also used to reduce the symptoms of heroin withdrawal.

codeine Methylmorphine, a pain reliever absorbed orally. It is also used as a cough suppressant.

community outreach programs A program to provide job counseling and psychological and medical help for addicts.

Darvon Propoxyphene, an opiate analgesic with little dependence potential.

Demerol Meperidine, a synthetic narcotic drug used as a pain reliever. It can be converted into a street drug called MPPP or China White.

Depakote A drug used to treat bipolar or manic-depressive disorder; a valproic acid.

Dilaudid Hydromorphone, a drug similar in structure to morphine and heroin but a legal analgesic.

Effexor The prescription drug name for venlafaxine, an antidepressant similar to the tricyclic antidepressants.

ephedra A plant orginially found in China that contains ephedrine. It has been used medically in China for centuries.

ergogenic aids Drugs used to enhance athletic performance and body build.

fen-phen A drug combination of dexfenfluramine and phentermine used to cause weight loss; now illegal.

gynecomastia Male breast development.

Harrison Narcotic Act of 1914 The legal basis for what eventually became the criminalization of narcotic drugs.

herbal remedies Methods of treating illnesses with different herbs.

heroin Diacetylmorphine, a potent derivative of morphine.

human pituitary factor A hormone secreted in the pituitary that is responsible for rapid growth of babies and adolescents; also known as human growth hormone.

ibuprofen An analgesic to relieve pain, fever, and inflammation. Ibuprofen can cause stomach upset and trigger asthma and hives.

LAAM A long-acting narcotics antagonist.

lithium A drug used to treat bipolar or manic-depressive disorder; a metal salt.

MAOI A kind of antidepressant with possible serious side effects.

medulla The area of the brain that controls breathing and other basic functions.

Meridia A serotonin reuptake inhibitor approved to treat severe obesity; silbutramine.

Methadone A synthetic analogue of morphine that is readily absorbed orally.

morphine A derivative of opium. Morphine is considered the standard for measuring the analgesic properties of narcotic drugs.

MPPP A designer drug synthesized from Demerol.

naloxone A narcotic antagonist that blocks the action of opiates and endorphins.

naltrexone Similar to naloxone but longer-acting.

naproxen An analgesic to relieve pain and fever. Naproxen can cause kidney and gastrointestinal problems.

Numorphan Ozymorphone, a drug similar in structure to morphine and heroin but a legal analgesic.

on the nod Twilight state between sleep and wakefulness when using heroin.

opium A tarlike substance found in the pod of the opium poppy.

Papaver somniferum Oriental or opium poppy.

Paxil The prescription name of paroxetine, an antidepressant that inhibits reuptake of serotonin.

periaqueductal gray area A structure in the base of the brain that inhibits incoming pain messages.

phenylpropanolamine An appetite-suppressant drug that resembles amphetamine.

prostaglandins Chemical substances secreted by cells in response to injury.

Prozac Prescription name of fluoxetine, an antidepressant that inhibits reuptake of serotonin.

psychopathic personality disorder A disorder involving a wide range of characteristics, including risk taking, need for immediate gratification, and lack of remorse.

rapid detoxification The use of clonidine and naloxone to displace the heroin molecule during heroin withdrawal.

Remeron Prescription name for mirtazepine, an antidepressant similar to the tricyclic antidepressants.

Rohypnol The "date rape drug."

rush   Drug-induced euphoria followed by relief from anxiety and tension.

Serzone   Prescription drug name for nefazodone, an antidepressant similar to the tricyclic antidepressants.

SSRI   Selective serotonin reuptake inhibitor. Antidepressant drugs that increase the amount of serotonin in the synapse by preventing its reuptake into the presynaptic neuron.

Tegretol   A drug used to treat bipolar or manic-depressive disorder; a carbamazepine.

testosterone   Male hormone responsible for muscle strength and endurance.

therapeutic communities   Programs that provide job counseling and psychological and medical help for addicts.

tricyclic antidepressants   Antidepressants that block the reuptake of catecholamines and serotonin.

ultrarapid detoxification   Detoxification of patient from heroin while unconscious.

Wellbutrin   The prescription drug name of bupropion, an "atypical" antidepressant.

Zoloft   The prescription name of sertraline, an antidepressant that inhibits reuptake of serotonin.

References

Face sheet: *Rohypnol (flunitrazemap)* (1997). Washington, DC: National Institute of Drug Abuse.

Altshuler, A., Conte, A., Sebok, M., Marline, R., & Winick, C. (1982). Three controlled trials of weight loss with phenylpropanolamine. *International Journal of Obesity, 6,* 549–556.

Beecher, H. K. (1956). Relationship of significance of wound to pain experienced. *Journal of the American Medical Association, 161,* 1609–1613.

Bickelman, C., Ferries, L., & Eaton, R. (1995). Impotence related to anabolic steroid use in a body builder. *Western Journal of Medicine, 162,* 158–161.

Brown, R. L., Fleming, M. F., & Patterson, J. J. (1996). Chronic opioid analgesic therapy for chronic low back pain. *Journal of the American Board of Family Practice, 9,* 191–204.

Calhoun, S. R., Wesson, D. R., Galloway, G. P., & Smith, D. E. (1996). Abuse of flunitrazepam (Rohypnol) and other benzodiazepines in Austin and South Texas. *Journal of Psychoactive Drugs, 28,* 183–189.

Carvey, P. M. (1998). *Drug action in the central nervous system.* New York: Oxford University Press.

Catlin, D. H. (1988). Anabolic androgenic steroids. In S. B. Karch (Ed.), *Drug Abuse Handbook* (pp. 653–670). Boca Raton, LA: CRC Press.

Chatham, L. R., Rowan-Szal, G. A., Joe, G. W., Brown, B. S., & Simpson, D. D. (1995). Heavy drinking in a population of methadone-maintained clients. *Journal of Studies on Alcohol, 56,* 417–422.

Chatham, L. R., Rowan-Szal, G. A., Joe, G. W., & Simpson, D. D. (1997). Heavy drinking, alcohol dependent vs nondependent methadone-maintenance clients: A follow-up study. *Addictive Behaviors, 22,* 69–80.

Comer, J. (1998). *Abnormal psychology.* Needham Heights, MA: Allyn & Bacon.

Cone, E., Holicky, B., Grant, T., Darwin, W., & Goldberger, B. (1993). Pharmacokinetics and pharmacodynamics of intranasal vs snorted cocaine. *Journal of Analytical Toxicology 17,* 327–337.

Courtwright, D. (1982). *Dark paradise: Opiate addiction in America before 1900.* Cambridge, MA: Harvard University Press.

Cuneo, R. C., Wallace, J. D., & Sonsken, P. (1998). Growth hormone abuse in elite athletes. In S. B. Karch (Ed.) *Drug Abuse Handbook* (pp. 690–719). Boca Raton, LA: CRC Press.

Dershewitz, R. A. (1998). Anabolic steroid use in females. *Journal Watch for Psychiatry, 4,* 15.

Dinwiddie, S. H., Cottler, L., Compton, W., & Abdallah, A. B. (1996). Psychopathology and HIV risk behavior among injection drug users in and out of treatment. *Drug and Alcohol Dependence, 43,* 1–11.

Dubovsky, S. (1997). Weight loss medications: More lost than gained. *Journal Watch for Psychiatry, 3,* 91–92.

Epstein, J. F., & Gfroerer, J. C. (1997). *Heroine abuse in the United States.* Washington, DC: Substance Abuse and Mental Health Services Administration: Center for Substance Abuse Research.

Galloway, G. P. (1997). Anabolic-androgenic steroids. In J. H. Lowinson, P. Ruiz, R. B. Millman, & J. G. Langrod (Eds.), *Substance abuse: A comprehensive textbook* (pp. 308–318). Baltimore: Williams & Wilkins.

Greenstein, R. A., Fudala, P. J., & O'Brien, C. P. (1997). Alternative pharmacotherapies for opiate addiction. In J. H. Lowinson, P. Ruiz, R. B. Millman, & J. G. Langrod (Eds.), *Substance abuse: A comprehensive textbook* (pp. 415–424). Baltimore: Williams & Wilkins.

Griboff, S., Berman, R., & Silverman, H. (1975). A double blind clinical evaluation of a phenylpronolamine-caffeine-vitamin combination and a placebo in the treatment of exogenous obesity. *Current Therapeutic Research, 17,* 535–543.

Hayter, A. (1988). *Opium and the romantic imagination: Addiction and creativity in De Quincey, Coleridge, Baudelaire, and others.* Northamptonshire, England: Crucible.

Hoberman, J., & Yesalis, C. (1995, February). The history of synthetic testosterone. *Scientific American,* pp. 76–81.

Hollinger, M. A. (1997). *Introduction to pharmacology.* Washington, D.C.: Taylor & Francis.

Hsu, J. H., & Shen, W. W. (1995). Male sexual side effects associated with antidepressants: A descriptive clinical study of 32 patients. *International Journal of Psychiatry in Medicine, 25,* 191–201.

Hung, O. L., & Hoffman, R. S. (1997). Reversal of opioid intoxication. *CNS Drugs, 7,* 176–186.

Inciardi, J. A. (1992). *The war on drugs II.* Mountain View, CA: Mayfield.

Jaffe, J. H., Knapp, C. M., & Ciraulo, D. Q. (1997). Opiates: Clinical aspects. In J. H. Lowinson, P. Ruiz, R. B. Millman, & J. G. Langrod (Eds.), *Substance abuse: A comprehensive textbook* (pp. 158–166). Baltimore: Williams & Wilkins.

Jaffe, J. H., & Martin, W. R. (1990). Opioid analgesics and antagonists. In A. G. Gilman, T. W. Rall, A. S. Nies, & P. Taylor (Eds.), *Goodman and Gilman's: The pharmacological basis of therapeutics* (pp. 485–521). New York: Raven Press.

Karch, S. B. (1996). *The Pathology of Drug Abuse, 2nd ed.* Boca Raton, LA: CRC Press.

Kim, S. C., & Seo, K. K. (1998). Efficacy and safety of fluoxetine, sertraline and clomipramine in patients with premature ejaculation: A double-blind, placebo controlled study. *Journal of Urology, 159,* 425–427.

Knight, K. R., Rosenbaum, M., Irwin, J., Kelley, M. S., Wenger, L., & Washburn, A. (1996). Involuntary versus voluntary detoxification from methadone maintenance treatment: The importance of choice. *Addiction Research, 3,* 351–362.

Lacey, C., Armstrong, L. L., Ingrim, N. B., & Lance, L. L. (1997). *Drug information handbook* (5th ed.). Hudson, OH: Lexicomp.

Leiken, J. B., & Paloucek, F. P. (1996). *Poisoning and Toxicology Handbook.* Hudson (Cleveland): Lexi-Comp Inc.

Lowinson, J. H., Payte, J. T., Salsitz, Joseph, H., Marion, I. J., & Dole, V. P. (1997). Methadone maintenance. In J. H. Lowinson, P. Ruiz, R. B. Millman, & J. G. Langrod (Eds.), *Substance abuse: A comprehensive textbook* (pp. 405–414). Baltimore: Williams & Wilkins.

Lukas, S. (1993). On anabolic-androgenic steroid abuse. *Trends in Pharmaceutical Sciences, 14,* 61–68.

Mathias, R. (1997). NIDA conferences aims 'preemptive strike' at increased heroin use among nation's young people. *NIDA Notes 12,* 1–2.

Mathias, R. (1997). Adolescent girls abuse steroids, too. *NIDA Notes 12,* 14–16.

Mendelson, J., Upton, R. A., Everhart, E. T., Jacob, P., & Jones, R. T. (1997). Bioavailability of sublingual buprenorphine. *Journal of Clinical Pharmacology 37,* 31–37.

Modell, J. G., Katholi, C. R., Modell, J. D., & DePalma, R. L. (1997). Comparative sexual side effects of bupropion, fluoxetine, paroxetine, and sertraline. *Clinical Pharmacology and Therapeutics, 61,* 476–487.

New antiobesity drugs appear in wake of phen/fen scare. (1998). *Psychopharmacology Update, 9,* 1,4.

Nurco, D. N., Blatchley, R. J., Hanlon, T. E., O'Grady, K. E., & McCarren, M. (1998). The family experience of narcotic addicts and the subsequent parenting practices. *American Journal of Drug and Alcohol Issues, 24,* 37–59.

Nurco, D. N., Kinlock, T. W., O'Grady, K. E., & Hanlon, T. E. (1996). Early family adversity as a precursor to narcotics addiction. *Drug and Alcohol Dependence, 43,* 103–111.

O'Brien, W. B., & Devlin, C. J. (1997). The therapeutic community. In J. H. Lowinson, P. Ruiz, R. B. Millman, & J. G. Langrod (Eds.), *Substance abuse: A comprehensive textbook* (pp. 400–404). Baltimore: Williams & Wilkins.

O'Connor, P. G., & Kosten, T. R. (1998). Rapid and ultrarapid detoxification techniques. *Journal of the American Medical Association, 279,* 229–234.

Owen, D. E. (1968). *British opium policy in China and India.* Hamden, CT: Archon Books.

Pope, H., & Katz, D. (1994). Psychiatric and medical effects of anabolic-androgenic steroid use. *Archives of General Psychiatry, 51,* 375–382.

Portnoy, R. K., & Payne, R. (1997). Acute and chronic pain. In J. H. Lowinson, P. Ruiz, R. B. Millman, & J. G. Langrod (Eds.), *Substance abuse: A comprehensive textbook* (pp. 563–590). Baltimore: Williams & Wilkins.

Preston, J. D., O'Neal, J. H., & Talaga, M. C. (1998). *Consumer's Guide to Psychiatric Drugs.* Oakland, CA: New Harbinger Publications, Inc.

Roy-Byrne, P. (1996). SSRI withdrawal syndrome. *Journal Watch for Psychiatry, 2,* 93.

Schanzer, W. (1998). Detection of exogenous anabolic androgenic steroids. In S. B. Karch (Ed.), *Drug Abuse Handbook* (pp. 671–689). Boca Raton, LA: CRC Press.

Schuckit, M. (1995). *Drug and alcohol abuse.* New York: Plenum Press.

Schwenk, T. L. (1998). A turbulent year for diet pills. *Journal Watch for Psychiatry, 4,* 16.

Scott, J. M. (1969). *The white poppy: A history of opium.* New York: Funk & Wagnalls.

Segura, J. (1998). Summary of International Olympic Committee regulations. In S. B. Karch (Ed.), *Drug Abuse Handbook* (pp. 710–719). Boca Raton, LA: CRC Press.

Shapiro, A. K., & Shapiro, E. (1997). The placebo: Is it much ado about nothing? In A. Harrington (Ed.), *The placebo effect: An interdisciplinary exploration.* Cambridge, MA: Harvard University Press.

Shen, W. W., & Hsu, J. H. (1995). Female sexual side effects associated with selective serotonin reuptake inhibitors: A descriptive clinical study of 33 patients. *International Journal of Psychiatry in Medicine, 25,* 239–248.

Simon, G. E., & VonKorff, M. (1998). Suicide mortality among patients treated for depression in an insured population. *American Journal of Epidemiology 147,* 155–160.

Sklair-Tavron, W., Shi, W. X., Lane, S. B., Harris, H. W., Bunney, B. S., & Nestler, E. J. (1996). Chronic morphine induces visible changes in the morphology of mesolimbid dopamine neurons. *Proceedings of the National Academy of Sciences, 93,* 11202–11207.

Soorani, E., & DeVincent, J. (1997). Bupropion may offset SSRI-induced sexual dysfunction. *Psychopharmacology Update, 8,* 1,5.

Stimmel, B. (1997). *Pain and its relief without addiction.* New York: Haworth University Press.

Strauss, R., Mariah, T., & Liggett, M. (1985). Anabolic steroid use and perceived effects in ten weight trained women. *Journal of the American Medical Association, 269,* 2871–2873.

Su, T., Pagliaro, M., Schmidt, P., Pickar, D., Wolkowitz, O., & Rubinow, D. (1993). Neuropsychiatric effects of anabolic steroids in male normal volunteers. *Journal of the American Medical Association, 269,* 2760–2764.

Thompson, C. J. S. (1993). *Quacks of Old London.* New York: Barnes & Noble.

Tretter, F., Burkhardt, D., Bussello-Spieth, B., Reiss, J., Walcher, S., & Buchele, W. (1998). Clinical experience with antagonist-induced withdrawal under anaesthesia. *Addiction, 93,* 269–275.

Use creative solutions to battle the sexual side effects of SSRIs. (1998). *Psychopharmacology Update, 9,* 1,4.

Wadler, G., & Hainline, B. (1989). *Drugs and the athlete.* Philadelphia: F. A. Davis.

Wesson, D. R., Smith, D. E., Ling, W., & Seymour, R. B. (1997). Sedative-hypnotics and tricyclics. In J. H. Lowinson, P. Ruiz, R. B. Millman, & J. G. Langrod (Eds.), *Substance abuse: A comprehensive textbook* (pp. 223–229). Baltimore: Williams & Wilkins.

Woods, J. H., & Winger, G. (1997). Abuse liability of flunitrazepam. *Journal of Clinical Psychopharmacology, 17* (Suppl. 2), 1s–57s.

Zacny, J. P. (1995). A review of the effects of opiods on psychomotor and cognitive functioning in humans. *Experimental and Clinical Psychopharmacology, 3,* 432–466.

Zacny, J. P., Conley, K., & Marks, S. (1997). Comparing the subjective, psychomotor and physiological effects of intravenous nalbuphine and morphine in healthy volunteers. *Journal of Pharmacology and Experimental Therapeutics, 280,* 1159–1169.

Zawertailo, L. A., Busto, U., Kaplan, H. L., & Sellers, E. M. (1995). Comparative abuse liability of sertraline, aprazolam and dextroamphetamine in humans. *Journal of Clinical Psychopharmacology, 15,* 117–124.

Ziegler, D. K. (1994). Opiate and opioid use in patients with refractory headache. *Cephalgia, 14,* 5–10.

Chapter Ten

Drugs and Social Policy

Chapter Objectives

When you have finished studying this chapter, you should

1. Be able to discuss the economic costs of the drugs you have studied.
2. Know why drug eradication programs for cocaine and tobacco are difficult to implement.
3. Know why it is so difficult to arrest dealers of LSD.
4. Be able to explain why the workplace is an important site for intervention.
5. Know how urine testing works and the limits of detection.
6. Be able to describe three other methods of drug testing and their strengths and weaknesses.
7. Be able to discuss the reasons that driving under the influence has declined.
8. Know the special difficulties involved in reducing the incidence of drinking and driving among motorcyclists.
9. Know how drinking and driving affects pedestrians.
10. Be able to describe which strategies work and which don't work to reduce drinking and driving.
11. Know how marijuana affects driving.
12. Know the relationship between prison overcrowding and drug arrests.
13. Be able to discuss the controversy over mandatory minimums.
14. Know why conspiracy laws are used in the fight against drugs.
15. Be able to discuss how seizure and forfeiture laws are used.
16. Know the difference between supply side and demand reduction strategies.
17. Be able to differentiate between school-based drug education and community action programs.
18. Be able to list the seven elements of a harm reduction program.
19. Know how needle exchanges fit into a harm reduction policy and why they are controversial.

The restrictions [on the sale of liquor] which the experience of many years and many places has proved to be desirable are chiefly these:

There should be no selling to minors, intoxicated persons, or habitual drunkards.

There should be no selling on Sundays, election days, or legal holidays in general. . . .

Saloons should not be allowed to become places of entertainment, and to this end they should not be allowed to provide musical instruments, billiard or pool tables, bowling alleys, cards or dice.

Every saloon should be wide open to public inspection from the highway, no screens or partitions being permitted. There should be a limit to the hours of selling, and the shorter the hours the better. . . .

It has been found necessary to prevent by police regulation the display of obscene pictures in saloons, and the employment of women as bartenders, waitresses, singers or actresses.

Excerpt from The Liquor Problem, *1905*

The use and abuse of both legal and illegal drugs is a problem for society as well as the individual. A society has the right to consider the good of the many as well as the privileges of the individual, and societies intervene in many situations when it has been determined that harm is occurring to the public good. In this chapter, we will consider the economic and legal aspects of both legal and illegal drugs, drugs in the workplace, drinking and driving, marijuana and driving, the role of drugs in violence, and the effects of drug policy. We will also consider the effects of our drug education and prevention programs.

The Economics of Drugs

The economic cost of drug abuse and addiction is staggering. Drug abuse impacts society at every level. Families are disrupted, job productivity suffers, and the legal system is overburdened. In parts of the world, the entire political system is corrupted. The amount of money generated by the drug trade is almost beyond belief. The problem is obvious, the solution is not.

Alcohol

The annual cost of alcohol misuse to U.S. society has been estimated at nearly $100 billion. You might expect that this is the cost of alcohol abuse, but about 70 percent of the social and personal problems brought on by alcohol are caused by social drinkers. At any given time about 7 percent of all drinkers are abusing alcohol. As a result, even though social drinkers do not often cause problems, their sheer numbers mean that most alcohol problems will be the result of their behavior (Single, 1996).

On the other hand, taxes on alcohol are an important part of local, state, and federal revenues. Taxation of alcohol has been an important part of U.S. fiscal policy throughout the nation's history (Kenkel & Manning, 1996). Alexander Hamilton, the first secretary of the treasury, proposed taxing whiskey to help pay off the costs of the Revolution. Ever since then, both federal and state governments have taxed alcoholic beverages. The federal government alone receives $8 billion a year from such taxes, and state and local governments receive slightly more. Not only do taxes provide income for the government, but evidence suggests that raising the price of alcoholic beverages by increasing taxes decreases consumption. Studies have found a relationship between increased liquor taxes and decreased death rates from cirrhosis of the liver and traffic fatalities (Kenkel & Manning, 1996).

The idea that the cost to society of alcohol abuse can be reduced by increasing taxes is controversial, but studies have shown that even heavy drinkers reduce their purchases when prices go up. Moderate drinkers are most responsive to price changes, and women are more responsive than men (Kenkel & Manning, 1996). Crime rates, drunken driving arrests, and mortality from alcohol-related problems also seem sensitive to increased taxes on alcohol. Increasing taxes is not going stop alcohol abuse, obviously, but it does seem to reduce the cost to society.

Another positive aspect of alcohol use is that more than 200,000 people are employed in the production and sale of beer, wine, and distilled beverages in the United States. If you include people working in restaurants and bars, an additional 6 to 7 million people derive their income in part from alcoholic beverages. All of these people contribute to the economy by paying taxes and purchasing goods and services. Furthermore, the alcohol industry spends millions on advertising and promotion. The combined positive revenue does not equal the cost of alcohol abuse, but alcoholic beverages do play an important role in our economy (Kenkel & Manning, 1996).

Cocaine and Methamphetamine

Estimates of the amount of money spent on cocaine are just that—estimates. Excise taxes on alcohol are a measure of how much alcohol is produced, but because the cocaine business is illegal and cocaine enters the country by smuggling, no one can be completely sure how much cocaine is in the United States each year. A frequently mentioned estimate is $40 billion worth. Coca is grown in Colombia, Ecuador, Brazil, and Bolivia and smuggled into the United States by way of Florida, California, Texas, and Arizona. Figure 10.1 shows the major routes of cocaine smuggling. Cocaine dealers own banks, soccer teams, and entire islands in their home countries.

The United States certifies countries in Latin America for making acceptable attempts to stop the flow of cocaine (Falco, 1997). This certification means that the countries are eligible for foreign aid. Many Latin American leaders think we are being hypocritical by "certifying" them when the United States is the major market. They also resent the corruption and destabilization of their political structure that comes about as a result of our seemingly insatiable demand for cocaine. The poor farmers who grow coca leaf are even more blunt. They shoot at helicopters they suspect carry narcotic agents and sabotage, or refuse to cooperate in, efforts to eradicate coca plantings. Their survival is at stake and they do not see why they should be punished with the loss of their coca crop because much of it is made into cocaine and sent to us.

If demand for cocaine continues to decline and demand for methamphetamine continues to rise, some of the problems that Latin American countries have faced could occur in the United States. Much of the production and distribution of crank is now controlled by criminals from Mexico, but most of those involved in the trade live in the United States (*Office of National Drug Control Policy*, 1997). How would our legal and political system respond if even part of the $40 billion spent on cocaine and sent back to Latin America were in the hands of those who manufacture and deal drugs in the United States? Would we see the same wholesale corruption and violence?

Marijuana

Marijuana might very well be the biggest cash crop in the United States. Once again, no one has any hard figures on how much marijuana is grown here. The U.S. Drug Enforcement Administration (DEA) estimate is about 3,000 metric tons (*Office of National Drug Control Policy*, 1994). The street value varies from location to location but $300 an ounce was about the average in 1997 (ONDCP, 1997). If you

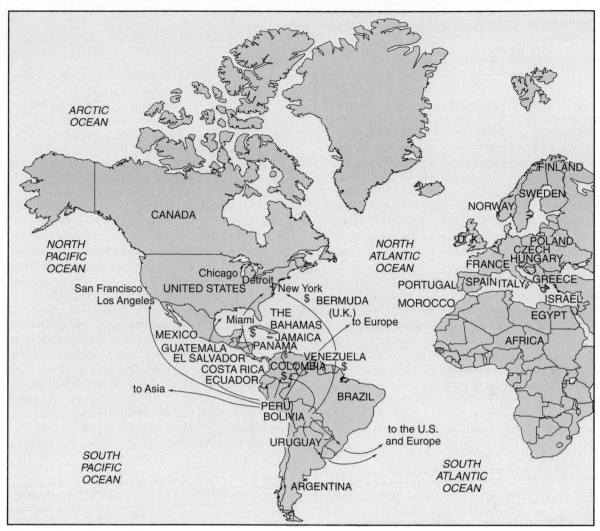

FIGURE 10.1
Major routes by which cocaine is smuggled into the United States. Coca leaves are usually shipped to Columbia, where they are processed into cocaine before being shipped to the United States.

combine these two estimates, the street value of the marijuana grown in the United States is more than $30 billion. The DEA estimates that about 15,000 metric tons are grown outside the United States (ONDCP, 1994). Assuming that all of the marijuana grown outside the States is smuggled into the country (and that it commands the same price), the two figures add up to $180 billion. All of these figures are estimates, of course, and the amount could be much smaller or much greater. As a famous U.S. senator once said, "A billion here, a billion there, pretty soon you are talking about real money."

Most of the smuggled marijuana is from Mexico, and Canada has recently become a major smuggling route (Crary, 1998). We have a very open border with Canada, making smuggling much easier. Agents are discovering that smugglers come in all shapes and sizes, from young couples with children to elderly couples who claim to be going to Canada just to buy medicine, which is cheaper there. Other major smuggling countries include Colombia and Jamaica.

How much of that marijuana is seized? Roughly 500 metric tons a year, a figure that includes both home grown and imported marijuana.

Tobacco

The economic cost of cigarette smoking has been in the news for the last few years. In 1998, Congress and the industry were in a confrontation over how much money the tobacco industry should pay to offset the cost of smoking-related illness. The amount of money being discussed is almost incomprehensible. One of the offers from the tobacco industry was to pay more than $350 billion over the next 25 years in exchange for immunity from lawsuits based on illnesses caused by smoking. Why would the tobacco companies be willing to part with that much money? They figure the cost will be less than contesting and perhaps losing individual lawsuits, they expect the money to be tax deductible, and they plan to raise the price of cigarettes and pass the cost

Cigarette Advertising

The cigarette industry claims that they are not trying to recruit new smokers, simply trying to get current smokers to change brands. Yet smokers have a very high brand loyalty. Fewer than 5 percent of smokers change brands yearly, so why all the advertising? More than one million people a year stop smoking. About half quit more or less permanently (80 percent relapse at least once) and the other half stop permanently because they die. The industry has to replace those who quit, or they lose money. Smokers rarely begin to smoke after 18 years of age. So where do the recruits come from?

The advertising that has been most criticized is the Joe Cool Camel campaign, which was halted in 1997. Joe Cool was a winner for the manufacturers of Camels. In 1988 only 0.5 percent of smokers under the age of 18 smoked Camels; just two years later, 32 percent did. How many of those were new recruits?

One way to attract new smokers is to keep the price low. Preteens who are not yet dependent on nicotine are affected by cigarette prices. Another way is through promotions. If you buy a pack of cigarettes you get a free lighter, a map, or a water bottle. If you get a lighter or a map, you might feel you are getting more value for your dollar. If you save up several hundred coupons, you get a "free" beach towel. What are you going to do with all those packs of cigarettes?

Tobacco companies pay retailers to display their cigarettes near checkout counters and place advertising at eye level for young people. Is this coincidence? They also place cigarettes in areas near the door of some retailers, knowing that the packs will be stolen. Of course, if they are stolen they will be smoked and the chances are good that the tobacco industry will more than make up for the loss of one pack when the person who stole them becomes a regular smoker. How many adults resort to stealing cigarettes?

Promotions also include sponsoring concerts and athletic events. The brand becomes associated with the event, increasing awareness of the product. It also enables the tobacco companies to get around the ban on advertising on all electronic media. When the announcer announces the Kool Jazz Series or the Winston Cup, or when the television camera pans onto the logo of the cigarette company, the company has managed to elude the ban on advertising.

---

on to the customer. You can be sure that they have done many studies to see how much per pack the average smoker is willing to pay.

As with alcohol, some of the cost of the harm tobacco does is regained by taxes on tobacco and, ironically, by the fact that cigarette smokers die at an earlier age and use up less of their retirement money. The cigarette industry has been diversifying for many years partly as a result of the decline in the number of smokers. The share of the companies' income that comes from tobacco sales has been declining. Even if all tobacco use were to stop tomorrow, the companies would undoubtedly survive.

Anti-tobacco programs are aimed primarily at young people, because very few individuals take up smoking after the age of 21. The average age at which people report having their first cigarette is about 15.7 years and has not changed since 1962. The average age at which smokers begin to smoke daily has remained about 17 years of age during the same time (SAMSHA, 1997). Antismoking strategies, therefore, must take into consideration the kinds of messages that work with young people rather than messages that might affect adults. These two are often different. Figure 10.2 shows some billboards designed by the state of California using money from an increase in state tobacco taxes. You might not think they are particularly effective, but they do appeal to the beginning smoker.

Like the coca farmers, many thousands of U.S. farmers earn their living from growing tobacco, and it is a very profitable crop. Some farmers whose families have been growing tobacco for generations feel much like the coca growers in South America. They point out that tobacco is legal and that what they are doing is legal. Many farmers would no doubt have to give up their livelihood and move from the farm if tobacco growing were to be substantially decreased. Of course, federal, state, and local governments would lose the income that comes from taxes on tobacco. The effect of cigarette smoking on national health is only one part of the problem, economic issues also come into play.

Hallucinogens

The manufacture of LSD is thought to be controlled by relatively few people who have developed an elaborate network of distribution to several layers of dealers, thus protecting themselves from discovery. The U.S. Drug Enforcement Administration has not been able to infiltrate the uppermost hierarchy, and they have not uncovered a single large laboratory dedicated to making LSD since 1981 (*National Narcotics Intelligence Consumers Committee,* 1993). Estimates of the amount of money spent on LSD are not necessarily any more accurate than estimates of the cost of

Studies have shown that young people who use drugs including tobacco at an early age are high risk takers. These young people respond to messages that are outrageous to others. The State of California has designed these billboard messages to make smoking less attractive to young people. Do you think they work?

other illicit drugs, but the DEA confiscates about 700,000 doses a year (NNICC, 1993). The general consensus is that no more than 10 percent of illegal drugs are confiscated, meaning that at least 7 million doses are manufactured every year. The street value of LSD ranges from $1 to $5 per dose. As you can see, somebody is making an incredible amount of money.

Narcotics

Heroin incurs many different types of costs to society. For example, there is the crime that is committed to get the money to buy heroin, the crime that is committed in the sale and distribution of heroin. The cost to society of unproductive workers and the cost to care for those who develop AIDs as a result of unsafe injection practices must also be included, as well as the cost of jailing those convicted of heroin-related crimes (Mahan 1997). In chapter 9 you read about methadone treatment for heroin addiction. In table 10.1 you can see a comparison of the costs to society of methadone treatment versus heroin addiction. You can make up your own mind as to which is preferable from an economic point of view.

Stop and Review

1. What are some strategies used to reduce alcohol consumption?
2. Where does most marijuana come from? How important is it to the economy?
3. Why is the tobacco industry willing to pay hundreds of billions of dollars for the damage tobacco has done?
4. How is tobacco farming similar to coca growing?
5. Why is LSD traffic so hard to stop?
6. How does methadone use effect the economics of heroin use?

The Workplace and Drugs

The extent of substance-abuse problems in the workplace and the cost to industry are difficult to estimate. Many problem drinkers and illicit drug users are able to function adequately at their jobs. When the user no longer can control the drug or alcohol use, the problem often becomes apparent at the workplace (Hoffman, Larison, & Sanderson, 1997). For some occupations, any problems associated with drugs or alcohol would be readily apparent; for others, behavior related to substance abuse would be hard to detect. Impairment in surgeons, airline pilots, and others whose occupations require exacting skill and considerable effort would be considerably easier to detect than impairment in jobs that have low visibility and output that is difficult to measure.

Because many substance abusers feel a stigma about their problem, the abuser is unlikely to ask for help and is likely to try to hide the problems. Coworkers and supervisors might cover up for the worker's inadequate performance out of a well-intended desire to help. Supervisors might feel uncomfortable confronting employees with suspected problems, and coworkers are even less likely to "snitch." Of course, this can worsen the employee's problem and delay the help that is often desperately needed (Engelhart, Robinson, & Kates, 1997).

An estimated $100 billion is lost each year in alcohol- and drug-related loss of productivity. Poor performance, in-

TABLE 10.1 Comparison of Illicit Heroin Addiction and Methadone Maintenance

Characteristics	Illicit Heroin	Methadone Maintenance
Duration of action	4–6 hours	24–36 hours
Routes of administration	Injection, snorting, smoking several times a day	Orally administered once a day
Overall safety	Potentially lethal	Medically safe
Withdrawal	Can be severe	Less severe but lasts longer
Euphoric effects	Approximately 2 hours duration	None
Narcotic craving	Recurring and high	Relieved and blocked
HIV transmission risk	Risk very high	None
Mood alteration	Constant swings	None
Sexual functioning	Impaired	Normalized during treatment
Emotional and intellectual functioning	Impaired	Normal
Employment	Virtually impossible	Functioning has been demonstrated at every level of occupation
Criminal activity	Constant high level	Greatly reduced
Personal relationships and social functioning	Greatly impaired	Normal with counseling
Cost to society	Estimated cost to the addict as much as $40,000/year. Est. cost as a result of crime to maintain addiction as much as $40,000/year. Est. cost for incarceration $30,000. Hospital costs for final stages of AIDS at least $100,000	$3,000/year

Sources: *Regan (1995), Woods (1994), Joseph (1994).*

creased absenteeism, bad morale, and increased medical benefit claims all contribute to this figure. Other disruptive factors include the time needed to handle disciplinary problems, high turnover, and increased recruiting and training costs (Engelhart, Robinson, & Kates, 1997). There is no doubt that substance abuse causes serious work-related problems. What is not clear is the cost of substance use. In the previous chapters you read that most users of illegal drugs do not go on to become abusers; typically they use the drug occasionally and eventually stop for a host of reasons. Do these users cause problems in the workplace?

Job Impairment

The Substance Abuse and Mental Health Services Administration (SAMHSA) has examined a number of issues involving illicit drug and heavy alcohol use among U.S. workers. The findings may surprise you. About 8 percent of full-time and 9 percent of part-time workers report current illicit drug use. Note that these percentages reflect *admitted* drug use. For the unemployed the figure is 16 percent. Turning the data around, 70 percent of users are currently employed full-time. The percentage of heavy alcohol use (five or more drinks on five or more occasions in the last month) is about the same. Current illicit drug users are more likely than nonusers to report that they had taken an unexcused absence from work in the past month, voluntarily quit a job, or

been fired within the last year (Hoffman, Larison, & Sanderson, 1997).

Illicit drug use is most common for young (18–25) white males compared to older workers, women, blacks, and Hispanics. Illicit drug users were more likely to report earnings of less than $9,000 and *$75,000 and more,* compared to those earning between these figures. Size of the company is also an important variable because illicit drug use is more common in workers employed in smaller establishments (1–24 employees) than larger establishments. Heavy alcohol use was the same regardless of the size of the company. Illicit drug use was most common among construction workers, precision production workers, and restaurant workers, especially bartenders. Not surprisingly, police and other protective services workers report the least drug use. By far, the most commonly used illicit drug is marijuana, with 7 percent of the workers reporting its use and more than 70 percent of those saying that marijuana was their only illicit drug (Hoffman, Larison, & Sanderson, 1997).

Keep in mind that these data do not prove a causal relationship between drug use and workplace problems. It might be that drug use is responsible for poor performance, but it also might be that these workers' drug use and poor performance are both related to other factors such as lack of motivation, psychological problems, or psychosocial disruption. It is also possible that workplace characteristics affect drug use. Perhaps some occupations are more conducive to drug and alcohol use. It is also possible that workers who use illicit drugs or are heavy drinkers tend to gravitate toward certain occupations (Hoffman, Larison, & Sanderson, 1997).

The pattern of use is also important. Workers are typically asked about drug and alcohol use within the last thirty days, with no attempt to determine whether the use occurred before, during, or after work. When this issue is addressed, it appears that for alcohol, at least, coming to work with a hangover or drinking on the job were related to workplace problems. Heavy drinking outside the workplace and overall consumption do not seem to be as important (Ames, Grube, & Moore, 1997). As you might guess from the discussion in chapter 4 on alcohol and health, moderate drinkers earn more than heavy drinkers, but they also earn more than nondrinkers (Hamilton & Hamilton, 1997).

Is there any reason to believe that the poor performance of the drug-using workers would be improved if they stopped? This expression (cleaned up for textbook purposes) is common in alcohol treatment: "If someone is a jerk when he is drunk and he stops drinking, what you have got is a sober jerk." The issue of poor work performance is a complex issue. Drug and heavy alcohol use might contribute to the problem, but it is unlikely they are the only cause of the problem. You should also know that heavy drinking and illicit drugs are not the only problems associated with workplace impairment; cigarette smokers typically earn 4 to 8 percent less than nonsmokers (Levine, Gustafson, & Valenchik, 1995).

Workplace Drug Testing

The issue of drug testing in the workplace is very complex. One element is timing. Testing can be conducted as part of the hiring procedure (preemployment screening), periodically during employment (random testing), or when job impairment has been documented (testing for cause) (Norman, Lempert, & O'Brien, 1994). Testing for cause is the least controversial. Preemployment and random screening, on the other hand, raise many serious questions. Because virtually everyone will be employed at some time in their lives, these issues affect you directly.

Legal Justification

The Fourth Amendment to the Constitution of the United States guarantees individuals the freedom from "unreasonable" searches. Various courts of law have ruled that the taking of blood and urine samples is a seizure. The issue is whether the seizure is unreasonable. The rights of an individual have to be weighed against the threat to public safety as well as the intrusiveness of the drug-testing policy (Norman, Lempert, & O'Brien, 1994). Where the threat to public safety is clear, testing is easier to justify. Drug testing is mandatory for government employees in sensitive positions, police officers, and those whose positions entail great public responsibility, such as pilots, truck drivers, and air traffic controllers.

Few would argue that testing in such sensitive jobs is justified, but what about testing supermarket baggers, insurance salesmen, ditch diggers, or college professors? The Fifth Amendment to the Constitution says that the *government* cannot deprive an individual of life, liberty, or property with due process, meaning that the method used must be fair. The courts have ruled that due process would be violated if the tests were unreliable (or were handled in an unreliable way) or if one cannot show some relationship to job impairment. The government is required to operate under stricter rules than the private sector. Once employed, an individual has certain rights of due process, but preemployment screening is almost unregulated.

If a government employee tests positive, the employee is guaranteed a fair "trial." The handling of a positive test in the private sector is almost unregulated. In the case of preemployment screening, there is no law forbidding an employer to refuse to hire someone because he or she wears brown shoes, has long hair, wears nose rings, or is the "wrong" blood type. The only rules relate to such things as age, gender, race, and religious preference. Once hired, an employee has legal recourse to sue for arbitrary firing, but such suits are expensive and rarely won. The private sector is under no real obligation to demonstrate the relevance of testing to job performance or the reliability of the test (Norman et al., 1997).

Types of Drug Tests

Nearly all (some estimates range as high as 98 percent) major corporations conduct some kind of drug testing (Crouch, 1998). The most common form is urine testing. There are two levels of urine testing: the immounoassay test and the gas chromatography/mass spectrometry (GC/MS). There are several types of immunoassay tests, but they all work in similar manner. The tests use antibodies designed to detect a specific drug or drug metabolite. The most widely available immunoassays test for marijuana, cocaine, amphetamine, methamphetamine, opiates, phencyclidine, barbiturates and benzodiazepines. They are easily automated and inexpensive. No extensive technical training is needed to run them.

The immunoassay tests have disadvantages as well. They will produce a positive response to various legal drugs and their metabolites (Crouch, 1998). They cannot detect how long ago a drug was used nor how much was taken. You may be surprised by the data in Table 10.2 which shows the detection limits for common drugs. Unless someone is a heavy user of a drug, its presence cannot be detected after a few days.

A positive reading on the immunoassay tests is not definitive unless the GC/MS is also positive.

An interesting folklore has developed concerning ways to "cheat" on the urine test. Various substances are supposed to produce a negative urine test for someone who has ingested drugs. For example, vitamin C, vinegar, and herbal preparations such as golden seal are supposed to do

TABLE 10.2 How Long since Last Use Drugs Are Detectable in Urine

Drug or Metabolite	Duration of Detectability
Amphetamine	1–3 days
Methamphetamine	2–4 days
Barbiturates	
Short acting	2–4 days
Long acting	up to 30 days
Benzodiazepines	up to 30 days
Cocaine (metabolites)	1–3 days
Cannabinoids	
Single use	1–3 days
Moderate smoker (4/week)	5 days
Heavy smoker (daily)	10 days
Chronic smoker (daily for years)	30 days
Methadone	2–4 days
Opiates	
Codeine	2–4 days
Heroin	2–4 days
Morphine	2–4 days

Note: The duration of detectability depends on the cutoff point used to determine a positive urine sample. The data given are for the most commonly used detection levels. Making the test more sensitive will result in slightly longer durations.

the trick, but there is no scientific evidence that any of these methods is effective (Eskridge & Guthrie, 1997). On the other hand, adding bleach, detergent, liquid hand soap, or certain eye drops to the urine will often result in a false negative (Eskridge & Guthrie, 1997). Most attempts to adulterate urine samples can be detected if proper procedures are followed. Proper procedure involves either direct or indirect observation of the sample being given. Direct observation means that an observer watches the act of urination. Indirect observation means that the person being tested is given a modicum of privacy. In such cases, dye is added to toilet water to prevent dilution, and bulky clothing (which could hide additives or a substitute urine sample) is prohibited. Taking the temperature of the sample will indicate whether the person being tested has substituted another person's urine. Testing the specific gravity will indicate dilution, and measuring the pH will test for the presence of adulterants (Vereby & Buchan, 1997). The good news is that there is one virtually infallible method of guaranteeing a clean urine: *don't do drugs!*

The limits of urine testing have led to the development of other techniques. The three that have received the most attention are tests on hair, sweat, and saliva. Examining hair for evidence of drug use works because hair follicles can absorb a drug through the bloodstream and the drug is then incorporated into the hair shaft. Hair grows at a rate of half an inch a month, so hair sampling can reveal drug use going back as far as six months or even longer (Verebey & Buchan, 1997). The major problem with hair testing is that

the hair shaft can be contaminated by external means (Kidwell & Blank, 1995). Environmental exposure to a drug can lead to a positive test. Other problems involve individual differences in rate of growth and racial differences in hair characteristics (Gygi, Joseph, Cone, Wilkins, & Rollins, 1996). Because of these and other limitations, the federal government has ruled that hair analysis cannot be used to test federal employees for illegal drug use. Hair analysis is used in the private sector, however (Verebey & Buchan, 1997).

Saliva testing has certain advantages. The sample is readily available and collection is not intrusive. Furthermore, drug concentrations in saliva are very close to drug concentrations in the bloodstream. On the other hand, saliva testing is effective during only a very short time range (about 12 to 24 hours after use of a drug). Although it is not commonly used at the present time, saliva testing is likely to become more popular in the future (Verebey & Buchan, 1997).

In addition to being metabolized in the liver, drugs are excreted through the sweat glands. Sweat testing can measure cumulative drug use for 1 to 4 weeks, much longer than either urine or saliva tests (Kintz, Tracqui, Mangin, & Edel, 1996; Verebey & Buchan, 1997). However, people sweat at different rates and sweating is temperature dependent. Sweat testing is still in the developmental stages and many questions are yet to be answered. However, it could prove a useful tool in drug screening.

Employee Assistance Programs

Because the vast majority of alcohol and other drug abusers are employed, the workplace is a logical place to initiate treatment. Employee Assistance Programs (EAPs) have proliferated in recent years. Some are voluntary, others are required as a condition of continued employment. EAPs are effective because they provide economic and social motivation. Many EAPs use a technique known as "constructive confrontation." Using this approach, a supervisor or counselor confronts an employee whose performance is unacceptable with a choice to "face up or face out" (Trice & Beyer, 1983). The employee now has an economic incentive to get treatment.

Why would an employer want to go to the trouble of confronting employees and arranging for their treatment? EAPs provide an economic benefit for employers. They reduce absenteeism, increase productivity in the impaired worker, and send a message to other employees (Engelhart et al., 1997). If the employee were simply fired, the employer would be faced with finding and training a replacement, and the fired employee would likely take his or her knowledge and experience to a rival company. EAPs are now being provided by prepaid health plans and medical insurance. Contracting with a provider is probably best for all companies except the largest, because an in-house drug and alcohol counselor can be expensive (Engelhart et al., 1997).

1. What are some ways drug abuse affects the workplace?
2. What kinds of drugs are tested in a urine test?
3. How can drug testing be legally justified?
4. What are some problems with urine testing?
5. What are the alternatives, and what are their strengths and weaknesses?
6. How do EAPs work?

Drinking and Driving

Drinking and driving is probably the biggest risk most Americans will take. The number of alcohol-related traffic deaths has declined from a peak of 24,050 in 1986 to 17, 274 in 1995, but the decline leveled off at 17,080 in 1996. Table 10.3 shows the figures for the last fifteen years. The decline has led to a perception that the problem has largely been solved. Organizations such as Mothers Against Drunk Driving (MADD) have lost members and funding. Public attention seems to have shifted to other topics. Nevertheless, the problem of drinking and driving is still with us. One alcohol-related traffic fatality occurs every 30 minutes.

Several approaches are being tried to reduce drinking and driving. One tactic is to lower the limit for blood alcohol concentration to .08 and make DUI a "per se" offense (*Drinking and Driving,* 1997). A man weighing 160 pounds could reach that BAL with as few as three drinks, and a woman weighing 120 pounds could be legally intoxicated after only two drinks. In order to become intoxicated, though, they would have to consume their drinks rapidly on an empty stomach. Spacing drinks and eating while drinking slows the rate of absorption of alcohol into the bloodstream. A "per se" offense means that if your BAL is .08 or greater, you are automatically guilty of driving under the influence, no matter how sober you act and appear.

TABLE 10.3 Alcohol-Related Fatalities, United States, 1982–1996

1982	25,165
1983	23,646
1984	23,768
1985	22,716
1986	24,045
1987	23,641
1988	23,626
1989	22,404
1990	22,084
1991	19,887
1992	17,858
1993	17,473
1994	16,580
1995	17,274
1996	17,080
1997	16,187

Two or three drinks might not seem like much, but even experienced drivers show impairment at .08 and often are unaware that their skills have deteriorated (*Drinking and Driving,* 1997). At present, fifteen states have a BAL limit of .08, and all states except Massachusetts and South Carolina have per se laws. Some studies have shown that lowering the BAL has led to a decrease in fatal crashes, although this finding is disputed. Most drivers involved in fatal crashes have a BAL far above .08. In fact, two-thirds have a BAL greater than .14, and the average is .18 (*Drinking and Driving,* 1997). Someone with that BAL is obviously impaired regardless of their driving and drinking experience.

Another strategy is to target drivers who are at greatest risk for drinking and driving. The greatest decline in alcohol-related fatalities has been for those under 21, and the smallest decline has been for those 21 to 34, who ac-

This crash is one example of how drinking and driving don't mix.

count for approximately half of all impaired drivers involved in alcohol-related fatal crashes. These drivers seem to ignore all of the advertising, enforcement, and laws. The worst offenders seem to be white male blue-collar workers who are responsible for more crashes than any other age group. They have the highest average BAL and are four times as likely to have had a suspended or revoked license. These men apparently view drinking as a reward after a hard day of work, and associate driving and drinking with feelings of control and freedom. Although they are typically in favor of harsher penalties for drunken drivers, they felt that they could safely drink and drive and are unlikely to get caught (*Drinking and Driving,* 1997)!

Motorcycle drivers are another group with high rates of alcohol-related fatalities. Thirty percent of all fatally injured motorcyclists were intoxicated, and another 11 percent had BALs lower than .10 (*Drinking and Driving,* 1997). In another study, 42 percent of all those killed or injured had alcohol present (Peeke-Asa & Kraus, 1996). Some of the problem stems from the motorcycle subculture. Drinking is often seen as a routine part of motorcycle events. Motorcyclists typically drink beer and think that they are better able to handle beer than wine or liquor. Many believe that their own ability to handle alcohol is far above average and that they would not be impaired at a BAL of .10. A sobering finding was that many said they would drive a car if they knew they were going to drink too much to ride their motorcycle (*Drinking and Driving,* 1997).

Deterrence is a particular problem with motorcyclists. Anyone who rides a motorcycle, or knows someone who does, knows that cyclists are even more careful about their vehicles than the average male car driver. The thought of being injured or killed didn't seem to be a deterrent, and they were often more concerned about damage to their machine than to themselves. Another problem is that the usual safe drinking strategies employed by car drivers do not operate for motorcyclists. To put it mildly, motorcyclists are unlikely to allow someone else to drive their motorcycle, which eliminates the designated driver strategy. Nor are they likely to be willing to leave their vehicle parked overnight in a public place and accept a ride home (*Drinking and Driving,* 1997).

It is not even safe to be a pedestrian around drinking drivers, especially if the pedestrian has been drinking. Pedestrian crash victims are often intoxicated themselves. About 25 percent had BALs higher than .20, and 31 percent registered higher than .10. The highest risk group was males between 25 and 34 (*Drinking and Driving,* 1997). Many of the intoxicated pedestrians were going to the store for cigarettes, food, or more alcohol. Drivers should be even more careful about driving at night near convenience stores and bars.

Even if you never drink and drive, remember that 20 percent of all such fatalities involved an intoxicated pedestrian and a completely sober driver. Those selling alcoholic beverages should also be careful. Few drink servers will serve an intoxicated person who is driving a car, but how many would sell a six-pack to an intoxicated walker? Simi-larly, law enforcement officers who would be likely to stop an apparent drunken driver might be reluctant to arrest a pedestrian for public intoxication.

Police officers must have probable cause to stop a driver. Table 10.4 lists some of the behaviors that give police officers probable cause for stopping a driver for drunk driving, and the probabilities that a driver showing this behavior has a BAL above .10. Obviously, if you see a driver exhibiting one or more of these behaviors, get out of the way. Some communities urge anyone with a cellular phone in their car to call the police and report the incident. You might get a drunk driver off the road and perhaps save someone's life.

There seems to be particular problems with drinking and driving among younger people. They are less experi-

TABLE 10.4 Driving Behaviors Associated with Drunk Driving

Driving Behavior	Probability That the Driver Is Drunk
Turning with a wide radius	65%
Straddling center or lane marker	65%
Appearing to be drunk Eye fixation Tightly gripping the steering wheel Slouching in the seat Gesturing erratically or obscenely Face close to windshield Drinking in the vehicle Driver's head protruding from window	60%
Almost striking an object or vehicle (e.g., a wall, a sign, another car)	60%
Weaving—a regular zigzag pattern of correction from one side of lane to the other	60%
Driving on other than a designated roadway—on the shoulder, through turn lanes	55%
Swerving—an abrupt turn after a drift or at the approach of another car	55%
Speed 10 mph less than speed limit	50%
Stopping without cause in traffic lane	50%
Following too closely	50%
Drifting	50%
Tires on center or lane marker	50%
Braking erratically	45%
Driving into opposing or crossing traffic	45%
Signaling inconsistent with driving action	40%
Slow response to traffic signals	40%
Turning abruptly or illegally	35%
Accelerating or decelerating erratically	30%
Headlights off	30%

Source: *National Highway Traffic Safety Administration DOT HS 805 711 8, 1994.*

enced drivers, and their age and gender also play a role. Adolescents 16 to 17 years old are more likely to be involved in an accident than those who are 18, and many studies show that women are less likely than men to be in an accident (Lang, Waller, & Shope, 1996). Raising the minimum age for drinking was not popular in many states, but the federal government threatened to withhold highway funds unless the states complied. The increase appears to have worked, because the rate of accidents involving drinking adolescents has declined substantially since the minimum age was raised (Klepp, Schmid, & Murray, 1996).

In forty five states, the permitted BAL for drivers under 21 is lower than for drivers over 21. Some states have zero tolerance, while most others permit a BAL of .02 (*Drinking and Driving*, 1997). These laws have not worked as well as most had hoped. The difficulties include limited space in which to hold offenders, problems of detection, and lack of serious penalties that will deter. North Carolina has a tough law: the legal BAL limit is .00, the offense is both an administrative and criminal violation, and the arrestee is processed like an adult DUI. The driver then receives a 1-year suspension and a fine, must attend 10 to 13 hours of education, and receives a mandatory assessment for drug and alcohol problems and mandatory treatment if determined necessary (*Impaired Driving Update*, 1997).

A few years ago, many states had mandatory jail sentences for convicted drunk drivers. Subsequent analysis revealed that jail sentences basically didn't work (Hingson, 1997). What seem to be greater deterrents are fines and license suspension. The license suspension should be for 12 to 18 months for maximum effect, and granting a limited license (to drive to work, for example) seems to detract from the effect. More than 50 percent of drivers with a suspended license drive, but they drive more carefully and less frequently.

A relatively new technique is to confiscate the driver's license plate or registration. A distinctive tag on the plate gives the police a right to stop the car and ask for a valid driver's license. Without probable cause, a police officer cannot stop even a known multiple DUI. Some states have tried ignition locks that prevent a car from being driven if the driver shows a positive BAL (*Drinking and Driving*, 1997). Both the tag confiscation and ignition lock seem to work, but not enough states have adopted these to be sure.

Sobriety checkpoints are considered effective ways of deterring drinking and driving. They seem to be effective if the public perception is that they are widespread and that drinking drivers will be detected. However, some research has called this effectiveness into question. Drivers who regularly drink and drive are more likely than nondrinking drivers to believe that they can escape detection. In fact, they are correct. In one study sobriety checkpoints missed more than 50 percent of drivers with BALs over .08 and 90 percent of those with a BAL over .05 (Wells, Greene, Foss, Ferguson, & Williams, 1997). Are you surprised to find out that women were less likely to be detected than men, and young women

were the least likely of all? Drivers who were alone in the car were less likely to be stopped than those with passengers (Wells et al., 1997).

Detecting that someone might be under the influence at a sobriety checkpoint is not easy. The police officer cannot take too much time with each car and cannot unduly delay those who have not been drinking. The police officer has not had the opportunity to observe the driver while driving or stopping and so must go on cues like slurred speech and the odor of alcohol. Typically individuals that do not fit the typical profile of the alcohol-impaired driver will be allowed to pass (Wells et al., 1997). The widespread use of sobriety checkpoints (in California, the locations are announced on radio and television) might deter drinking and driving if it draws the attention of the driver to the fact that the police are actively watching.

One technique geared to the multiple offender seems to lower the rate of alcohol-related crashes. When Maine set the legal limit for driving at .04 for persons with a previous DUI, alcohol-related crashes decreased by 38 percent. For those who cause injury or death, a wide range of penalties can be assessed. Most people do not realize that a drunk driver who causes death can be tried for murder. In most cases the charge is vehicular homicide, but two states have charged impaired drivers with first-degree murder. One legal justification for a charge of murder is that the driver's behavior was so completely beyond the norm that it constituted an implied intent to kill (*Drinking and Driving*, 1997). Another involves laws that hold that a person can be charged with murder if a victim dies during the commission of a felony, even if the death is not intended.

Marijuana Use and Driving

It is not safe to drive under the influence of any substance that will impair functioning. The degree of danger is a reflection of the amount of impairment the drug causes. Marijuana use affects coordination, tracking, reaction time, and performance in other tasks that are required for safe driving (Smiley, 1986). Reports suggest that drivers try to compensate for being under the influence by driving more carefully (Hindrick et al, 1993). Nevertheless, studies in several various cities have shown that between 9 to 37 percent of injured drivers tested positive for marijuana (Crouch, 1998). It is one thing to show that an injured driver tests positive for marijuana and another to demonstrate that the marijuana caused impairment that led to the crash. Drinking and driving, using drugs and driving, and risky driving might all be part of a context of risky behavior in general (Donnovan, 1993).

Surprisingly few experimental studies of the effects of THC on driving have been done. Many of those that have been done have used inexperienced smokers and closed driving courses. The finding that a third of the injured drivers tested positive for marijuana is difficult to interpret, because marijuana use can cause a positive urine test for several days after use, but the behavioral effects of marijuana last only a few hours. More research is needed to determine the extent to which marijuana impairs driving ability. However, it is safe to say that driving under the influence of marijuana is dangerous and combining marijuana with other drugs leads to even greater impairment.

Stop and Review

1. How has the rate of DUI changed? What are some reasons?
2. Who is at greatest risk for DUI?
3. What kinds of changes have occurred in the definition of DUI and the way it is enforced?
4. What special problems are associated with drinking and driving by motorcyclists?
5. What are some deterrents to DUI?
6. How does marijuana affect driving, compared to alcohol?

Drugs and Crime

How does the drug use relate to criminal activity? There are three kinds of relationship: psychopharmacological, economic-compulsive, and systemic (U.S. Department of Justice, 1992). A psychopharmacological relationship exists when someone commits a crime because of some drug-induced change in mood or physiological function. A psychopharmacological relationship is also implied when a drug increases impulsivity. Economic-compulsive reasons involve committing a crime to obtain money to buy drugs. Systemic reasons involve drug-related drive-by shootings, rip-offs of buyers and sellers, murders to eliminate rivals, and bribery or perjury to avoid conviction (Falco, 1997).

More than 1.2 million people are currently in federal and state prisons and jails with over half of that number in-

carcerated for drug-related offenses. Moreover, anywhere from 25 to 40 percent of inmates report being under the influence of a drug at the time the crime was committed. Two-thirds of arrestees tested positive for drugs at the time of arrest. In jail or prison, drug-abuse treatment is rare or nonexistent. About 10 percent of state prison and county jail inmates received treatment. In the federal prisons, the situation is even worse. As a result, nine out of ten prisoners return to crime and drugs, and the majority are arrested again within three years (Falco, 1997).

Mandatory Minimums

Mandatory minimum sentences require that a judge sentence a convicted felon to a predetermined sentence. This policy makes a statement that a given crime will result in a given penalty. Many judges are opposed to mandatory minimums because they take all discretionary power away from the courts, which can lead to incomprehensible effects. One man was sentenced to a ten-year mandatory minimum sentence because he accepted $5 to drive a friend to a fast-food restaurant. He claims (and evidence supports the claim) that he did not know that his friend was delivering crack. The disparity in sentences between crack and powder cocaine create another problem. Despite many years of recommendation by judges, scholars, and federal commissions, the penalty for crack is 100 times greater than the penalty for powder cocaine. Table 10.5 shows the federal mandatory minimums for several drugs.

Conspiracy Laws

A conspiracy involves two or more persons agreeing to commit a criminal act. The agreement becomes the crime, and the crime itself need not be carried out. The only requirement is that one of the conspirators must commit a single act to further the conspiracy. Buying fertilizer with the purpose

---

TABLE 10.5 Federal Mandatory Minimum Drug Sentences—First Offenders

Type of Drug	5 Years without Parole	10 Years without Parole
LSD	1 gram	10 grams
Marijuana	100 plants or 100 kilos	1,000 plants or 1,000 kilos
Crack cocaine	5 grams	50 grams
Powder cocaine	500 grams	5 kilos
Heroin	100 grams	1 kilo
Methamphetamine	10 grams	100 grams
PCP	10 grams	100 grams

Offense	Penalty (Added to Drug Sentence)
Possession of a gun during a drug offense	5 years
Armed career-criminal act (felon in possession of a gun)	15 years
Continuing criminal enterprise offense	20 years
These are federal mandatory minimums; those of local states differ.	

of using it on marijuana plants would constitute an act of conspiracy. The penalty for conspiracy is often greater than the penalty for the crime that was intended. Conspiracy laws were passed to break up criminal mobs, but they have been liberally applied to relatively simple drug cases.

Seizure and Forfeiture

Property (including money) used in the commission of a crime or "secured with the fruits of criminal activity" can be confiscated. The technical term is **derivative contraband.** The concept behind it is that criminals should not be allowed to profit from criminal activity. The enormous profits from drug dealing have made the "fruits of criminal activity" confiscation laws very popular. Forfeitures have been a valuable tool in combatting drug trafficking. What is troubling to many is that the forfeiture is a civil process. Criminal forfeiture requires that the defendants be convicted of a criminal offense before their property can be seized. Civil forfeiture is a different process. Forfeiture of assets can occur even if the defendant is found not guilty, and in fact forfeiture often takes place before the defendant's trial even begins. Finally, the prosecutor need only prove a "preponderance" of evidence that a crime has been committed. In criminal cases, guilt must be proved beyond the shadow of a doubt (Grantland, 1992).

Stop and Review

1. What are the three types of relationships between drugs and criminal activity?
2. What are some criticisms leveled at mandatory minimums?
3. What are some other strategies used to reduce crime rates?

Drug Policy

In 1998, the federal government spent more than $17 billion on antidrug efforts. These funds were primarily aimed at illegal drugs. Since 1981, taxpayers have spent nearly $75 billion on federal efforts to reduce illegal drug supply, referred to as **supply-side strategy.** Yet heroin and cocaine are more available at lower prices than ever before. Heroin, which currently is of much higher purity, costs half of what it did in 1981 and cocaine prices have dropped by two-thirds. Worldwide, opium production and cocaine growing have more than doubled in that time (Falco, 1997). Despite this apparent utter failure, some critics argue that the failure is based on a lack of resources. In other words, *much more money should be spent!*

One way of looking at the problem of stopping drugs at the border is to consider that the total amount of heroin needed by U.S. addicts each year could be carried on three small commercial jets and the amount of cocaine could be carried on three large jets. Furthermore, the profits from drug sales occur at the street-sale end of the drug chain. Even if we were successful in confiscating half of the cocaine smuggled into the United States, cocaine prices would increase only about 5 percent and consumption probably would remain the same (Falco, 1997).

Demand reduction attacks the drug problem from the other end. As you read in chapter 5, leaders from the drug-trafficking countries have pointed out that if we didn't buy it, they couldn't sell it. Part of demand reduction involves drug education, which we will look at shortly. Another element of this approach is to make treatment widely available. The federal government spends on treatment less than a third of the amount devoted to supply-side policies, even though studies have clearly shown that every dollar invested in drug-abuse treatment returns more than $7 in decreased taxpayer expenses (Falco, 1997).

According to the most recent report of the Substance Abuse and Mental Health Services administration, only 26 percent of the population who need treatment receive treatment in a given year (Gerstein, Foote, & Ghadialy, 1998). Overall, about five million individuals had been treated for drug problems as of 1992–1993 (Gerstein et al, 1998). Those who did receive treatment had the most extreme patterns of drug use: the highest numbers of times used, and early initiation of alcohol and marijuana use. About 30 percent of individuals treated were covered by health insurance, about 25 percent paid for treatment from earnings or savings. Only 16% of individuals treated were covered by Medicare or Medicaid (Gerstein et al., 1998).

Most prisoners cannot get treatment while they are in jail, and most cannot get treatment on parole. If addicts can't get treatment before jail, during jail, or after release, what do you think are their chances of going back to jail? The few programs that do exist are at least modestly effective. Intensive treatment programs in jails reduce recidivism at a cost of $5,000 to $8,000 per inmate. On parole, effective treatment has been shown to cost about $1,000 (Falco, 1997). The return on such a modest investment would repay the expense many times over.

Drug Education and Prevention

How does society go about reducing demand? The obvious answer would be through education. However, proving that drug education is effective in reducing drug use has proven difficult. What is meant by "reducing drug use"? Can we realistically expect a prevention program to prevent drug use altogether? Nonuse is a goal of nearly all programs, but would a drug program still count as effective if some participants took one trial puff of marijuana out of curiosity? If we permit experimentation, where do we draw the line? How many puffs make a person a user as opposed to an experimenter? The peak years for reported drug use by adolescents was around 1979–1980. The decline in drug use that followed began before massive implementation of drug educa-

Drugs and Law Enforcement Strategy

In Depth

It is extremely unlikely that drugs will be legalized in the foreseeable future, so the problem of law enforcement strategy will remain. How do we reduce the manufacture, distribution, and sale of illegal drugs? Should we concentrate on the low-level dealers, the gangs involved in distributing the drugs, or the kingpins of the drug culture—the narcotraficantes, in Spanish? There are serious difficulties with each of these approaches.

The low-level dealers are easily replaced. Cracking down on low-level sales involves intervening at the point of purchase. This method is time consuming for law enforcement and clogs the judicial system with petty criminals. The result is a revolving-door policy of arresting and releasing low-level dealers who go right back to dealing. Attempts to crack down on dealers have led to the recruitment of young children as couriers or sellers. Children typically are exempt from prosecution, and arresting them makes no significant impact on drug sales. Because point of sale is the target for law enforcement strategies aimed at low-level dealers, this approach can result in harassment of law-abiding citizens who happen to be in areas where drugs are sold. Drugs are usually sold at night, when police are busy with other emergencies, and in smaller cities and towns there might be only a few police officers on duty at any time. How can they be expected to deal with drunk driving arrests, assault and battery cases, burglaries, robberies, and accidents, all of which peak during the same hours as drug sales?

Distributing drugs is a business, with the same characteristics as distributing any other product. However, with illegal drugs, gangs often act as distributors. These gangs use their profits to buy arsenals of weapons, which have escalated the level of crime and intergang warfare. Gangs are difficult to infiltrate because members often are recruited from the local neighborhood. Some gangs are restricted to a single ethnic groups and sometimes speak a particular language or dialect. Finding and training officers to infiltrate gangs is far from easy, especially because most police forces require that officers be nonusers of drugs themselves, at least for a few years before recruitment. Officers are often out of touch with the present drug culture and can place themselves in seri-

ous danger if they use the wrong terms or speak a different dialect. Of course, when a gang is broken up, another usually takes its place. If the weaker and less cohesive gangs are eliminated, the stronger and more ruthless gangs might take over.

Concentrating on the narcotraficantes is extremely time consuming, expensive, and dangerous. Agents must infiltrate the drug network with informants, set up elaborate undercover operations, search through financial records, and maintain surveillance. Often the agents are required to either sell or buy large quantities of drugs to prove that they are "honest" dealers and not police. What happens to drugs that are distributed with the assistance of police officers is a troublesome issue to many. Narcotraficantes got to the top because they were smart and ruthless. They are not easy to catch, and, like with gangs, it is often the least capable that are captured, expanding the market for the smarter and more vicious.

Most law enforcement officials acknowledge that it is impossible to completely stop the smuggling of drugs into the United States. No matter how vigilant they are, a percentage of drugs is going to get through. In the 1970s, there was a very brief attempt to search every car entering the United States from selected border crossings from Mexico. The resultant traffic jams backed up cars for miles and infuriated honest citizens. The attempt was hastily abandoned. Imagine the cost and logistical difficulty of having narcotics agents stationed a few feet apart along the thousands of miles that constitute the borders of the United States. How many property owners would permit police officers to be permanently stationed on their land? Law enforcement agents cannot inspect every ship, plane, train, and car legally coming into the United States, not to mention the impossibility of maintaining constant surveillance to prevent illegal flights and shipments.

Winning the war on drugs by interdicting supply is demonstrably impossible. Law enforcement can only hope to get a small fraction of the drugs smuggled into the United States. Of course, preventing distribution and sale within the United States is even more difficult.

tion programs (Gorman, 1997). The recent increase in drug use is among the adolescents that have received extensive drug education. None of the programs that are widely known, including SMART, DARE, and ALERT have been shown to be effective in reducing drug use (Gorman, 1998).

One program has been shown to be effective (Botvin et al., 1996). This program focuses on a wide variety of strategies that can be considered life styles training. Even this program, however, has been criticized for methodological flaws (Gorman, 1998).

School-Based Programs

School-based programs are aimed at stopping drug use before it starts. These programs, also called primary prevention programs, are geared toward middle school and junior high school students. School-based programs have a long but not especially successful history. The early programs were based on the not unreasonable assumption that if young people find out that drugs are bad for them, they will not take them (Botvin & Botvin, 1997). The scare tactics did not work because they were often exaggerated and, in some cases, might have appealed to the risk-taking students and even increased drug use. In fact, none of the widely known programs has been shown to have real impact on drug taking. The best-known program, Drug Abuse Resistance Education (DARE), has been studied a number of times and the results have been uniformly negative (Dusenbury, Falco, & Lake, 1997). Although everyone, including students, seems to like the DARE program, it has no lasting impact on drug initiation or drug use later in school.

Community Action Programs

Community action programs are aimed at more than reducing drug use. Prevention is one part of an overall strategy aimed at promoting neighborhood cohesion, strengthening social norms of nonuse, and providing opportunities such as neighborhood youth recreation services. Community action programs related to drugs involve neighborhood groups that form to drive out drug dealers and establishing community-wide patrols (Winick & Larson, 1997).

Community action programs employ a number of strategies to improve their neighborhoods. They try to reduce the sale of alcoholic beverages by reducing the number of licenses issued, by insisting on strict enforcement of existing laws, and by cooperating with police to reduce public drunkenness and drunken driving. Of course, driving drug dealers out of the neighborhood or preventing the licensing of more liquor stores might just push the problems over into the next community. Presumably, however, the next community will also become organized. The major role that community action programs play is to foster norms of nonuse (Winick & Larson, 1997).

Harm Reduction Strategy

Harm reduction is a controversial topic with professionals, politicians, and the public. At the same time there is no definition that all of its advocates would agree upon. The principal is relatively simple: Although eliminating illicit drug use is a valuable goal, the fact remains that some people will continue to use drugs and it is impossible to completely eliminate the supply of drug. Society must protect itself from those who cannot or will not stop. Therefore addicts should be provided with whatever help is necessary to reduce the danger that they pose. The suggestions below (based on Des Jarlais, 1995) represent the most essential and least controversial elements of the harm reduction strategy:

1. Permit needle exchanges.
2. Provide free medical treatment and counseling for needy drug abusers.
3. Permit marijuana use for compassionate reasons for persons who have a medical condition that justifies its use.
4. Require jails and prisons to offer counseling on alcohol and other drugs.
5. Eliminate mandatory minimums for drug offenses.
6. Offer alternatives to jail sentences for possession of small quantities of most drugs.
7. Make methadone treatment available at no cost to the addict, even if the abuser remains dependent.

These suggestions might not seem particularly startling, but each one of them is opposed by one or more groups. Many critics see the harm reduction strategy as giving in to drug users, many feel that harm reduction will result in greater drug use, and others feel that harm reduction is a stalking horse for complete legalization (Nadelman, McNeely, & Drucker, 1997). The advocates of harm reduction claim that none of the criticisms are valid.

Needle Exchanges

The purpose of needle exchanges is to provide clean injection equipment to intravenous drug users. Overall, about one-third of all AIDS cases are the result of intravenous drug injection with contaminated needles. Two-thirds of all cases of AIDS in women are the result of intravenous drug use, and more than half of all cases of AIDS in babies can be attributed to intravenous use. Someone dying of AIDS deserves care regardless of how they contracted HIV, and it costs approximately $100,000 to care for AIDS patients in the last year of their lives. Even though needle exchange programs are illegal in most states, more than sixty cities have them.

In 1988, Congress prohibited the use of federal funds to support needle exchange programs, fearing that needle exchanges might encourage addiction by making needles more available. They were also concerned that needle exchanges might somehow indicate social approval of intravenous use. They also wanted to get reelected and perceived that the public was opposed to them. In 1992, Congress extended the ban until the surgeon general determines that needle exchanges prevent the spread of AIDS and do not increase drug use. A comprehensive evaluation by the U.S. Centers for Disease Control and Prevention (a government agency) indicated that needle exchanges reduce the spread of AIDS without increasing drug use.

On the basis of these findings, the National Academy of Sciences recommended that the surgeon general should state officially that needle exchange works. The National Academy of Science is the nation's most prestigious organ-

The Issue of Legalization

Despite billions of dollars spent on fighting the war on drugs, cocaine, heroin, and marijuana are at least as available now as they were twenty years ago. In addition, there are the enormous problems associated with incarcerating those convicted of drug-related offenses, the potential for bribery and corruption, and a growing sense of futility that is felt throughout the criminal justice system. The combination of these and other factors has led some to suggest making drugs legal. The proponents of legalization maintain that drug use should be treated the same way as other unhealthy activities such as cigarette smoking, heavy alcohol use, or even overeating—as a medical and social, not a legal, issue.

Those proposing legalization come from the entire political spectrum of American politics. In addition, many professionals in the fields of economics, criminology, and medicine have added their voices (Boaz, 1990). What would drug legalization entail? Could you stop off at the nearest convenience store for a pack of marijuana cigarettes? Would crack and heroin be advertised on television? Would there be magazine ads extolling the various hallucinogens? Some very libertarian proponents would say legalization should include just such freedoms. Others have a much more restrictive point of view. They would limit drug distribution to government-controlled facilities, and availability would be very time-limited. Still others would have drugs like heroin dispensed by physicians only. Some would limit the sale of drugs to government-regulated centers that would control the time and amount of sale. Some have even proposed licensing drug users and requiring users to demonstrate an understanding of what drugs can do (Nadelman, 1994; Kleber, Califano, & Demers, 1997).

The arguments of proponents of legalization include the following:

1. The cost of drug law enforcement would be substantially reduced.
2. The cost of drugs would decrease, reducing the need for criminal activity to acquire them.

3. Criminal organizations that now benefit from the distribution of illegal drugs would go out of business.
4. Taxes could be levied on drug sales, and the money raised could be used to treat addicts.
5. Users who are presently addicted could lead more normal lives.
6. The medical costs of illegal drug use, especially for AIDS and other diseases, would be greatly reduced (Nadelman, 1994; Kleber et al., 1997).

Those who oppose legalization maintain the following:

1. Legal access to drugs would encourage those who are presently deterred by legal sanctions, and drug use would increase.
2. Decreasing prices would lead to increased use.
3. Minors would have increased access to drugs, like they now have to alcohol and cigarettes.
4. The increase in drug use would inevitably lead to an increase in addicts.
5. The money raised by taxation would be insufficient to pay for treating an increased number of users and addicts.
6. Violence and crime would increase because of the pharmacological effects of drugs such as cocaine and methamphetamine.
7. An increase in drug users would have a significant negative impact on the workforce, because drug users tend to be less responsible employees (Kleber et al., 1997).

There are other arguments, as well as counterarguments to each of the points of both sides. Can you think of arguments to refute each of these positions? Do you think drugs should be legalized? Should drugs be decriminalized, meaning that penalties for possession would be eliminated while criminal penalties might remain for sale and distribution? If so, where would users get their drugs?

What do you think?

---

ization for scientists. Their recommendation has been supported by the American Medical Association and many other professional groups. As of this writing, federal funding of needle exchange is still prohibited.

Stop and Review

1. How do supply side strategies differ from demand reduction strategies?
2. What are some characteristics of the new school-

based programs that make them different from older programs?
3. What do community action programs do, and how does this affect drug use in the community?
4. What are the basic concepts of harm reduction?
5. How is harm reduction related to needle exchanges?

As you finish the material in this book, you should be much more aware of the complicated issues surrounding drug use and abuse. You should be able to distinguish true from false claims about drugs. You should be able to make an informed decision as to what needs to be done in the future. If your position on these issues reflects the material you learned in this course, the book will have served it purpose.

Summary

Alcohol and drug abuse affect our society in many ways, not the least of which is their impact on the economy. Alcohol abuse and cigarette smoking, although legal, cost taxpayers billions of dollars a year. Illegal drugs are big business and the profits are staggering.

Drinking under the influence has decreased for many reasons, but still is a major problem. The strategies to reduce DUI have been more successful with some parts of society than with others. Drinking and driving is dangerous to passengers, pedestrians, and drivers. Deterrents for drinking and driving include sobriety checkpoints and administrative per se laws. The cost of a DUI arrest is a significant deterrent. Motorcyclists create their own special problems regarding deterrence. The effect of marijuana on driving is complex. Most people who smoke marijuana also drink, and the combination is particularly dangerous.

Alcohol abuse and drug use affect the workplace. Drug users are more likely to be problem employees. Drug testing is quite popular and several methods of testing have been developed. Employee assistance programs have been shown to be economically sound and save money in the long run.

Illegal drug use is closely linked to other crimes. A large percentage of people in jail are there for drug-related activities. Mandatory minimums, forfeitures and seizures, and conspiracy laws are intended as deterrents to crime. Although they seem to work, they also create problems.

Our drug policy has many critics. The government focuses on the supply side more than on demand reduction. Drug prevention gets a smaller share of the federal dollar. School-based programs seem to be ineffective. Community action strategies attempt to get everyone involved in changing many factors that lead to drug abuse.

Harm reduction is a difficult concept to define and is controversial. Two major areas of focus of harm reduction are methadone maintenance and needle exchanges. Even though needle exchanges work to reduce the number of new cases of AIDS, there is much opposition to them.

Key Terms

community action program A prevention program on the community level based on promoting neighborhood cohesion.

demand reduction Eliminating or reducing the demand for drugs.

derivative contraband Any property associated with drug sale or smuggling, such as automobiles and airplanes.

school-based programs Programs at the middle and junior high school levels aimed at educating the adolescent on drugs.

supply-side strategy Federal efforts to reduce the illegal drug supply.

References

Pulse Check: National trends in drug abuse (1997). In Rhodes, W., Scheiman, P., Pittayathikhun, T., Collins, L., & Tsarfaty, V. (Eds.) *What America's users spend on illegal drugs 1988–1993.* Office of National Drug Control Policy.

The supply of illicit drugs to the United States (1993). National Narcotics Intelligence Consumers Committee: Drug Enforcement Administration.

Ames, G., Grube, J. W., & Moore, R. S. (1997). The relationship of drinking and hangovers to workplace problems: An empirical study. *Journal of Studies on Alcohol, 58,* 37–47.

Boaz, D. (1990). *The crisis in drug prohibition.* Washington, DC: Cato Institute.

Botvin, G. J., Baker, E., Dusenbury, L., Botvin, E. M., & Diaz, T. (1995). Long term followup results of a randomized drug abuse prevention trial in a white middle-class population. *Journal of the American Medical Association 273,* 1106–1112.

Botvin, G. J., & Botvin, E. M. (1997). School based programs. In J. H. Lowinson, P. Ruiz, R. B. Millman, & J. G. Langrod (Eds.), *Substance abuse: A comprehensive textbook* (pp.764–774). Baltimore: Williams & Wilkins.

Blumenson, E., & Nilsen, E. (1998). Policing for profit: The drug war's hidden economic agenda. *The University of Chicago Law Review, 65,* 35–114.

Calhoun, S. R., Wesson, E. R., Galloway, G. P., & Smith, D. E. (1996). Abuse of flunitrazepam (Rohypnol) and other benzodiazepines in Austin and south Texas. *Journal of Psychoactive Drugs, 28,* 183–190.

Chalsma, A. L., & Boyum, D. (1994). *Marijuana situation assessment.* Office of National Drug Control Strategy.

Committee of Fifty (1903). *The Liquor Problem: A Summary of Investigations 1893–1903.* Boston and New York: Houghton Mifflin Company. Reprint (1970). New York: Arno Press.

Crary, D. (1998, April 18). Drug warriors go after Canadian Pot. *San Francisco Chronicle,* p. A8.

Crouch, D. (1998). Alternative drugs, specimens, and approaches for non-regulated drug testing. In S. B. Karch (Ed.), *Drug abuse handbook* (pp. 776–783). Boca Raton, LA: CRC Press.

DeLeon, G. (1994). Some problems with the antiprohibitionist position on the legalization of drugs. *Journal of Addictive Diseases 13,* 35–57.

Des Jarlais, D. (1995). Harm reduction: A framework for incorporating science into drug policy [Editorial]. *American Journal of Public Health, 85,* 10–11.

Drinking and driving: Facts. (1997). Washington, DC: U.S. Department of Transportation and Highway Safety.

Dusenbury, L., Falco, M., & Lake, A. (1997). A review of the evaluation of 47 drug abuse prevention curricula available nationally. *Journal of School Health 67,* 127–132.

Engelhart, P. F., Robinson, H., & Kates, H. (1997). The workplace.

In J. H. Lowinson, P. Ruiz, R. B. Millman, & J. G. Langrod (Eds.), *Substance abuse: A comprehensive textbook* (pp. 874–883). Baltimore: Williams & Wilkins.

Eskridge, K. D., & Guthrie, S. K. (1997). Clinical issues associated with urine testing of substances of abuse. *Pharmacotherapy, 17,* 497–510.

Falco, M. (1997). Federal policy. In J. H. Lowinson, P. Ruiz, R. B. Millman, & J. G. Langrod (Eds.), *Substance abuse: A comprehensive textbook* (pp. 16–21). Baltimore: Williams & Wilkins.

Gerstein, D. R., Fotte, M. L., & Ghadialy, F. (1998). *The prevalence and correlates of treatment for drug problems.* Substance Abuse and Mental Health Services Administration Office of Applied Studies: US Department of Health and Human Services Document H-2.

Gorman, D. M. (1997). The failure of drug eduction. *The Public Interest 129,* 50–60.

Gorman, D. M. (1998). The irrelevance of evidence in the development of school-based drug prevention policy, 1986–1996. *Evaluation Review 22,* 118–146.

Grantland, B. (1992). Asset forfeiture: Rules and procedures. *Drug Law Report, 3,* 37–48.

Gygi, S. P., Joseph, R. E., Cone, E. J., Wilkins, E. G., & Rollins, D. E. (1996). Incorporation of codeine and metabolites into hair. *Drug Metabolism and Disposition, 24,* 495–501.

Hamilton, V., & Hamilton, B. H. (1997). Alcohol and earnings: Does drinking yield a wage premium? *Canadian Journal of Economics, 30,* 135–151.

Hindrick, W., Robbe, R., & O'Hanlon, J. (1993). *Marijuana and actual driving performance.* Washington, DC: Department of Transportation publication No. HS-808-878.

Hingson, R. (1996). Prevention of drinking and driving. *Alcohol Health and Research World, 20,* 219–229.

Hoffman, J. P., Larison, C., & Sanderson, A. (1997). *An analysis of worker drug use and workplace policies and programs.* Washington, DC: Department of Health and Human Services.

Hoyt, D., Finnigan, T., Nee, T., Schults, T., & Butler, T. (1987). Drug testing in the workplace—are legal methods defensible? *Journal of the American Medical Association 258,* 504–509.

Joseph, H. (1994). Methadone maintenance treatment and clinical issues. In H. Joseph (Ed.) *Methadone treatment works: a compendium for methadone maintenance treatment* (pp. 22–36). New York: New York State Office of Alcoholism and Substance Abuse Treatment.

Kenkel, D., & Manning, W. (1996). Perspectives on alcohol taxation. *Alcohol Health and Research World, 20,* 230–238.

Kidwell, M. J., & Blank, D. L. (1995). *Hair testing for drugs of abuse: International research on standards and technology.* Washington, DC: National Institute on Drug Abuse.

Kintz, P., Tracqui, A., Mangin, P., & Edel, L. M. (1996). Sweat testing in opioid users with a sweat patch. *Journal of Analytical Toxicology, 20,* 393–397.

Kleber, H. D., Califano, J. A., & Demers, J. C. (1997). Clinical and societal implications of drug legalization. In J. H. Lowinson, P. Ruiz, R. B. Millman, & J. G. Langrod (Eds.) *Substance abuse: a comprehensive textbook* (pp. 855–864). Baltimore: Williams & Wilkins.

Klepp, K., Schmid, L., & Murray, D. (1996). Effects of the increased minimum drinking age law on drinking and driving behavior among adolescents. *Addiction Research, 4,* 237–244.

Lang, S., Waller, P., & Shope, J. (1996). Adolescent driving: Characteristics associated with single-vehicle and injury crashes. *Journal of Safety Research, 27,* 241–257.

Levine, P. B., Gustafson, T. A., & Valenchik, A. D. (1995). *More bad news for smokers? The effects of cigarette smoking on labor market outcomes.* Cambridge, MA: National Bureau of Economic Research.

Mahan, N. (1997). Treatment in prisons and jails. In J. H. Lowinson, P. Ruiz, R. B. Millman, & J. G. Langrod (Eds.), *Substance abuse: A comprehensive textbook* (pp. 455–457). Baltimore: Williams & Wilkins.

Mathias, R. (1997). National conference showcases effective drug abuse prevention programs. *NIDA Notes, 12,* 8–9.

Nadelman, E. (1994). Thinking seriously about alternatives to drug prohibition. *Questioning prohibition: 1994 international report on drugs.* Brussels: International Antiprohibitionist League.

Nadelman, E., McNeely, J., & Drucker, E. (1997). International Perspectives. In J. H. Lowinson, P. Ruiz, R. B. Millman, & J. G. Langrod (Eds.), *Substance abuse: A comprehensive textbook* (pp. 22–40). Baltimore: Williams & Wilkins.

Norman, J., Lempert, R. O., & O'Brien, C. (1994). *Under the influence? Drugs and the American work force.* Washington, DC: National Academy Press.

Peeke-Asa, C., & Kraus, J. (1996). Alcohol use, driver and crash characteristics among injured motorcycle drivers. *Journal of Trauma: Injury, Infection, and Critical Care, 41,* 989–993.

Regan, C. (1995). Harm reduction as a middle step in the drug war. *Justica,* 1–2.

Shope, J., Waller, P., & Lang, S. (1996). Alcohol-related predictors of adolescent driving: Gender differences in crashes and offense. *Accident Analysis and Prevention, 28,* 755–764.

Single, E. (1996). Harm reduction as an alcohol prevention strategy. *Alcohol Health and Research World, 20,* 239–243.

Smiley, A. (1986). Marijuana: Onroad and driving simulator studies. *Alcohol, Drugs, and Driving: Abstracts and Review 2,* 121–134.

Trice, H., & Beyer, J. (1987). Social control in the workplace: Using the constructive confrontation strategy with problem drinking employees. In D. Ward (Ed.), *Alcoholism: Introduction to theory and research.* Dubuque, IA: Kendell/Hunt.

Verebey, K. G., & Buchan, B. J. (1997). Diagnostic laboratory screening for drug abuse. In J. H. Lowinson, P. Ruiz, R. B. Millman, & J. G. Langrod (Eds.), *Substance abuse: A comprehensive textbook* (pp. 369–376). Baltimore: Williams & Wilkins.

Wells, J., Greene, M., Foss, R., Ferguson, S., & Williams, A. (1997). Drinking drivers missed at sobriety checkpoints. *Journal of Studies on Alcohol, 58,* 513–517.

Winick, C., & Larson, M. J. (1997). Community action programs. In J. H. Lowinson, P. Ruiz, R. B. Millman, & J. G. Langrod (Eds.), *Substance abuse: A comprehensive textbook* (pp. 755–763). Baltimore: Williams & Wilkins.

Wood, J. (1994). Neuroscience questions and answers by Jocelyn Woods. In H. Joseph (Ed.), *Methadone treatment works: a compendium for methadone maintenance treatment* (pp. 9–11). New York: New York State Office of Alcoholism and Substance Abuse Services.

To my fellow students:

I use the term *fellow students* because I am still learning about this subject. Even after thirty years of teaching, research, and writing, I am daily discovering something. I hope that you, as you begin your learning process, will find the same joy as I get from acquiring knowledge. The purpose of this study guide is to help you learn as much as you wish to and to do well in your course. The more you know about both legal and illegal drugs, the better prepared you will be to meet the challenges that drug use presents. I have tried to be as objective as possible in evaluating these drugs and writing about these topics. I hope you will be challenged by some of the things I have written, and, I issue a challenge. If you think I am wrong, write to me and tell me why you think I am wrong. Be prepared to support your position with facts, not opinion. I promise you I will respond. Despite all the hard work of the fine staff at McGraw-Hill Higher Education, there is a chance that you will still find errors in some parts of the book. If so, I ask you to contact me.

    Dr. Harry Avis
    Department of Psychology
    Sierra College
    5000 Rocklin Road
    Rocklin, CA 95677

Finding Information About Drugs on the Internet

There are literally thousands of places on the Internet where you can find information about drugs, including alcohol and tobacco. They cover every possible range of opinion. Rather than attempt to list them all, I have chosen a few of the most comprehensive or representative sites. Each has links to other sources as well. The Internet addresses below will provide useful information about the psychological and physiological effects of alcohol and other drugs, as well as information about social and legal policy related to drugs. Look these over and be prepared to answer the questions about them in the study guide. I have included sites that cover a wide range of perspectives. You might not agree with them all but you should at least know that they exist.

    All of the addresses (URLs) listed below are accurate at the time of this writing. Keep in mind that the addresses change. If you cannot find the organization by using the address, try one of the Internet search engines.

Web Sites for Drug and Alcohol Information

Address: www.	Name	Description
well.com/user/woa	Webb of Addictions	Probably the best overall nongovernmental drug-related site on the Internet. You can find factual information about drugs, recovery, and nearly every other related topic.
jointogether.org	Join Together	A prevention Web site with many links to other sites.
lingmag.com/bacchus	Bacchus and Gamma	A Web site oriented toward prevention among college students.
gran-net.com/MADD/MADD.htm	Mothers Against Drunk Driving	The Web site for MADD, one of the oldest and best organizations fighting drinking and driving.
alcoholics-anonymous.org	Alcoholics Anonymous	The official AA Web site.
uhs.bsd.uchicago.edu	Psychopharmacology Tips	Information about all prescription psychoactive drugs plus excerpts of questions and answers from physicians using these drugs.
cts.com/crash/habtsmrt	Habit Smart	A harm-reduction oriented Web site.
pitt.edu/~mmv/cedar.html	CEDAR	An excellent Web site for a wide range of drug-related material.
ca.org	Cocaine Anonymous	The Cocaine Anonymous Web site.
marijuana-anonymous.org	Marijuana Anonymous	Just what the name implies.
desh.oreg/SOS/	SOS	Save OurSelves, or Secular Sobriety. An alcohol-abuse-related organization for agnostics and atheists.
mediapulse.com/wfs	Women for Sobriety	The official WFS Web site.
ash.org	ASH	A Web site devoted to reducing tobacco health-related problems.
turnpike.net/~jnr/wodarts.htm	War on Drugs	An alternative Web site that has information opposed to the war on drugs.
soros.org/lindesmith/+icweb.html	Lindesmith Center	Probably the most comprehensive harm-reduction Web site.
frw.uva.nl/sq/drugs	Center for Drug Research	A Web site originating in The Netherlands. It provides a different perspective.
casacolumbia.org	CASA	This organization is well funded and provides lots of information about drug use.
ncbi.nlm.nih.gov/pubmed	PubMed	The Library of Medicine has made available their entire information base on every conceivable medical topic. This one is not to be missed. You can search the entire world's medical literature for free.
niaaa.nih/gov	National Institute on Alcoholism and Alcohol Abuse	The Web site of NIAAA. Many links and lots of information on alcohol abuse.
nida/org	National Institute of Drug Abuse	The federal government's primary Web site for all drug- and alcohol-related information. Provides many links to other sites.
deausdoj.gov/dea/dea/home.html	Drug Enforcement Administration	Find out what the DEA is focusing on and how they try to stop the distribution of drugs.
winternet.com/~publish	Drugs for DARE officers	Information from the DARE antidrug program.
radial.com/night	Recovery Alternatives	Web site for help for drug and alcohol abuse. Useful for those who don't find AA helpful.
samhsa.gov	Substance Abuse and Mental Health Services Administration	A website for surveys and other drug and alcohol information. A government agency.

CHAPTER ONE

An Overview

Chapter Objectives

When you have finished studying this chapter, you should

1. Understand why the term *addiction* is difficult to define.
2. Know the difference between *pharmacological* and *behavioral* definitions of addiction.
3. Understand what *craving* is and how it differs from *withdrawal.*
4. Know the description of substance abuse according to the *DSM-IV.*
5. Be able to distinguish among four kinds of tolerance.
6. Be able to state the criteria used in the CDCA to list drugs on various schedules.
7. Know why heroin, LSD, and marijuana are Schedule I drugs while cocaine is Schedule II.
8. Understand why nicotine and marijuana are often placed in their own separate categories.
9. Know what the two major drug surveys are and how they differ.
10. Be able to describe how drug use changes across the life span.
11. Be able to describe the three kinds of drug use.
12. Know the stages of recovery and the role that relapse plays.
13. Be able to state the three primary reasons for relapse.
14. Distinguish between lapse and relapse.
15. Be able to state the differences between inpatient and outpatient treatment.
16. Be able to differentiate between negative and positive reinforcement.
17. Know what role religion plays in drug use.
18. Be able to describe how availability affects drug choice and use.
19. Know why *expectancy* has become an important concept in explaining drug use.
20. Be able to define the term *dual diagnosis* and show how it complicates treatment.

Key Terms

Define these without referring to the textbook.

abstinence

action stage

behavioral addiction

caffeine

contemplation stage

craving

dependence

detoxification

experimental use

heavy user

maintenance stage

negative reinforcement

positive reinforcement

precontemplation stage

preparation stage

pharmacological addiction

psychoactive drug

regular use

relapse

relapse prevention

therapeutic communities

tolerance

withdrawal

Key Concepts

The term *addiction* is so overused that it has lost its original meaning. *Pharmacological addiction* refers to physiological processes of tolerance and physical dependence. *Behavioral* definitions stress drug-seeking behavior, use in spite of problems, and craving. Craving can occur long after physical withdrawal is completed.

The *Diagnostic and Statistical Manual of Mental Disorders,* fourth edition (*DSM-IV*), of the American Psychiatric Association sets the standard by which drug treatment can be made available. The *DSM-IV* differentiates between drug abuse and drug dependence and provides objective criteria for all substance abuse.

Tolerance can take many forms, including reverse tolerance, meaning that the user becomes more, not less, affected by a drug. *Cross-tolerance* means that the user is affected the same way by different drugs in the same class. *Physical tolerance* refers to the biological process by which the brain adapts to the presence of the drug, and *behavioral tolerance* refers to the learned behavior that users develop.

The Controlled Substances Act distinguishes among drugs on the basis of their dependence potential and their medical usefulness. Some drugs that are relatively harmless are Schedule I because they are illegal.

Drug use peaks for most people in late adolescence and early adulthood. The risk of abuse is increased during other major transitions in life as well, including divorce and retirement. Only a small percentage of users of any drug go on to abuse; most users either experiment or use in a controlled fashion.

Recovery is a long ongoing process, and relapse is common. However, relapse is not inevitable and does not signal failure. The risk for relapse can continue for a long time after withdrawal is accomplished.

In many cases relapse is associated with negative emotions and interpersonal conflict. It can also occur when the user is confronted with the abused drug and has not worked out a strategy to avoid its use.

There is a trend in managed care toward outpatient treatment because it is considerably less expensive, and has about the same success rates, as inpatient treatment.

Both negative and positive reinforcement play a role in drug use. Positive reinforcement occurs when the user finds that the drug produces a pleasurable experience. Negative reinforcement occurs when the drug relieves an unpleasant condition.

A number of factors influence drug use, including availability and family influences. The expectation that a drug will have a given effect on the user seems to be related to drug use.

Many substance abusers have psychological problems that can occur independently of abuse or might be the result of it. The need to treat both conditions is recognized but difficult to implement.

Self-Test

Multiple Choice

1. Instead of addiction, the *DSM-IV* uses which of the following two terms?
   a. *physical dependence* and *physical tolerance*
   b. *psychological dependence* and *physical tolerance*
   c. *abuse* and *dependence*
   d. *withdrawal* and *tolerance*
2. In the case of most drugs, physical withdrawal
   a. lasts a matter of hours.
   b. can continue for many months.
   c. is never completely resolved.
   d. is over in a week or so.

3. Of the four kinds of tolerance, which would explain why a person who had taken LSD for several days did not experience anything upon switching to hallucinogenic mushrooms?
   a. cross-tolerance
   b. behavioral tolerance
   c. physical tolerance
   d. reverse tolerance

4. Which of the following in a Schedule I drug?
   a. Ecstasy
   b. morphine
   c. cocaine
   d. methamphetamine

5. Nicotine is different from most other drugs in that
   a. it is a stimulant only at low doses.
   b. users consider it to be both stimulating and relaxing.
   c. it has properties of both marijuana and alcohol.
   d. it is a Schedule I drug except when used as tobacco.

6. Johann just turned 22. He occasionally binges on alcohol and has smoked marijuana, but does not smoke cigarettes. If he is typical of most young adults, ten years from now he
   a. is likely to be a heavier drinker.
   b. is more likely to be a smoker.
   c. will have "forgotten" about past illegal drug use.
   d. will have cut down on his drinking considerably.

7. Mary stopped smoking cigarettes one week ago. Which of the stages of change is she most likely in?
   a. maintenance
   b. contemplation
   c. action
   d. precontemplation

8. Which of the following situations is most likely to trigger a lapse (or relapse) in Clyde, who used to be an alcohol abuser?
   a. he finds out he just won $1 million in the lottery
   b. he just reached his fortieth birthday
   c. he is to undergo surgery in a week
   d. he has an argument with his wife

9. Inpatient treatment for alcohol and other drug abuse
   a. has been shown to result in a lower relapse rate.
   b. is usually offered only to those who are physically dependent.
   c. is available on demand with most managed care companies.
   d. is cost effective.

10. Which of the following people is *least* likely to experiment with a drug such as marijuana or LSD?
   a. Lisa, who has perfect church attendance but wonders about the depth of her faith
   b. Bob, who is on the church basketball team but rarely goes to church
   c. Anthony, who rarely goes to church but considers himself devout
   d. Monica, who is not a believer but has high ethical and moral values

11. Which of the following is an example of negative reinforcement?
    a. taking an aspirin for a headache
    b. getting arrested for driving under the influence
    c. having a bad experience with LSD
    d. talking a policeman out of arresting you for marijuana possession

12. Increasing the price of cigarettes would be considered
    a. an example of negative reinforcement.
    b. a way of making cigarettes more attractive and increasing their use.
    c. a way of reducing availability.
    d. a form of positive taxation.

13. Which of the following young adults would be most likely to get drunk at a party?
    a. Albert, who came with a designated driver
    b. Miguel, who is just beginning to drink
    c. Charlotte, whose parents are strict nondrinkers
    d. Amber, who believes that alcohol reduces anxiety

14. Which psychological disorder is most common among alcohol abusers when they stop drinking?
    a. depression
    b. panic attacks
    c. anxiety
    d. paranoia

15. Which of the following terms does not belong in a definition of pharmacological addiction?
    a. *physical tolerance*
    b. *physical withdrawal*
    c. *physical dependence*
    d. *craving*

True/False

T   F   1. The concept of addiction is important in the *DSM-IV.*
T   F   2. Physical withdrawal is necessary for a definition of pharmacological addiction.
T   F   3. Cross-tolerance might be expected between prescription anesthetics and morphine given during surgery.
T   F   4. Marijuana is a Schedule II drug.
T   F   5. Middle age is the time when heaviest alcohol use occurs.
T   F   6. Social/recreational users of many drugs continue moderate use for long periods.
T   F   7. Negative emotional states rarely cause a relapse.
T   F   8. In the contemplation stage of change, there are attempts to cut down use.
T   F   9. Negative reinforcement accounts for much of the drug taking when someone becomes dependent.
T   F   10. Inpatient treatment is typically more effective than outpatient treatment.

Exercise Your Critical Thinking Skills

1. How do you explain the fact that people who take morphine for a long period of time for chronic pain usually become dependent but rarely become "addicted"?

2. How does craving differ from withdrawal?

3. Think of a time when you tried to stop some habit and relapsed. Did any of the common reasons given in the textbook apply in your situation?

4. Why do you think that depth of religious conviction is more important than religious observance in reducing drug use?

5. What are the various ways in which psychological disorders and substance-abuse disorders interact?

On the Internet

Look up at least three of the Web sites listed that deal with recovery and see if you can find differences in their approach based on what you have read in the textbook about theories of drug abuse.

CHAPTER TWO

Biological Basis of Drug Action

Chapter Objectives

When you have finished studying this chapter, you should
1. Be able to label the principle parts of the neuron.
2. Understand what happens at the synapse.
3. Be able to describe the lock-and-key principle.
4. Know the difference between the first and second messenger systems.
5. Know how inhibitory and excitatory neurotransmitters work.
6. Know how neurotransmitter action is terminated.
7. Be able to distinguish between agonists and antagonists.
8. Know the function of the following neurotransmitters: acetylcholine, dopamine, norepinephrine, serotonin, the amino acid neurotransmitters, adenosine, the opioid peptides, and anandamide.
9. Be able to describe at least one function for the prefrontal cortex.
10. Know why the diencephalon is so important in understanding drug use.
11. Know where the substantia nigra and nucleus accumbens are and how they relate to drug abuse.
12. Be able to describe at least two functions of the brain stem.
13. Understand how the routes of administration are important in determining a drug's abuse potential.
14. Know the role played by lipid solubility in drug action.
15. Know the advantages and disadvantages of each of the routes of administration.
16. Be able to explain what first-pass metabolism is and why it is important.
17. Understand what a half-life is.
18. Be able to explain how the action of a drug is terminated.
19. Know why gender, age, and weight play a role in determining a drug's actions.
20. Be able to distinguish among set, setting, and placebo effects.

Key Terms

Define these terms without referring to the textbook.

absorption

acetylcholine

agonist

antagonist

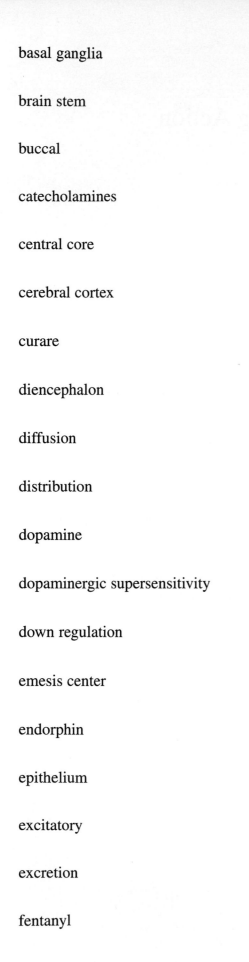

basal ganglia

brain stem

buccal

catecholamines

central core

cerebral cortex

curare

diencephalon

diffusion

distribution

dopamine

dopaminergic supersensitivity

down regulation

emesis center

endorphin

epithelium

excitatory

excretion

fentanyl

first messenger system

first-pass metabolism

half-life

inhalation

inhibitory

insufflation

intramuscular route

intravenous route

ligand-gated channel receptor

lipid solubility

limbic system

lock-and-key principle

medulla

metabolism

mucous membrane

mules

muscarinic

neuromodulator

neurotransmitter

nicotinic

norepinephrine

oral route

parenteral

patient-controlled anesthesia

placebo

prefrontal cortex

receptor

reticular formation

reuptake

routes of administration

second messenger system

set

setting

skin popping

subcutaneous

sublingual

transdermal route

titration

up regulation

urinalysis

vesicles

visual cortex

Key Concepts

The neuron is the principal building block of the brain. Messages travel from the dendrite to the cell body and then down the axon to the end button. At the synapse there is a release of neurotransmitters, which cross the synapse.

The neurotransmitters fit into the postsynaptic receptor like a key fits into a lock. They then open ion channels on the postsynaptic dendrite or cell body. The first messenger system works by directly opening the channels. The second messenger system works by changing the internal environment of the postsynaptic neuron. Inhibitory neurotransmitters increase the resting potential and excitatory neurotransmitters decrease it.

Drugs that increase firing in a cell are called agonists, those that decrease it are called antagonists. The principal neurotransmitters in the brain are the monoamines, acetylcholine, the amino acid neurotransmitters, and the opioid peptides.

The prefrontal cortex of the brain performs the functions of inhibiting responses, organizing thinking, and controlling other structures. The most important structure in the diencephalon is the pathway between the substantia nigra and the nucleus accumbens. Dopamine is the primary neurotransmitter in the nucleus accumbens, and the pathway just described is believed to be responsible for the rewarding effects of drugs as well as the adaptation that produces dependence.

The brain stem is the part of the brain that controls functions of which we are usually unaware, such as heart rate and breathing. Death due to overdose usually involves inhibiting the functions of the brain stem.

The faster a drug reaches the brain, the greater its dependence potential. The fastest route of administration is inhalation. The oral route is slow, and absorption of the drug is subject to a number of variables. Inhalation and intravenous injection produce the greatest dependence potential.

Most drugs are metabolized in the liver and excreted in the urine through the kidney. First-pass metabolism occurs when the drug passes through the liver before reaching the other parts of the body.

The time required for half of the available quantity of a drug to be metabolized is the drug's half-life. Drug action is terminated when the drug is metabolized. Factors such as body weight, percentage of body fat, and age play a role in determining what effect a drug will have.

Set and setting are extremely important concepts in understanding drug action. Set is the expectation of what a drug will do, and setting is the environment in which the drug's effects are felt.

Self-Test

Multiple Choice

1. The primary site of drug action is the
   a. axon.
   b. dendrite.
   c. cell body.
   d. synapse.
2. Vesicles are found
   a. in the synapse.
   b. throughout the axon.
   c. in the end button.
   d. in the postsynaptic neuron.
3. The lock-and-key principle refers to
   a. the action of ions on the axon.
   b. the action of neurotransmitters on the postsynaptic receptor.
   c. the process by which a neurotransmitter is taken back up into an end button.
   d. the second messenger system.
4. An example of a drug that acts on the second messenger system is
   a. caffeine.
   b. cocaine.
   c. heroin.
   d. nicotine.
5. The action of catecholamines in the synapse is terminated by
   a. leakage out of the synapse.
   b. reuptake in the presynaptic neuron.
   c. enzymatic degradation.
   d. post receptor fatigue.
6. Which is the most common neurotransmitter in the brain?
   a. acetylcholine
   b. norepinephrine
   c. GABA
   d. serotonin
7. Which drug acts on the anandamide receptor?
   a. LSD
   b. cocaine
   c. alcohol
   d. THC
8. The brain reward system is believed to be the pathway between the
   a. thalamus and the prefrontal cortex.
   b. reticular formation and the thalamus.
   c. substantia nigra and the nucleus accumbens.
   d. basal ganglia and the thalamus.
9. Which structure is most responsible for a fatal drug overdose?
   a. brain stem
   b. prefrontal cortex
   c. basal ganglia
   d. thalamus

10. Which of the following routes of administration is the fastest?
   a. oral
   b. intramuscular
   c. inhalation
   d. transdermal
11. Drug *X* is more lipid soluble than drug *Y*. This means that
   a. drug *X* is more likely to be an antagonist.
   b. drug *X* will be taken up into the brain more rapidly.
   c. drug *X* will be less likely to be a drug of abuse.
   d. drug *X* is more likely to be a stimulant.
12. Which organ in the body is responsible for first-pass metabolism of most drugs?
   a. liver
   b. small intestine
   c. stomach
   d. kidney
13. THC has a longer half-life than cocaine. This means that
   a. cocaine is more lipid soluble.
   b. THC leaves the body more slowly.
   c. cocaine is less lipid soluble.
   d. THC gets into the brain more rapidly.
14. When a drug has been metabolized in the liver, it is typically
   a. released through perspiration.
   b. exhaled through the lungs.
   c. excreted from the large intestine.
   d. eliminated in the urine.
15. Drinking a beer in a warm dark room usually makes you sleepy, but a beer at a fraternity party seems to give you energy. Which term best describes this phenomenon?
   a. *set*
   b. *setting*
   c. *placebo effect*
   d. *drug antagonism*

True/False

T F 1. The neurotransmitter fits into the postsynaptic receptor.
T F 2. First messenger systems are typically faster than second messenger systems.
T F 3. The action of acetylcholine is terminated by reuptake.
T F 4. Glutamate is an inhibitory neurotransmitter.
T F 5. Serotonin is released in the nucleus accumbens.
T F 6. Titration is easy with the oral route of administration.
T F 7. The sublingual route of administration bypasses first-pass metabolism.
T F 8. Most drugs are metabolized in the kidney.
T F 9. THC is an example of a drug with a short half-life.
T F 10. *Set* refers to expectancy about what a drug will do.

Exercise Your Critical Thinking Skills

1. What would be the likely effect of a drug that antagonized the action of serotonin?

2. Not every expert agrees that the pathway between the substantia nigra and the nucleus accumbens is responsible for abuse or addiction. Why?

3. Why are very few illicit drugs administered transdermally?

4. Under what circumstances would a drug with a long half-life be more appropriate than one with a short half-life?

5. What is the difference between set and placebo?

On the Internet

Go to PubMed and look up information on a neurotransmitter and on a drug that works on that neurotransmitter. Try to find five or more articles on the subject that were published since 1998. What new information do they contain?

CHAPTER THREE

Alcohol: Pharmacological and Physiological Effects of Use and Abuse

Chapter Objectives

When you have finished studying this chapter, you should.

1. Know where in the gastrointestinal tract alcohol is absorbed.
2. Be able to discuss three factors that affect absorption in the stomach.
3. Understand the harmful effects that heavy drinking can cause in the gastrointestinal tract.
4. Know why the liver is so important for the process of metabolism.
5. Be able to discuss the three common types of liver damage caused by heavy drinking.
6. Be able to name two other organs related to digestion and excretion that are also affected by alcohol.
7. Have your own opinion about the health benefits of drinking alcohol and be able to support your position.
8. Know what effect alcohol has on male and female sexual performance.
9. Be able to describe how alcohol affects the fetus.
10. Know what happens in the brain of a person who drinks heavily.
11. Be able to describe the effects of alcohol on the amino acid neurotransmitter systems.
12. Know how alcohol's effects of serotonin relate to depression and violence.
13. Describe the rationale behind prescribing SSRIs for recovering alcoholics.
14. Understand and be able to discuss the controversy surrounding the disease concept of alcoholism.
15. Know what inherited characteristics make alcohol abuse more common in the sons of alcoholic fathers.
16. Be able to list the genetic markers for alcohol abuse that have been demonstrated in research animals.
17. Understand the concept of recovery without treatment.
18. Be able to describe the main characteristics of alcohol-abuse treatment and differentiate between inpatient and outpatient treatment.
19. Know what craving is and understand the important role of motivation in recovery.

Key Terms

Define these terms without referring to the textbook.
acetaldehyde

alcohol dehydrogenase

alcohol-related neurodevelopmental disorder (ARND)

Antabuse (disulfiram)

ascites

concordance

delirium tremens

fetal alcohol syndrome (FAS)

French paradox

holiday heart syndrome

Korsakoff's syndrome

monoamine oxidase (MAO)

Naloxone

Post alcohol withdrawal syndrome (PAWS)

Type 1 (milieu-limited) alcoholism

Type 2 (male-limited) alcoholism

Key Concepts

Alcohol is primarily absorbed in the small intestine. Metabolism of alcohol begins in the stomach, where alcohol dehydrogenase is found. Men have more alcohol dehydrogenase than women. Food, particularly fatty food, will slow absorption of alcohol in the stomach.

Alcohol can affect the entire gastrointestinal tract. The liver is the primary site of alcohol metabolism. Abusive drinking can damage the liver, leading to alcoholic fatty liver, hepatitis, and cirrhosis. The pancreas and kidney are also affected by alcohol abuse.

Light drinking (1 or 2 drinks a day) can help prevent heart disease, whereas heavy drinking shortens lives. Any amount of alcohol will decrease sexual performance.

Mothers who drink heavily during pregnancy run the risk of harming the developing fetus. The most serious effect is fetal alcohol syndrome.

Alcohol can cause diffuse brain damage if taken in excess. The effects of alcohol on the brain depress serotonin levels and can lead to depression. Because serotonin is involved in this form of depression, antidepressants are frequently prescribed for the recovering alcohol abuser.

The disease concept of alcoholism seems to make good sense, but it has significant flaws. Most researchers do not accept the traditional view of the disease process of alcoholism.

A strong argument can be made that alcohol abuse has a genetic component. Sons of alcoholic fathers seem to have a greater innate tolerance and to be less affected by other stimuli. Animal studies have confirmed a genetic component based on the dopamine model.

Type 1 alcoholics get into trouble a great deal and begin abusive drinking at an early age. On the other hand, Type 2 alcoholics typically are older and display fewer symptoms.

No one knows just how many, but a large percentage of heavy drinkers seem to recover on their own. For those who cannot, both inpatient and outpatient treatment have proven effective.

Relapse is common in alcohol abusers, and craving can be strong. Antabuse and naloxone are available to prevent relapse.

Self-Test

Multiple Choice

1. Alcohol is primarily absorbed in the
   a. large intestine.
   b. small intestine.
   c. stomach.
   d. esophagus.
2. Which of the following is likely to have the least alcohol dehydrogenase in their stomach?
   a. a woman who drinks only once a year
   b. a woman who is a heavy drinker
   c. a man who drinks only with meals
   d. a man who prefers liquor to wine or beer
3. Which of the following nearly always occurs after a period of heavier than usual drinking?
   a. hepatitis
   b. cirrhosis
   c. alcoholic fatty liver
   d. biliary adhesions
4. Which condition is usually the result of heavy drinking?
   a. asthma
   b. duodenal ulcer
   c. pancreatitis
   d. kidney stones
5. Fetal alcohol syndrome is most likely to occur if the mother drinks heavily
   a. during the first trimester of pregnancy.
   b. during the last trimester of pregnancy.
   c. just prior to conception.
   d. during the second trimester of pregnancy.
6. The effect of alcohol on the brain is most similar to the effect of?
   a. an antidepressant
   b. an antianxiety drug
   c. an antimanic drug
   d. a narcotic drug

7. The lower levels of _____ contribute to the depression experienced by many heavy drinkers.
   a. norepinephrine
   b. dopamine
   c. acetylcholine
   d. serotonin
8. Type 1 alcoholics are more likely than Type 2 alcoholics
   a. to be young.
   b. to have been arrested.
   c. to have a later onset of abuse.
   d. to show signs of severe alcohol dependence.
9. What percentage of the sons of alcoholics become alcohol abusers?
   a. 40 percent
   b. nearly all
   c. 20 percent
   d. 75 percent
10. Which drug has recently been developed to reduce craving and relapse among alcohol abusers?
    a. Xanax
    b. Prozac
    c. Antabuse
    d. naloxone
11. Which drug causes nausea when alcohol is taken?
    a. Antabuse
    b. naloxone
    c. Xanax
    d. Prozac
12. Which neurotransmitter is linked to alcohol-induced violence?
    a. dopamine
    b. GABA
    c. serotonin
    d. norepinephrine
13. Which of the following is most likely to be experienced by the sons of alcoholic fathers?
    a. they have less ability to control their emotions
    b. they seem to be affected less by alcohol
    c. they often show signs of mild neurological damage
    d. they are more likely to be involved in criminal behavior
14. The strongest criticism of the disease concept of alcoholism is the
    a. fact that many alcohol abusers appear to recover without treatment.
    b. lack of a specific genetic marker for alcohol abuse.
    c. results of studies of identical twins.
    d. popularity of Alcoholics Anonymous.
15. What characteristic seems to best predict success in recovery from alcohol abuse?
    a. the social background of the abuser
    b. the degree of motivation
    c. the severity of the alcohol abuse
    d. the presence of medical problems brought on by drinking

True/False

T   F   1. Alcohol is metabolized exclusively in the liver.

T   F   2. One way to reduce the absorption of alcohol is to eat a fatty meal before drinking.

T   F   3. Cirrhosis can be reversed if the alcohol abuser stops drinking.

T   F   4. To maximize any possible health benefit from drinking, men should have no more than one or two drinks a day and women no more than one drink a day.

T   F   5. Alcohol decreases sexual performance in men only at a BAL over .08.

T   F   6. Alcohol exerts part of its effect by blocking the neurotransmitter GABA.

T   F   7. The depression experienced by many alcohol abusers is related to an alcohol-induced decrease in serotonin.

T   F   8. The disease concept of alcohol is virtually universally accepted.

T   F   9. Sons of alcoholic fathers tend to be less sensitive to the effects of alcohol.

T   F   10. Recent evidence suggests that a large number of people who were at one time alcohol abusers stopped or moderated their use without help.

Exercise Your Critical Thinking Skills

1. Why do you think that many people are opposed to liver transplants for alcohol abusers?

2. Would you urge someone who didn't drink and who had a family history of cardiovascular problems to have one or two drinks a day? Why or why not?

3. The antidepressants that increase serotonin in the brain help some alcohol abusers, but the effect is not large. Why do you think this is the case?

4. You are giving a talk in a speech class, and the topic you were assigned is the disease concept of alcoholism. You know several people who used to drink heavily but now attend AA and believe firmly in the disease concept of alcoholism. How would you present your material so that you explain the controversy and at the same time do not offend your classmates?

5. What differences do you think exist between those who recover from alcohol abuse without recovery and those who feel they need treatment?

On the Internet

Go to a Web site with a harm-reduction approach and a government site. Compare their information about moderate drinking and health. Which makes more sense to you?

CHAPTER FOUR

Alcohol: Social and Psychological Aspects of Use and Abuse

Chapter Objectives:

When you have finished studying this chapter, you should

1. Know what a standard drink is and decide whether the drinks you have are standard.
2. Know what percentage of people are abstainers, light drinkers, and heavy drinkers.
3. Know why five drinks or more is considered binge drinking.
4. Be able to describe the harmful effects of binge drinking on college students.
5. Be able to discuss the pattern of drinking over the life course.
6. Be able to discuss alcohol use by the following groups: women, gay men and lesbians, the elderly, Native Americans, African Americans, Asians and Latins, and the homeless.
7. Know how alcohol affects driving and know what strategies are being used to combat driving under the influence.
8. Be able to discuss the relationship between depression and alcohol abuse.
9. Understand how alcohol affects the family.
10. Be able to describe the role of the family in alcohol abuse treatment.
11. Know why the search for the "alcoholic personality" has been unsuccessful.
12. Be able to describe how the antisocial personality trait might predispose someone to alcohol abuse.
13. Understand the concept of relapse prevention.
14. Know what triggers for relapse are specific to alcohol.
15. Know why Alcoholics Anonymous has been so successful and what some criticisms of it might be.
16. Be able to name three other groups that offer support for alcohol abusers.

Key Terms

Define these terms without referring to the textbook.

addictive voice recognition training (AVRT)

Alcoholics Anonymous (AA)

al kohl

antisocial personality disorder

binge drinking

blood alcohol level (BAL)

brief intervention

chicha

consensus estimate

dual diagnosis

Moderation Management

per capita

proof

Rational Recovery

Secular Organization for Sobriety (SOS)

shared ideology

SMART

Women for Sobriety

Key Concepts

Most people who drink alcohol are light drinkers. Heavy drinkers account for a large percentage of the total amount of alcohol consumed. The greatest problems occur when either light or heavy drinkers consume more than five drinks at a setting, which is called binge drinking.

College students are especially prone to binge drinking. Binge drinkers have lower grades, get in more trouble, and create problems for others. For most people the years of late adolescence and early adulthood constitute the heaviest drinking period. Marriage seems to decrease drinking more in men than in women.

Different groups have different drinking habits. Gays and the homeless are the heaviest drinkers. Although heavy drinking is a serious problem for some African Americans and Native Americans, it is not the norm.

Alcohol abuse can trigger depression or make an ongoing depression worse. In most cases, however, it appears that heavy drinking and depression are independent problems.

Alcohol abuse in a family can lead to serious problems. The family plays an important role in cessation of drinking.

Most researchers have been unable to identify common personality characteristics of most heavy drinkers. Persons with certain personality disorders, however, are prone to be alcohol abusers.

Relapse prevention has become an increasingly important part of alcohol recovery. Groups such as AA and others play an important role in aftercare for the recovering alcoholic.

Self-Test

Multiple Choice

1. Officially, a typical can of beer, mixed drink, or glass of wine contains how much absolute alcohol?
   a. 1 ounce
   b. .60 ounce
   c. 2 ounces
   d. .40 ounces
2. Heavy drinkers make up about what percentage of society?
   a. more than 20 percent
   b. less than 5 percent
   c. about 10 to 15 percent
   d. the percentage is unknown
3. The point at which problems with alcohol consumption begin to rise sharply occurs after
   a. three standard drinks
   b. five standard drinks
   c. six standard drinks
   d. eight standard drinks
4. What important factor has been identified as a reason for the high rate of drinking among college students?
   a. the stress of college, such as taking exams and preparing for the future
   b. the immaturity of most college students
   c. the fact that families of most college students are also heavy drinkers
   d. the fact that society has given subtle approval of heavy drinking in college
5. A typical alcohol abuser
   a. displays a pattern of heavy drinking followed by abstention and then more heavy drinking.
   b. increases drinking between age 30 and 50.
   c. almost always begins a pattern of heavy drinking in early adolescence.
   d. rarely continues to drink heavily after age 40.
6. Students who are heavy drinkers in college
   a. continue their heavy drinking but do not seem to suffer the consequences.
   b. typically taper off when they graduate but return to heavy drinking during middle age.
   c. usually do not go on to become alcohol abusers.
   d. almost invariably become alcohol abusers.
7. Which group is generally believed to have the lowest rate of alcohol abuse?
   a. Asians
   b. Latinos
   c. African Americans
   d. Homeless

8. African Americans who have achieved upper-class status
   a. drink less than whites.
   b. drink more than Latinos, but less than Native Americans.
   c. have high rates of alcohol abuse.
   d. drink more than whites.

9. CAGE is a mnemonic used to
   a. estimate the severity of liver damage.
   b. evaluate the presence of fetal alcohol syndrome.
   c. identify the sons of alcoholics.
   d. identify those who may be alcohol abusers.

10. Which neurotransmitter is believed to link alcohol abuse and depression?
    a. dopamine
    b. norepinephrine
    c. GABA
    d. serotonin

11. Persons with antisocial personality disorder
    a. are likely to abuse alcohol because they are sensation seekers and need immediate gratification.
    b. do not typically abuse alcohol, because they have a need to remain in control.
    c. become alcohol abusers because they are almost invariably depressed.
    d. are likely to become alcohol abusers because of their feelings of isolation from others.

12. Relapse prevention, among other things, emphasizes the
    a. disease concept of alcoholism.
    b. inevitability of relapse.
    c. need to recognize triggers for drinking.
    d. idea that one drink almost always leads to a serious relapse.

13. The effectiveness of Alcoholics Anonymous is difficult to evaluate because
    a. nearly everyone who goes stays sober.
    b. they actively discourage research.
    c. they do not keep records on who attends.
    d. members rarely admit to being members.

14. Which drug is used to treat craving in alcoholics?
    a. naloxone
    b. Antabuse
    c. Xanax
    d. Prozac

15. Those who take Antabuse
    a. have less craving because of the effect of the drug on the endorphin system.
    b. become seriously ill if they consume alcohol.
    c. often stop its use because of side effects.
    d. rarely remain abstinent.

True/False

T   F   1. A martini made by a bartender in a bar contains more absolute alcohol than a glass of wine.

T   F   2. About 15 percent of all Americans are abstainers.

T	F	3.	Binge drinking refers to the consumption of five or more drinks in a sitting.
T	F	4.	The elderly are rarely alcohol abusers.
T	F	5.	Alcohol abusers are incapable of being abstinent for more than a day or so.
T	F	6.	Many alcohol abusers experience depression during recovery.
T	F	7.	Daughters of alcoholic fathers do not have as high a rate of alcohol abuse as do sons of alcoholic fathers.
T	F	8.	According to relapse prevention strategies, any amount of drinking is considered a relapse.
T	F	9.	Alcoholics Anonymous believes that spirituality plays an important part in recovery.
T	F	10.	Naloxone, a drug that reduces craving in alcohol abusers, is used to treat heroin overdose.

Exercise Your Critical Thinking Skills

1. How would you go about discouraging heavy drinking at your college?

2. Why do you think that alcohol abusers often experience long periods of sobriety but then relapse?

3. What role do you think poverty and social inequality play in the heavy drinking of some members of some groups such as Native Americans and African Americans?

4. What validity is there to the idea that alcohol abusers are self-medicating themselves?

5. What kind of personality do you think would be attracted to AA?

On the Internet

Go to the Web sites for AA and for Recovery Alternatives. Using the links, if necessary, compare three different positions on recovery.

CHAPTER FIVE

Stimulants: Cocaine, Amphetamine, and the Xanthines

Chapter Objectives

When you have finished studying this chapter, you should
1. Be able to trace the history of cocaine from the Incas to the present.
2. Know why the Incas thought coca leaf was so valuable.
3. Know how cocaine acts in the synapse.
4. Be able to list the physiological effects of cocaine.
5. Know how cocaine use produces dependence.
6. Be able to discuss what happens when someone who is using cocaine also drinks alcohol.
7. Know why crack has created so many problems.
8. Know how cocaine use can lead to depression.
9. Be able to discuss the effects of cocaine use in pregnant women.
10. Know how cocaine dependence is treated.
11. Know how amphetamine works in the brain.
12. Be able to explain the difference between crack and crank.
13. Be able to discuss the problems associated with the illegal manufacture of methamphetamine.
14. Know the physiological effects of methamphetamine abuse.
15. Know why people coming down from amphetamine can be dangerous.
16. Be able to discuss the role that adenosine plays in the effects of caffeine.
17. Understand what caffeine dependence is and how it differs from dependence on cocaine or amphetamine.
18. Be able to decide whether and to whom caffeine use is harmful.

Key Terms

Define these terms without referring to the textbooks.
adenosine

amphetamine

bingers

butylcholinesterase

caffeinism

cocaethylene

cocaine

coca leaves

crack

crack babies

crack lung

crank

crystal

dopamine transporter

ephedrine

freebasing

go-fast

high-intensity users

ice

low-intensity users

meth

P2P

pseudoephedrine

speed

speed freaks

spiralling distress

theobromine

theophylline

tweaking

xanthines

Key Concepts

The coca leaf has played an important role in the culture of the indigenous peoples of Central and South America for centuries.

Cocaine inhibits reuptake of catecholamines and serotonin in the synapse. It produces euphoria and sympathetic nervous system arousal. The depression that follows cocaine use leads to dependence.

Many cocaine users also consume alcohol, and the combination can produce serious problems. Cocaine users are at risk for seizures, stroke, and heart attack in addition to dependence. Use of large amounts of cocaine over several days can lead to hallucinations.

Crack is a form of freebase cocaine. It reaches the brain quickly, and its effects last for a short time. Users of crack often neglect their health and well-being to maintain their dependence.

Cocaine depletes the brain of dopamine, and cocaine abusers are often depressed when they attempt to stop using. Treatment for cocaine dependence is difficult because cocaine users are depressed and respond to many environmental cues that trigger craving.

Pregnant women who use cocaine can harm their fetus, but proper social and medical care after birth usually can overcome the effects.

The effects of amphetamine last longer than the effects of cocaine. Amphetamine produces its effects by release of dopamine and norepinephrine in the synapse. Crank is a form of methamphetamine that can be smoked, and its use appears to be increasing.

The distribution of methamphetamine is increasingly being controlled by Mexican narcotics traffickers. A method of making methamphetamine from over-the-counter medicine has been developed. It is easier to obtain the necessary chemicals in Mexico. The manufacture of crank involves many chemicals that are environmentally toxic.

Methamphetamine produces many of the same effects as cocaine and creates the same problems. Users who have been abusing crank for several days and are on the downside are said to be "tweaking" and can be dangerous.

Caffeine is a mild stimulant that inhibits adenosine instead of affecting the catecholamine system. Dependence is possible with caffeine but withdrawal is relatively mild. There are very few health consequences from prolonged use of caffeine.

Tea also contains the stimulant theophylline in addition to caffeine. Recent studies suggest that drinking tea might provide some protection from cancer.

Self-Test

Multiple Choice

1. The Incas of South America
   a. considered the coca leaf indispensable.
   b. had developed dependence on the coca leaf by the time of the Spanish Conquest.
   c. rarely used coca leaf after the Conquest.
   d. developed a highly effective method of smoking the leaf that yielded high levels of cocaine.
2. The first medical use of cocaine was
   a. to relieve depression.
   b. to decrease appetite.
   c. to treat diseases such as malaria.
   d. as a local anesthetic.
3. In the synapse, cocaine acts to
   a. decrease levels of dopamine.
   b. increase the release of catecholamines from the vesicles.
   c. block the inhibitory postsynaptic receptors.
   d. inhibit reuptake of catecholamines and serotonin.
4. Cocaine abuse leads to a short period of elation followed by
   a. nausea and vomiting.
   b. depression.
   c. anxiety.
   d. paranoia.
5. Cocaethylene
   a. is an enzyme that metabolizes cocaine in the liver.
   b. is a contaminant of street cocaine.
   c. produces more serious dependence than cocaine.
   d. is the substance formed when cocaine is taken in combination with alcohol.
6. Crack is made by
   a. combining cocaine with baking soda.
   b. mixing cocaine with ephedrine.
   c. dissolving cocaine in ether and then heating it.
   d. adding methamphetamine to cocaine.
7. The depression following cocaine use
   a. can last for weeks or months.
   b. is over in a few days.
   c. is related to the increased release of dopamine in the nucleus accumbens.
   d. is easily treated.
8. Cocaine use by pregnant women
   a. almost always causes serious and permanent birth defects.
   b. usually results in a spontaneous abortion.
   c. can harm the fetus, although most seem to recover.
   d. increases the risk that the baby will become a substance abuser when he or she matures.

9. Amphetamine causes its effects by
   a. inhibiting reuptake of catecholamines.
   b. directly stimulating the postsynaptic receptor.
   c. causing a direct release of catecholamines.
   d. blocking the enzyme that metabolizes catecholamines.
10. _____ refers to amphetamine abusers who have been using for several days.
   a. Tweakers
   b. Cranksters
   c. Speedsters
   d. Tipsters
11. Methamphetamine differs from cocaine in that
   a. cocaine is longer acting.
   b. methamphetamine users do not experience hallucinations.
   c. methamphetamine is longer acting.
   d. cocaine has a greater abuse potential.
12. Methamphetamine can be made from which over-the-counter medicine?
   a. Benadryl
   b. ephedrine
   c. dextromethorphan
   d. phenylpropanolamine
13. Caffeine works by
   a. inhibiting reuptake of GABA.
   b. inhibiting adenosine.
   c. increasing glutamate in the brain.
   d. increasing dopamine levels in the synapse.
14. The major symptom of caffeine withdrawal is
   a. depression.
   b. irritability.
   c. headache.
   d. anxiety.
15. The health benefits of tea appear to be associated with
   a. a decreased risk of cancer.
   b. a reduction in cholesterol.
   c. an increase in clotting time in the blood.
   d. a reduction in blood pressure.

True/False

T   F   1. The Incas learned how to extract cocaine from the coca leaf.
T   F   2. Cocaine was the first general anesthetic discovered.
T   F   3. Cocaine increases the amount of catecholamines in the synapse.
T   F   4. The depression caused by cocaine use is long lasting.
T   F   5. The legal penalties for cocaine use are greater than for crack use.
T   F   6. Amphetamine has no valid medical use.
T   F   7. Methamphetamine use seems to be increasing.
T   F   8. Paranoia and delusional thinking seldom occur with methamphetamine abuse.
T   F   9. Caffeine can produce physical dependence.

T F 10. High levels of caffeine consumption have been linked to increased risk of intestinal cancer.

Exercise Your Critical Thinking Skills

1. Why do you think that chewing coca leaf rarely leads to dependence while snorting cocaine often does?
2. Why do you think cocaine caught on with middle-class whites in the 1980s?
3. What factors do you think have led to the decline in cocaine use and the increase in methamphetamine use?
4. Why do you think the penalties for crack use are so much greater than those for cocaine use?
5. Why is caffeine dependence acceptable while amphetamine use is not?

On the Internet

Use a search engine to see what you can find about methamphetamine abuse (try using the term *"methamphetamine abuse")* that has been posted since 1998. Is my prediction correct?

CHAPTER SIX

Marijuana

Chapter Objectives

When you have finished studying this chapter, you should
1. Be able to trace the use of marijuana from its earliest use to the present.
2. Know the various types of cannabis and how marijuana is used.
3. Know how THC is absorbed, metabolized, and eliminated.
4. Understand the difference between testing positive for THC and being under the influence of THC.
5. Know the physiological effects of THC.
6. Know what anandamide is and how it is related to marijuana.
7. Understand how the distribution of anandamide in the brain helps explain the effects of marijuana.
8. Be able to decide whether marijuana produces dependence as serious as the dependence produced by other drugs of abuse.
9. Be able to discuss the ways in which marijuana use harms the body.
10. Understand the controversy over medical use of marijuana.
11. Be able to decide whether marijuana could have any valid medical use.
12. Know how hemp and marijuana are related.

Key Terms

Define the key terms without referring to the textbook.

amotivational syndrome

anandamide

California Buyers Club

cannabinoids

Cannabis indica

Cannabis ruderalis

Cannabis sativa

delta-9-tetrahydrocannabinol (THC)

EMIT

false negative

false positive

hashish

hashishiyya

hash oil

hemp

hemp oil

hemp seed

The Mahabharta

sinsemilla

Thai sticks

Key Concepts

The plant called marijuana has been used for many centuries as a source of clothing and rope, as a medicine, and for recreational purposes. There are three varieties of the cannabis plant.

The varieties of cannabis differ in their manner of growth and in the amount of THC they produce. THC (tetrahydrocannabinol) is the psychoactive chemical found in cannabis.

Although marijuana can be eaten, most users in the United States smoke it so the THC reaches the brain quickly. It is very lipid soluble, which means it is taken up and stored in fatty tissue. As the concentration in the blood decreases, THC is released from fatty stores.

THC is metabolized in the liver, and the metabolite is excreted in the urine. Testing for marijuana can produce positive results for several days after regular use. However, a positive test for marijuana does not indicate how much the person has used or when they used it.

The physiological effects of marijuana are not striking. Bloodshot eyes, clumsiness, and short-term memory difficulties are the most common. The short-term memory difficulties typically are present only while the person is under the influence of the drug, although there might be some long-lasting effect with heavy users.

THC acts on a specific receptor on the neuron. The brain produces a THC-like substance called anandamide. Anandamide and the receptors for it are found in the frontal cortex, hippocampus, and cerebellum. These structures are associated with the effects of THC.

Some people are unable to stop using marijuana, so it can produce dependence. Most users, however, do not show indications of either pharmacological or behavioral addiction. Physical withdrawal does not lead to serious symptoms.

It is clear that smoking marijuana is harmful, just as all smoking is, but some of the other problems associated with marijuana use might be overstated. Panic attacks and even psychosis have been attributed to its use, but these are rare. Whether it affects the immune system in a clinically significant way and whether it causes amotivational syndrome are issues that are still being debated.

Marijuana does reduce nausea, and proponents have called for compassionate use for those who need it. It can also reduce the risk of blindness from glaucoma and might have some pain-relieving properties. Opponents of compassionate use see the movement as a cover for legalization.

Some enthusiasts have advocated hemp, which is *Cannabis sativa* grown to produce fiber rather than THC. Opponents see this movement as a cover for legalization as well. The arguments for legalization are not strong, but neither are the arguments for continuing criminal penalties.

Self-Test

Multiple Choice

1. In the past, the plant from which marijuana is derived has been used
   a. as a source for rope and clothing.
   b. for its medical properties.
   c. for recreational purposes.
   d. All of the above.
2. Which of the following has the shortest growing season?
   a. *Cannabis sativa*
   b. *Cannabis ruderalis*
   c. *Cannabis indica*
   d. *Cannabis siniensis*
3. Titration of marijuana is easiest when it is
   a. smoked.
   b. injected.
   c. taken orally.
   d. used rectally.
4. The endogenous neurotransmitter that resembles THC is
   a. serotonin.
   b. endorphin.
   c. anandamide.
   d. GABA.
5. The fact that THC is lipid soluble means it
   a. has a short half-life.
   b. is taken up readily into muscle tissue.
   c. passes the blood-brain barrier very slowly.
   d. is taken up into fatty tissue.

6. Use of marijuana
   a. is harmful to the lungs.
   b. has been clearly linked to amotivational syndrome.
   c. causes brain damage to the frontal lobes.
   d. can result in long-lasting psychoses.
7. Dependence on marijuana
   a. is stronger than for nicotine.
   b. occurs even when small amounts are used.
   c. does not occur.
   d. does not produce dramatic withdrawal symptoms.
8. Receptors for anandamide are found in the
   a. hippocampus.
   b. caudate nucleus.
   c. hypothalamus.
   d. corpus callosum.
9. There have been no verified cases of death due to marijuana overdose. This is probably because
   a. the marijuana available in the United States is not strong enough.
   b. THC is rapidly metabolized in the liver.
   c. THC stimulates the sympathetic nervous system.
   d. there are few or no anandamide receptors in the brain stem.
10. One explanation for the memory deficits that result from marijuana use is that THC
    a. causes brain damage.
    b. binds to receptors in the frontal cortex.
    c. binds to receptors in the hippocampus.
    d. causes temporary "electrical storms" that interfere with memory.
11. One clear indication that marijuana can cause dependence is that
    a. some users are unable to stop even though they want to.
    b. some users experience strong physical withdrawal symptoms.
    c. some users find themselves committing crimes to obtain money to buy marijuana.
    d. some heroin users switch to marijuana when they cannot get heroin.
12. Studies showing that marijuana can affect the immune system
    a. find that the immune system still functions within normal limits.
    b. account for the increase in infectious diseases that marijuana users experience.
    c. indicate that marijuana use might be a risk factor for AIDS.
    d. have not been verified by studies of the anandamide receptors.
13. The main distinction between hemp and marijuana is that
    a. hemp and marijuana are different species of the same genus.
    b. hemp has male and female blossoms on the same plant, marijuana does not.
    c. hemp is grown for long fibers rather than high potency.
    d. hemp contains no THC.
14. Proponents of the medical use of marijuana claim that smoking marijuana is preferable to taking Marinol orally because Marinol
    a. is not readily absorbed into the bloodstream.
    b. causes gastrointestinal problems.
    c. is a pill and difficult to swallow.
    d. cannot be made strong enough to have an effect.

15. The evidence for a beneficial effect of marijuana for medical purposes is most clearly shown with marijuana used
    a. to relieve nausea.
    b. as an antidepressant.
    c. as a sedative.
    d. for muscle spasms.

True/False

T F   1. THC is found in several other plants besides marijuana.
T F   2. All existing types of marijuana are variations of the same species.
T F   3. THC remains in the body for a long time because it is lipid soluble.
T F   4. THC can cause permanent memory loss in occasional smokers.
T F   5. Anandamide is a chemical that blocks the effect of THC.
T F   6. Receptors for THC are found mainly in the hypothalamus and brain stem.
T F   7. Physical dependence on marijuana can cause severe withdrawal symptoms.
T F   8. The lethal dose of THC is unknown.
T F   9. Most researchers agree that smoking a marijuana cigarette results in more harmful substances getting into the lungs than smoking a tobacco cigarette does.
T F   10. Marijuana is useful in treating the symptoms of ulcers.

Exercise Your Critical Thinking Skills

1. Many drugs cause more obvious harm than marijuana, so why do you think the federal government has expressed so much concern about marijuana?

2. If it were legal to grow hemp, but illegal to grow marijuana to smoke, how would authorities discriminate between the two?

3. Knowing what you know about marijuana from this chapter, what would you advise a 15-year-old who wants to try it?

4. If anandamide is a naturally occurring substance in the brain that is similar to THC, what purpose does it serve?

5. If marijuana were made available for medical purposes, what controls could you devise to prevent it from being diverted to street use?

On the Internet

What does the Marijuana Anonymous site have to say about marijuana dependence? What do government sites say? What do the harm reduction sites say? Can you integrate all three perspectives?

CHAPTER SEVEN

Nicotine

Chapter Objectives

When you have finished studying this chapter, you should
1. Be able to trace the history of tobacco use from the time of Columbus to the present.
2. Be able to describe how the modern cigarette is designed to deliver nicotine.
3. Know how cigarettes, smokeless tobacco, and cigars differ.
4. Know the different trends of cigarette use for males and females.
5. Know how nicotine affects the body.
6. Know why nicotine is addicting.
7. Be able to discuss the rewarding effects of cigarette smoking.
8. Be able to list the three main ways in which cigarette smoking harms the body.
9. Know the role cigarette smoking plays in heart disease, COPD, and cancer.
10. Know how nicotine and cigarette smoking affect pregnancy and the developing fetus.
11. Be able to discuss the link between nicotine and psychological disorders.
12. Understand what the controversy over environmental tobacco smoke is all about.
13. Be able to discuss why addiction is not the only reason smoking is difficult to stop.
14. Be able to define nicotine replacement therapy.
15. Understand the role nicotine replacement therapy plays in smoking cessation.
16. Be able to list the health benefits of smoking cessation.

Key Terms

Define these terms without referring to the textbook.
acetylcholine

benzene

branded discounts

carbon monoxide

chemical trigger zone

chronic bronchitis

chronic obstructive pulmonary disease (COPD)

cilia

clove cigarettes

cotinine

contingency management

cue exposure

emphysema

environmental tobacco smoke

epinephrine

eugenol

exhaled smoke

fading

formaldehyde

generic

glutamate

lung cancer

mainstream smoke

nicotine

nicotine inhaler

nicotine nasal spray

nicotine polacrilex

nicotine replacement therapy

nitrosamines

nucleus accumbens

relapse prevention

relative risk ratios

sidestream smoke

smokeless tobacco

tar

up regulation

Key Concepts

Despite many attempts to stop it, tobacco use has spread to virtually every part of the world. No society that has taken up smoking has ever given it up completely.

The modern cigarette is designed to permit easy inhalation and requires inhalation to get nicotine into the system. Nicotine can be absorbed buccally by means of smokeless tobacco or by means of pipe and cigar smoke. Smoking pipes and cigars or using smokeless tobacco is only slightly less dangerous than smoking cigarettes.

Smoking has declined among males and persons with higher education. It has leveled or is increasing among women and persons who are less educated. People working at some vocations are far more likely to smoke than others.

Nicotine is a stimulant and a potent poison. It can affect the heart and many other structures in the body. It increases the amount of dopamine released into the nucleus accumbens, which could account for the difficulty people have in trying to stop.

Cigarettes provide many individual rewards every day, with every puff. Smoking itself is an activity that many find pleasurable.

Most of the harm from smoking comes from carbon monoxide, tars, carcinogens, and nicotine itself. Smokers run a much higher risk for a number of cancers, chronic obstructive pulmonary disease, and heart disease. Cigarette smoking can also harm the developing fetus.

Many people who smoke cigarettes have psychological disorders such as anxiety, depression, and schizophrenia. Trying to stop smoking is often associated with an increase in the symptoms of these disorders.

Environmental tobacco smoke is harmful to nonsmokers. Virtually everyone is exposed to cigarette smoke, and most people have measurable levels of its metabolite cotinine in the bloodstream. The harmful effects are seen most often in young children.

Because nicotine is addicting, nicotine replacement therapy focuses on treating withdrawal symptoms while the user concentrates on breaking the habit of smoking. Various forms of nicotine replacement have been developed, and they seem to work if the smoker is motivated to stop.

Regardless of how long a person has smoked, stopping results in an improved health outcome. Stopping cannot reverse certain conditions, but it can keep them from getting worse.

Self-Test

Multiple Choice

1. When tobacco was first introduced in Europe
   a. cigarettes were the most popular way to take it.
   b. it was considered useful for medicinal purposes.
   c. it was mixed with opium.
   d. very few people took up the habit.
2. When a cigarette is smoked, absorption of nicotine
   a. begins in the mouth.
   b. begins in the esophagus.
   c. takes place sublingually.
   d. begins in the lungs.
3. Nicotine is considered addicting because it
   a. increases dopamine in the nucleus accumbens.
   b. is taken up rapidly into the brain.
   c. acts on a naturally occurring neurotransmitter.
   d. acts as a stimulant.
4. Cigarette smoking is declining in every group except
   a. middle-aged men.
   b. middle-aged women.
   c. men over 65.
   c. young women.
5. One of the reasons dependence on smoking is so strong is that
   a. cigarettes contain many additives that add to its addiction potential.
   b. smokers are rewarded for every puff.
   c. smoking is seen as desirable behavior.
   d. nicotine in a cigarette can readily be absorbed in the mouth.
6. Chronic obstructive pulmonary disease is a combination of
   a. pneumonia and bronchitis.
   b. pulmonary hypertension and pneumonia.
   c. pneumonia and emphysema.
   d. emphysema and bronchitis.

7. Smoking is particularly common among
   a. overweight men.
   b. the homeless.
   c. alcohol abusers.
   d. middle-aged women.
8. People with emphysema cannot breathe well because
   a. their lungs are distended.
   b. of pulmonary edema.
   c. of the effect of nicotine on the heart.
   d. of obstruction in the esophagus.
9. The harm that cigarette smoking does to the heart comes from
   a. the combination of tars and nicotine.
   b. the damage to the lungs, which makes the heart work harder.
   c. carbon monoxide and nicotine.
   d. carbon monoxide and tars.
10. Nicotine is an agonist for the neurotransmitter _____.
   a. serotonin
   b. acetylcholine
   c. dopamine
   d. glutamate
11. Babies born to mothers who smoke are
   a. born with lung damage.
   b. born with preexisting cancers.
   c. of lower birth weight.
   d. addicted to nicotine.
12. The first form of nicotine replacement therapy was the
   a. nicotine gum.
   b. nicotine nasal spray.
   c. nicotine patch.
   d. nicotine but smokeless cigarette.
13. Stopping smoking can lead to a worsening of the symptoms of
   a. emphysema.
   b. depression.
   c. heart disease.
   d. obsessive compulsive disorder.
14. Environmental smoke poses the greatest hazard for
   a. the elderly.
   b. people drinking in bars where smoking is permitted.
   c. young children living with smokers.
   d. former smokers.
15. Which of the following health problems associated with smoking improves the least when the smoker stops?
   a. the risk of heart attack
   b. the risk of damage to the fetus
   c. the risk of blood clots
   d. the risk of lung cancer

True/False

T   F   1. Tobacco smoking took a long time to catch on in Western Europe.
T   F   2. The nicotine in the modern cigarette is in an acidic form.
T   F   3. Cigar smokers have little risk of most smoking-related disorders.
T   F   4. Females have reduced their smoking more than males have.
T   F   5. Nicotine is a vasodilator.
T   F   6. Nicotine is used as an insecticide.
T   F   7. Schizophrenics have high rates of smoking.
T   F   8. Nicotine gum provides the same spike of nicotine as smoking does.
T   F   9. When people with emphysema stop smoking, their lungs return to normal within one year.
T   F   10. The carbon monoxide in the bloodstream of smokers can damage the heart.

Exercise Your Critical Thinking Skills

1. Why do you think Native Americans did not recognize the dangers of smoking?

2. Why do you think cigar smoking is less socially objectionable than cigarette smoking?

3. Why do you think young people who are not yet addicted continue to smoke despite knowing the harmful effects?

4. Can you think of some reasons that depression and smoking are linked so closely?

5. Your friend is using nicotine replacement therapy to avoid withdrawal. What kind of plan should she or he follow to break the habit of smoking?

On the Internet

ASH is an anti-tobacco group. Look up their Web site and find out as much as you can about the effects of the most recent legislation on the tobacco industry. What has been happening in Congress recently?

CHAPTER EIGHT

Hallucinogens and Inhalants

Chapter Objectives

When you have finished studying this chapter, you should
1. Understand the role hallucinogens have played in history.
2. Be able to differentiate between the two major types of hallucinogens.
3. Be able to trace the history of LSD.
4. Understand the relationship between LSD and serotonin.
5. Be able to discuss the reasons why LSD does not produce physical tolerance.
6. Be able to decide whether the dangers of LSD have been overstated.
7. Know the psychological effects of LSD.
8. Know how peyote is used and why.
9. Be able to discuss the similarities and differences among MDMA, mescaline, and amphetamine.
10. Be able to discuss the possibility that MDMA produces brain damage.
11. Know who uses inhalants.
12. Be able to list the four main classes of inhalants.
13. Know the dangers of inhalant use.

Key Terms

Define these terms without referring to the textbook.
acacia

Adam

anesthetics

angel dust

aerosols

ARRRT

ayahuasca

Banisteriopsis

belladonna

bufotenine

butane

datura

desmanthus

DOM

DMT

Ecstasy

entheogen

epena

ether

Eve

fenfluramine

flashbacks

fly agaric

gamma-hydroxybutyrate (GHB)

glutamate

harmala alkoids

ipomoea

jimson weed

Lactuca virosa

liquid ecstasy

lobelia

lysergic acid diethylamide (LSD-25)

mace

MDA

MDE

mescaline

Methylenedioxymethamphetamine (MDMA or Ecstasy)

mimosa

Native American Church

nitrous oxide

nutmeg

peace pill

Peganum harmala

peyote

phencyclidine

phenethylamines

post hallucinogenic perceptual disorders

prodrug

psilocybin

raves

Stirpa robusta

STP

synesthesia

teonanacatl

toluene

volatile nitrites

volatile solvents

yage

Key Concepts

In the past, hallucinogenic plants and drugs were used by shamans and others to foretell the future, cure illnesses, and communicate with the gods. Because these drugs were considered sacred, their recreational use was minimal.

The drug LSD set the scene for the social and political upheaval of the 1960s. It was first discovered during World War II, and many studies were done to determine whether it had medical uses. In structure, LSD and similar hallucinogens resemble the neurotransmitter serotonin. When LSD passed into the street scene, it was made illegal and most research ceased.

Mescaline and other hallucinogenic drugs that structurally resemble the catecholamines and amphetamine constitute the other major class of hallucinogens. Peyote, which contains mescaline, has long been used in sacred ceremonies. It is presently legal for use during rituals of the Native American Church.

LSD appears to block the action of the 5-HT2 receptor, one of several receptors for serotonin, and most of its actions can be explained in terms of this receptor. It is active at a very low dose and is highly lipid soluble.

LSD produces many effects, including synesthesia and depersonalization. The "hallucinations" are better described as perceptual distortions. Tolerance to LSD occurs very rapidly and so no dependence occurs.

Many of the harmful effects of LSD have been exaggerated, although it can cause very serious problems in users that are not stable to begin with. Unpleasant experiences, known as bad trips, can also create problems. Flashbacks are poorly understood and do not apparently pose a serious threat.

Other substances similar to LSD can be found in some mushrooms and in morning glory seeds. The effects of psilocybin, found in mushrooms, are similar to those of LSD.

When the peyote cactus is consumed, the mescaline creates experiences similar to those from LSD. Neither peyote nor mescaline has been a significant drug of abuse. Other mescaline-like substance can be found in some common cooking spices.

MDMA, or Ecstasy, does not actually produce hallucinations and has been on the scene for a relatively short time. While it does cause brain damage in animals, the relevance of these studies to humans is not yet clear. MDMA use is popular at raves.

PCP (phencyclidine) is an anesthetic that in low doses causes disorientation and can be accompanied by neurological difficulties. GHB can cause euphoria and was popular with athletes because it was supposed to release human growth factor. High doses can result in coma and death.

Inhalants are often the first psychoactive drug used by young people. They are readily available in the form of gasoline, paint thinner, and other household products. Other inhalable substances include anesthetic gases such as halogen and nitrous oxide. These drugs produce disorientation rather than hallucinations.

A few individuals continue to abuse inhalants as young adults. Prolonged long-term use can have serious physical consequences. Nitrous oxide, an inhalable anesthetic, is particularly popular among certain groups. In young people, significant inhalant abuse is predictive of use of illegal drugs later in life.

Self-Test

Multiple Choice

1. In the past, hallucinogenic drugs were
   a. used as much for recreational purposes as they are today.
   b. recognized as dangerous substances.
   c. used by shamans and others strictly for religious purposes.
   d. confined to Western society.
2. Most of the most commonly used hallucinogenic drugs resemble the neurotransmitter
   a. norepinephrine.
   b. dopamine.
   c. acetylcholine.
   d. serotonin.
3. The psychoactive chemical found in peyote is
   a. LSD.
   b. mescaline.
   c. psilocybin.
   d. harmaline.
4. The early research on LSD focused on its
   a. use in preventing nausea from cancer therapy.
   b. characteristics as an anesthetic.
   c. actions on the dopamine receptor.
   d. use in psychotherapy.

5. One important reason LSD use does not result in dependence is that
    a. tolerance develops very rapidly.
    b. high doses are toxic.
    c. LSD releases dopamine in the nucleus accumbens.
    d. LSD is too hard to obtain.
6. The hallucinations caused by LSD are
    a. very similar to those that occur in schizophrenics.
    b. primarily auditory.
    c. more accurately called perceptual distortions.
    d. often last for several days after the drug has been metabolized.
7. The anxiety, terror, and depersonalization caused by bad trips
    a. should be immediately treated by medical personnel.
    b. frequently trigger a permanent psychosis.
    c. are more common nowadays than in the past.
    d. usually can be diminished with reassurance and a quiet environment.
8. Which one of the following does the textbook indicate is an LSD myth?
    a. LSD causes flashbacks.
    b. LSD can lead people to stare at the sun and go blind.
    c. LSD can trigger a psychosis in unstable people.
    d. LSD produces synesthesia.
9. So-called magic mushrooms are found
    a. primarily in South America.
    b. in large parts of Southern United States.
    c. in Mexico and the American Southwest.
    d. only in the jungle areas of Southern Mexico.
10. Synesthesia is best defined as
    a. seeing sounds and hearing colors.
    b. the feeling that one is no longer connected with reality.
    c. the perception that objects are much smaller or larger than they really are.
    d. the result of damage to the serotonin-containing neurons in the brain.
11. The effects of MDMA most closely resemble those of
    a. LSD.
    b. psilocybin.
    c. amphetamine.
    d. the ingredient in morning glory seeds.
12. Research has shown that MDMA can cause
    a. brain damage in laboratory animals.
    b. a lasting memory loss in users.
    c. a schizophrenic-like condition.
    d. permanent loss of touch with reality.
13. The most commonly abused inhalant is
    a. amyl nitrite.
    b. toluene.
    c. myristicin.
    d. butane.

14. Most of the users of inhalants are
    a. in their early teens.
    b. college age.
    c. blue-collar workers aged 18 to 25.
    d. users of other drugs such as cocaine and methamphetamine.
15. The primary danger from the use of nitrous oxide is
    a. neurological damage to the peripheral nervous system.
    b. damage to the liver.
    c. the development of dependence.
    d. asphyxiation due to failure to combine it with oxygen.

True/false

T   F   1. Use of hallucinogens was widely accepted by the Spanish who conquered Latin America.
T   F   2. Psilocybin resembles the neurotransmitter serotonin.
T   F   3. Mescaline is the active ingredient in morning glory seeds.
T   F   4. LSD was first discovered in the early 1960s.
T   F   5. LSD acts as an antagonist in the brain.
T   F   6. The belief that morning glory seeds are hallucinogenic is a myth.
T   F   7. MDMA (Ecstasy) causes hallucinations much like those caused by LSD.
T   F   8. One danger of MDMA use is hyperthermia.
T   F   9. Poppers are used to come down from the effects of cocaine.
T   F   10. The main psychoactive ingredient in gasoline and paint thinner is toluene.

Exercise Your Critical Thinking Skills

1. Many reports indicate that the healers and shamans in Mexico disliked the hippies who visited them to find out more about their use of hallucinogenics. Why do you think that was the case?

2. Why do you think that use of hallucinogenics caught on with so many people during the 1960s?

3. You are at a party where someone who has taken LSD is having a bad experience. How would you handle the situation?

4. Why do you think that most people who try MDMA are enthusiastic about it at first but soon stop using it?

5. Why do you think inhalants are so popular with young adolescents?

On the Internet

Go to the Web of Addictions site and find their section on hallucinogens. Compare it to the material in the textbook. Do you find any differences in fact or emphasis?

CHAPTER NINE

Use and Abuse of Prescription Drugs

Chapter Objectives

When you have finished studying this chapter, you should
1. Be able to describe the path from opium use to heroin addiction.
2. Know the two primary components of opium and how they differ.
3. Know how heroin is related to morphine.
4. Be able to describe how narcotic drugs interact with the endorphin system.
5. Be able to discuss how management of pain with narcotics is changing.
6. Be able to discuss neurochemical and psychological theories of narcotic addiction.
7. Know how heroin withdrawal is managed.
8. Be able to discuss the role of methadone and other drugs that are used to treat addiction.
9. Know what therapeutic communities are and how they work.
10. Know how heroin use has changed.
11. Be able to describe how aspirin relieves pain and how its alternatives work.
12. Be able to list the three main types of antidepressants and discuss how they differ.
13. Know the role of benzodiazepines in managing anxiety and insomnia.
14. Be able to discuss the controversy over the use of fen-phen.
15. Understand what ergogenic aids are and how they work.

Key Terms

Define these terms without referring to the textbook.

acetaminophen

ambien

amygdala

anabolic steroids

anterograde amnesia

aspirin

benzodiazepines

bipolar disorder

buprenorphine

Buspar

clonidine

codeine

community outreach programs

Darvon

Demerol

Depakote

Dilaudid

Effexor

ephedra

ergogenic aids

fen-phen

gynecomastia

Harrison Narcotic Act of 1914

herbal remedies

heroin

human pituitary factor

ibuprofen

LAAM

lithium

MAOI

medulla

Meridia

methadone

morphine

MPPP

naloxone

naltrexone

naproxen

Numorphan

on the nod

opium

Papaver somniferum

Paxil

periaqueductal gray area

phenylpropanolamine

prostaglandins

Prozac

psychopathic personality disorder

rapid detoxification

Remeron

Rohypnol

rush

Serzone

SSRI

Tegretol

testosterone

therapeutic communities

tricyclic antidepressants

ultrarapid detoxification

Wellbutrin

Zoloft

Key Concepts

Opium has been used for centuries as a medicine and for recreational purposes. After morphine was isolated from opium and the hypodermic syringe was invented, the door was open to narcotic abuse. The introduction of heroin increased the problem because heroin gets into the brain faster than morphine.

Heroin is diacetylmorphine. Morphine and codeine are derived from opium. Heroin is converted into morphine in the brain. All of the narcotic drugs act as agonists in the endorphin system.

Physicians have been reluctant to prescribe narcotics out of fear that patients will become addicted. Most have come to realize that while long-term use can result in dependence, it rarely results in addiction. Physicians have been increasingly willing to use the patient's report as an indicator of the effectiveness of pain relief.

Heroin addiction is very difficult to overcome. Methadone, which is a substitute, is widely used in the belief that methadone users will commit fewer crimes than heroine users. Withdrawal from heroin is unpleasant but not life threatening, and virtually all the symptoms can be prevented.

Smoking heroin is rapidly becoming more popular than injecting. As a result the potency of heroin has risen.

Aspirin works by inhibiting prostaglandins. It is useful in the treatment of pain, fever, and inflammation and as a preventive against heart attack and other conditions.

Antidepressants increase the amount of the norepinephrine, dopamine, and serotonin present in the synapse. The first antidepressants had significant drawbacks; the side effects of the newer ones are considered less serious. The most popular are selective serotonin reuptake inhibitors.

Antianxiety drugs work by increasing the availability of GABA. Properly used they have little abuse potential, but some abusers of other drugs can become dependent on these. Antianxiety drugs are not meant for long-term use, because they can cause dependence.

Most diet drugs work on either norepinephrine or serotonin. They do not create willpower, and they are supposed to be used only in cases of severe obesity. They do not work independently of diet and exercise.

Ergogenic aids are drugs used to increase athletic performance. Their use has remained stable for males but has increased for females. There are significant risks to their use, especially in high doses.

Self-Test

Multiple Choice

1. Opium use
   a. marked the beginning of the modern concept of medical treatment.
   b. in ancient times was primarily for recreational purposes.
   c. goes back to the beginning of recorded history.
   d. was never popular until morphine was discovered.
2. What two events brought about an increase in narcotic addiction in the late nineteenth century?
   a. the isolation of morphine and the development of the hypodermic syringe
   b. the discovery of heroin and the development of the hypodermic syringe
   c. the development of a method of smoking narcotics and the isolation of morphine
   d. the discovery of the endogenous receptor for morphine in the brain and the development of powerful anesthetics
3. What are the two components of opium that have wide medical use?
   a. heroin and codeine
   b. heroin and morphine
   c. codeine and morphine
   d. codeine and Demerol

4. Which of the following drugs gets into the brain fastest?
   a. morphine
   b. codeine
   c. heroin
   d. Demerol
5. Most patients who use narcotics for long-term pain relief
   a. become addicted to morphine.
   b. move on to illicit heroin use.
   c. are unable to function normally because of their narcotic use.
   d. become dependent but not addicted.
6. Which of the following is an accepted neurochemical theory of narcotic addiction?
   a. narcotics block the action of dopamine.
   b. narcotics cause a release of dopamine in the nucleus accumbens.
   c. narcotics use leads to a decrease in the production of endorphins.
   d. narcotics block the ability to feel pleasure.
7. When pain patients experience withdrawal, they
   a. consider it a minor annoyance.
   b. are incapacitated for about two weeks.
   c. experience craving for narcotics.
   d. must be hospitalized because of the severe reaction.
8. When methadone is substituted for heroin, heroin addicts
   a. are able to get high again.
   b. dislike it so much they stop using it.
   c. can function normally.
   d. divert large quantities to street use.
9. Most of the alternative treatments for heroin addiction mentioned in the textbook involve
   a. twelve-step programs such as Narcotics Anonymous.
   b. requiring the addict to experience withdrawal so that he or she will remember the discomfort.
   c. drugs that would make the addict extremely ill if she or he tried to take heroin.
   d. drugs similar to methadone that remain longer in the body.
10. How has heroin use changed in the last few years?
    a. heroin use has declined because of the fear of AIDS.
    b. heroin users have switched from intravenous to subcutaneous injection.
    c. heroin users have begun to smoke heroin.
    d. heroin users have switched to designer drugs.
11. Aspirin is effective in preventing second heart attacks because it
    a. reduces cholesterol levels.
    b. lowers blood pressure.
    c. increases clotting time.
    d. strengthens heart muscle.
12. The most popular antidepressants, the SSRIs, work by
    a. blocking the reuptake of serotonin in the synapse.
    b. blocking the action of serotonin on the postsynaptic receptor.
    c. increasing firing in the nucleus accumbens (the pleasure center in the brain).
    d. inhibiting monoamine oxidase.

13. The most important side effect of the SSRIs is
    a. increased risk of stroke.
    b. increased risk of spontaneous violence.
    c. decreased blood pressure.
    d. decreased sexual desire and function.
14. Antianxiety drugs work on which neurotransmitter system?
    a. serotonin
    b. GABA
    c. endorphin
    d. dopamine
15. Significant side effects of steroids in men include
    a. severe kidney problems.
    b. decreased bone density.
    c. breast development.
    d. intestinal tumors.

True/False

T F 1. Morphine and codeine are the two primary components found in opium.
T F 2. Heroin is less lipid soluble than morphine.
T F 3. Morphine exerts its action primarily on the mu receptor for endorphin.
T F 4. Long-term use of narcotics for pain relief nearly always results in physical dependence.
T F 5. If not properly treated, heroin withdrawal can be fatal.
T F 6. Most younger users of heroin either smoke it or inject it.
T F 7. Aspirin acts on the endorphin system in the periphery.
T F 8. The most widely prescribed antidepressants increase serotonin in the synapse.
T F 9. Both benzodiazepines and alcohol work on the amino acid glutamate.
T F 10. The combination of drugs called fen-phen was removed from the market because it has been associated with brain damage.

Exercise Your Critical Thinking Skills

1. You have a friend who is experiencing severe chronic pain. He is reluctant to take the narcotics that his doctor has prescribed because he is afraid of becoming "addicted." What would you tell him?

2. If heroin addiction is a disease brought on by some neurochemical deficit in the brain and the heroin addict is unable to stop using because of it, why do you think so many people are opposed to methadone therapy? Can you think of arguments against using methadone?

3. Would you admit to your employer that you were taking an antidepressant? If so, what would you say to her? If not, why?

4. Suppose a new drug were to come on the market that completely eliminated all feelings of hunger without any significant side effects. Should it be made an over-the-counter drug that anyone could buy? Why or why not?

5. Assume an athlete is taking an ergogenic aid and signs a statement indicating awareness of the dangers of these drugs. Should the athlete be permitted to compete with athletes who did not take the ergogenic drug? Should the record of the event indicate which athletes took ergogenics?

On the Internet

Go to the Psychopharmacology Tips site and look up a psychoactive drug that you or someone you know has taken. How is what you read different from what the physician who prescribed the drug said.

CHAPTER TEN

Drugs and Social Policy

Chapter Objectives

When you have finished studying this chapter, you should

1. Be able to discuss the economic costs of the drugs you have studied.
2. Know why drug eradication programs for cocaine and tobacco are difficult to implement.
3. Know why it is so difficult to arrest dealers of LSD.
4. Be able to explain why the workplace is an important site for intervention.
5. Know how urine testing works and the limits of detection.
6. Be able to describe three other methods of drug testing and their strengths and weaknesses.
7. Be able to discuss the reasons that driving under the influence has declined.
8. Know the special difficulties involved in reducing the incidence of drinking and driving among motorcyclists.
9. Know how drinking and driving affects pedestrians.
10. Be able to describe which strategies work and which don't work to reduce drinking and driving.
11. Know how marijuana affects driving.
12. Know the relationship between prison overcrowding and drug arrests.
13. Be able to discuss the controversy over mandatory minimums.
14. Know why conspiracy laws are used in the fight against drugs.
15. Be able to discuss how seizure and forfeiture laws are used.
16. Know the difference between supply side and demand reduction strategies.
17. Be able to differentiate between school-based drug education and community action programs.
18. Be able to list the seven elements of a harm reduction program.
19. Know how needle exchanges fit into a harm reduction policy and why they are controversial.

Key Terms

Define these terms without referring to the textbook.

community action programs

demand reduction

derivative contraband

school-based programs

supply-side strategy

Key Concepts

The use of illegal drugs, alcohol, and nicotine generates an enormous amount of income from their production, manufacture, and sale, so the economic aspect of drug use is very important. Marijuana is a major crop in the United States, as is tobacco. Coca and opium poppy growing play a similar role in other countries.

The criminal activity associated with illicit drugs is difficult to control. Those distributing the drugs are very careful about allowing others into their group. Interdiction of drugs entering the country is virtually impossible; authorities can hope to stop only a small percentage.

The workplace has become an important area for control of illegal drugs. Most large companies test for illegal drugs but not alcohol.

Drinking and driving has decreased among most groups in our society. Blue-collar young adults are an exception. Jail terms for DUI are not as effective as economic penalties in preventing drinking and drugged driving.

Both alcohol and marijuana can impair the skills necessary for safe driving. Alcohol seems to be the worst culprit.

The current drug laws have resulted in massive overcrowding of jails and prisons. Very few prisoners can get drug treatment while incarcerated. Mandatory minimum laws are seen by many as an impediment to the legal control of drug use.

Conspiracy laws and seizure and forfeiture laws are being used to take away the economic incentive for illegal drug sales and distribution. On occasion these laws can be misused.

Many experts believe that supply-side attempts to reduce drug use are unsuccessful and want to substitute demand reduction strategies. These strategies would include education about the effects of drugs.

Drug education in our society has not yet proven successful. Although there are a few programs that seem to work, most have little effect on drug use.

Self-Test

Multiple Choice

1. Attempts to stop drug smuggling into the United States
   a. would work if we were willing to spend more money.
   b. would work but we are handicapped by treaties with other countries.
   c. will never be completely successful.
   d. have, on the whole, been successful.
2. Those who manufacture LSD are rarely caught. This is because
   a. many who are manufacturing it have connections in the government.
   b. most LSD is manufactured in foreign countries.
   c. there are so many that it is impossible to identify them.
   d. manufacture is in the hands of a very few people who are very close to each other.
3. Which of the following statements is true?
   a. most drug users are on welfare
   b. the majority of illicit drug users are employed
   c. because of privacy issues, workers cannot be tested once on the job
   d. for preemployment screening all positive urine tests must be confirmed with the GC/MS test

4. Which of the following drugs is not included in the typical workplace urine test?
   a. alcohol
   b. marijuana
   c. cocaine
   d. narcotics
5. The most effective sanction against drinking and driving is
   a. jail terms of at least one week.
   b. license suspension.
   c. public flogging.
   d. fines and other economic costs.
6. Which group has responded least to the campaign to reduce drinking and driving?
   a. young women between 16 and 20
   b. upper-class executive males
   c. the eIderly
   d. blue-collar workers in their twenties
7. What percentage of inmates are currently in jails and prisons for drug-related offenses?
   a. fewer than 10 percent
   b. more than half
   c. about 40 percent
   d. about 90 percent
8. Two people agree to cultivate marijuana and one of them buys the necessary fertilizer. They are arrested before they even purchase the seeds. Both individuals can be charged with
   a. felony possession.
   b. possession with intent to sell.
   c. conspiracy.
   d. being career criminals.
9. Possession of one gram of which of the following drugs would result in the longest jail term?
   a. cocaine
   b. marijuana
   c. methamphetamine
   d. crack
10. If you are arrested for drug sales, the government can confiscate
    a. only the funds you have in U.S. banks.
    b. all of your assets and cash.
    c. all of your assets and cash that were the result of illegal activities.
    d. only your land and other nonliquid assets.
11. Reducing the amount of drugs smuggled into the United States is referred to as
    a. suppIy-side strategy.
    b. demand reduction strategy.
    c. harm reduction strategy.
    d. the scorched-earth strategy.
12. Which drug test can identify users for the longest period of time after use?
    a. the urine test
    b. the saliva test
    c. hair analysis
    d. skin testing

13. Which group is least likely to use the designated driver strategy?
    a. blue collar males
    b. motorcyclists
    c. executive females
    d. older, retired males
14. Drug education programs that emphasize the dangers of drugs that
    a. have been proven very effective in reducing drug use.
    b. have a "sleeper effect"—they do not have an impact until several years later.
    c. are a new development in drug education programs.
    d. are ineffective in reducing drug use.
15. Harm reduction strategies are controversial because
    a. they encourage use of some drugs.
    b. they advocate strategies such as needle exchanges.
    c. They demand complete abstinence from all drugs.
    d. They advocated legalization of drugs.

True/False

T　F　1. Growing of coca leaf is important to the economy of several South American countries.

T　F　2. Tobacco companies expect to recoup the costs of legal action by raising the price of cigarettes.

T　F　3. The distribution of methamphetamine is increasingly controlled by Mexican narcotics traffickers.

T　F　4. The sale of LSD is controlled by the Mexican mafia.

T　F　5. Motorcyclists have lower rates of DUI than automobile drivers.

T　F　6. Very few people who have been drinking and driving can fool the experts at a sobriety checkpoint.

T　F　7. Mandatory minimums are in part responsible for the overcrowding of jails.

T　F　8. If you plot with someone to distribute marijuana, you can be charged for merely having the conversation.

T　F　9. Drug education programs are considered an element of the demand reduction strategy.

T　F　10. Needle exchanges have been shown to encourage intravenous drug use.

Exercise Your Critical Thinking Skills

1. How would you counter the argument of tobacco growers that because their product is legal and results in high profits, they have the right to grow as much as they want to?

2. How would you design a program to discourage motorcycle riders from drinking and driving?

3. What do you think would be the result if individuals who were arrested for nonviolent drug-related crimes were given drug treatment instead of jail?

4. How would you distribute the federal government's anti-drug funds? Would you emphasize stronger legal sanctions? Would you pay for treatment on demand? What would you do?

On the Internet

Go to the DEA Web site and find the most recent report on smuggling drugs into this country. Is there any evidence of success in stopping the traffic?

Answers to Study Guide Questions

Chapter 1

Multiple Choice

1. C	6. D	11. A
2. D	7. C	12. C
3. A	8. D	13. D
4. A	9. B	14. A
5. B	10. C	15. A

True-False

1. F	6. T
2. T	7. F
3. T	8. T
4. F	9. T
5. F	10. F

Chapter 2

Multiple Choice

1. D	6. C	11. B
2. A	7. D	12. A
3. B	8. C	13. B
4. A	9. A	14. D
5. B	10. C	15. B

True-False

1. T	6. F
2. T	7. T
3. F	8. F
4. T	9. T
5. F	10. T

Chapter 3

Multiple Choice

1. B	6. B	11. A
2. B	7. B	12. C
3. C	8. C	13. B
4. C	9. A	14. A
5. A	10. D	15. B

True-False

1. T	6. F
2. T	7. T
3. F	8. F
4. T	9. T
5. F	10. T

Chapter 4

Multiple Choice

1. B	6. C	11. A
2. C	7. A	12. C
3. B	8. A	13. C
4. D	9. D	14. A
5. A	10. D	15. B

True-False

1. F	6. T
2. F	7. T
3. T	8. F
4. F	9. T
5. F	10. T

Chapter 5

Multiple Choice

1. A	6. A	11. C
2. D	7. A	12. B
3. D	8. C	13. B
4. B	9. C	14. C
5. D	10. A	15. A

True-False

1. F	6. F
2. F	7. T
3. T	8. F
4. T	9. T
5. F	10. F

Chapter 6

Multiple Choice

1. A	6. A	11. A
2. B	7. D	12. A
3. A	8. A	13. C
4. C	9. D	14. C
5. D	10. C	15. A

True-False

1. F	6. F
2. T	7. F
3. T	8. T
4. F	9. T
5. F	10. F

Chapter 7

Multiple Choice

1. B	6. D	11. C
2. D	7. C	12. A
3. A	8. A	13. C
4. D	9. C	14. C
5. B	10. B	15. D

True-False

1. F	6. T
2. T	7. T
3. F	8. F
4. F	9. F
5. F	10. T

Chapter 8

Multiple Choice

1. C	6. C	11. C
2. D	7. D	12. A
3. B	8. B	13. B
4. D	9. C	14. A
5. A	10. A	15. D

True-False

1. F	6. F
2. T	7. F
3. F	8. T
4. F	9. F
5. F	10. T

Chapter 9

Multiple Choice

1. C	6. C	11. C
2. A	7. A	12. A
3. C	8. C	13. D
4. C	9. D	14. B
5. D	10. C	15. C

True-False

1. T	6. T
2. F	7. F
3. T	8. T
4. T	9. F
5. F	10. F

Chapter 10

Multiple Choice

1. C	6. D	11. A
2. D	7. B	12. C
3. B	8. C	13. B
4. A	9. D	14. D
5. D	10. C	15. B

True-False

1. T	6. F
2. T	7. T
3. T	8. F
4. F	9. T
5. F	10. F

Chapter 1

p. 12 Courtesy of Gregory Saenz
p. 13 © James L. Shaffer

Chapter 4

p. 59 (left & right) National Gallery of Art

Chapter 5

p. 78 (top) courtesy of the National Museum of the American Indian, Smithsonian Institution
p. 78 (bottom) Courtesy of Kevin McEnnis
p. 80 © Eugene Richards/Magnum Photo Library
p. 86 © Eugene Richards/Magnum Photo Library

Chapter 6

p. 98 (left) courtesy of Drug Enforcement Agency
p. 98 (right) © Hiroji Kubota/Magnum Photo Library

Chapter 7

p. 110 (left) Arents Collection, The New York Public Library, Astor, Lenox, and Tilden Foundations
p. 110 (right) © Gertrude Duby Blom, NaBolom Fund, The Hofman Foundation
p. 111 The Bettmann Archive
p. 113 (top) National Library of Medicine

Chapter 8

p. 130 (upper bottom) © Robert H. Wright/National Audubon Society Collection/Photo Researchers, Inc.
p. 130 (lower bottom) Courtesy of Drug Enforcement Agency
p. 130 (top) AP/Wide World Photos
p. 137 (right) James Price

Chapter 9

p. 144 Photo by Dan Hodges

Chapter 10

p. 171 AP/Wide World Photos

Ferguson, S., 173
Fermented beverages, 58
Fernandez, A., 93
Fernandez-Sola, J., 63
Ferries, L., 158
Fetal alcohol syndrome (FAS), 44*f*, 46, 46*f*
Feucht, T. E., 88
Feverfew, 145
FHN. *See* Family history negative
FHP. *See* Family history positive
Fields, H. L., 35
Figueredo, M., 45
Figueredo, V. M., 45
Finagrette, H., 8
Finn, D., 52
Finnegan, L., 46
Finney, J., 69, 72
Fiorella, D., 131
First messenger system, 21
First pass metabolism, 33
Fischman, M. W., 82–83, 87, 92, 105
Flanders, W. D., 118
Flashbacks, 132
Fleming, M. F., 4, 8, 68, 149
Flemming, D., 139
Flushing, and alcohol use, 51
Fly agaric, 129
Fogerson, R., 106
Folsom, A. R., 45
Foltin, R. W., 87, 92, 105
Foltz, R., 101
Food and Drug Administration, 90
Foote, M. L., 175
Forbes, A., 115
Fordyce, W. E., 34
Forfeiture, 175
Formaldehyde, 118
Fortman, S. P., 4
Fortner, N., 106
Foss, R., 173
Fowler, J. S., 81
Fox, B. S., 85
Fox, D. R., 131
Francheschi, D., 83
Frazer, A., 53
Frederick, S. L., 138
Free will, and addiction, 28
Freebasing, 82
French, M. T., 61
French paradox, 44
French, T. L., 85
Freund, G., 48
Fried, P. A., 103
Friedman, S. R., 83
Frost, H., 98
Frost, J. J., 84
Fudala, P. J., 151
Fuller, J. G., 129
Furnas, J. C., 39

GABA, 25–26
    and benzodiazepines, 155
    effects of alcohol on, 48
    and fetal alcohol syndrome, 46, 46*f*
Gabrielli, W., 10, 52–53
Galen, L. W., 69
Galletly, D. C., 92
Galloway, G. P., 138, 156, 158
Galloway, M. P., 135

Gambert, S., 8, 47, 65–66
Gamma-hydroxy-butyrate (GHB), 138
Gammon, M. D., 45
Gardner, C. O., 12
Garfinkel, L., 111
Gargon, N., 117
Garlic, 145
Garrett, B. E., 26
Gartz, J., 128
Gastrointestinal tract, effects of alcohol on,
    41–42
Gattey, C. N., 1
Gauthier, R., 93
Gavaler, J., 43
Gays and lesbians, alcohol abuse among, 65
Gaziano, J. M., 45
GBH, 138
Gefter, M. L., 85
Gender
    and alcohol abuse, 50, 63–65, 64*t*
    and metabolism, 34
Generalized anxiety disorder, and caffeine,
    92–93
Generic cigarettes, 114
George, W., 45–46
Georgopoulus, S. K., 117
Gerlach, K. K., 113
Gerstein, D. R., 175
Gfroerer, J., 7, 120, 152
GGT test, 68
Ghadialy, F., 175
GHB. *See* Gamma-hydroxy-butyrate
Gianetta, J., 85
Gibson, J., 51
Gilbert, R. M., 91
Gillman, M. A., 139
Gilpin, E., 113–114
Gin, 58
Ginger, 145
Gingko biloba, 145
Giovannucci, E., 93
Glantz, K., 120
Glass, W. J., 130–132
Glover, E., 113
Glover, P., 113
Glutamate, 26
    effects of alcohol on, 48
    and nicotine, 115–116
    and PCP, 137
Glynn, R. J., 45
Gobbi, M., 25
Goddard, D., 12
Godlaski, T., 9, 52
Go-fast, 88
Gold, M. S., 3, 81–85
Goldberger, B., 152
Goldbohm, A., 45
Golding, J., 119
Goldman, M. D., 83
Goldman, M. S., 14
Goldschmidt, L., 85
Goldstein, D., 128
Goldstein, M. G., 120
Gomberg, E. S., 34
Gonzales, M., 138
Gonzales, R., 48
Gooberman, L., 11
Goodman, J., 110
Goodwin, D., 52–53
Gordon, A., 26
Gordon, R., 43

Gorelick, D. A., 84–85
Gorman, D. M., 176
Gosnell, B., 93
Gottlieb, A., 84
Gourlay, S. B., 115, 122
Graceffo, T. J., 105
Gradner, C. P., 27
Graham, S., 45
Grant, B. F., 45
Grant, T., 152
Grantland, B., 175
Graves, W., 85
Greden, J. F., 91–92
Greenbaum, P. E., 14
Greene, M., 173
Greenstein, J. L., 85
Greenstein, R. A., 151
Greenwald, P. G., 117–118, 123
Griboff, S., 157
Grievous Bodily Harm, 138
Griffiths, R. R., 3, 26, 92
Grimes, W., 58
Grinspoon, L., 99–103, 105
Groark, K. P., 128
Grob, C. S., 136
Grobbee, D., 93
Grodstein, F., 45
Grover, L., 26
Groves, P. M., 86
Growth hormones, 158
Grube, J. W., 169
Gruenewald, P. J., 103
Guitierres, S., 66
Gunpowder proof, 58
Gustafson, T. A., 169
Guthrie, S. K., 169
Gygi, S. P., 170
Gynecomastia, 158

Ha, C. N., 47
Haaga, J., 6
Hagan, H., 83
Hagan, T. A., 10
Hainline, B., 158
Half-life, 33
Halikas, J. A., 4
Halldin, H., 100
Hallucinations, 132
Hallucinogenic drugs, and tolerance, 4
Hallucinogenic use, and culture, 5
Hallucinogens, 7*t*
    betacarbolines, 129
    classification of, 129–138
    distribution of use, 128, 128*f*
    economics of, 166–167
    history of, 127–129
    indole-like, 129
    isoxasoles, 129
    phenethylamine-like, 129
    tryptamines, 129
    types of, 129
    in Western society, 133
Halstead, William, 146
Hamel, S. C., 85
Hamilton, B. H., 169
Hamilton, V., 169
Haney, M., 92
Hanlon, T. E., 149–150
Hanna, E. Z., 45
Hannan, P., 67

Oral route of administration, 30
Oscar-Berman, M., 47–48
Ostrea, E., 85
Ott, J., 5, 90, 128, 130, 133
Ott, W. R., 113
Ouimette, P., 69, 72
Outpatient treatment, 10
Over-the-counter analgesics, 152
Owen, D. E., 143
Owen, H., 31

Pagliaro, M., 158
Paloucek, F. P., 24, 114, 137, 152
Pancreas, effects of alcohol on, 42–43
Panic disorder, and caffeine, 92–93
Paone, D., 67
Papaver somniferum, 144
Paranoia, 132
Pare, J., 63
Parenteral route of administration, 30f, 30–31
Paria, B., 103
Parker, R. B., 82
Parks, K., 64
Parmley, W., 120
Passey, R. B., 93
Patch, nicotine, 121
Patches, 31–33
    transdermal, 31–33, 33f
Patient-controlled anesthesia, 31
Patterson, J. J., 4, 149
Patton, G. C., 119
Paul, B. D., 100
Pava, J., 69
Pavia, D., 112
PAWS. See Post alcohol withdrawal syndrome
Paxil, 25
Payne, R., 148
Payte, J. T., 150–151
PCP, 136–138
Peace pill, 136–138
Peacock, L., 45
Pechnick, R. N., 131–134
Peeke-Asa, C., 172
Peer pressure, 12
Peganum harmala, 137
Pendryx, D. G., 117
Penta, C., 53
Per capita, 59, 60f
Performance enhancement, 12
Periaqueductal gray area, and narcotics, 148
Peripheral nervous system, 20, 20f
Perlman, D. C., 31
Personality, and drug use, 13
Pertwee, R. G., 26
Peterson, E., 119
Pettinati, A., 68
Pettinati, H., 50, 53
Peyote, 133
Pfefferbaum, A., 47
Pharmacologic addiction, 2
Pharmacology, of drug action, 29–35
Phencyclidine, 136–138
    street/trade names for, 7t
Phenethylamines, 133
Phenylpropanolamine (PPA), 157, 157f
Phillips, S., 81
Physical dependence, 4
Pickar, D., 158
Pickworth, W. B., 31

Pierce, C., 22, 131
Pierce, J. P., 113–114
Pierce, R. C., 27
Pincomb, G. A., 93
Pinel, J., 27
Placebo effect, 34–35
Plummer, J., 31
Poceta, J., 47
Poland, R. E., 136
Pollack, R., 45
Pomerleau, C. S., 119
Pontieri, F., 27, 102
Pope, H., 158
Portnoy, R. K., 148
Positive reinforcement, 11
Post alcohol withdrawal syndrome
        (PAWS), 53
Post hallucinogenic perceptual disorders, 132
Potischman, N., 45
Potter, J. D., 45
Pouch tobacco, 112–113
PPA. See Phenylpropanolamine
Precontemplation stage, of recovery, 8f, 8–9
Prefrontal cortex, 27, 27f
Pregnancy, smoking and, 118
Preparation stage, of recovery, 8f, 9
Prescott, C., 12, 50
Prescription drugs, 143–162
Presley, C., 63
Preston, J. D., 153–154
Preston, K. L., 92
Price, D. D., 35
Prochaska, J. O., 8
Prodrug, 133
Prohibition, 62
Proof, 58
Prostaglandins, 152
Prozac, 25
Przybeck, T., 13
Pseudoephedrine, and methamphetamine, 88
Psilocin, structure of, 129f
Psilocybin, 132–133
    street/trade names for, 7t
    structure of, 129f
Psychiatric disorders
    and alcohol use, 67–69
    smoking and, 119–120
Psychoactive drugs, 7t
    definition of, 4
Psychological dependence, 4
Psychological disorders, and drug use, 14f,
        14–15
Psychological tolerance, 4t
Psychopathic personality disorder, 150
Psychopharmacology Update, 154, 157
Psychotherapy, 11
    for alcohol abuse, 69–71
Psychotic reactions, 132
P2P (phenyl-2-propanol), 88
Pucak, M. L., 22
Puddley, I., 44
Pulaski, J., 47
Pulse Check, 78, 87–89
Purdie, G. I., 92

Quaid, K., 51
Quaraishi, M. S., 31
Questionnaires, 6–7
Quinn, D., 29
Quinn, V. P., 119

Rabin, R. A., 131
Rabinovitz, M., 43
Ramlow, B. E., 14
Randall, M., 10
Rapid detoxification, 149
Rational Recovery, 73
Raub, W. A., 103
Ravert, H. T., 86
Ravert, J. T., 84
Raves, 136
Ray, A., 93
Rebec, G. V., 22, 26–27
Receptor, 20
Recovery, 8–9
    abstinence and, 52, 73
    from alcohol abuse, 52–53
        with treatment, 52–53
        without treatment, 52
    medical treatment in, 53
    moderation and, 73
    psychological factors in, 67–73
    role of family in, 69
    stages in, 8f, 8–9, 10f
    support during, 71–73
Reductionism, 28
Regan, C., 150, 168
Regular drug use, 8
Reinforcement
    negative, 11
    positive, 11
Reiss, J., 149
Reith, M.E.A., 25
Relapse, 2
    definition of, 9
Relapse prevention, 9, 10f
    and alcohol abuse, 71
    for nicotine dependence, 122
Relative risk ratios, 117
Religion, and drug use, 12
Remeron, 154
Repace, J. L., 113
Reproductive system, effects of alcohol on,
        45–47
Reticular formation, 26–27, 29
Reuptake, 22–23, 23f
Reverse tolerance, 4t
Ricaurte, G. A., 86
Rich, M., 12
Richards, T., 6
Richardson, G. A., 85
Richardson, M. A., 119
Riggs, R., 47
Rimm, E., 63, 93
Ritchie, T., 51
Rivard, G., 93
Rivier, C., 82
Rivinus, T., 84
Robbe, R., 173
Roberts, L., 63
Robinson, H., 167, 170
Robinson, J., 69, 105
Rode, S., 49, 53
Rodin, J., 69
Roerich, L., 14
Roffman, R., 101–103
Rohypnol, 156
Roizen, J., 71
Rollins, D., 101, 170
Rome, E. S., 12
Romero, A., 85
Roosa, M., 69